Lecture Notes
in Business Information Processing

62

Series Editors

Wil van der Aalst
Eindhoven Technical University, The Netherlands

John Mylopoulos
University of Trento, Italy

Michael Rosemann
Queensland University of Technology, Brisbane, Qld, Australia

Michael J. Shaw
University of Illinois, Urbana-Champaign, IL, USA

Clemens Szyperski
Microsoft Research, Redmond, WA, USA

W0235230

Miguel-Angel Sicilia   Christian Kop
Fabio Sartori (Eds.)

Ontology, Conceptualization and Epistemology for Information Systems, Software Engineering and Service Science

4th International Workshop, ONTOSE 2010
held at CAiSE 2010,
Hammamet, Tunisia, June 7-8, 2010
Revised Selected Papers

 Springer

Volume Editors

Miguel-Angel Sicilia
University of Alcalá
Computer Science Department
Ctra. Barcelona km. 33.6, 28871 Alcalá de Henares, Madrid, Spain
E-mail: msicilia@uah.es

Christian Kop
Alpen-Adria-Universität Klagenfurt
Angewandte Informatik/Application Engineering
Universitätsstraße 65-67, 9020 Klagenfurt, Austria
E-mail: chris@ifit.uni-klu.ac.at

Fabio Sartori
University of Milan-Bicocca
Department of Computer Science, Systems and Communication (DISCo)
viale Sarca, 336, 20126 Milan, Italy
E-mail: sartori@disco.unimib.it

Library of Congress Control Number: 2010937278

ACM Computing Classification (1998): J.1, H.3.5, I.2.4, I.2.11

ISSN   1865-1348

ISBN   978-3-642-16495-8 Springer Berlin Heidelberg New York

springer.com

© Springer-Verlag Berlin Heidelberg 2010

Typesetting: Camera-ready by author, data conversion by Scientific Publishing Services, Chennai, India
Printed on acid-free paper   06/3180   5 4 3 2 1 0

Preface

As in the previous editions, ONTOSE 2010 once again was a discussion platform for all kinds of aspects on ontologies, service sciences, information systems and software engineering. The ONTOSE 2010 proceedings reflect this open discourse and hence contain contributions on various aspects of the above-mentioned research areas. A total of 25 contributions were received. These contributions underwent a full peer review with at least two referees, and finally 10 papers were presented at the Workshop and collected in these proceedings. The presentations particularly focused on enterprise and service architectures, ontology application, visualization and query expansion as well as on ontologies for services.

In the area of enterprise and service architecture the paper written by Thomas Kohlborn, Christian Luebeck, Axel Korthaus, Erwin Fielt, Michael Rosemann, Christoph Riedl and Helmut Krcmar outlines how relationships between services can be a basis for service bundling. The work of Remigijus Gustas describes an approach which better supports the integration of static and dynamic aspects in service architectures. The third paper by Sabine Buckl, Florian Matthes, Christopher Schulz and Christian M. Schweda addresses research questions concerning interrelating enterprise architecture (EA) (i.e., questions concerning the structure of the framework for interrelating EA, the types of relationship used, utilization of the framework for development and evolution of EA).

The three papers in the Ontology Application section are devoted to ontologies as formal descriptions for several applications. The first paper, written by Benjamin Diemert, Marie-Hélène Abel and Claude Moulin, discusses the usage of ontologies for digital information exchange. In the second paper, Jinsongdi Yu, Xia Wang and Peter Baumann present its usage for geospatial coverage information. Finally, Diego Bernini, Daniela Micucci and Francesco Tisato present their research work about an interoperability model based on spatial concepts, which can be used in software components in the ubiquitous computing domain.

Two papers were subsumed to the third section of these proceedings. The first one, written by Juan Garcia, Francisco Garcia and Roberto Theron, focuses on several strategies to view the coupling between ontology elements. In the second paper, Fabio Sartori and Matteo Palmonari describe query expansion and how ontologies can be used therein.

The last section, Ontology for Services, completes these proceedings and focuses once again on the two key topics of the workshop (i.e., ontology and services). Florie Bugeaud and Eddie Soulier present a formalization of service upstream in the telecommunication domain. Finally, Miguel-Angel Sicilia and Manuel Mora address the need to use the REA enterprise ontology.

The production of these proceedings, with all these interesting research results, was possible because many people supported the workshop. We would like to thank the authors for their valuable contributions, the reviewers for their substantial reviews and the CAiSE workshops organization chairs Jolita Ralyté and Pierluigi Plebani who supported the process.

June 2010

Miguel-Angel Sicilia
Christian Kop
Fabio Sartori

Organization

Workshop Co-chairs

Miguel-Angel Sicilia	University of Alcalá, Spain
Christian Kop	Alpen-Adria-Universität Klagenfurt, Austria
Fabio Sartori	University of Milano–Bicocca, Italy

Sponsoring Institution

Department of Computer Science, Systems and Communication (DISCo), University of Milano–Bicocca, Milano

Program Committee

Sudhir Agarwal	Universität Karlsruhe (TH), Germany
José Angel Olivas	Universidad de Castilla–La Mancha, Spain
Stefania Bandini	University of Milano–Bicocca, Italy
Djamal Benslimane	LIRIS, Université Claude Bernard, Lyon, France
Pierre Bourque	Engineering School of the Université du Québec, Canada
Pierre-Jean Charrel	Université Toulouse le Mirail, France
Jürgen Ebert	University of Koblenz, Germany
Werner Esswein	TU Dresden, Germany
Johann Eder	Alpen-Adria-Universität Klagenfurt, Austria
Sergio España Cubillo	Universidad Politecnica de Valencia, Spain
Raimund Feldmann	Fraunhofer Center for Experimental Software Engineering, Maryland, USA
Alexander Felfernig	Graz University of Technology, Austria
Anthony Finkelstein	University College London, UK
Gerhard Friedrich	Alpen-Adria-Universität Klagenfurt, Austria
Faïez Gargouri	l'Institut Supérieur d'Informatique et du Multimédia de Sfax, Tunisia
Olly Gotel	New York City, USA
Nicola Guarino	Laboratory of Applied Ontology, ISTC–CNR, Italy
Remigijus Gustas	Karlstad University, Sweden
Peter Haase	Universität Karlsruhe (TH), Germany
Wolfgang Hesse	Philipps–Universität Marburg, Germany

Table of Contents

Identification and Specification of Relationships as the Foundation for Service Bundling

Thomas Kohlborn[1], Christian Luebeck[2], Axel Korthaus[1], Erwin Fielt[1],
Michael Rosemann[1], Christoph Riedl[2], and Helmut Krcmar[2]

[1] Faculty of Science and Technology, Queensland University of Technology,
126 Margaret Street, 4000 Brisbane, Australia
{t.kohlborn,axel.korthaus,e.fielt,m.rosemann}@qut.edu.au
[2] Lehrstuhl für Wirtschaftsinformatik, Technische Universität München
85748 Garching b. München, Germany
{luebeckc,riedlc,krcmar}@in.tum.de

Abstract. Service bundling can be regarded as an option for service providers to strengthen their competitive advantages, cope with dynamic market conditions and heterogeneous consumer demand. Despite these positive effects, actual guidance for the identification of service bundles and the act of bundling itself can be regarded as a gap. Previous research has resulted in a conceptualization of a service bundling method relying on a structured service description in order to fill this gap. This method addresses the reasoning about the suitability of services to be part of a bundle based on analyzing existing relationships between services captured by a description language. This paper extends the aforementioned research by presenting an initial set of empirically derived relationships between services in existing bundles that can subsequently be utilized to identify potential new bundles. Additionally, a gap analysis points out to what extent prominent ontologies and service description languages accommodate for the identified relationships.

Keywords: Service bundling, service description language and ontology.

1 Introduction

The creation of bundled offers of services and goods with distinguishing and superior characteristics compared to existing offers has long been recognized as an opportunity for companies to increase their competitive advantages over rival contenders in the market [1]. Generally, a bundle represents a package that contains at least two elements and presents a value-add to potential consumers. In the travel industry, for example, bundling is common and well-known. For instance, a travel business might offer a service bundle that combines three nights of accommodation in a hotel on a tropical island together with a one-day diving trip. Consumers might perceive the diving trip as a distinguishing characteristic of the offer and a decisive factor for selecting this bundle.

While a considerable amount of literature addressing the process of service design or new service development can be found today, much less is known about approaches

M.-A. Sicilia, C. Kop, and F. Sartori (Eds.): ONTOSE 2010, LNBIP 62, pp. 1–16, 2010.
© Springer-Verlag Berlin Heidelberg 2010

that facilitate the creation of adequate service bundles. Despite the fact that companies across all industry sectors with increased market pressures are challenged by the issue of service bundling [2], only little guidance has been provided so far for the identification of potential bundle candidates and for the actual process of bundling. Previous research introduced a service bundling approach that can be positioned within the area of Semantic Science as it utilizes the description of a service to identify relationships to reason about the suitability of a potential new service bundle [3, 4].

In this paper, we aim to extend the aforementioned research by providing empirical insights into a first set of relationships and its coverage by existing service description languages and ontologies. Not only do we provide insights into foundational aspects and the process of bundling, we also extend the proposed service bundling method that will support organizations in finding service bundles that could potentially be offered to service consumers. The overall research can be positioned in the area of Design Science: by extending a service bundling method, the objective is to develop an "artifact" to "solve a contemporary problem" [5]. However, the evaluation of the artifact, although it is a constituent part of Design Science, is not in scope of this paper, since we report on research in progress.

The remainder of this paper is structured as follows. Based on the problem description that has been provided in this section, we will briefly introduce our service bundling method to provide the means to position the remainder of this paper appropriately. Subsequently, a first set of relationships derived from existing bundles is presented that can be utilized by our service bundling method to identify potential new bundles. Then, existing, prominent service description languages and ontologies are analyzed in regard to their coverage of the identified relationships. The paper ends with a conclusion and directions for further research.

2 Positioning Previous Research

The proposed method is targeted at the identification of possible service bundles by supporting the early stages of the bundle creation process. The method therefore focuses on limiting the solution space of possible bundles, using indicators that express some form of bundling motivation. It is important to point out that this method is not supposed to omit the evaluation of bundles by a domain expert. It has to be acknowledged that the domain expert is still needed to evaluate the overall feasibility of bundles, since this requires complex analysis, often utilizing tacit knowledge across a range of different disciplines (e.g. economy, marketing, legal). Rather, the aim of this method is to limit the scope of the necessary evaluation for the domain expert. This is in particular relevant with a large number of services and, therefore, many bundling options. The proposed approach leverages existing service descriptions and does not necessitate a time-consuming step of (manually) explicating relationships between services as it is the case with the method described by Baida [6], for example. Instead, commonalities of attributes indicate such a relationship. As long as services are consistently described and attributes relevant for this bundling approach are present, the proposed method can be employed. Moreover, Baida [6] relies on a given customer demand to drive the creation of service bundles. While useful for situations where customer demand is well known and understood, poor performance can be expected from this approach when demand is hard to capture or anticipate. Furthermore, the economically desirable situation where customer demand is induced by a new service offering is not supported at all. Our proposed method explicitly targets the latter case by focusing on the creation of new and innovative service bundles. Therefore, customer demand is not utilized to reason about the suitability of potential bundles in this method. Instead, the driving source of this method is a repository of services that are available for bundling. Depending on the given context, this repository might consist of the services of a single provider, a provider network or even contain all available services in a service ecosystem.

Herrmann et al. [7] found that functionally complementary components in a bundle lead to high intentions to purchase compared to bundles in which no complementary components are present. The authors state that, *"as the relationship among the components increased from 'not at all related' through 'somewhat related' to 'very related', intention to purchase also increased"*. The proposed method builds upon these findings and the conjecture that other commonalities or relationships between services can also indicate potentially useful bundles. We define the term relationship as *a connection, whose existence can be evaluated by a logic expression* utilizing service description attributes. Every relationship refers to previously specified attributes (e.g. location of the hotel, destination of the flight) and evaluates them using a given logic (e.g. distance between destination airport and location of the hotel). This evaluation can be realized ranging from simple value comparisons of single attributes to complex algorithms using multiple attributes.

We distinguish between two types of relationships, namely *generic relationships* and *specific relationships*. A generic relationship is used independently of a concrete domain and is applied on *possible bundles*, which comprise any combination of two or more different services to one package. These relationships evaluate connections of a general nature that can be found across a range of different domains. The evaluation of generic relationships does not require a domain-specific awareness and will lead to *generic bundles*. A specific relationship only applies to certain domains and can be tailored for concrete bundling scenarios. As visualized in Fig. 1, applying generic and specific relationships leads to the derivation of potential *specific bundles*. As pointed out previously, those bundles have to be evaluated by a domain expert to check the feasibility of the proposed bundle. Therefore, *domain knowledge* is utilized to get from specific bundles to *feasible bundles*.

As this method represents a structured, explicable approach, it is possible to develop a tool to support the identification of service bundles. The tool requires an explicit service description language, clearly defined relationships and corresponding

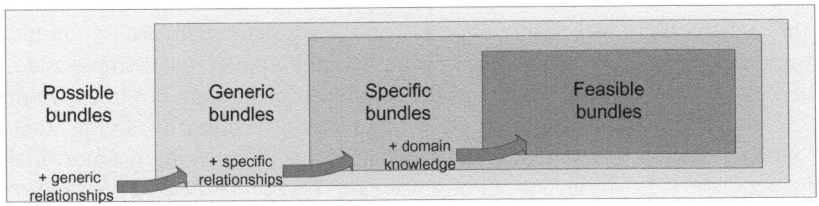

Fig. 1. Constraining the Solution Space to Derive Service Bundles

logic as well as consistently described services. A tool could evaluate chosen relationships for all possible service bundle combinations, therefore creating a short-list of feasible bundles.

3 Empirical Derivation of an Initial Set of Generic Relationships

3.1 Analysis of Existing Service Bundles

The previous section has introduced the notion of relationships in a bundling context and explained the difference between generic and specific relationships. This section aims at deriving a first working set of generic relationships.

An empirical approach was chosen to analyse existing service bundles and to identify relationships that exist between the components of the bundle. For this purpose, a survey in form of a questionnaire was designed listing a total of 28 bundles. The following description of the empirical derivation generic relationships in inspired by [8].

The objective of this questionnaire was to collect a set of generic relationships among components a part of bundles as perceived by ordinary people. For this purpose we provided a list of 28 bundles. These bundles were either concrete existing real-world bundles (e.g. Flight Brisbane to Frankfurt + Accommodation in Hotel Savigny**** Frankfurt City) or generic representations for common combinations (e.g. Phone Landline + ADSL). Since it is possible that relationships between goods might be identified that are also valid for services, the questionnaire has not been limited to services. Instead it contains bundles that are composed of services, goods or a combination of both. For each bundle the participant had to identify which relationship among the components probably influenced most the designer of the bundle. The survey took place at the end of 2009, after ensuring that appropriate resources would be available to administer the survey and analyse the results. The survey was sent out as an attachment to an email, so that responses were either in the form of filled-out print-outs of the survey or electric scans of those filled-out versions. After an initial analysis of the first version of the survey, which included proof reading and discussing the potential understanding of certain bundles by participants, we decided to provide an initial example. For the first bundle of the questionnaire *Flight Brisbane to Frankfurt + Hotel Savigny**** Frankfurt City* the example was given that both bundle components have a common location, since the arrival city of the flight is the same as the location of the hotel. The questionnaire was completed by five people from different backgrounds based on convenience sampling.

3.2 General Findings

Since the questionnaire was highly explorative, the results varied strongly in terms of quality and creativity. Some participants were biased by the given example and evaluated the bundles mostly with regard to the relationships already provided by the example. Some participants focused on customer demand. While it is obvious that most of the bundles relate to a certain customer demand, this information is not available in a service repository. Positioned as a bottom-up approach, this method does not require a previously defined customer demand and findings related to customer demand were disregarded.

3.3 Identified Generic Relationships

Location: Apart from the given example, all participants identified other bundles with location relationships. This was mainly found in service bundles that included a transportation service. In one instance a location relationship was also identified for a service bundle that required the customer's physical presence for service invocation and consumption. One participant also noted varying degrees of the relationship stating that within one bundle the locations are 120km apart.

Time: Two participants indicated that relationships in terms of timing are also present. The mentioned bundles contain services that are consumed in a certain order. Therefore, along the lines of the location relationship, the time relationship indicates temporal availability, a requirement for the sequential consumption of bundle components.

Resource: Three participants found relationships regarding the resources of a bundle. For example in the bundle *Phone Landline + ADSL* it was noted that both components share the same transport medium. For the bundle *Phone Landline + Unlimited Local & Nation Calls* and the bundle *Wii Gaming Console + Game Wii Sports* one person noted that the first component is a required resource for the second component. Along these lines, two participants identified that all products in the Bundle *Multi Purpose Cleaner, Windscreen Wash, Wash & Wax, Paint Protector, Glass Wipes, Bucket, Sponge* target the same object, a customer's car. These findings are all based on the fact that services can require external resources. Hence this relationship is called Resource relationship.

Event: Two participants found that the components in some bundles support certain Events. In the bundle *Cup of Coffee + Cake of the Day* the events *Break* or *Snack* were seen, while the bundle *2 Pizzas + 2 Movie Tickets* might apply for the events *Night with friends* or *Going out*. The notion of an event can be seen as a generic type of customer demand, since a general context is applied.

Customer group: Two participants also identified bundles with components targeting a certain customer segment or group. For example the bundle Wii *Gaming Console + Game Wii Sports* was classified as targeting *gamers*. One participant indicated that most bundles target either a business or leisure customer segment.

Compensation: Two participants stated that some bundles contain components to counterbalance disadvantages of another component. This relationship was seen in the bundle *Flight Brisbane to Frankfurt + Single-Trip Essentials-Travel Insurance Worldwide*, where the insurance is a means to compensate for the risk of international travel. Within the bundle *Flight Brisbane to Frankfurt + Expedia Global Calling Card*, the calling card was seen as a means to ease communication challenges imposed by the long distance and within the bundle *Flight Brisbane to Frankfurt + Fly-Green with Terrapass (Carbon Offset Program)*, the carbon offset program was seen as a countermeasure to the increased personal carbon footprint due to the flight.

Capability: Two participants also found bundles with components related to their purpose, usage or capability. For example, the components in the bundle *Multi Purpose Cleaner, Windscreen Wash, Wash & Wax, Paint Protector, Glass Wipes, Bucket, Sponge* were all identified as serving the purpose of cleaning a car.

Complementarity: Four participants also indicated some form of general complementarity relationship between the components.

Compatibility: One participant evaluated the bundles in terms of the compatibility of the components. He stated that within multiple bundles the components are technically compatible.

Customer demand: One participant indicated that nearly all bundles have related components, as they satisfy a certain customer demand.

Category: Two participants also indicated that most bundle components reside in the same or a similar category.

The set of generic relationships derived from existing service bundles will have to be supplemented by domain-specific relationships. The identification of the latter type of relationships, however, is beyond the scope of this paper and remains subject to future work.

4 Detailing the Identified Relationships

The previous section has identified relationships between bundle components based on real-world services. This section will discuss the usability of these findings for a first working set of generic relationships. This first set does not aim to be complete. Rather its purpose is to serve as a starting point for the development of the prototype. It has to be seen as a creative artifact of design science, which can evolve over time. Furthermore, it should be noted that a certain degree of interpretation was applied to categorize the findings.

The relationships *location* and *time* have been identified by multiple participants. It seems logical that the spatial and temporal availability of services plays an important role for many service bundles. This is especially relevant for services provided by brick-and-mortar providers like restaurants, cinemas or transportation providers. Both relationships will therefore be included in this first working set. The *resource* relationship has also been mentioned multiple times. Since bundling services, that share certain resources, might lead to efficiencies on service provider and consumer side, this relationship will be included in this first set. The relationships *event* and *customer* have also been discovered by multiple participants. Both relationships are regarded as relevant for bundling and will therefore also be included. The relationships *compensation*, *complementarity* and *compatibility* have distinct characteristics. The evaluation of these relationships is complex and very domain specific. For example, it seems unrealistic to create an explicit logic for the complementarity of two services solely based on their service description, since complementarity can be based on multiple domain dependent factors. These relationships therefore have to be evaluated by a domain expert. Once a domain expert has identified explicit relationships between services, this information can be fed into the service description. This working set will therefore cover all explicit connections between services as a *linkage* relationship. The relationships *category* and *capability* will not be included in this set. Although the questionnaire results indicated promising results, it would be necessary to create a taxonomy of categories and capabilities before services could be sufficiently described. The creation of classification schemes for these relationships would go beyond the scope of this paper and should therefore be considered future work. Lastly, the relationship *customer demand* was identified. Since this method is a bottom-up approach, which explicitly avoids customer demand for multiple reasons as already outlined in section 2, this relationship will not be included in the set.

Our first working set of relationship therefore includes a total of six relationships, i.e. the location, time, resource, event, customer and linkage relationship. To utilize these relationships in a prototype, attributes for the service description have to be specified. Based on these attributes, logic has to be developed that is capable of evaluating the relationships. The following paragraphs will cover each relationship in detail. An exemplary model for appropriate attributes and the associated logic is given.

Location
A location relationship exists between two services, if both services are available at the same location or within a previously specified range. The service description needs to include the spatial availability of a service to evaluate this relationship. This has to be described by a list of locations, which can be either political or geographical. Political locations can be captured on different detail levels, namely continent, country, state, city, street, building and unit. A location implicitly covers all detail levels that are not described. If, for example a service is available everywhere within one city, the attributes for street, building and unit are left empty. A geographic location can be described as a coordinate specifying longitude and latitude. These details should be provided using WGS84, a reference system used by the Global Positioning System (GPS). The location can also be described as a shape using a minimum of 3 coordinates. Using shapes, any spatial area can be almost perfectly described. It is therefore possible to describe single points of service availability as well as complex areas, politically as well as geographically. A UML-Model visualizing the described attributes is shown in Fig. 2.

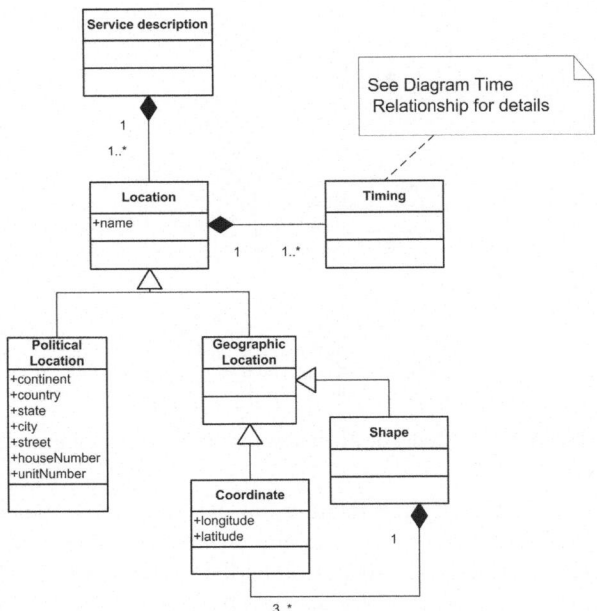

Fig. 2. UML-Model of Attributes for the Location Relationship

The logic evaluates the distance between any two given services. If services have multiple locations, the closest distance is used. If political locations are used, they will be geo-coded, so that calculations on distances are possible. If the spatial availability is described by shapes, the closed distance from any point in the shape is used. The calculated distances between the services are compared with the maximum allowed distance, which has to be set as a parameter of the relationship. To allow for varying degrees of strength, the logic scores the relationship on a scale from 0 to 100, 100 meaning both services have the same location and 0 meaning the distance between the services locations is greater than the specified maximum distance.

Time
Along the lines of spatial availability, the time relationship covers the temporal availability of a service. A time relationship between two services exists when both services can be consumed at the same time or within a specified time frame. The service description needs to include a list of all time periods in which the service is available. These periods can be specified on two levels for all specified locations and separately for each location. To specify the timing for one specific location, time periods can be added to the location-element as visualized in Fig. 2. A time period consists of the start and end time of the day. A recurrence pattern can also be specified to easily describe multiple instances. The recurrence can be limited using a start and end date. In addition to the availability of the service, the typical duration of service consumption also has to be specified. This is required to evaluate sequences of services. A model of the relevant attributes for this relationship, including the possible recurrence pattern, is shown in Fig. 3.

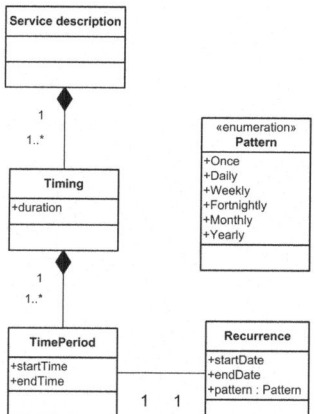

Fig. 3. UML-Model of Attributes for the Time Relationship

The logic for evaluating a time relationship can operate in two distinct modes, namely parallel and sequential mode. In parallel mode, the logic evaluates whether services are available at the same time, meaning there is an overlap in temporal availability. The strength of the relationship depends on how big the overlap is. The logic scores 100 if both services are available at the same times and 0 if both services are never available at the same time. In sequential mode the logic evaluates whether the services can be arranged as a sequence. In this mode a maximum time span between the service consumption has to be specified. The logic then tries to accommodate both services in a sequential order, taking into account this time span and the specified durations of service consumption. The highest score of 100 is reached if both services can be brought into a sequence without a gap in between. The greater the gap, the lower the score is. If the gap is greater than the specified maximum time span the specified maximum 0 is scored.

Resource
Services may also be related because they share the same resources. Resources can play different roles for a service. In this model a resource might be used as the input, output or the target object of a service. Resources can also vary in their importance for a service. For example, resources, which the customer has to bring into the process, might be of higher importance.

The service description has to include a list of all used resources. For every resource, the type of usage (input, output or target) and the importance in form of a weight have to be specified. The weight provides a generic way of expressing the relevance of a resource for a given service. The attributes are visualized in Fig. 4.

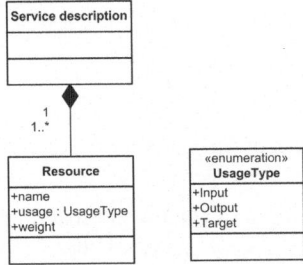

Fig. 4. UML-Model of Attributes for the Resource Relationship

The logic for the resource relationship can operate in different modes. It can be configured to evaluate the used resources regardless of the type of usage (input, output or target object) or specifically target only one specific usage type. It can also be configured to identify resources with different usages (for example a resource is output of one service and acts as input for another service). The different operating modes can be combined in any order to support complex requirements. Independent from the chosen mode, the strength of the relationship is always scored based on the relation of matched resources to total resources used by both services. The more resources that are used by both services, the higher the score will be. A score of 100 denotes a perfect match. The weights assigned to the resources are used to weigh the overall score according to the importance of the resources.

Customer
Services can be interrelated because they are consumed by the same or similar type of customer. To evaluate this relationship the properties of the targeted customers have to be described.

The service description has to include a list of relevant attributes that describe the properties of targeted customers. These attributes can be of a generic nature (e.g. age, gender, income) or they can be domain-specific (e.g. movie preferences, willingness to take financial risks). In the current model an attribute can be specified either as a value range (e.g. age, income) or as a simple value (gender, movie category). Apart from attributes, the problems and goals that are targeted by a service can also be described. Attributes necessary for the customer relationship are visualized in the UML-Model in Fig. 5.

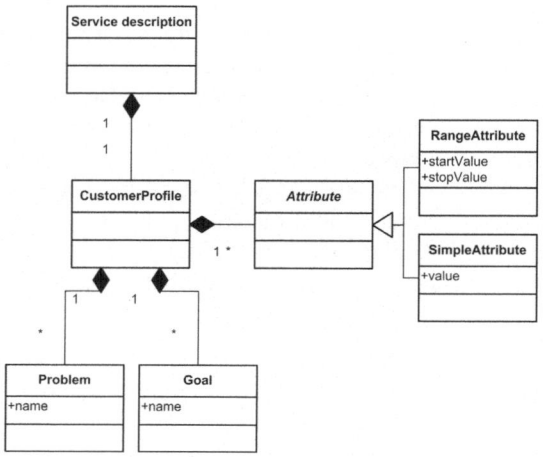

Fig. 5. UML-Model of Attributes for the Customer Relationship

The customer relationship logic evaluates the listed problems and goals and attributes of both services and scores how many of these can be found in both services. Value range attributes contribute towards the score in proportion to the overlap between the compared ranges.

Linkage

The linkage relationship is special and has distinct characteristics compared to the former relationship types. This relationship covers all ex ante and explicitly specified relationships between two services. Two types of relationships are relevant in this context, positive and negative relationships. Positive relationships might be enhancing, complementing, compatible or compensating. These relationships indicate bundling opportunities. Negative relationships might be substituting or excluding/ incompatible. These relationships discourage bundling.

The service description has to include links between related services specifying the types of relationships. Fig. 6 visualizes this relationship.

To evaluate the linkage relationship, the score value of each relationship has to be specified beforehand. The logic then assigns the applicable score between 0 and 100 to each service relationship (e.g. a service enhancement might be valued at 100 points, while a complementing link might be worth 70 points).

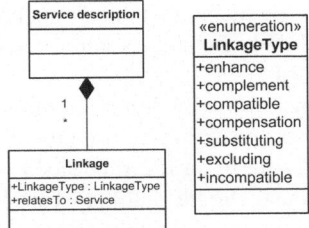

Fig. 6. UML-Model of Attributes for the Linkage Relationship

Event

The event relationship can be used to identify services that are used for specific occurrences. Events can be defined for any kind of happening, incident or occurrence (e.g. bushfire, merger and acquisition, Christmas).

For the event relationship the service description has to include a list of events that have relevance for the service. This is visualized in Fig. 7.

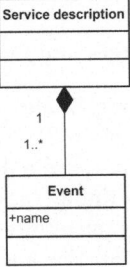

Fig. 7. UML-Model of Attributes for the Event Relationship

The logic for the event relationship evaluates the count of events that apply to both services. The relation of matched events to total events determined the score, ranging between 0 and 100. A score of 100 means that both customer profiles are identical and 0 means that no similarities in the profiles exist.

5 Analyzing Service Description Languages and Ontologies

5.1 Contrasting Description Languages and Ontologies

Description languages and ontologies are used as a structured approach to describe services. Ontologies are used to define high level concepts and the relationship between these concepts and therefore can be used for service discovery and analysis as well as enabling reasoning about services. Ontologies can be created for multiple purposes with varying characteristics. One common scenario is to define a taxonomic structure of terms associated with their definitions, so-called lightweight ontologies. On the other hand, foundational ontologies such as the Descriptive Ontology for Linguistic and Cognitive Engineering (DOLCE) use Axioms in order to remove terminological and conceptual ambiguities and to facilitate mutual understanding and inter-operability among people and machines [9]. Ontologies can often be extended, refined or inter-connected using mediators [10].

Efforts that do not employ a formally described ontology are commonly referred to as description languages. These efforts often use modeling languages such as UML or XML, or describe their concepts in an informal fashion. Multiple efforts to describe services can currently be found. Some ontology based efforts aim at extending the ideas of the semantic web to services, mainly to enable machine-based agents to se-mantically discover services and to reason about integrational aspects [11]. Other ontologies and description languages try to facilitate topics such as service bundling or target a business-oriented view.

Since the evaluating logic of a relationship is based on the service description, it is desirable to have an overview of the available options to describe a service as well as whether the necessary attributes for the previously introduced generic set of relation-ships are supported. Therefore, prominent efforts will be described and analyzed re-garding how these efforts are generally suited for the bundling identification method. Following this, all efforts will be evaluated regarding their support for the needed attributes.

5.2 Analyzing Description Languages and Ontologies

WSMO. The Web Service Modeling Ontology (WSMO) [10] is based on the Web Service Modeling Framework (WSMF) [12], which it extends. It is comprised of 4 main areas: Ontologies, providing the terminology; goals that are reached using a service; Web service descriptions, defining various aspects of a service, and media-tors, bridging the gap between different terminologies. WSMO acts as meta-model layer and does not go into great detail. For non-functional properties WSMO refer-ences the Dublin Core, an organization providing interoperable metadata standards that support a broad range of purposes and business models [13]. Using the Dublin Core concept *dc:coverage*, WSMO can be used to add information about the temporal and spatial availability of a service. The duration of a service consumption can be specified using *dc:format*. The concept of a relation can be utilized to express link-ages between services. WSMO capability to import or mediate between other ontolo-gies can be used to define the necessary concepts for the remaining attributes.

OWL-S. The Semantic Ontology Web Language (OWL-S) [14] uses a similar ap-proach to WSMO. Based on the Ontology Web Language (OWL), OWL-S provides a framework to describe capabilities and properties of a web service. OWL-S aims at supporting a high level of automation throughout the complete lifecycle of a service. It is structured in 3 main parts: The service profile describing capabilities and functions used for advertising and discovery; the process model gives a detailed description of a services methods and the grounding providing technical details on how to access the service. OWL-S has a highly technical view and is mostly concerned with the auto-mated discovery of web services by matching input, output, preconditions and results of services. Only the notion of resources in the form of input and output is present in OWL-S. With OWL-S being based on OWL, providing high-level semantic concepts, all necessary attributes could be implemented by deriving the concepts of OWL.

USDL. The Universal Service-Semantics Description Language (USDL) is very similar to OWL-S, but is based on a universal ontology using WordNet, a lexical database semantically linking related words/concepts [15], instead of having domain-specific ontologies and therefore avoiding the semantic aliasing problem [16]. USDL defines high level concepts to semantically annotate WSDL-Documents and also aims for automated service discovery and composition. None of the required attributes are explicitly described in USDL, but through utilizing WordNet it is possible to describe all necessary attributes. That being said, it has to be acknowledged that the evaluation of concepts described through WordNet might prove difficult, since the semantic richness of a lexical approach offers various ways of expressing one fact. USDL is therefore categorized as not describing any of the required attributes.

WSDL-S. The Semantic Web Service Description Language (WSDL-S) by Akkiraju et al. [17] uses XML to enrich WSDL with semantics. The authors describe how to use the extensibility elements of WSDL to create semantic annotations. WSDL-S is a very high level of abstraction and aims purely at web services. Rather than an actual description language it provides a method to combine XML-based WSDL descriptions and ontology based OWL descriptions. Hence, no description on actual attributes is present.

Oberle et al. [11]. The service ontology described by Oberle et al. [11] uses a modular approach. It is based on the Descriptive Ontology for Linguistic and Cognitive Engineering (DOLCE) [9] as the foundation. This foundation can be extended by so-called core modules, providing semantics for various areas including functional and legal aspects, core service descriptions, and business models. The ontology can then be further refined using industry modules. This ontology aims at services in the internet of services. It is high level and does not go into the details of concrete modules, as the focus of this work is the modular use and inter-linkage of ontologies. No description for the required attributes is present in this work, but all attributes can be implemented as a new module based on DOLCE.

OBELIX. The OBELIX (Ontology-Based Electronic Integration of Complex Products and Value Chains) project [2] developed a service ontology to describe service bundles. It is component-based and allows a description of services and their relationship to each other. The ontology offers three top-level viewpoints, service value, service offering and service process. It defines a concept to describe the functions of individual services within a bundle. The project aims at describing real-world services making this ontology particularly relevant for this review. Within the service offering viewpoint, the concept of service bundles comprised of other service bundles or elementary services is defined. Furthermore services or service bundles can be linked to express a certain dependency (i.e. enhancing, supporting, bundle, substitute, excluding, optional bundle). The notion of a customer profile is also present. The service value viewpoint describes the customer perspective by a customer's demands and sacrifice. The sacrifice (what the customer is willing to give up for receiving the service) can be monetary or some kinds of relationship costs. OBELIX is developed to support the configuration of service bundles using customer demand and explicated service dependencies. It therefore does not explicitly provide any extension mechanism, but it is possible to extend the ontology itself.

Ferrario & Guarino [18]. The ontology by Ferrario and Guarino [18] tries to model a service as a layered set of interrelated events. It identifies five different layers,

14   T. Kohlborn et al.

i.e. service value exchange, service process, service acquisition, service bundling and presentation, and service commitment. The ontology is business oriented and tries to provide a framework that fits real world services. This effort has to be considered as early work and does not go into much detail on specific layers. A concrete representation of a description is missing and none of the necessary attributes are described.

Colombo et al. [19]. The description language by Colombo et al. [19] uses UML as the foundation for modeling. The author aims at providing a conceptual model describing actors, activities and entities involved in a Service Oriented Architecture. In contrast to WSMO or OWL-S, this work tries to provide information for human-readers. The model specifically states the entity Service Description but leaves specifying the details of the entity to the user of the model. It is therefore regarded as having a high level of abstraction. It partially supports the notion of resources, as they can be used as the output of a service. Services can also be linked to each other, but only in the form of a composition. The model does not provide any extension mechanisms.

O'Sullivan [20]. The effort by O'Sullivan [20] focuses on non functional properties of a service. He addresses the research question of what would be a domain independent taxonomy that is capable of representing the non-functional properties of conventional, electronic and web services. He analyzed services from various domains and created 80 conceptual models in 10 different categories. The author aims at describing each category in as much details as possible to cover any kind of existing service characteristic in terms of non function properties. Therefore this work exposes a high level of details. The work includes all required concepts to model the spatial and temporal availability required for the relationships. The remaining attributes concerning resources, events, customer profiling and linkage are not described.

5.3 Comparative Analysis

A comparative overview regarding the performance of each description language or ontology in respect to its coverage of identified relationships and specified attributes is visualized in Table 1.

Table 1. Gap Analysis of Service Ontologies and Description Languages

Approach	Location			Time			Resource		Event	Customer			Linkage
	Political	Geo-graphical	Geo. Shapes	Periods	Duration	Recurrence	Type	Weight		Problems	Goals	Attributes	
WSMO [8]	S	S	S	S	S	-	-	-	-	-	P	-	S
OWL-S [12]	-	-	-	-	-	-	P	-	-	-	-	-	-
USDL [13]	-	-	-	-	-	-	-	-	-	-	-	-	-
WSDL-S [15]	-	-	-	-	-	-	-	-	-	-	-	-	-
Oberle et al. [9]	-	-	-	-	-	-	-	-	-	-	-	-	-
OBELIX [2]	-	-	-	-	-	-	P	-	-	P	P	-	S
Ferrario Guarino [16]	-	-	-	-	-	-	-	-	-	-	-	-	-
Colombo et al. [17]	-	-	-	-	-	-	P	-	-	-	-	-	P
O'Sullivan [18]	S	S	S	S	S	S	-	-	-	-	-	-	-

(S=Supported, P=Partially Supported/Similar Concept, - =Not Supported/Not Described)

Summarizing the findings in the previous section, it has to be said that no ontology or description language currently implements all required attributes or employs similar concepts. Most ontology approaches aim at providing a semantic foundation to enrich the technical descriptions of web services, without going into detail on concrete attributes. Furthermore, most approaches can be extended or enriched to include the required attributes.

As indicated in Table 1, WSMO, already employing concepts for spatial and temporal availability, seems to be a good starting point, although it has to be acknowledged that profound knowledge in the area of ontologies is required to correctly implement these extensions.

6 Conclusion

This paper describes the logical extension of previous research related to defining a novel approach to identifying service bundle candidates. Because of its potential to combine innovation with cost-effective re-use of existing services, we envision that service bundling will become as important as new service development as, for example, can be seen in the growing attention for mash-ups. However, while the process of new service development has been extensively researched and conceptualized, the process of finding suitable service bundling candidates is still ill-defined. The proposed method is a contribution to Design Science research in the field of Information Systems. It represents an innovative artifact that extends the academic knowledge base related to service management.

The method utilizes service description languages as they provide the means to analyze relationships between services to identify potential new bundles. In this paper we presented an empirically derived set of initial relationships that can be used to derive generic bundles. Each identified relationship has been described in detail and specified regarding associated attributes. Finally, relationships and attributes have built the foundation to conduct a gap analysis involving prominent service description languages and ontologies. Findings indicate that none of the analyzed languages and ontologies provides sufficient scope and depth to cover the identified relationships and attributes.

Thus, research in the area of service descriptions has to be conducted to develop a universal service description language that is applicable across industries and covers business as well as software services or extend existing approaches such as WSMO. While we have shown that generic relationships can be derived from existing service bundles, it also remains further work to validate the general utility of these relationship constructs and to derive specific relationships for different domains. At this stage, the proposed relationships have to be seen as a working set, which will evolve as additional studies and evaluations are carried out. Further research should also be conducted in the area of analyzing the suitability of different bundling approaches in different application scenarios and their utilization of existing service description languages.

Acknowledgements. This research was carried out as part of the activities of, and funded by, the Smart Services Cooperative Research Centre (CRC) through the Australian Government's CRC Programme (Department of Innovation, Industry, Science and Research).

References

1. Lawless, M.W.: Commodity Bundling for Competitive Advantage: Strategic Implications. Journal of Management Studies 28, 267–280 (1991)
2. Akkermans, H., Baida, Z., Gordijn, J., Peiia, N., Altuna, A., Laresgoiti, I.: Value Webs: Using Ontologies to Bundle Real-World Services. IEEE Int. Systems 19, 57–66 (2004)
3. Kohlborn, T., Luebeck, C., Korthaus, A., Fielt, E., Rosemann, M., Riedl, C., Krcmar, H.: Conceptualizing a Bottom-up Approach to Service Bundling. In: Pernici, B. (ed.) CAiSE 2010. LNCS, vol. 6051, pp. 129–134. Springer, Heidelberg (2010)
4. Kohlborn, T., Luebeck, C., Korthaus, A., Fielt, E., Rosemann, M., Riedl, C., Krcmar, H.: How Relationships Can Be Utilized for Service Bundling. In: Proceedings of the Americas Conference on Information Systems (AMCIS), Lima, Peru (2010)
5. Hevner, A.R., March, S.T., Park, J., Ram, S.: Design Science in Information Systems Research. MIS Quarterly 28, 75–105 (2004)
6. Baida, Z.: Software-Aided Service Bundling. Intelligent Methods & Tools for Graphical Service Modeling. In: Dutch Graduate School for Information and Knowledge Systems. Vrije Universiteit, Amsterdam (2006)
7. Herrmann, A., Huber, F., Coulter, R.H.: Product and Service Bundling Decisions and Their Effects on Purchase Intention. In: Fuerderer, R., Herrmann, A., Wuebker, G. (eds.) Optimal Bundling: Marketing Strategies for Improving Economic Performance, pp. 253–268. Springer, Heidelberg (1999)
8. Pfleeger, S.L., Kitchenham, B.A.: Principles of Survey Research: Part 1: Turning Lemons into Lemonade. SIGSOFT Softw. Eng. Notes 26, 16–18 (2001)
9. Masolo, C., Borgo, S., Gangemi, A., Guarino, N., Oltramari, A.: Wonderweb Deliverable D18. Ontology Library (Final) (2003), http://www.loa-cnr.it/Papers/D18.pdf
10. Roman, D., Lausen, H., Keller, U.: D2v1.3. Web Service Modeling Ontology (WSMO): WSMO Final Draft (2006), http://www.wsmo.org/TR/d2/v1.3/
11. Oberle, D., Bhatti, N., Brockmans, S.: Countering Service Information Challenges in the Internet of Services. Business & Information Systems Engineering 1, 370–390 (2009)
12. Fensel, D., Bussler, C.: The Web Service Modeling Framework WSMF. Electronic Commerce Research and Applications 1, 113–137 (2002)
13. Dublin Core Metadata Initiative Ltd.: Dublin Core Metadata Initiative (2010)
14. Martin, D., Burstein, M., Hobbs, J., Lassila, O., McDermott, D., McIlraith, S., Narayanan, S., Paolucci, M., Parsia, B., Payne, T., Sirin, E., Srinivasan, N., Sycara, K.: Owl-S: Semantic Markup for Web Services (2004), http://www.w3.org/Submission/OWL-S
15. Fellbaum, C.: Wordnet: An Electronic Lexical Database. MIT press, Cambridge (1998)
16. Bansal, A., Kona, S., Simon, L., Hite, T.D.: A Universal Service-Semantics Description Language. In: Third European Conference on Web Services, pp. 214–225. IEEE Computer Society, Los Alamitos (2005)
17. Akkiraju, R., Farrell, J., Miller, J.A., Nagarajan, M., Sheth, A., Verma, K.: Web Service Semantics - WSDL-S (2005), http://lsdis.cs.uga.edu/projects/METEOR-S/WSDL-S
18. Ferrario, R., Guarino, N.: Towards an Ontological Foundation For Services Science. In: Domingue, J., Fensel, D., Traverso, P. (eds.) FIS 2008. LNCS, vol. 5468, pp. 152–169. Springer, Heidelberg (2009)
19. Colombo, M., Di Nitto, E., Di Penta, M., Distante, D., Zuccala, M.: Speaking a Common Language: A Conceptual Model for Describing Service-Oriented Systems. In: Benatallah, B., Casati, F., Traverso, P. (eds.) ICSOC 2005. LNCS, vol. 3826, pp. 48–60. Springer, Heidelberg (2005)
20. O'Sullivan, J.: Towards a Precise Understanding of Service Properties. Queensland University of Technology (2006)

Conceptual Modeling and Integration of Static and Dynamic Aspects of Service Architectures

Remigijus Gustas

Department of Information Systems, Karlstad University, Sweden
Remigijus.Gustas@kau.se

Abstract. The concept of service is comprehensible in various domains and it can be used for integrated modeling of business process and business data. Service-oriented modeling approach, which is presented in this paper, is based on a single type of diagram. It helps to reason about semantic integrity of different modeling dimensions across organizational and technical system boundaries. A well-known case study is analyzed to demonstrate how service interactions among enterprise organizational components can be represented for detecting the essential similarities and differences of business processes. The ultimate goal of this paper is to overview deficiencies of conventional modeling approaches and to present generic principles for computation neutral modeling of service architectures. Conceptual models of service interactions between organizational and technical components enable separation of crosscutting concerns in enterprise engineering without requirement to specify a complete solution. However, most information system methodologies are projecting the structural, interactive and behavioral aspects into totally different modeling dimensions. If service architectures are represented as loose collection of models, it is difficult to detect integrity problems of various diagrams.

Keywords: Service interactions, value flows, decomposition and generalization, static and dynamic aspects of service architecture.

1 Introduction

Enterprise business processes can be defined on different modeling levels of granularity and in various projections, which are typically defined by using totally different types of diagrams. It is common to the industrial versions of system analysis and design methods to distinguish disparate views and dimensions of enterprise architecture [28]. The Zachman Framework can be viewed as taxonomy for understanding different types of diagrams that are used for representation of organizational and technical system architecture. It defines separate dimensions of business application and data architecture such as Why, What, How, Who, Where and When. Detection of inconsistency and incompleteness among different architecture views and dimensions is a fundamental problem in most information system (IS) methodologies. This is one obvious reason of integrity problems in information system specifications. For instance, semiformal IS modeling methods such as structured analysis and design [11], [4] , [27] suffer from paradigm mismatch in the diagrams, which analyze business processes and business data in isolation.

M.-A. Sicilia, C. Kop, and F. Sartori (Eds.): ONTOSE 2010, LNBIP 62, pp. 17–32, 2010.

Unified Modeling Language (UML) [25] was developed with the ultimate goal for unifying the best features of the graphical modeling languages and creating a de facto industry standard for system development. However, semantic integration principles of different UML diagram types are not totally clear. UML notation has several some accidental, essential and fundamental weaknesses [13]. The fundamental deficiencies can be summarized as follows:

- Value flows between actors and service interactions cannot be explicitly captured in UML,
- It is unclear how to combine interactive, structural and behavioral aspects together in a single view.

Data flow modeling was the strength of structured analysis and design methods [11], [27]. UML also supports various types of associations between classes, actors and use cases, or between objects such as software or hardware components. However, it is not suitable for modeling direct associations between actors that define actor interaction flows outside technical system boundary. Modeling of service or data flows between organizational enterprise subsystems is awkward in UML. It is not clear how rich context of actor interactions can be expressed. If actor interaction flows cannot be explicitly captured, then they are viewed as tacit knowledge, which is hidden from enterprise architects. In this case, such important relations cannot be maintained by CASE tools.

One of the benefits of enterprise modeling is to analyze business processes for reaching consensus on how and by whom the processes are carried out. Most conceptual modeling methods that are intended for business process modeling are not using explicitly the concept of value flow. Value models, which include resource exchange activities among actors, can be viewed as design guidance in enterprise reengineering [21]. Declarative nature of value flows is very useful from system analysis point of view for one reason that flows have very little to do with the dependencies between business activities. The particular strength of value flows is separation of crosscutting concerns among organizational and technical subsystems. Each value flow between service requester and service provider can be further refined in terms of more specific interaction dependencies among organizational components. Service flows are suitable for discussing new configurations of processes with business developers, enterprise architects, system designers and users. Typically, business stakeholders distinguish among the past, current and future structure of processes that can be expressed on different levels of abstraction. Typically, business process modeling is not dealing with the notion of value flow, which demonstrates value exchange among actors involved in business processes [18]. Most information system methodologies are quite weak in representing the alternative value flow exchange scenarios and consequences if commitments are broken.

The treatment of fundamental deficiencies would require modification of the UML foundation. Introducing fundamental changes in UML constructs with the purpose of semantic integration of collection of models is a complex research activity. However, such attempts would allow using UML as an enterprise modeling language for developing computation neutral type of diagrams, which are more suitable for understanding and reasoning about enterprise system architectures [10]. It is recognized that

UML support for such task is vague, because semantic integration principles of different diagram types are lacking [20].

This paper demonstrates how service interactions can be integrated with behavioral and structural aspects of conceptual representations. The well-known example of Ford's case [19] is used to explain the benefits of the service-oriented approach [15], which was developed for conceptual modeling of information systems. We are not discussing advantages of service-oriented enterprise architectures [23], because they are quite obvious [26]. Nevertheless, given the central role of service concept in this study, we will focus on what is essential and most stable core in conceptual modeling of enterprise system, which is composed of the organizational or technical parts. Conceptual models of services should make sense not just for IS designers in the implementation-oriented domains, but also for business modeling experts, which are focused on computation neutral analysis of organizations. The presented service-oriented modeling approach shares many similarities with ontological foundation of service process [9]. The internal behavior of services is described by using basic principles of an ontological framework, which is developed by Bunge [3].

2 Value Flows and Service Interactions

Service flow modeling is quite intuitive way of system analysis that is easy to understand for business professionals and information system designers. Value models clarify why actors are willing to exchange business objects with each other. Actions are required for exchanging the physical, decision and data flows. Actions and exchange flows can be viewed as fundamental elements for defining business scenarios. A scenario is an excellent means for describing the order of service interactions. Scenarios help the enterprise system architects to express business processes in interplay with elementary service interactions between enterprise system components. Each service can be analyzed separately as is required by the principle of separation of concerns. In such way, value flows and service interactions provide a natural way of process decomposition.

Value flows are special types of concepts that represent moving things such as information or materials. Solid rectangles will be used for denotation of physical flows and light boxes will indicate data flows. Actions are performed by actors, which will be represented by ellipses. Actions are necessary for transferring flows between subsystems, which are represented as organizational actors. Actors will be represented by square rectangles. Two value flows between customer and vendor are illustrated in figure 1.

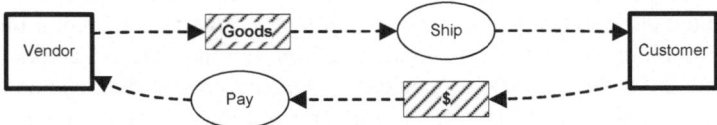

Fig. 1. Value flows between a Customer and Vendor

Direction of the material flow of Goods indicates that the Ship action is initiated by Vendor. Customer is a recipient of Goods flow. In contrary, money flow (represented by $) is initiated in exchange to Goods by Customer with the help of the Pay action. If so, then Vendor is the recipient of money flow. An action with a missing data or physical flow component will be understood as a decision or control flow.

Organizational actor is a unit of functionality exposed to environment that is conceptualized for representation of an enterprise subsystem. It depends on the individual actor role and his goals whether he considers some received information, materials or decisions as value flows. So, value flow is relative notion. Ideally, any elementary interaction must be motivated by the resulting value flow and vice versa a value flow typically requires initiation of some coordinating interactions, which are necessary for provision of value flows. Service interactions take place between service requester and service provider. In the DEMO theory [5], service requesters and service providers are viewed as active elements, which are represented by individuals or subjects. The DEMO approach distinguishes between two kinds of actions: production acts and coordination acts. Coordination acts are normally initiated by service requesters. Coordination acts are necessary to make commitment regarding the corresponding production act, which is supposed to bring a value flow to service requester. Production acts are normally performed by service providers. Therefore, they should be always associated with value flows.

Interaction dependencies can be used to conceptualize services between various enterprise system actors. Since all actors are implemented either as organizational or technical system components, they can use each other according to the prescribed service interaction patterns to achieve their goals. The simplest service interaction pattern can be represented by two interaction dependencies into opposite directions between service requester and service provider [16]. It is very similar to a well-known communication action loop. This idea is illustrated graphically in figure 2.

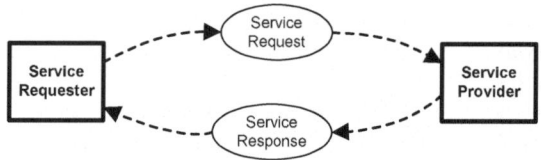

Fig. 2. Elementary service interaction loop

Interaction loop between two actors indicates that these two depend on each other by specific actions. Service providers are actors that typically receive service requests, over which they have no direct control, and initiate service responses that are sent to service requesters. Service requests and service responses can be used to define more complex interaction loops. In this way, designers are able to construct a blueprint of interacting components, which are represented by various types of actors across organizational and technical system boundaries. An enterprise system can be defined as a set of interacting loosely connected components [16], which are able to perform specific services on request. One example of service interaction loop, which consists of two interaction flows in two opposite directions, is presented in figure 3.

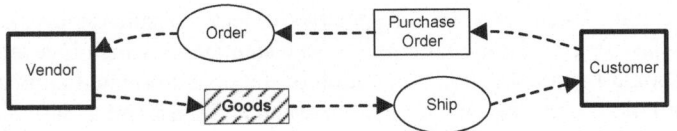

Fig. 3. Example of the elementary service interaction loop

This example can be considered as graphical description of elementary service interaction loop between Customer and Vendor. It defines two actions, which are available to the organizational actors. A customer may be interested to order goods. A vendor is able to ship goods. Coordinating actions can be viewed by actors as possibilities. Set of possibilities, which are delegated to one organizational actor, may help to understand his organizational power. By using such actions, the actors are entering into commitments regarding their obligations. For instance, the Order action can be viewed as a possibility for sending a purchase order by Customer to Vendor. If a Vendor would accept it, then he is obliged to ship Goods to the customer. In this way, service interactions can be used to analyze possibilities and obligations of the enterprise actors.

3   Enterprise System Decomposition Principles

Enterprise systems can be analyzed as compositions of technical and organizational components, which can be represented by various types of actors. Organizational components are interacting subsystems such as individuals, organizations and their divisions or roles, which denote groups of people. Technical components are represented by enterprise subsystems such as machines, software and hardware. We distinguish between two types of concepts: active and passive [17]. An actor can only be represented by an active concept. An instance of an actor is an autonomous subsystem. Its existence can only be motivated by a set of interaction dependencies with other actors that keep enterprise system viable. Passive concepts are represented by entities or classes of objects, which represent data at rest. All passive concepts are characterized by mandatory attributes. Objects of passive concepts can be affected by interacting subsystems, which are able perform specific services on request. Passive concepts are not the focus of this chapter, because they have no influence on system decomposition principles.

The ontological foundation of our modeling approach is based on the set of semantic dependencies between active concepts, which are viewed as enterprise actors. Actors are represented by subsystems that are non-overlapping in functionality. Active concepts can be related by the static dependencies such as inheritance, composition and classification [15]. Graphical notation of semantic dependencies, which are used to represent decomposition of enterprise system, is represented graphically in figure 4.

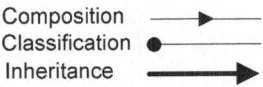

Fig. 4. Notation of static dependencies between actors

Classification dependency (•—) specifies objects or subsystems as instances of concepts. Classification is often referred to as instantiation, which is reverse of classification. It should be noted that classification of the object-oriented approaches is more restricted relation. It can be only defined between an object and a class. A class cannot play a role of meta-object, which is instantiated in another class, in the conventional IS modeling approaches. Instances of concepts propagate to the more generic concepts in the inheritance hierarchy. This feature is defined by the following rule:

If A •— B and B ➡C then A •— C.

Here: ➡ is inheritance dependency and •— is classification dependency.

Actors have their own instances, which play role of subsystems. For example, Ford Motor Company is an instance of an Organization. Instances can be basic or derived. These two types of actor instances are represented in figure 5.

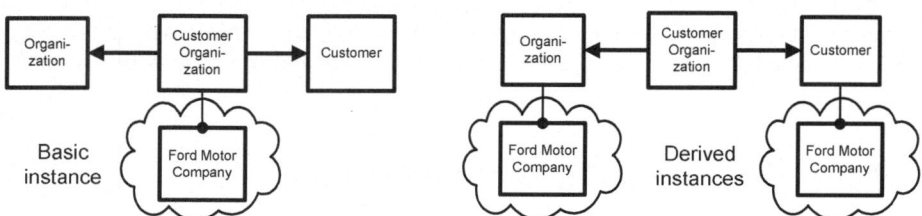

Fig. 5. Basic and derived instances of actors

For example, if (Ford Motor Company •— Customer Organization) and (Customer Organization ➡ Customer) then (Ford Motor Company •— Customer). Every instance of an actor is subsystem, which is characterized by the set of possibilities and obligations that are defined for this actor. Conceptual models of service interactions can be used to analyze possibilities and obligations, which are represented by the interaction dependencies. For instance, the Order action can be viewed as a possibility for sending a purchase order by Ford Motor Company to Vendor. If Vendor would accept it, then it is obliged to ship Goods to Ford Motor Company (see figure 3).

Composition (—▶—), which is presented in this paper, differs significantly from the object-oriented composition [17]. A—▶—B indicates that objects of the concept A are viewed as parts of composite B. is It is a much stricter form of aggregation, which allows just either 1 or 1..* multiplicities between wholes and parts. Other cases of conventional composition are not legal. It means that a part cannot be optional. Very important distinctive features of the presented composition dependency, that differentiate it from the other types whole-part dependencies, are as follows: (1) part is existent dependent on a whole, (2) if a whole has a single part, then this part has coincident lifetime with a whole, (3) if a whole has more than one part, then the creation of a first part is coincident with creation of a whole, creation and removal of additional parts can take place any time, but the removal of a last part is coincident with removal of a whole [14], (4) coincident creation and removal of a whole together with all parts is a special case of composition, (5) part can belong to only one whole of the same type. It should be noted that the optional cases of aggregation and composition can be always transformed into this stricter type of composition with the help of special modeling techniques [17].

Composition hierarchies can be used for detection of inconsistent interaction dependencies between actors. If the actors are loosely coupled, they never belong to the same decomposition hierarchy. Interaction dependencies of loosely coupled actors on the lower level of decomposition hierarchy are propagated to compositional wholes. So, composition links can be used for reasoning about derived interaction dependencies between actors on the higher granularity levels of conceptualization. Interaction dependencies between actors, which are placed in two different composition hierarchies, are characterized by the following inference rules:

1) If A −▶− B and R(A ▪▪▪▪▶C) then R(B ▪▪▪▪▶C),
2) If A −▶− B and R(C ▪▪▪▪▶A) then R(C ▪▪▪▪▶B).

Interaction dependency R(B ▪▪▪▶C) between two actors B and C indicates that subsystem denoted by B is able to perform action R on one or more subsystems of C. Two subsystems of Customer Organization together with their interaction dependencies are represented in figure 6.

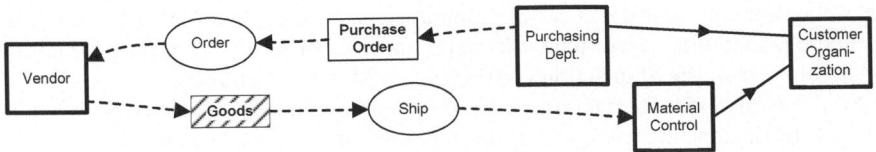

Fig. 6. Service interaction loop on the lower level of decomposition

Service interaction loops, which are specified on different granularity levels, must be consistent. Actors, actions and flows of consistent service interaction loops cannot be contradictory. For instance, if (Purchasing Department −▶− Customer Organization) and Order(Purchasing Department ▪▪▪▪▶Vendor) then Order(Customer Organization ▪▪▪▪▶Vendor). Note that service interaction flows, which are represented in figure 7, are consistent with the interactions of the previous diagram.

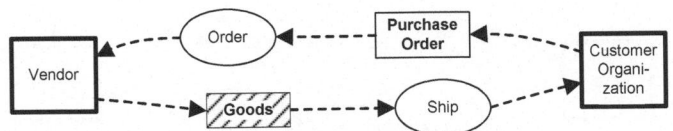

Fig. 7. Service interaction loop on the higher level of decomposition

Inheritance dependency between two actors indicates that these actors share structural and interactive similarities. More specific actors inherit the composition and interaction dependencies from more generic actors. It should be noted that in the object-oriented approaches, the inheritance link is defined just for associations, attributes and operations. Inheritance dependency is convenient for sharing service interaction loops of more generic actors. Interaction dependencies are inherited according to the following inference rules:

1) If A ➡ B and R(B ···· ▶ C) then R(A ···· ▶ C),
2) If A ➡ B and R(C ···· ▶ B) then R(C ···· ▶ A).

If (Customer Organization ➡ Customer), then Customer Organization inherits all service interaction links, which are specified for the actor of Customer (see figure 3). For example, if (Customer Organization ➡ Customer) and Order(Customer ···· ▶ Vendor) then Order(Customer Organization ···· ▶ Vendor). Customer Organization has possibility to send a purchase order to a Vendor and Vendor is obliged to ship goods to the Customer Organization. Please note that possibilities and obligations of these two actors must be consistent with the interaction flows, which were already presented in figure 6 and 7. It is not difficult to find out that the presented dependencies are consistent with the service request (Order) and response (Ship) of figure 3. They can be specified as follows: if Order(Customer Organization ···· ▶ Vendor) then Ship(Vendor ···· ▶ Customer). This example is based on a well-known case study [19]. Ford Motor Company (see figure 5) is playing a role of customer organization, which is decomposed into two departments (Purchasing and Material Control). Customer Organization concept is additionally defined as the specialization of two other active concepts such as Customer and Organization. Therefore, same service interaction loop, which is discussed in the previous chapter (see figure 3), is consistent with the other diagrams of the lower level of granularity (see figure 6 and 7). The only difference here is that initiation of the Order action is delegated to a Purchasing Department and acceptance of the Ship action is delegated to Material Control.

All derived service interaction loops of the enterprise system cannot be in conflict with the other dependencies, which are represented by a set of diagrams on various levels of abstraction. Inconsistency can be detected by identifying action or flow naming conflicts. For instance, two service interaction loops, which are presented in figure 8, are inconsistent.

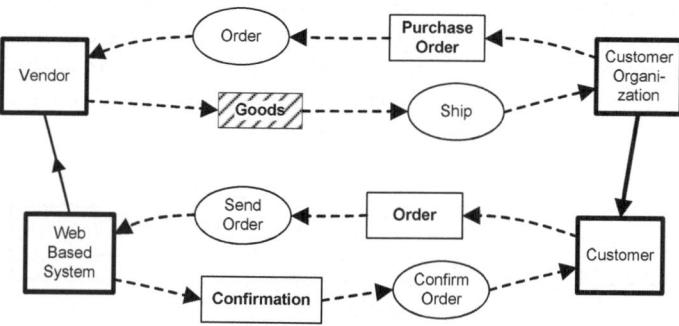

Fig. 8. Two inconsistent service interaction loops

Adding more specific actors into an enterprise system specification, must be justified by additional possibilities or obligations, which can be specified in terms of complementary interaction dependencies. It must be noted that the presented inference rules are useful, but not sufficient for reasoning about consistency of service interactions, which are specified on different levels of abstraction. To understand deep semantic structure of service interactions, the behavioral and related structural aspects of communication actions must be analyzed. How to express the interplay between business interactions and object transition effects is demonstrated in the next chapter.

4 Interplay of Structural and Behavioral Aspects of Service Architectures

Good principles of decomposition are not sufficient for systematic analysis of enterprise architectures. To understand the internal service interaction effects between service requesters and service providers, graphical representations of actions must be integrated with data descriptions. The dynamic aspects of service interactions can be expressed by defining structural changes of passive concepts. Passive concepts are classes of objects that are characterized by mandatory attributes. Values of such attributes are created or consumed in service requests and service responses. Structural aspects of data at rest are fundamental for understanding the semantic aspects of service choreographies and service architectures. From an ontological perspective, when two subsystems interact [3] one may affect the state each other. Changes in object state are characterized in terms of object properties. Interaction dependency R(A••••▶B) between two active concepts indicates that A subsystem can perform action R on one or more B subsystems. Actions are able to manipulate object properties. Property changes may trigger objects transitions from one class to another.

The internal effects of objects can be expressed by using transition links (——▶) between passive concepts. There are three fundamental ways for representing object behavior by using reclassification, creation and termination actions [16]. If termination and creation action is performed at the same time, then it is called a reclassification action. Graphical notation of these three variations of actions is graphically represented in figure 9.

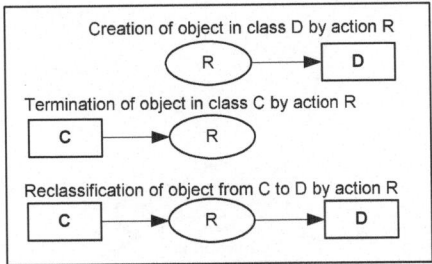

Fig. 9. Three variations of transition dependencies

Creation action is represented by a transition to an initial class. Termination action can be represented by a transition link from a final class. For instance, initiation of the Order action is typically used to create a Customer Order in a Vendor database or archive (see the diagram in figure 10). If Customer Order is accepted, then it may be used for triggering the shipping action. Creation and termination actions can be expressed by using object flows. A diagram showing operations and object flows with states has most of the advantages of activity diagrams without most of their disadvantages [1]. A transition arrow to action or transition arrow from action represents a

26   R. Gustas

control flow. In this way, any communication action can be used to superimpose interactions and control flow effects in the same diagram.

To demonstrate how service interactions can be used to analyze service architectures, we take well-known example of Ford's case [19]. The problematic situation of enterprise system was described as follows: *When Ford's purchasing department wrote a purchase order, it sent a copy to accounts payable. Later, when material control received the goods, it sent a copy of the receiving document to accounts payable. Meanwhile, the vendor sent an invoice to accounts payable. It was up to accounts payable, then, to match the purchase order against the receiving document and the invoice. If they matched, the department issued payment. The department spent most of its time on mismatches, instances where the purchase order, receiving document, and invoice disagreed. In these cases, an accounts payable clerk would investigate the discrepancy, hold up the payment.* The effects of described actions are expressed by using passive classes, which are represented in figure 10.

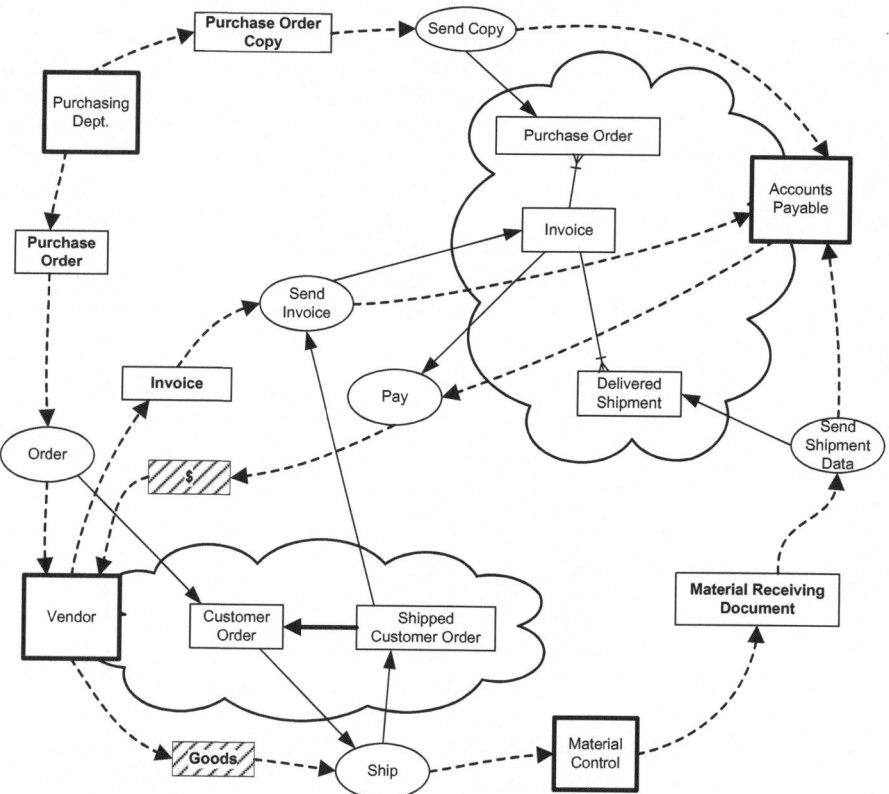

Fig. 10. Service architecture before radical change

This diagram represents conceptualization of two service loops. Purchasing Department is entitled to order goods by sending a purchase order. If it is accepted by vendor, then a Customer Order is archived. Vendor is obliged to ship goods for every outstanding Customer Order (service loop 1). Creation of Shipped Customer Order object is necessary precondition to generate another service request. It is used to trigger Send Invoice action. If Invoice flow is accepted by Accounts Payable, then the Pay action must be initiated (service loop 2). There are two explicit post-conditions for creating an Invoice. Every Invoice object must be linked with at least one Purchase Order and with at least one Delivered Shipment (see two mandatory associations from Invoice). Purchase Order object cannot be created without involvement of Purchasing Department. Creation of Delivered Shipment object is triggered by Material Control. This diagram also indicates that Send Copy and Send Shipment Data actions must precede Send Invoice action.

Most IS methodologies are not integrating interactive and behavioral aspects of service architectures, which were illustrated in the previous diagram. Failure to visualize interaction and object transition effects in a single diagram makes it difficult to understand the essential semantic differences of a deep business process structure. This example demonstrates how interactions should be linked together with structural changes of passive classes of objects. Transition dependencies between passive concepts help designers to reason about sequences, alternatives, synchronizations or iterations of service interaction flows [16]. We are not going into details of various control patterns for the reason of space limitations.

Structural changes of objects are manifested via object properties. Properties can be understood as mandatory attribute values. If diagrams are used to communicate unambiguously semantic details of a conceptualized system, then optional properties should be proscribed [12]. In the presented method, the attributes are defined by the total single-valued ($\longrightarrow\!\!>$) or by the total multi-valued attribute dependency ($\longrightarrow\!\!\gg$). If $A\longrightarrow\!\!> B$ or $A\longrightarrow\!\!\gg B$, then concept A is viewed as a class and concept B - as a mandatory property of A. One significant feature of our approach is that the association ends of static relations are nameless. Association ends cannot be used to denote mappings in two opposite directions. Semantics of dependencies are defined by cardinalities, which represent a minimum and maximum number of objects in one class (B) that can be associated to objects in another class (A). Expression $A\longrightarrow\!\!\gg B$ can be used to represent the following cardinalities: (0,1;1,1), (0,*;1,1) and (1,1;1,1). Expression $A\longrightarrow\!\!> B$ corresponds to (0,1;1,*) or (1,1;1,*) cardinalities. Graphical notation of an attribute dependency between A and B is represented in figure 11.

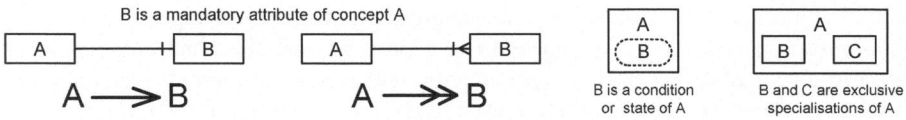

Fig. 11. Notation of attribute dependencies

Any passive concept can be defined as an exclusive complete generalization of two concepts. Passive concept can also be characterized by state [7] or condition [16]. Example of exclusive generalization and example of state is presented in the next diagram.

We will apply our approach to illustrate service architecture after the radical change in Ford Motor Company. The reengineering of the enterprise system in Ford was possible to make in two ways. These two alternatives are described as follows [19]:

One way to improve things might have been to help the accounts payable clerk investigate more efficiently, but a better choice was to prevent the mismatches in the first place. To this end, Ford instituted 'invoice-less processing'. Now when the purchasing department initiates an order, it enters the information into an online database. It doesn't send a copy of the purchase order to anyone. When the goods arrive at the receiving dock, the receiving clerk checks the database to see if they correspond to an outstanding purchase order. If so, the receiving clerk accepts them and enters the transaction into the computer system. If receiving can't find a database entry for the received goods, it simply returns the order. Computation neutral graphical description of the new situation is represented in figure 12.

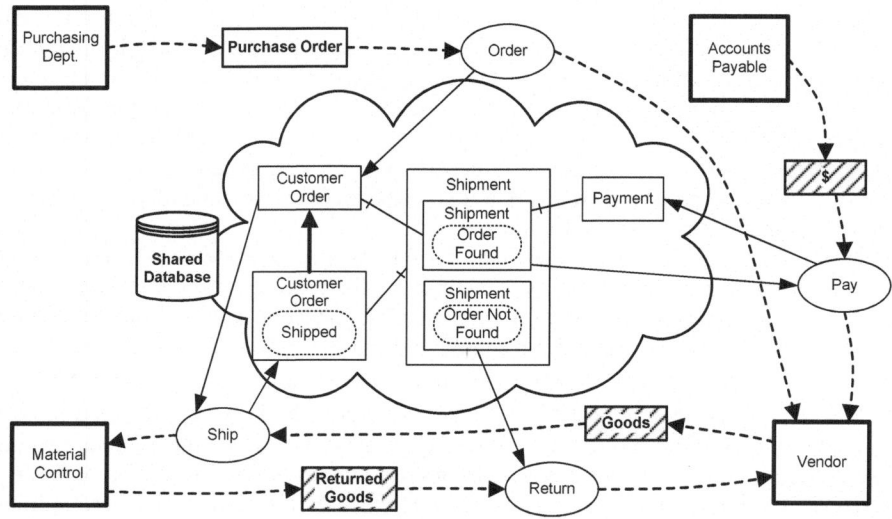

Fig. 12. Service architecture after radical change

Concepts and their static dependencies of a shared database are represented by cloud (it is used just for illustration purposes). Please note that this cloud is an implementation specific notion, which should not be represented in this diagram. Any interaction dependency represents creation (Order action), termination (Return action) or reclassification (Ship and Pay actions). Fundamentally, two kinds of changes occur during reclassification: removal of an object from a precondition class and creation of an object in a postcondition class. Object creation without any properties does not make sense. Sometimes, postcondition class may require preservation of some precondition class object. Such requirements can be specified by the static dependencies. Examples of such preserved classes of objects are Customer Order and Shipment [Order Found]. Preservation of Customer Order is required by the postcondition of Customer Order[Shipped] object (see Ship action). Creation of Payment requires preservation of the Shipment[Order Found] object. Quite often objects should not be preserved like in the presented case. They are passing several classes and then are destroyed.

A missing postcondition class represents termination, which is a special case of the reclassification. Termination action is supposed to remove all object properties, which are represented by attributes of a precondition class. In the presented diagram, the Return action not only initiates Returned Goods flow, but it also removes Shipment[Order Not Found] object. Note that Shipment is a property of Customer Order[Shipped]. So, if Shipment is removed, then the related Order[Shipped] object must be removed as well. The creation action is represented with a missing precondition class. Creation must bring all object properties, which are represented by attributes of a post-condition class, into existence. Creation event is illustrated by the Order action. Please note that this diagram is incomplete. Customer Order properties are not shown.

5 Discussion and Concluding Remarks

Service interaction dependencies are essential for understanding similarities of business processes. However, interaction flow analysis is not sufficient for studying the fundamental semantic differences of processes when reengineering the organizations. The structural and behavioral aspects of service architectures need to be analyzed in terms of object properties and object transitions between various types of classes. For instance, the essential similarities and differences of service architectures, which are presented in figure 10 and figure 12, can be identified by analyzing conceptualizations of two situations in Ford Motor Company. They illustrate not just interactions, but also some related behavioral and structural aspects of service architectures.

Essential similarities of service architectures are not difficult to identify by the help of inference rules, which are presented in this paper. The similarities of two situations in Ford are graphically expressed by the diagram, which is represented in figure 13.

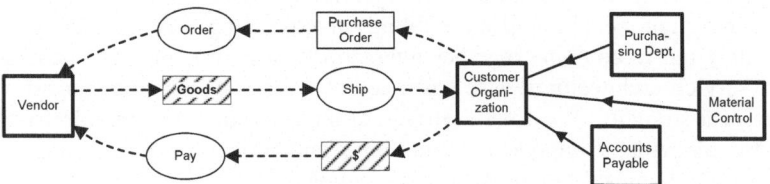

Fig.13. Essential similarities before and after radical change

This diagram characterizes in a concise form the basic enterprise system structure, which is defined in terms of actors and their interaction dependencies. The overlapping of interactions before and after the radical change, demonstrate that the generic business process structure is stable. Analysis of the same case with DEMO approach confirms stability of the essential model as well [6]. However, our service-oriented diagrams demonstrate some important differences between two situations. It is not difficult to understand that one service loop before the radical change is different. Pay action follows Ship action in both diagrams (see figure 12 and 10). However, the main difference is in Send Invoice action. In the service architecture before radical change, one complementary interaction is necessary, because an Invoice class object cannot be created directly by the Ship action (see figure 10). Invoice is required as a precondition for triggering of the Pay action. The related service requests and responses before the radical change can be expressed as follows:

1) if Order(Customer Organization ···· ▶ Vendor)
    then Ship(Vendor ···· ▶ Customer Organization),
2) if SendInvoice(Vendor ···· ▶ Customer Organization)
    then Pay(Customer Organization ···· ▶ Vendor).

If Send Invoice action before radical change could be replaced by Ship action, then triggering events and effects would be equivalent to what is represented in figure 13. The first service interaction loop is exactly the same in both situations and the second service loop is quite different. After the radical change, this service loop is as follows:

> if Ship(Vendor ···· ▶ Customer Organization)
> then Pay(Customer Organization ···· ▶ Vendor).

There is one more essential difference in the service architecture after radical change. It clearly reveals an alternative interaction flow of Returned Goods, which is missing in the architecture before radical change (see figure 12). New service requests and responses can be expressed as follows:

> if Ship(Vendor ···· ▶ Customer Organization)
> then Pay(Customer Organization ···· ▶ Vendor),
> otherwise Return(Customer Organization ···· ▶ Vendor).

The alternative prescribes what happens if Pay action fails. Please note that Return action is missing in service architecture before radical change, because conditions on returning of goods were unclear (see textual description of the situation). After radical change, Shipment is defined as non-overlapping generalization of two concepts with mutually exclusive conditions. If newly created shipment order cannot be found (figure 12), then the Return action must be triggered by Material Control. Most information system design methodologies are 'blind' in expressing such alternative behavior, because they fail to combine together interactions with structural and behavioral aspects of service architectures. Use case, activity and state diagrams are difficult to integrate in a straightforward way. Structural analysis methods provide some possibilities for modeling components, data flows and processes on different levels of decomposition, but resulting hierarchies are clumsy.

Visual analysis of semantic differences between two conceptualizations reveals that the service architecture before radical change is more complicated in a variety of ways. Success of Ship action (with condition Order Found) is not sufficient for triggering the Pay action by Accounts Payable. Pay action before radical change requires creation of an Invoice flow by Vendor. It is obvious from the presented diagram (see figure 10), that Invoice action may fail more often, because of some other reasons:

1) Failure to trigger Send Copy action by Purchasing Department or to receive Purchase Order Copy by Accounts Payable (Purchase Order object is not created),
2) Failure to trigger Send Shipment Data action by Material Control or to receive the Material Receiving Document by Accounts Payable (Delivered Shipment is not registered).
3) Failure to link Invoice object with at least one Purchase Order or to link it with at least one Delivered Shipment in the Accounts Payable archive.

According to the presented diagram, these three situations cannot take place in the service architecture after radical change, because unnecessary coordinating interactions are removed and each Shipment object must only be associated with exactly one Customer Order (see figure 12). It is unclear how these semantic differences can be expressed by the DEMO method [5], because it is not taking into account interplay between service control flows and static dependencies of conceptualizations. To the best of our knowledge, expressing parallel, alternative and iterative behavior of service interactions in combination with structural properties is a challenge for most business process modeling methods.

Conceptual modeling methods, which put into foreground active concepts, are typically focusing on analyzing interactivity between organizational and technical components. The DEMO approach as well as the enterprise modeling language ArchiMate [23] are stemming from a similar modeling tradition. It is quite successful in analyzing an external behavior of enterprise system components. In contrary, the object-oriented paradigm is based on modeling of the static and dynamic aspects of passive concepts, which are represented by various classes of objects. Majority of the textbooks in the area of systems analysis and design recommend concentrating first on domain modeling [1], which is based on analyzing classes, attributes, relationships, state transitions and related effects. Most conventional system analysis and design approaches put into foreground modeling of passive concepts. Only few emerging approaches are making attempts to express deep semantics of interplay between active and passive structures [7]. Conventional information system analysis and design methods are projecting the structural, interaction and state-transition aspects into totally different types of diagrams. It makes very difficult verification of integrity between the static and dynamic aspects of various enterprise architecture dimensions. UML individual diagram types are clear enough, but integrated semantics among models is missing. That is why object-oriented diagrams are difficult to apply for business logics alignment with design for making both organizational and technical system parts more effective.

References

1. Blaha, M., Rumbaugh, J.: Object-Oriented Modelling and Design with UML. Pearson, London (2005)
2. Booch, G., Rumbaugh, J., Jacobsson, I.: The Unified Modelling Language User Guide. Addison Wesley Longman, Inc., Massachusetts (1999)
3. Bunge, M.A.: Treatise on Basic Philosophy. Ontology II: A World of Systems, vol. 4. Reidel Publishing Company, Dordrecht (1979)
4. De Marco, T.: Structured Analysis and System Specification. Prentice Hall, NJ (1979)
5. Dietz, J.L.G.: DEMO: Towards a Discipline of Organisation Engineering. European Journal of Operational Research (128), 351–363 (2001)
6. Dietz, J.L.G.: The Deep Structure of Business Processes. Communications of the ACM 9(5), 59–64 (2006)
7. Dori, D.: Object-Process Methodology: A Holistic System Paradigm. Springer, Berlin (2002)
8. Evermann, J., Wand, Y.: Ontology Based Object-Oriented Domain Modeling: Representing Behavior. Journal of Database Management 20(1), 48–77 (2009)
9. Ferrario, R., Guarino, N.: Towards an Ontological Foundation for Service Science. In: Domingue, J., Fensel, D., Traverso, P. (eds.) FIS 2008. LNCS, vol. 5468, pp. 152–169. Springer, Heidelberg (2008)

10. Finkelstein, C.: Enterprise Integration Using Enterprise Architecture. In: Linger, H., et al. (eds.) Constructing the Infrastructure for the Knowledge Economy, pp. 43–82. Kluwer Academic/Plenum Publishers (2004)
11. Gane, C., Sarson, T.: Structured System Analysis. Prentice Hall, NJ (1979)
12. Gemino, A.: To be or maybe to be: An empirical comparison of mandatory and optional properties in conceptual modeling. In: Proc. Ann. Conf. Admin. Sci. Assoc. of Canada, Information Systems Division, Saskatoon, pp. 33–44 (1998)
13. Glinz, M.: Problems and Deficiencies of UML as a Requirements Specification Language. In: Proc. of the 10-th International Workshop on Software Specification and Design, San Diego, pp. 11–22 (2000)
14. Guizzardi, G.: Modal Aspects of Object Types and Part-Whole Relations and the de re/de dicto distinction. In: Krogstie, J., Opdahl, A.L., Sindre, G. (eds.) CAiSE 2007. LNCS, vol. 4495, pp. 5–20. Springer, Heidelberg (2007)
15. Gustas, R., Gustiene, P.: Pragmatic – Driven Approach for Service-Oriented Analysis and Design. In: Information Systems Engineering - from Data Analysis to Process Networks. IGI Global, USA (2008)
16. Gustas, R., Gustiene, P.: Service-Oriented Foundation and Analysis Patterns for Conceptual Modelling of Information Systems. In: Information System Development: Challenges in Practice, Theory and Education, vol. 1, Springer, Heidelberg (2009)
17. Gustas, R.: A Look behind Conceptual Modeling Constructs in Information System Analysis and Design. International Journal of Information System Modeling and Design 1(1), 79–108 (2010)
18. Gordijn, J., Akkermans, H., van Vliet, H.: Business Process Modelling is not Process Modelling. In: Mayr, H.C., Liddle, S.W., Thalheim, B. (eds.) ER Workshops 2000. LNCS, vol. 1921, pp. 40–51. Springer, Heidelberg (2000)
19. Hammer, M.: Reengineering work: Don't Automate, Obliterate. Harvard Business review, 104–112 (1990)
20. Harel, D., Rumpe, B.: Meaningful Modeling: What's the Semantics of 'Semantics'? IEEE Computer, 64–72 (October 2004)
21. Johannesson, P., Andersson, B., Weigand, H.: Resource Analysis and Classification for Purpose Driven Value Model Design. International Journal of Information System Modeling and Design 1(1), 56–78 (2010)
22. Krogstie, J., Lindland, O.I., Sindre, G.: Defining Quality Aspects of Conceptual Models. In: Proceedings of the IFIP8.1 Working Conference on Information Systems Concepts (ISCO3): Towards a Consolidation of Views, Marburg, Germany, March 28-30, pp. 216–231. Chapman & Hall, London (1995)
23. Lankhorst, M., et al.: Enterprise Architecture at Work. Springer, Berlin (2005)
24. Lindland, O.I., Sindre, G., Solvberg, A.: Understanding Quality in Conceptual Modelling. IEEE Software 11(2), 42–49 (1994)
25. OMG: Unified Modeling Language Superstructure, version 2.2. (2009), http://www.omg.org/spec/UML/2.2/ (retrieved January 19, 2010)
26. Steen, M.V.A., Strating, P., Lankhorst, M.M., ter Doest, H., Iacob, M.E.: Service-Oriented Enterprise Architecture. In: Service-Oriented Software System Engineering: Challenges and Practices, pp. 132–154. Idea Group Inc., USA (2005)
27. Yourdon, E., Constantine, L.L.: Structured Design. Prentice Hall, NJ (1979)
28. Zachman, J.A.: A Framework for Information System Architecture. IBM Systems Journal 26(3) (1987)

Exemplifying a Framework for Interrelating Enterprise Architecture Concerns

Sabine Buckl, Florian Matthes, Christopher Schulz, and Christian M. Schweda

Chair for Software Engineering of Business Information Systems (sebis),
Technische Universität München,
Boltzmannstr. 3, 85748 Garching, Germany
{sabine.buckl,matthes,christopher.schulz,schweda}@in.tum.de
http://wwwmatthes.in.tum.de

Abstract. In recent years, enterprise architecture (EA) management
has gained increasing attention as means to support enterprises in adapting to changing markets and in seizing new business opportunities. A
multitude of approaches and frameworks making prescriptions on how
to document the different states of the EA have been developed. These
approaches target different purposes and correspondingly different concerns (areas of interest) in the architecture. Hence, an enterprise seeking
to develop or evolve an organization-specific EA documentation technique most likely runs into difficulties to understand the interdependen-
cies between different frameworks and approaches.

The paper addresses the aforementioned challenge by presenting a
framework for EA concern interrelations, which can be used to system-
atically analyze the concern relationships of different approaches. The
applicability of the framework is demonstrated by means of a case study
from the automotive industry, in which the framework is used for the development and enhancement of an EA description for risk management.

1 Introduction and Motivation

The increasing frequency of change, modern enterprises face in today's globalized
and competitive environments, leads to a rising internal complexity of the socio-
technical system *enterprise*. A promising and commonly accepted instrument
to deal with this complexity and to foster business-IT-alignment is enterprise
architecture (EA) management [1,2,3]. Originating from the field of information
systems architecture (cf. [4]), EA management takes a holistic perspective targeting all areas of an enterprise from business and organizational via application
and information to infrastructure and data aspects. EA is thereby in the sense of
the ISO Standard 42010 understood as the "fundamental organization of a system [enterprise] embodied in its components, their relationships to each other,
and to the environment, and the principles guiding its design and evolution" [5].
A multitude of methods to EA management has been developed by researchers
(cf. [6,7,2,8,3]), practitioners (cf. [9,10,11]), and standardization bodies (cf. [12]).
Although differing in respect to the selected scope, reach, and focus, the

M.-A. Sicilia, C. Kop, and F. Sartori (Eds.): ONTOSE 2010, LNBIP 62, pp. 33–46, 2010.

proposed methods usually distinguish the following activities of the EA management function: a) document and maintain the current state of the EA, b) develop and describe planned and target states of the EA, c) enact and communicate planned EAs and architectural principles, and d) analyze and evaluate architectures.

A central challenge arising during the aforementioned typical activities of EA management is *stakeholder involvement* [12,13]. To address this challenge the architectural documentations referring to the current, planned, or future states of the EA, need to represent the corresponding concerns of the stakeholders. Thereby, concerns are defined in accordance with the ISO Standard 42010 as "those [areas of] interests which pertain to the system's [enterprise's] development, its operation or any other aspect that are critical or otherwise important to one or more stakeholders" [5]. Put in other words, a concern can be understood as the area of the enterprise that the respective stakeholder is interested in. Whereas, a product manager for instance is interested in the performance of the business process and the services responsible for creating the product, an application manager is concerned with the standard conformity of the business applications.

In the holistic perspective of EA management the two aforementioned concerns are clearly interrelated. Crosspoints are the terms service and business application. The thereby denoted concepts are most likely related – a service is provided by business applications – or may even be identical – two terms referring to the same concept. The differences in terminology can be explained by the different language communities the two stakeholders belong to. To develop a comprehensive EA description, covering the different concerns of the stakeholders, the relations between concerns should be made explicit. Furthermore, these relations between concerns could be utilized to decide on a maturity roadmap for the evolution of the EA management function. In an initial step an enterprise might decide to stick to a more simple concern, while after first results have been achieved the concern is expanded to support a more detailed investigation. This directly yields the research questions that our paper addresses:

– *How does a framework for interrelating EA concerns look alike?*
– *What types of relationships between EA concerns exist?*
– *How can the framework be utilized in developing and evolving EA models?*

In the remainder of the article above research questions are answered by developing a conceptual framework for EA concern relationships. The framework is derived and presented in a step-wise manner (see Section 2). A real world case study form the automotive industry is utilized to illustrate the applicability of the framework in answering the aforementioned research questions in Section 3. Complementingly, prominent approaches from literature to EA management in general and EA modeling in special are revisited to ensure comprehensiveness of the approach (see Section 4). In Section 5, we conclude with a critical reflection of the achieved results and an outlook on future research directions.

2 A Framework for EA Concern Relationships

In line with the ISO 42010 [5], descriptions of architectures are comprised of viewpoints that conversely reflect areas of interest in the corresponding architecture. These areas of interest, called *architectural concerns* in the terms of the ISO 42010, not only define the part of the architecture that should be considered, but also bring along a conceptualization of the EA. Put in other words, a concern builds and centrally employs an underlying domain ontology targeting a specific part of the overall EA. Considering two or more different architectural concerns, it may be beneficial to understand, in which ways the corresponding areas of interest relate. In order to facilitate in-depth discussions on concern relationships, we subsequently present are more precise definition of what an architectural concern means. A concern can be described by two fundamental properties, namely

– a **selection** of relevant architectural elements, i.e. of *things* and their *properties* in an ontological sense, that are in the area of interest, and
– a **conceptualization** describing the architectural *types* and *property types* abstracted from the selected (relevant) architectural elements.

Illustrating above definition of an architectural concern in the EA context, we formulate a CONCERN A that describes the

> *business applications in relationship to their responsible organizational units* (conceptualization) of an enterprise, *restricted to organizational units located in Germany* (selection).

In the light of the above definition, we can derive different types of relationships between concerns. A basic relationship expresses the fact that two concerns have at least one type in common, i.e. that their conceptualizations share at least one type. This entails a more sophisticated discussion on the question of how to understand 'share' in this context. In more detail, two ways to understand the term exist: *syntactic* and *semantic*. While sharing in the latter sense means that two concerns have a type with similar meaning in common, syntactic sharing describes that two concerns are related via a concept with a common name. To qualify these two different understandings of the term 'share', we use the term *intersection* to denote syntactic sharing.

Based on the intersection-relationship, we establish the notion *compatibility* as a relationship between two concerns, indicating that all intersecting types and property types of two concerns are also semantically shared. If in contrast at least one intersecting type or property type is assigned distinct meanings in both concerns, the concerns are called *incompatible*. Introducing a CONCERN B describing

> *business applications and their standardization level* (conceptualization)
> of an enterprise,

we can exemplify the aforementioned concern relationships in the following. Both concerns are clearly intersecting, as they both employ the type 'business application'. At this point nothing can be said on the compatibility of these concerns.

To answer this question, one would have to delve into the contexts, in which these concerns were raised. With concerns being described as sentences in real language, such investigation would employ analyses of the linguistic communities (cf. Kamlah and Lorenzen [14]) from which the concern descriptions originate. We abstain here from going into the details of interpersonal testing techniques, but call for an intuitive understanding of *equivalent meanings*, based on the assumption that each type described in the concerns was backed by a defini-tory sentence in a glossary or an ontologically richer structure. Based on the glossary, equivalence of meaning can be understood as stakeholder consensus in accordance to Kamlah and Lorenzen [14]. Two types thereby share a common meaning, if "any informed member of [both] linguistic communities would [...] say so". Given the fact that both concerns referred to a single definitory glossary, explaining what a business application is, we can state that the two concerns are compatible.

Grounded on the basic relationship of compatibility, we establish a *super*-relationship between architectural concerns. One concern is superconcern of an-other, if the concerns are compatible and all types and property types of the second are intersecting ones. Put more colloquially, the conceptualization of the first concern completely covers the conceptualization of the second one. Intro-ducing another CONCERN C that describes the

> *business applications in relationship to their responsible organizational units and their supported business processes* (conceptualization) of an enterprise.

We further assume that CONCERN A and CONCERN C are *maximally* compati-ble, i.e. that all shared concepts each have an equivalent meaning. Under these premises, CONCERN C completely covers CONCERN A, exemplifying supercon-cern relationship with CONCERN C being super to CONCERN A.

Above, we introduced three types of concern relationships based on an intu-itive understanding of the concern's underlying conceptualization. In the context of EA management such conceptualizations are frequently described as object-oriented meta-models, see e.g. Buckl et al. in [15], Johnson and Ekstedt in [16], and Österle et al. in [17]. Subsequently, we shall call these meta-models in ac-cordance with Buckl et al. *information models*. Based on such more formally described conceptualizations the aforementioned types of concern relationships can be defined more concisely and described in more detail. We nevertheless abstain from discussing the subtleties of such definitions, an application of the concern relationships along exemplary information models is given in Section 3. Some additional remarks on concern relationships based on their corresponding conceptualizations are described by Buckl et al. in [18].

Concluding the exposition of the concern relationship framework in this sec-tion, we discuss on relationship types that ground in the selection that con-stitutes a concern. The first relationship type to devise, is the one of *instance level intersection*. Two concerns are related in this way, if they – applied to the same EA – cover at least one common element, i.e. thing, from the architecture. Refraining the examples from above, we display CONCERN D that describes the

organizational units (conceptualization) of an enterprise.

Assuming that both CONCERN A and CONCERN D have a common understanding what the term "organizational unit" means, the concerns are intersecting on instance level. Complementing, we can define a *non-intersection* relationship. In addition, we can derive an *instance level superconcern* relationship, expressing that one concern – applied to the same EA – covers all elements that another concern – applied to this EA – covers.

We complement the above framework with a discussion on the utilization of the relationships in the context of EA management. Refraining an argument put forward by Aier et al. in [19], an enterprise-specific EA description technique must match the requirements of the using enterprise in two directions, namely in "width" and "depth". Width in this context means, that the technique must cover the relevant parts of the EA embracingly, i.e. must be able to answer questions of all relevant EA stakeholders. Complementing, the criterion of depth accounts for the fact that for answering certain EA questions more detailed information about the EA may be needed. While in the context of initially devising an EA description technique, multiple different approaches, also ones not using concern relationships, might be helpful, we expect that the relationships especially simplify the evolution of the EA description technique in response to changing demands of the EA stakeholders. To illustrate how this can be achieved, we build on the EA management pattern catalog of Technische Universität München [20,21]. This catalog expatiates a set of practice-proven EA relevant concerns that are complemented with information models reifying the underlying information demands. If the concerns were related using the aforementioned relationship types, an enterprise willing to evolve its own EA description technique based on the information models would have the following advantages:

- Feeling the need to "widen" the scope of the EA description technique, the enterprise could search the set of concerns that are *compatible* with the currently employed ones. These concerns and their complementing information models should easily integrate into the current description technique.
- Feeling the need to "deepen" the scope of the EA description technique, the enterprise could traverse the *superconcern*-relationships, in order to determine concerns that employ the currently described concepts, but cover additional information.

Summarizing the above, concern relationships provide decision support for developing an enterprise-specific EA description technique. Illustrating this fact, we subsequently provide an application example from a practice case, where we applied concern relationships to prepare decision making on the appropriate EA description technique for addressing an EA challenge in both 'right width and depth'.

3   Application Example

An international manufacturer from the automotive industry intends to construct a new overseas production plant. Thereby, the local market should be served in a customer friendlier manner, while currency fluctuations have to be mitigated in order to remain competitive. Part of this large-scale project is the deployment and roll-out of approximately 170 partly interconnected applications supporting a modern and up to date assembling of vehicles. For the sake of profitability, existing applications are duplicated and slightly adjusted to the local conditions before being deployed and tested. These applications are typically referred to as *group applications*, meaning they are used in a slightly adapted manner at different production plants. Thereby, those new applications are also connected with their counterparts on the other side of the globe, enabling a company-wide business intelligence, monitoring, and controlling capability.

The local production and sales of vehicles is constrained by country-specific laws and regulations. In the case of our international car manufacturer, the disclosure of company-internal information is regulated by the *antitrust law*. Once a piece of information is revealed to one supplier or customer, it must be automatically made accessible to other third parties. Contrastingly, if a *class action suits* succeeds, hence an objection raised by several plaintiffs is sustained, lawyers will have the possibility to access different company-internal information as well.

As a matter of fact, information is mostly stored within applications nowadays allowing an effective and efficient data organization and retrieval. These applications directly and indirectly support the execution of different business processes (e.g. car construction process, car sales process, etc.). Due to above alluded rules and regulations, external lawyers and auditors would have unimpeded access to those applications as well as their contained data. As second consequence, the attorneys were also allowed to retrieve information not only stored locally on those applications, but also on other applications which are connected via network technology. Hence, the real set of information being also transitively accessible through the 170 applications would be much broader than anticipated before, representing a danger for corporate secrets.

To respond to this challenge, the international manufacturer launched a project targeting at modifying those applications also granting access to data, which is not explicitly needed for the production plant. Initially, 35 applications as well as their exported and imported interfaces providing access on data not relating to the overseas factory where identified and marked as inherently critical. The classification thereby was mostly based on the experience application owners and users had with those applications. Subsequently, the 35 applications classified as critical will undergo time-consuming analysis and complex functional modifications aiming at restricting their data scope to the information relevant for the local context. The remaining 135 applications not classified yet, will be analyzed in a two step approach. To reduce workload, a quick but comprehensive interface analysis of the 135 applications will be performed in a first step to identify those applications, which need to be considered in more detail. In a second step, the applications classified as critical will be analyzed as described before.

When being confronted with the application interface analysis, the car manufacturer asked us for help. The problem description of our cooperation reads as follows:

> How can criticality of application systems interfaces be determined? Which concepts and relationships are decisive for criticality of interfaces exported by applications.

After thoroughly studying a list of factors all determining if an interface is critical, we suggested three different concerns, which are detailed in the following.

As a first step, we generally defined an interface as being critical whenever it has no authorization mechanism available. Hence, once an interface possesses such a mechanism, its criticality is set to low and it needs no further investigation. Figure 1 illustrates the underlying information model I-1 consisting only of one single entity named `interface` and the attributes `hasAuthorization`, `hasAuthentication`, and `criticality`. Thereby, the attribute `criticality` is a derived attribute, whose value is influenced by the two other attributes. This fact is illustrated utilizing the notation of *feature dependency relationship* as defined by Buckl et al. in [22].

An alternative way to assign a specific criticality to an application interface is to closely examine the security type of the data the interface exchanges. This can be expressed through a second concern, which is described in the information model I-2 depicted in Figure 2 by showing two entities, `interface` and `data`. Thereby, an `interface` is regarded as being low critical whenever it is used for exchanging public data only. If the data is either internal, confidential, or secret, the interface's criticality shifts to medium or high. Again the notation of the *feature dependency relationship* (cf. [22]) is used.

Compared to our aforementioned framework for interrelating EA concerns, both models are compatible. The entity `interface` is semantically and syntactically equal within the two concerns, both models could complement each other.

After further consideration, we proposed a third concern whose information model I-3 also addresses the goal of determining critical and non-critical interfaces. Thereby, an interface may only be deemed as being critical when it is from the type 'exporting' with regards to the interface's underlying application.

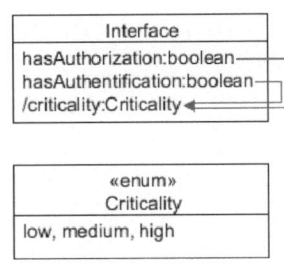

Fig. 1. Interface criticality defined by an available authentication mechanism

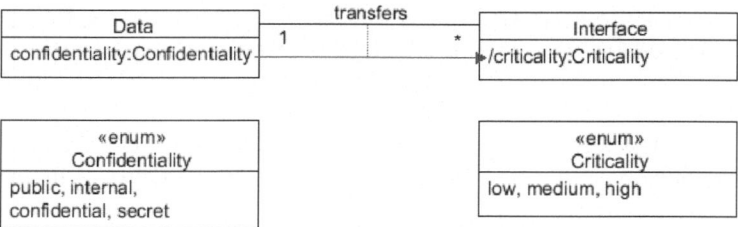

Fig. 2. Interface criticality contingent on the security type of exchanged data

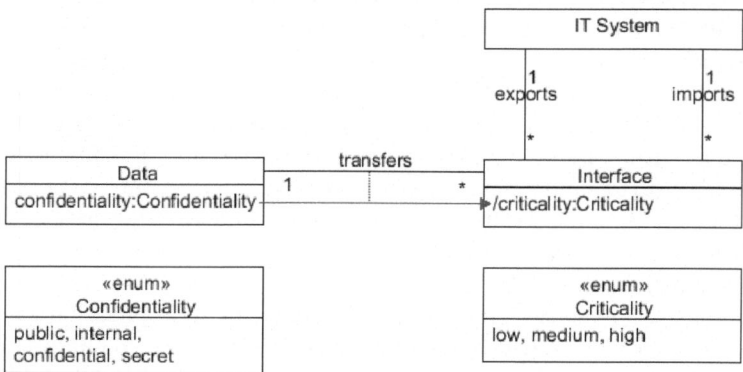

Fig. 3. Interface criticality depending on interface and exchanged data security type

In addition, the interface has to transfer non-public data, thus data which is either internal, confidential, or secret.

As expatiated on in Section 2, Figure 3 represents a super concern with regards to the concern specified in Figure 2. Additional relationships between information model I-1 and I-2, respectively I-3 exist. Each of the above pair describes two compatible concerns. The interrelations between the different concerns worked out so far, are depicted in the map presented in Figure 4. In the map, we further added an "artificial" concern I-3', as the integration of I-1 and I-3.

When discussing the results with the international car manufacturer, two further fields of work arose. Firstly, we identified additional attributes, which may be regarded as being relevant for the criticality of an application and its

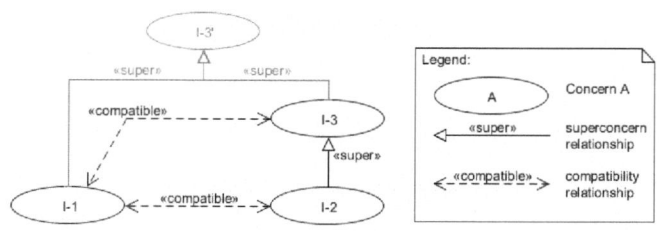

Fig. 4. Concern map for the exemplary concerns

interfaces, i.a. multi-client capability on different application layers, concrete data content (i.e. business objects and their criticality), configurability of the interface, etc. Those aspects could be either directly incorporated in existing information models or new concerns had to be created. Secondly, we had to find out which of the required information addressing the concerns of application interface criticality presented above is already stored in existing EA management tools. If the specific date is not available it has to be gathered, e.g. through interviews with the according application owners or an online survey. In all, the goal of determining the criticality of application interfaces was addressed through several interrelating EA concerns, summarized by a concern relationship map, which follows the presented framework.

4   Concern Relationship in the State-of-the-Art in EA Descriptions

In addition to the first successful application of the framework for EA concern relationship in practice as discussed in the preceding section, we analyzed existing literature on EA management. EA management is a research topic with an increasing number of publications [23], in which especially the fields of EA modeling and EA analysis are heavily researched. Central to both activities is the notion of the architectural description reflecting the corresponding architectural concerns. Subsequently, we explore the state-of-the-art in EA modeling and analysis with a special emphasis on the EA descriptions used thereby as well as their underlying concerns in order to validate the framework for interrelating EA concerns as presented in Section 2.

The approach of *multi-perspective enterprise modeling (MEMO)* was initially presented by Frank in 2002 [6]. Therein, Frank outlines a modeling framework, which is based on an extendable set of special purpose modeling languages. The special purpose modeling languages correspond to the different language communities, which typically exist in an enterprise, e.g. salespersons or project managers. By further providing a common meta-language, the *MEMO meta modelling language (MML)* [24], which the special purpose languages rely on, the integration of the different languages can be facilitated. Examples for special purpose languages are e.g. the *strategy modelling language (MEMO-SML)* [25] and the *organization modelling language (MEMO-OrgML)* [26]. Concepts of two different languages can be associated, i.e. are common to both languages. Therefore, the different concerns addressed by the MEMO special purpose languages can be regarded as being *intersected* and *compatible*.

The communication challenge already mentioned in the approach presented by Frank, is further discussed by Buckl et al. in [27], Schelp and Winter in [28], and Schönherr in [13]. While the first publication refers to the communication challenge within an enterprise, the latter two publications discuss the different language communities mirroring the academic groups conducting research in the area of EA management. Due to the absence of a standardized terminology and a commonly-accepted description language for EA management, the different approaches and communities have developed their own terms, leading to *incompatibility* issues, when different approaches are combined.

A systemic perspective on EA modeling is presented by Wegmann et al. in [29]. They provide a method and a tool to formalize the alignment of the multiple levels that constitute an EA. In particular, they propose to organize the different concepts that constitute the EA in *organizational* and *functional levels*. Thereby, the functional levels represent behavioral and the organizational levels the constructional hierarchy. Within each organizational level, two different viewpoints are available, the *information viewpoint* – a black box view on the respective concern – and the *computational viewpoint* – a white box specification of the concern. These viewpoints can be refined, which results in a hierarchy of viewpoints and the underlying information, respectively. Based on this understanding, a *super-* and *sub-relationship* between different viewpoints and concerns can be identified. Furthermore, Wegman et al. point out that a "vocabulary mapping" [29] between related concepts on different organizational levels has to be performed, which can be ascribed to the already mentioned *compatibility* question.

In [7] Kurpjuweit and Winter present a *systemic approach to meta model engineering*, which consists of five steps: 1) Identification of relevant concerns, 2) requirements elicitation, 3) viewpoint relationship overview, 4) meta model[1] fragment selection or design, and 5) meta model fragment integration. For the identification of relationships between concerns, especially the last step is of importance. Kurpjuweit and Winter allude to two different types of relationships between concerns as mirrored in the corresponding meta model fragments. Firstly, concerns can be *intersected*, which rises the challenge that the terminology must be adjusted. Secondly, a generalization or specialization may be necessary, which is caused by a *superconcern* or *subconcern* relationship between different concerns.

In [16] Johnson and Ekstedt discuss an approach to EA decision making based on EA models and analyses. Based on the current documentation of the EA, future EA scenarios are derived and assessed in respect to selected quality attributes, as e.g. performance, interoperability, availability, security, or usability. For each of these quality attributes, an *influence diagram* is presented by the authors, which details on causal dependencies between architectural properties. If for instance availability is considered, the reliability or recoverability of the system under consideration influences the overall availability. Thus, the concerns included in an influence diagram have a *subconcern/superconcern* relationship to each other, while concerns of different influence diagrams may be *intersected*.

Central ideas for a language for describing EAs are outlined by Jonkers et al. in [30] and further elaborated in [31]. They discuss two requirements that relate to the notion of the concern, namely *meta model flexibility* and *integration of heterogeneous models*. Meta model flexibility is thereby meant to demand that general EA description concepts can be refined to organization-specific concepts and standards. Conversely, a language for describing EAs must facilitate the

---

[1] The term *meta model* thereby corresponds to the term *information model* as used in this paper.

integration of heterogeneous models, as special purpose languages for specific parts of the EA exist, whose concepts can be 'translated' into or 'associated' with concepts for EA description. Jonkers et al. further discuss in [30] the distinct levels of detail, on which the corresponding descriptions may act. In this sense, one or more concerns from special purpose modeling languages might be 'aggregated' into a single concern at the EA description level. In [31] Jonkers et al. provide a core meta-model for architectural descriptions, more precisely behavioral aspects thereof, based on a dichotomy of *service-* and *implementation-aspects*. The corresponding basic concepts *service* and *behavior element* are refined to specific *business*, *application* and *infrastructure-layer* concepts, respectively. Nevertheless, the basic modeling language allows to omit concepts on some of these layers, if they are not of interest for the specific modeling purpose. Put in the terminology of our concern-discussion, the language implicitly allows for the derivation of *subconcerns*.

Summarizing the state-of-the-art in EA concern relationship modeling it can be stated, that the framework presented in Section 2 can be used to classify the different relationships as explicitly or only implicitly proposed in current publications. Furthermore, it provides a framework for conceptual interrelation as well as proposes the *concern map* for making the relations explicit.

5   Conclusion and Outlook

In this paper, we discussed the concept *concern* in the context of EA modeling and EA management, respectively. Concerns thereby represent distinct information demands in respect to the described architecture and can hence be reflected by information models that provide a 'schema' for the information to be modeled and collected during the corresponding EA management process. Based on this model-centric understanding of concern, we developed a framework for interrelating EA concerns and showed its applicability in a real world case study from the automotive industry. Thereby, especially the utility for evolving modeling techniques was discussed. Complementingly, we revisited the state-of-the-art in EA modeling and analysis.

This paper presents itself as a research-in-progress paper, that outlines the idea of concern relationships. From this point different directions for further development and research are open. At first, the informal presentation of the relationship types in this paper should be complemented with a more formal understanding thereof. In this respect, the semantics of the different relationship types could be formally defined based on a formal understanding of architectural descriptions. This would then allow for more intricate considerations on the relationships between information models that reflect the corresponding concerns. Secondly, concern relationships might not only be an issue of theoretical interest, but may prove to be interesting for supporting maturity considerations for EA management functions. In this respect, the relationships could also be beneficial for evolving an already existing EA management function towards a 'broader' and 'deeper' coverage of the overall EA. This subject has yet not been investigated in practice, although the notion of the "related" concerns as outlined by Ernst in [32] and in [21] have shown to be beneficial during the process of establishing and evolving an EA management function.

Acknowledgement

The case study research presented in this paper was possible thanks to the support of Volkswagen AG, Wolfsburg. The authors of the document wish to acknowledge the industry partners for their help and important contributions.

References

1. Henderson, J.C., Venkatraman, N.: Strategic alignment: leveraging information technology for transforming organizations. IBM Systems Journal 32(1), 472–484 (1993)
2. Lankhorst, M.: Enterprise Architecture at Work: Modelling, Communication and Analysis. Springer, Heidelberg (2005)
3. Ross, J.W., Weill, P., Robertson David, C.: Enterprise Architecture as Strategy. Harvard Business School Press, Boston (2006)
4. Zachman, J.: Extending and formalising the framework for information systems architecture. IBM Systems Journal 31(3) (1992)
5. International Organization for Standardization: Iso/iec 42010:2007 systems and software engineering – recommended practice for architectural description of software-intensive systems (2007)
6. Frank, U.: Multi-perspective enterprise modeling (memo) – conceptual framework and modeling languages. In: Proceedings of the 35th Annual Hawaii International Conference on System Sciences (HICSS 2002), Washington, DC, USA, pp. 1258–1267 (2002)
7. Kurpjuweit, S., Winter, R.: Viewpoint-based meta model engineering. In: Reichert, M., Strecker, S., Turowski, K. (eds.) Enterprise Modelling and Information Systems Architectures – Concepts and Applications, Proceedings of the 2nd International Workshop on Enterprise Modelling and Information Systems Architectures (EMISA 2007), Bonn, Germany, Gesellschaft für Informatik, October 8-9, LNI, pp. 143–161 (2007)
8. van der Raadt, B., van Vliet, H.: Designing the enterprise architecture function. In: Becker, S., Plasil, F., Reussner, R. (eds.) QoSA 2008. LNCS, vol. 5281, pp. 103–118. Springer, Heidelberg (2008)
9. Dern, G.: Management von IT-Architekturen (Edition CIO). Vieweg, Wiesbaden (2006)
10. Keller, W.: IT-Unternehmensarchitektur. dpunkt.verlag, Heidelberg (2007)
11. Niemann, K.D.: From Enterprise Architecture to IT Governance – Elements of Effective IT Management. Vieweg+Teubner, Wiesbaden (2006)
12. The Open Group: TOGAF "Enterprise Edition" Version 9 (2009), http://www.togaf.org (cited 2010-02-25)
13. Schönherr, M.: Towards a common terminology in the discipline of enterprise architecture. In: Aier, S., Johnson, P., Schelp, J. (eds.) Pre-Proceedings of the 3rd Workshop on Trends in Enterprise Architecture Research, Sydney, Australia, pp. 107–123 (2008)

14. Kamlah, W., Lorenzen, P.: Logische Propädeutik: Vorschule des vernünftigen Redens, 3rd edn. Metzler, Stuttgart (1996)
15. Buckl, S., Ernst, A.M., Lankes, J., Schneider, K., Schweda, C.M.: A pattern based approach for constructing enterprise architecture management information models. In: Wirtschaftsinformatik 2007, pp. 145–162. Universitätsverlag Karlsruhe, Karlsruhe (2007)
16. Johnson, P., Ekstedt, M.: Enterprise Architecture – Models and Analyses for Information Systems Decision Making. Studentlitteratur, Pozkal (2007)
17. Österle, H., Winter, R., Hoening, F., Kurpjuweit, S., Osl, P.: Der St. Galler Ansatz des Business Engineering: Das Core Business Metamodel. Wisu – Das Wirtschaftsstudium 2(36), 191–194 (2007)
18. Buckl, S., Matthes, F., Schweda, C.M.: Interrelating concerns in ea documentation – towards a conceptual framework of relationships. In: 2nd European Workshop on Patterns for Enterprise Architecture Management (PEAM 2010), Paderborn, Germany (2010)
19. Aier, S., Kurpjuweit, S., Saat, J., Winter, R.: Enterprise Architecture Design as an Engineering Discipline. AIS Transactions on Enterprise Systems 1, 36–43 (2009)
20. Buckl, S., Ernst, A.M., Lankes, J., Matthes, F.: Enterprise Architecture Management Pattern Catalog (Version 1.0, February 2008). Technical report, Chair for Informatics 19 (sebis), Technische Universität München, Munich, Germany (2008)
21. Chair for Informatics 19 (sebis), Technische Universität München: Eam pattern catalog wiki (2010), http://eampc-wiki.systemcartography.info (cited 2010-02-25)
22. Buckl, S., Ernst, A.M., Schweda, C.M.: An extension to the essential meta-object facility (emof) for specifying and indicating dependencies between properties. Technical report, Technische Universität München (2008)
23. Langenberg, K., Wegmann, A.: Enterprise architecture: What aspect is current research targeting? Technical report, Laboratory of Systemic Modeling, Ecole Polytechnique Fédérale de Lausanne, Lausanne, Switzerland (2004)
24. Frank, U.: The memo meta modelling language (mml) and language architecture (icb-research report). Technical report, Institut für Informatik und Wirtschaftsinformatik, Duisburg-Essen, Germany (2009)
25. Frank, U.: Memo: Visual languages for enterprise modelling. Technical Report 18, Arbeitsberichte des Instituts für Wirtschaftsinformatik Koblenz (1999)
26. Frank, U., Jung, J.: The memo organisation modelling language (memo-orgml). Technical Report 26, Arbeitsberichte des Institut für Wirtschaftsinformatik der Universität Koblenz-Landau (2001)
27. Buckl, S., Ernst, A.M., Lankes, J., Matthes, F., Schweda, C.M.: State of the art in enterprise architecture management 2009. Technical report, Chair for Informatics 19 (sebis), Technische Universität München, Munich, Germany (2009)
28. Schelp, J., Winter, R.: Language communities in enterprise architecture research. In: DESRIST 2009: Proceedings of the 4th International Conference on Design Science Research in Information Systems and Technology, pp. 1–10. ACM, New York (2009)
29. Wegmann, A., Balabko, P., Lê, R.G., Rychkova, I.: A method and tool for business-it alignment in enterprise architecture. In: Pastor, Ó., Falcão e Cunha, J. (eds.) CAiSE 2005. LNCS, vol. 3520, pp. 113–118. Springer, Heidelberg (2005)

30. Jonkers, H., van Burren, R., Arbab, F., de Boer, F., Bonsangue, M., Bosma, H., ter Doest, H., Groenewegen, L., Scholten, J., Hoppenbrouwers, S., Iacob, M.E., Janssen, W., Lankhorst, M., van Leeuwen, D., Proper, E., Stam, A., van der Torre, L., van Zanten, G.: Towards a language for coherent enterprise architecture descriptions. In: 7th International Enterprise Distributed Object Computing Conference (EDOC 2003), Brisbane, Australia, IEEE Computer Society, Los Alamitos (2003)
31. Jonkers, H., Goenewegen, L., Bonsangue, M., van Buuren, R.: A language for enterprise modelling. In: Lankhorst, M. (ed.) Enterprise Architecture at Work, Springer, Heidelberg (2005)
32. Ernst, A.M.: A Pattern-Based Approach to Enterprise Architecture Management. PhD thesis, Technische Universität München, München, Germany (2010)

Ontology Representations for Information Exchange between Communities

Benjamin Diemert, Marie-Hélène Abel, and Claude Moulin

Heudiasyc UMR 6599 - Université de Technologie de Compiègne
Centre de Recherches de Royallieu
BP 20529 60205 Compiègne cedex, France
{benjamin.diemert,marie-helene.abel,claude.moulin}@hds.utc.fr
http://www2.hds.utc.fr/

Abstract. Exchange and repurposing of digital information and content raise language variations issues between communities. Indeed, producer and consumer may not share the same practices and languages. TV producers tend to have more and more collaborative workflows and uses amateur contributions to diversify their content's sources. However, amateurs may not understand the audiovisual jargon. In this paper, we introduce a conceptual model and its OWL formalization to deal with these issues. We show that our approach extends the thesaurus approach and is able to attach various labels to any kind of ontological element (class, property, instance). We find our motivations in information exchange between professionals and amateurs as well as in multilingual search. We study digital archiving and cultural heritage model and use them as the foundations of our work. We show how these models tend to focus on material exchange and are not sufficient to deal with a comprehensible exchange of information. We propose to use personal and contextual parameters to make a selection of comprehensible label and other kind of information for a given user. We finish by demonstrating the OWL formalization of our model.

Keywords: knowledge representation, thesaurus, denomination, digital archiving, TV production.

1 Introduction

The massive introduction of digital content on public and private networks has considerably increased the amount of documents and information available. However, digitisation and network availability have not yet kept their promises to ease content's exploitation and repurposing [1]. The TV production field is not an exception. The task is even more difficult as the production process is segmented into various stages. From script writing through funding, shooting, editing to post-production, each stage has its own specialized know-how and jobs. Nevertheless, each stage re-use audiovisual content or information from the previous ones.

M.-A. Sicilia, C. Kop, and F. Sartori (Eds.): ONTOSE 2010, LNBIP 62, pp. 47–62, 2010.

Dedicated Information Systems have been developed to meet these various needs one step at a time. They usually focus on content processing and leave aside the transportation of associated information valuable for production, archiving and repurposing. Indeed, information such as compositional metadata, – describing the content's structure – descriptive metadata – describing the context of production – and the description of intentions may lead to significant efficiency gains to describe the content's and ease its production and repurposing [2].

The few metadata available are produced in various manners. Some are produced automatically by systems – GPS coordinates, camera lens information etc. Others are automatically extracted from the audiovisual content – shot detection, speech recognition etc. Some others are manually filled in by the various protagonists engaged in the production chain. These information are usually lost or trapped into proprietary formats. The lack of integration between systems leads to a loss of information as the production goes on [3]. Thus, we believe there is a strong need to design a system which can wrap up both content and metadata and transport them without loss throughout the production chain. The package will need to hold the required metadata for repurposing.

In addition to interoperability issues, the diversity of protagonists engaged in the TV production process leads to language variations (vocabulary, spelling, abbreviation etc.) in the production of information, which may be critical for content's description. Even though they may share common concepts there are always language differences which make the content's description even more difficult to use and understand for the one which is searching. This problem increases with the use of archive and content from other organizations. The issue could be defined at a terminology level where we need to consider various denominations for the same concept, each one having a given scope of use.

It is also essential to build up a model capable of integrating and join these language variations whatever the syntax or jargon used. This feature is needed in order to carry on content and its description along the chain and ensure that these information will be comprehensible and re-usable. An ontology could tackle this issue provided that it considers and connects communities with their own variation. Multilingualism is thus dealt as a specific case of a more generic concern.

In this article, we present the advantages of modelling denomination's variations for information exchange between community of users. We consider two use-cases, the first one with two communities having different level of understanding of the same jargon, the second one exemplifies a search in a multilingual corpus – see Section 2. We introduce then some related works at the roots of our model and explain why they are not sufficient to address the language variations issue – see Section 3. We define the key concepts and relations of our model and illustrate its principles through the modelling of our two use-cases – see Section 4. Eventually, we discuss our OWL representation with these two examples – see Section 5 – and conclude on future works.

2   Motivations

This work takes place in the MediaMap project[1] which make use of Semantic Web technologies to promote collaborative production and audiovisual content repurposing. The consortium includes the two Belgian public broadcasting network[2] as main users. Thus, multilingual aspects are more like a requirement than a feature.

Moreover, the arrival of new competitors from the telecommunication field urges these organizations to develop collaborative production, to diversify their content's supply source (shooting, internal archive, purchase) and find new opportunities to exploit their productions. Description of the organization's content, search and integration of content from other organizations and even amateurs become crucial needs. Exchange of content and related information has gone beyond the scope of the organization and take place at various stages of the production chain. As the chain becomes more and more versatile there is a strong need for indexation since pre-production and all along the chain in order to support these exchanges.

2.1   Amateur and Professional Collaboration

Calls for amateur's contribution constitute one promising way to purchase original and sometimes exclusive content. This raises however a quality issue as the content may not meet the professional quality requirements. One pro-active approach to address this issue is to provide the amateur with editorial guidance written by professionals. But a shooting script written by a director is not sufficient as the amateur may not have a sound knowledge of professional's jargon and know-hows. For instance, shot values such as *American Shot*, *Medium Close-Up* or *Medium Shot* refer to a given framing of a character which needs to be explained to the amateur cameraman – see Figure 1.

We face here an information exchange issue between two communities with different levels of knowledge of the same jargon. We indicate in this figure how one concept could be presented differently for a (**P**)rofessional cameraman and an (**A**)mateur one.

2.2   Multilingual Information Retrieval

In some cases, we may consider the multilingual issue [4] as spelling variations denoting the same concept or instance. A proper name may have various acknowledged spellings which all refer to the same individual. For instance, there are many spellings for the name of the *Swan Lake's* composer – see Figure 2. Suppose now a French user makes a search on the composer with the French spelling. English and Russian documents will not be part of the results set even though the user understands these languages. Unless all spellings refering to the same instance are connected together and the user's capabilities are described.

---

[1] http://www.mediamapproject.org/
[2] The Flemish Radio- and Television Network (VRT), the French-speaking Radio- and Television Network(RTBF).

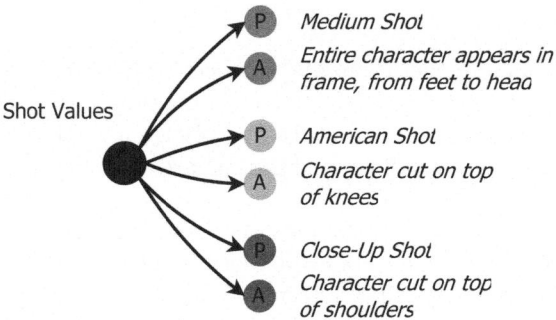

Fig. 1. A sample of shot values used in the audiovisual (**P**)rofessional jargon and their explanations for the (**A**)mateur

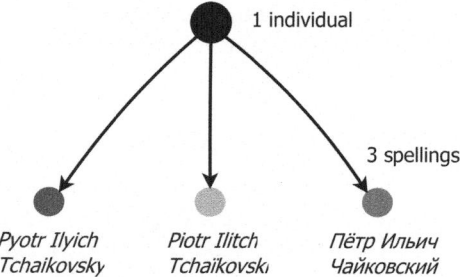

Fig. 2. English, French and Russian spellings for the proper name of the Swan Lake's composer

In order to connect these spellings we first have to distinguish them. Obviously, each spelling may be characterised by its natural language transcription. Also, the first two are written in the Latin alphabet, the last one is in Cyrillic. In other cases, we may eventually need to consider geographical locations to distinguish between local variations – English versus American spelling for instance.

3 Related Works

Among the works we have studied, *Acquisition, eXchange, Indexing and Structuring* (Axis) has brought us the best foundations to describe audiovisual description all along the chain. Axis is both a model and an architecture developed during the Memories project[3] to deal with exchange and archiving of media assets. Axis bases itself on principles brought by *Open Archive Information System* (OAIS), a digital archiving norm. We introduce in the next section the archiving principles of OAIS that have been used in Axis in order to address the exchange issue of media assets.

---

[3] http://www.memories-project.eu/

3.1 Digital Archiving and Information Exchange

Archiving may be defined in a documentary perspective as the intentional will to constitute and preserve a memory [6]. This is achieved through two indivisibles kind of preservation: (1) the material preservation of documents against physical deterioration, (2) the preservation of a reading tradition to convey the ability to interpret and understand the content of documents. Thus, archiving ensures us a sensible and comprehensible access to documents. We want to introduce in the next section the OAIS definition of archiving and its relation with information exchange.

Archiving as a service. The OAIS norm defines digital archiving as an information exchange service provided to various communities [5]. OAIS gives recommendations for setting up an organization which can provide such a service. Figure 3 shows the functions assumed by the organization as well as the data flows.

The main focus of this organization is to act as a middleman between a Producer and a Consumer community and take care of every aspects of the information exchange. In this perspective, *Preservation Planning* is charged to monitor changes in information representation technologies and practices in both communities. Additional information to ensure future exploitation and understanding is included in various *Information Package* (IP) which are used as conveyors. We detail first the information flow and then information requirements which define the IP's structure.

Information exchange management. The *Ingest* function is the first step of the chain. Its purpose is to gather the Producer's data and transform them in conformity with Preservation Planning quality requirements. A *Submission* IP (SIP) is defined conforming to previous agreements with the Producer. After ingestion, an internal format is used, the *Archival* IP (AIP). The information to be preserved is stored by the *Archival Storage*. Its description is handled separately

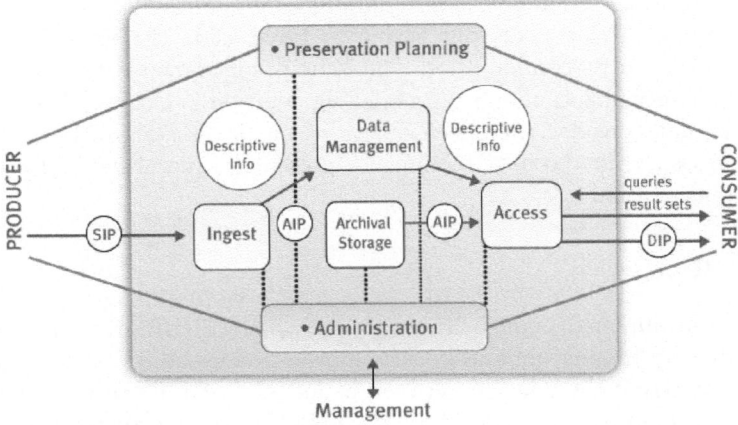

Fig. 3. OAIS functional organization and information flow

by the *Data Management* function to meet search needs. Indeed, the *Access* function uses these descriptions to handle the interaction – search, order, retrieve – with the Consumer community. Once the information needed is ordered, the AIP is transformed into a *Dissemination* IP (DIP). Notice that each IP is intended for a different use which may require format transformations or restructuring according to the general information requirements defined by OAIS.

Information's description requirements. OAIS defines four kind of requirements for its IP in order to ensure material and comprehensible access to information to be preserved:

- *Content Information* is the information to be preserved along with the descriptions needed for the Consumer community to exploit it. The descriptions deal with data structures, their meanings and the knowledge required to understand it. It could be as much detailed as needed, this decision belongs to Preservation Planing. For instance, a PDF file of a musical score may need first a plain text file for describing the PDF format, provided that the designated community is able to read such a file. Then another plain text file is required to explain the musical notation used.
- *Preservation Description Information* are identification and traceability information. Identification is needed for the whole and each part of the Content Information. Traceability starts with a description of the production's context, the author's original intentions, a processing history and integrity indicators.
- *Package Description* is used for search and exploration of the Content Information.
- *Packaging Information* is the information needed to bind and identify each part of the Content Information to its physical location on an information carrier.

As we have shown, OAIS define organizational and description requirements to handle information exchange between various communities. These requirements also consider archiving goals but seems to leave aside the issue of language variations between its communities. The issue is somehow raised but left to be solved by the organization and no modelling solution is expressed. Eventually, OAIS does not consider the specific case of media assets which raises other description issues. In the next section, we present a general model for cultural object representation.

3.2   FRBRoo

Functional Requirements for Bibliographic Records (FRBRoo) is a conceptual model dedicated to museum and library information exchange [7]. Its main purpose is to represent the relation between people engaged in the various stage of cultural object production, from the very first idea to the concrete realisation. Each cultural object is described on three levels:

- the abstract level of ideas that have no concrete existence outside an individual's mind, a melody or a story for instance (*Work* class in FRBRoo).
- the expression level where there may exist various possible expressions of the same idea (*Expression* class in FRBRoo). For instance a written novel, its translations and a screenplay adaptation of the novel.
- the carrier level which holds the various material manifestations of expressions (*Item, Manifestation Product Type, Manifestation Singleton* classes in FRBRoo). For instance, a book, a score or a cd-rom.

These basic distinctions are particularly helpful to describe the contribution of each individual in the production process of a media asset. It gives a very detailed view on the production context, so precise that it is hardly used in other context than cultural heritage. The Axis model represents media assets in pursuance of these distinctions and specialized them for its own use. The next section presents how Axis takes a stand on these norms and inspires us in our own work.

3.3   Axis

Axis is an implementation of OAIS which focuses on media assets description and exchange between organizations. As a consequence, Axis needs to consider the media industry concerns and specificities. Hence, the architecture has been exploded to consider more flexible information flows than proposed in OAIS. For instance, each organizations taking part in the flow may provide one or more functions, sometimes redundantly. Moreover, Axis deal only with one information package which holds for each kind of exchange (submission, archival, dissemination). The idea is that one package conforming to archival recommendations may also conform to interoperability requirements.

Concerning media assets description, the Axis model borrows the FRBRoo basic distinctions and use them to build its core ontology. Dedicated specializations are added in order to handle the specificities of temporal media such as audio or video. The base is to distinguish between a conceptual level (*Entity* in the Axis Core), a sign level (*Document* in Axis Core) and a physical or digital carrier level (*PhysicalClip* in Axis). Each element in a higher level may be related to several elements of the next lower level. For instance, one concept may be expressed in a variety of documents, each corresponding to a given facet of the concept. In a similar way, each document may be represented on several digital or physical carriers. For instance, the *Little Night Music* from Mozart has several interpretations played by various orchestra stored on various carriers.

On the sign level however, Axis restricts itself to a thesaurus approach to handle language variations. This approach enables for each concept to bind various alternate labels to a unique reference or preferred label in the same way that the W3C's *Simple Knowledge Organization System* (SKOS). The OWL Full representation of SKOS enables to define relations between concepts (broadMatch, narrowMatch, relatedMatch, exactMatch, closeMatch) to structure a scheme and enable mapping between them in a Semantic Web fashion [8].

The thesaurus approach does not seem sufficient for our concern, as it does not provide any way to characterize a label's scope of use, aside from the *xml:lang* attribute. Thus, natural language is the only hold to select a label for a given user. The automatic selection of a label pertaining to a specific jargon is not possible. Even though the label could be bound with the preferred label, there will still lack an attribute to characterize it.

In a way, we could say that the thesaurus objective is to normalize the use of language whereas our goal is to provide each community with a dedicated access to information – without losing the ability to exchange with and understand information from other communities. With SKOS thesaurus, the only manner to provide that kind of service is to define one thesaurus for each community and make the mappings between them. We define in the next section our modelling solution to overcome this issue.

4   Modelling

We first present the general principles which underly our modelling – section 4.1 – then we will illustrate them with the two use-cases previously described – section 2 for their descriptions, section 4.2 for their modelling. We finish by defining in details the main concepts and relations of our conceptualization – section 4.3.

4.1   Principles

We found with Axis a good model to deal with the majority of the MediaMap project issues. Hence, we have used their Core as the basis of our work. However, the thesaurus approach does not cover our concerns about language variations between community of users engaged in a production process. Our modelling extends the thesaurus approach to all kind of information and makes it more flexible so as to select the most comprehensible information for a given user engaged in a given context.

Our approach relies on the articulation of an information model, a user model and a context model. Figure 4 presents each part of the model. The idea is to bind a description of the information's production context to a description of the information access context, including a user description. Contextual parameters help us to select more precisely the most comprehensible information for a given user.

The selection of a denomination (instance of the Term class) is first made upon condition of the user's (instance of the PhysicalPerson class) personal abilities (instance of the Skill class). These abilities may refer to either a know-how or the knowledge of a jargon, a natural language, a syntax (instance of the Notation class). Other contextual parameters may help to make a finer selection. For instance, the membership in an organization (instance of the CorporateBody class) which may have its own practices – vocabulary, specific syntax etc. The job or position (instance of the Role class) is another indicator which may indicate the user's practical or linguistic knowledge. Locations may also help to identify the linguistic skills of a user. This example is extendable to other kind of information such as documents.

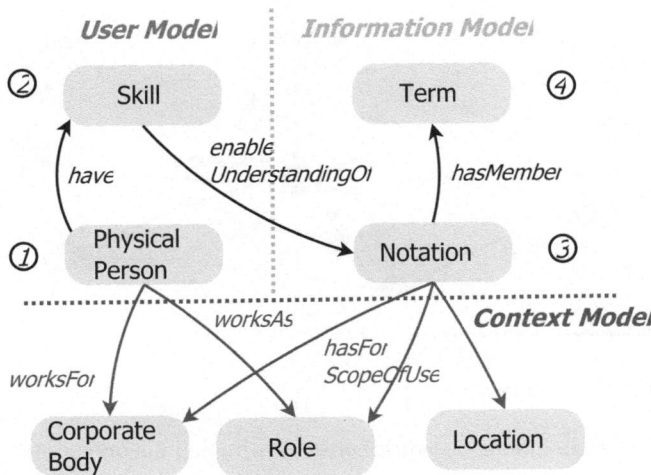

Fig. 4. Main concepts and relations between the User model, the Information model and the Context model

4.2   Use-Case Modelling

In this section we show the modelling of the use case of section 2, their OWL representation are described in section 5. The first use-case illustrates two French-speaking user, a professional cameraman and a amateur one, both accessing to the same script and in particular a shot value – see Figure 5. There are two distincts denominations for this shot value, the first is concise, the second one is more explanatory. The distinction between those two users is made on their skill level (amateur, professional) which gives them access to distinct Notations and thus a distinct or custom-tailored view on the script. Each denomination (instance of the Term class) is member of one of these Notations. Both denominations are related by a similarity relation when they refer to the same shot value. The Figure shows the connection between a given user and a given denomination.

The Tchaikovksi use-case illustrates the modelling of a multilingual search. Suppose one user requesting in French information about the famous composer. In this case, the request first brings us to the individual, to whom other pieces of information are attached. The real improvement comes from the user description – we know he understands both French and English – which enables us to bring a new source of information to the fore – English B document – aside from the French A document.

We may complicate the example by adding other attributes to the documents, such a character encoding parameters – ISO 8859-1 for Latin alphabet, ISO 8859-5 for Cyrillic alphabet. This kind of attributes may be useful when not only the user but also its device's abilities have been described. We define in the next section the concepts and relations of our model.

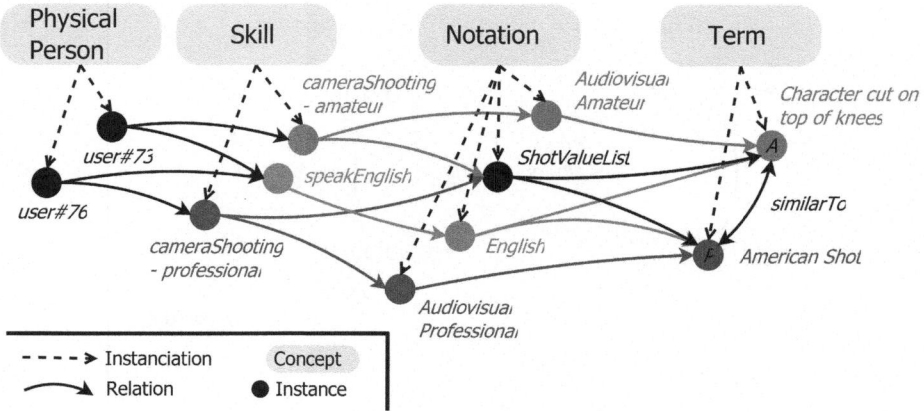

Fig. 5. Relations' network between users and denominations

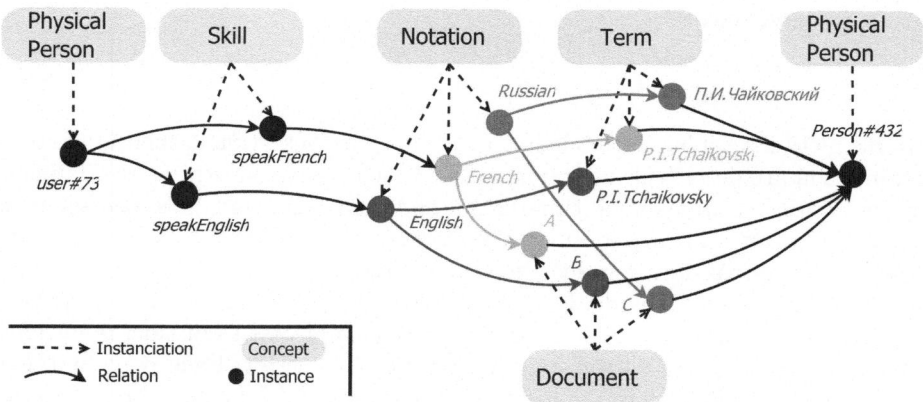

Fig. 6. Multilingual search and documents' selection

4.3   Conceptualization Definition

We divide the presentation of our conceptualization by its three different parts.

Information Model's concepts and relations. A term (instance of the Term class) wraps a property's value which would usually be considered as a string. We also attached various attributes to provide a description of its context of use. The real datatype of the value could be anything, word, date, number etc.

A document (instance of the Document class) denotes information related to a concept. Concepts are abstract entities which only exist through the material manifestations of documents. Contrary to FRBRoo, manifestation is not a concept but a relation (isAManifestationOf) between a document and an entity.

A notation (instance of the Notation class) designates a set of terms sharing common characteristics. They may refer to each other to build richer Notation and thus models the different aspects of a term. The Notation class have several specializations that we detail below:

- a naturalLanguage (instance of the NaturalLanguage class) models the membership of a term to a natural language – e.g. French, English, Flemish etc. Country code may be added to model geographical variations of a language – English & UK or English & USA.
- a syntaxEncodingScheme (instance of the SyntaxEncodingScheme class) models a specific way to encode bits. This include character encoding system (UTF-8), datatype encoding (xsd:string) or more complex syntax such as date format (ISO 8601 : 1988 (E)[4]) or even file formats (jpg, pdf).
- a vocabularyEncodingScheme (instance of the VocabularyEncodingScheme class) models a chosen set of terms such as a professional thesaurus. It may be used in a general way to model naming conventions within a business, organisational or geographic context. A metadata description scheme such as Dublin Core[5] is one example.
- an authorityList (instance of the AuthorityList class) models a finite list of terms which values have been arbitrarily chosen. For instance, the ISO 639-2 norm is a list of three-letters code referring to a language name, e.g. *eng* stands for english.

A term is member of a notation (isMemberOf relation) when it shares the corresponding characteristics. The membership is not exclusive so we may refine the description of a term at will. This relation is specialized by the natural language's membership (inLanguage relation). For instance, the value *Tchaikovsky* may be described both as member of the English naturalLanguage and encoded in ISO 8859-1. A notation is in conformity with (conformsTo) a SyntaxEncodingScheme when it uses its encoding rules. A notation may of course conform to several schemes.

User Model's concepts and relations. An agent (instance of the Agent class) models any acting entity. This class has three specializations:

- a physicalPerson (instance of the PhysicalPerson class) models an individual, e.g. *Tchaikovksy.*
- A corporateBody (instance of the CorporateBody class) models an organization composed of other agents, e.g. the *Minneapolis Symphony Orchestra.*
- A proxy (instance of the Proxy class) models a system acting on behalf of another kind of agent, e.g. a web server.

A skill (instance of the Skill class) models an agent's ability to perform a given task or to understand an information related to that task, e.g. setup instructions. This class has two specializations:

---

[4] W3C standard for date format, see http://www.w3.org/TR/NOTE-datetime for further details
[5] http://dublincore.org/documents/dcmi-terms/

- a linguisticSkill (instance of the LinguisticSkill class) is an agent's ability to understands a given natural language.
- a professionalSkill (instance of th ProfessionalSkill class) models an agent's ability to perform specific task and understand professional notations. For instance, *Framing* is an agent's ability to handle a camera given shot value instructions. These shot values are grouped together in an authorityList.

A physicalPerson is defined as skilled (isProficient relation) when the management considers him so.

Context Model's concepts and relations. Skills helps to define jobs or position (instance of the Role class). An agent – individual, organization or system – playing a given role is assigned a set of rights and duties in a project's scope. An individual may be employed by an organization (workFor relation) in a given position (workAs relation). A location (instance of the Location class) denotes a geographical or political entity. Location is a generic concept that may be specialized if needed.

Relations between the model's part. There are three major relations connecting each other part of the model. The first one connects a user with notations, the second one binds notations with contextual parameters and the third one links a term with any ontological element:

- a skill designates the ability of an agent to understand a notation (enablesUnderstandingOf relation)
- a notation may be used in various context (hasForScopeOfUse relation), an organization, a location or a role.
- a term may be attached to any ontological element to label it (isNamedBy relation), instance, concept or property.

5   OWL Formalization

The use of ontology seems to be profitable on several points. First, it requires the model's semantic to be explicit and well documented which will thus ease its understanding by the users and its maintenance by the designers. Moreover, the fact to focus on domain objects rather than a particular task may improve the flexibility and extensibility of the model [9]. When it comes to search on instances, query extension has proven valuable [10]. Eventually, reasoning capability and data integration between various models are particularly precious when dealing with information interchange and interoperability issues [11]. Knowledge Representation languages such as RDF and OWL offer us a way to express our ontology. We have chosen the OWL-DL species to ensure a good expressiveness without losing computational completeness. We discuss details of our formalization in the next section.

5.1   Denominations for Amateur and Professional

We present here an OWL representation of the shot value use-case in N3[6]. We have an authorityList with two terms referring to the same shot value. This shot value has no existence by itself, there is only these two terms which belongs either to an amateur or professional vocabularyEncodingScheme. On one side we distinguish the two terms by their membership in a different scheme (isMemberOf, inLanguage relations) and then on the other side we need to identify their equivalence (similarTo relation).

```
// ==== NOTATIONS ===== //
mm:shotValueList
        a          mm:AuthorityList ;
   mm:hasMember mm:AmericanShot-a, mm:AmericanShot .
mm:Audiovisual-Professional
        a          mm:VocabularyEncodingScheme ;
        mm:hasMember mm:AmericanShot .
mm:Audiovisual-Amateur
        a          mm:VocabularyEncodingScheme ;
        mm:hasMember mm:AmericanShot-a .
mm:English
        a          mm:NaturalLanguage .


// ==== TERM ===== //
mm:AmericanShot
        a          mm:Term ;
        mm:inLanguage mm:English ;
        mm:isMemberOf mm:shotValueList , mm:Audiovisual-Professional ;
        mm:similarTo mm:americainShot-a ;
        mm:value "American Shot"^^xsd:string .
mm:AmericanShot-a
        a          mm:Term ;
        mm:inLanguage mm:English ;
        mm:isMemberOf mm:shotValueList  , mm:Audiovisual-Amateur ;
        mm:similarTo mm:AmericanShot ;
        mm:value "A shot in which the character appears
          from head to knee"^^xsd:string .
```

The user's description is made through their skills and skill level. The skillLevel is an attribute which can take two values, amateur or professional. Therefore, each skill may have two versions, each of which enables to understand a different notation – here Audiovisual-Amateur and Audiovisual-Professional vocabularyEncodingScheme. However, each version may grant access to a common notation – here the shotValue authorityList.

```
// ==== PHYSICAL PERSON ===== //
mm:user_73
        a          mm:PhysicalPerson ;
        mm:isProficient mm:cameraShooting-a , mm:speakEnglish .
```

---

[6] http://www.w3.org/DesignIssues/Notation3.html

```
mm:user_76
      a        mm:PhysicalPerson ;
      mm:isProficient mm:cameraShooting-p , mm:speakEnglish .


// ==== SKILLS ===== //
mm:speakFrench
      a        mm:LinguisticSkill ;
      mm:enablesUnderstandingOf
            mm:English .

mm:cameraShooting-p
      a        mm:BusinessSkill ;
       mm:enablesUnderstandingOf
            mm:Audiovisual-Professional , mm:shotValueList ;
      mm:SkillLevel "professional"^^xsd:string .
mm:cameraShooting-a
      a        mm:BusinessSkill ;
      mm:enablesUnderstandingOf
            mm:Audiovisual-Amateur , mm:shotValueList;
      mm:SkillLevel "amateur"^^xsd:string .
```

5.2 Denominations and Multilingual Search

The multilingual use-case gives us the opportunity to talk about the OWL representation of the naming relation (isNamedBy). It has to be an Annotation Property so as to be attached to any kind of ontological element. Therefore, it is a good substitute for the *rdfs:label* relation. The OWL-DL species implies some constraints on the use of annotation property, but this has no impact in our case. Indeed, we only build triplet in the form `subject mm:isNamedBy term` where the subject may be an owl:class, an owl:property or an instance. The next example shows two terms carrying various spellings for Tchaikovski's proper name, and three documents related to the Composer (isAManifestationOf relation). There are also the natural language used.

```
// ==== NOTATIONS ===== //
mm:French-NL
      a        mm:NaturalLanguage .
mm:English-NL
      a        mm:NaturalLanguage .
mm:Russian-NL
      a        mm:NaturalLanguage .
// ==== TERM ===== //
mm:Tchaikovsky-EN-Term
      a        mm:Term ;
      mm:inLanguage mm:English-NL ;
      mm:value "Pyotr Ilyich Tchaikovsky"^^xsd:string .
mm:Tchaikovsky-FR-Term
      a        mm:Term ;
      mm:inLanguage mm:French-NL ;
      mm:value "Piotr Ilitch Tchaikovski"^^xsd:string .
```

```
// ==== DOCUMENT ===== //
mm:Document_A
        a          mm:Document ;
        mm:inLanguage mm:French-NL ;
        mm:isAManifestationOf
                mm:Tchaikovsky .
mm:Document_B
        a          mm:Document ;
        mm:inLanguage mm:English-NL ;
        mm:isAManifestationOf
                mm:Tchaikovsky .
mm:Document_C
        a          mm:Document ;
        mm:inLanguage mm:Russian-NL ;
        mm:isAManifestationOf
                mm:Tchaikovsky .
```

An individual's name may have several variations (isNamedBy relation). We have here one user having two different linguisticSkill which may eventually help us to select two comprehensible documents (A and B) out of three – see section 4.2.

```
// ==== PHYSICAL PERSON ===== //
mm:Tchaikovsky
        a          mm:PhysicalPerson ;
        mm: isNamedBy mm:Tchaikovsky-FR-Term , mm:Tchaikovsky-RU-Term ,
        mm:Tchaikovsky-EN-Term .
mm:user_73
        a          mm:PhysicalPerson ;
        mm:isProficient mm:speakEnglish , mm:speakFrench .
```

```
// ==== SKILLS ===== //
mm:speakFrench
        a          mm:LinguisticSkill ;
        mm:enablesUnderstandingOf
                mm:French-NL .
mm:speakEnglish
        a          mm:LinguisticSkill ;
        mm:enablesUnderstandingOf
                mm:English-NL .
```

6 Conclusion

In this article, we have presented a conceptual model which enables us to characterize a given denomination's scope of use. We use contextual parameters (job, organization, location) as well as personal parameters (skill, skill level) to make a selection of comprehensible information for a given user. This approach is extendable to any ontological element (class, property, instance) and to other kind of information (such as documents).

We have first shown the relevancy of this approach in the context of collaborative TV production, where amateur contributions to professional workflows are bound to widespread. As the ability to exchange and repurpose information and content becomes a major challenge for organizations, there is a strong need for a system and conceptual model to support them. Models we have studied usually focus on the ability to exchange and transform data between various formats and neglect language variations issues. From a basic distinction between concept, sign and physical carrier we have defined a model which enables us to represent the language variations of user communities and find a way to ease information search and interpretation.

Acknowledgement. The Eureka framework is funding the MediaMap project in which our work takes place.

References

1. Abel, M., Leblanc, A.: Knowledge Sharing via the E-MEMORAe2.0 Platform. In: 6th International Conference on Intellectual Capital, Knowledge Management & Organisational Learning, Montreal, Canada, pp. 10–19 (2009)
2. Rayers, D.J.: Metadata in TV Production: Associating the TV Production Process with relevant Technologies. IBC White Paper, BBC R&D UK (2003)
3. Devlin, B.: What is MXF? Ebu Technical Review, 1–7 (2002)
4. Moulin, C., Sugawara, K., Fujita, S., Wouters, L., Manabe, Y.: Multilingual Collaborative Design Support System. In: 13th International Conference on Computer Supported Cooperative Work in Design (CSCWD 2009), Santiago, Chile, pp. 312–318 (2009)
5. Consultative Committee for Space Data Systems (CCSDS): Reference Model for an Open Archival Information System (2002)
6. Bruno, B.: L'archive numérique: entre authenticité et interpretabilité. archivistes.qc.ca (2000)
7. Aalberg, T., Barthélémy, J., Boutard, G., Görz, G., Iorizzo, D., Jacob, M., et al.: Definition of Object-Oriented FRBR. CIDOC (2008)
8. Summers, E., Isaac, A., Redding, C., Krech, D.: LCSH, SKOS and Linked Data. CoRR (2008)
9. Spyns, P., Meersman, R., Jarrar, M.: Data Modeling Versus Ontology Engineering. SIGMOD Record 31(4), 12–17 (2002)
10. Guarino, N.: Formal Ontologies and Information Systems. In: Proceedings of FOIS 1998, pp. 3–15. IOS Press, Amsterdam (1998)
11. Garcia, R., Celma, O.: Semantic integration and retrieval of multimedia metadata. In: 5th International Workshop on Knowledge Markup and Semantic Annotation, Ireland (2005)

A Specification-Oriented Geospatial Coverage Ontology Study

Jinsongdi Yu, Xia Wang, and Peter Baumann

Jacobs University Bremen,
Campus Ring 1, 28759 Bremen, Germany
{j.yu,xia.wang,p.baumann}@jacobs-university.de

Abstract. In earth sciences, the term "geospatial coverage" denotes a space/time-varying geographic object, that is: multi-dimensional raster data such as 2-D satellite images, 3-D or 4-D seismic data. Web coverage services (WCS) as standardized by the Open Geospatial Consortium (OGC) provide access to such detailed and high-volume sets of information being used in a wide variety of earth system applications, such as in solar, atmosphere, oceans, cryosphere, solid earth, and biosphere research. However, different service implementations sometimes turn out to be incompatible because of incompleteness and a lack of conciseness in the current WCS 1.1.2 standard. The main reason for this is that the specification is written without formal testing procedures. To overcome this, we propose a specification-oriented Ontology for coverages. This work is a part of the development of the new WCS 2.0 standard. In this way, an improved sharing of geospatial coverage data is expected in future.

Keywords: WCS geospatial coverage, raster images, Ontology, OGC WCS.

1 Introduction

Geo data classically are subdivided into vector, raster, and metadata. Vectorial data consist of points, lines, and polygon-bounded areas denoting, e.g., the points of interest, roads, and water areas. Raster data represent regularly spaced observations aligned on a spatio-temporal grid; examples include hyperspectral (i.e., multi-channel) airborne and satellite images, image time series, elevation and bathymetry data, and scanned maps. Metadata encompasses any kind of alphanumeric data attaching further description to the geographic elements, such as parcel ownership, type of road, or date when an image was taken.

To allow for reasoning, ontologies have been modeled on the metadata level as since some time [1][2][3]. To a lesser extent but conceptually convincing, the same has been done with vector data. Raster data, however, currently are not considered and, hence, no inference on the pixel contents is possible at all. Notably, reasoning on raster data does not necessarily mean image understanding. For applications in e-government as well as e-science a pixel-based semantics is used regularly to aid in geo decision making. For example, geo raster users are frequently interested in classification tasks like cloud, snow, and vegetation coverage. Often there is a well-accepted analytical definition for doing such derivations; the Normalized Difference

M.-A. Sicilia, C. Kop, and F. Sartori (Eds.): ONTOSE 2010, LNBIP 62, pp. 63–74, 2010.

Vegetation Index (NDVI) is evaluated for each pixel of the red and near-infrared (NIR) channel of an earth observation image a based on the following formula:

$$NDVI(a) = (a.red - a.nir) / (a.red + a.nir)$$

The result is an image of the same resolution containing pixel values between -1 and +1. The closer a value comes to +1 one, the more likely the pixel location contains vegetation.

The Open GeoSpatial Consortium[1] (OGC) Web Coverage Service (WCS) Standard defines an interface to give clients access to such data in a platform and vendor independent manner. Functionality is organized in a modular manner and ranges from simple access operations (e.g., subsetting) in the core to an open-ended raster query language [4]. In this way, WCS gives access to the original data suitable for further client-side processing, rather than rendering images which are suitable only for display, as it is done, e.g., with Google Maps and OGC WMS.

Obviously, a well-defined data model is of critical importance to achieve true interoperability. The term "coverage" is defined in [5][2] as a space-time varying phenomenon represented by a function which maps points within the space/time extent of the coverage to values, such as spectral intensity or altitude. Raster data are a special case of coverages; further coverage types include, for example, triangulated irregular networks. In Section 3 we will give a detail view on coverages.

Definitions in [5] give only an abstract model, which is refined by WCS to become practically usable. Not always was the coverage model sufficiently well defined. For example, while WCS 1.0.0 [6] elaborated extensively on the metadata, there was no specification of the image contents to be returned – a WCS 1.0.0 server which always delivers a black image is perfectly conformant to this standard version. In its current version WCS 1.1.2 [7], an informal evaluation model is given which, however, does not allow for conformance testing. In the coverage definition of the new version WCS 2.0 [4][8], a formal model of both coverage model and access functions is provided which allows for automated testing.

In this paper, we present an ontology-based modeling of WCS 2.0 coverages which allows to do inference. Ultimately, this will pave the way for including coverage data into the overall orchestration of semantic services. As a short-term goal, we investigate the automated conformance testing to study reasoning on coverages.

Consider the following simple cutout retrieval. Assume that a request is sent to a WCS2.0 service entry for obtaining a subset area with corner points (50,100) and (500,400) from a 2-D raster image of interest (a false color image), see Fig. 1.

The result is a WCS coverage [8] in some image encoding format. The question remains as to how a machine can digest this result and verify whether the response coverage is correct.

The current OGC Compliance & Interoperability Testing & Evaluation[3] (CITE) program uses OGC's Test, Evaluation, and Measurement (TEAM) Engine[4], which is fed with Compliance Test Language [9] (CTL) to digest the geospatial information

---

[1] http://www.opengeospatial.org
[2] This is a joint work between the OGC and ISO.
[3] http://cite.opengeospatial.org/cite
[4] http://cite.opengeospatial.org/teamengine/

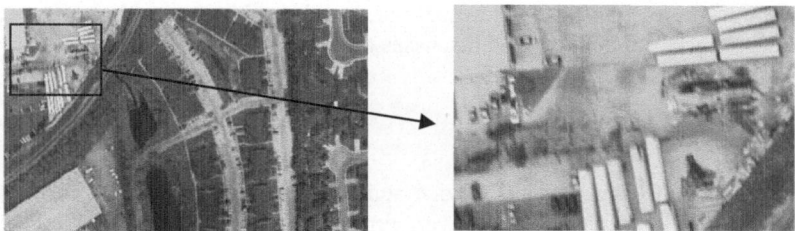

Fig. 1. False color image of a city (left) and cutout obtained from this image (right) (source: http://www.earthlook.org/)

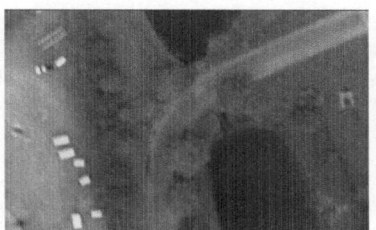

Fig. 2. a. Result with different area   **Fig. 2. b.** Result with rotated coordinate system

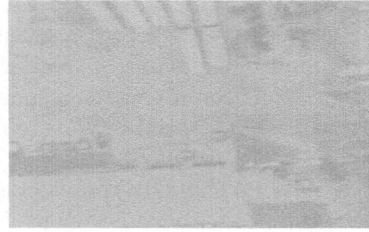

Fig .2. c. Result with wrong pixel intensities   **Fig. 2. d.** Otherwise wrong result

provided. The CTL uses the eXtensible Stylesheet Language[5] (XSL) to probe the geospatial XML.

However, this approach is not aware of the underlying geospatial semantic. Therefore, it will accept a pseudo-specification compliance implementation. For example, the above retrieval image is just about a 2-D image of the same size as request, but in a different spatial area (see Fig.2.a), rotated coordinate system (see Fig.2.b), false pixel values (see Fig.2.c) or other unknown image result (see Fig.2.d). Without a semantic guarantee, these results will be accepted by a machine.

The specification conformance test needs to check the response GML coverage not only from a syntax level, but also from a semantic level. The geospatial coverage ontology is a formal and machine-understandable representation to address the above mentioned issues. The remaining parts of this paper are organized as follows: Section 2 introduces the related research work, section 3 provides the formalized geospatial

---

[5] http://www.w3.org/TR/1999/REC-xslt-19991116

coverage definition, section 4 addresses the ontology implementation, and finally, section 5 summaries this paper and discusses the future work.

2   Related Work

There are researches on the geo service semantic to guarantee the information retrieval, such as [10] and [11]. However, further research at geospatial information semantic level is needed to make sure that the retrieval information is correct.

[12] formalized the Conceptual Spaces [13] (CS) model, and used it to bridge between the real-world and symbolic representations. However, such a CS model provides a means to represent the knowledge in geometrical vector spaces, but it does not provide the geospatial coverage knowledge.

[5] describes the coverage knowledge in a semi-formal way, and this needs further development before machines can directly reason on that. XML-schema-based GML serves as a modeling language to express geographical phenomenon, but current GML3.2.1 [17] only provides a conformant, partial implementation of the coverage knowledge.

The existing related ontologies, such as Cyc Open Geospatial Consortium, Cyc Terrain ontology and Drexel ontology only provide some partially related knowledge [14]. Cyc ontologies have not covered some specific concepts, such as coverage domain, range and function [5]. By comparison, the initial aim of this research is to support geospatial semantic digestion in the scope of specification-based geospatial web services formal testing procedures. Drexel developed an OWL representation of a subset of GML 3.0 [15], which is specialized for encoding places of specific types, whereas this geo ontology needs to encode places that occur at a more detailed level, ranging from standardized ISO coverage knowledge to specific WCS coverage knowledge.

Moreover, OGC Web Coverage Processing Service (WCPS) [16] provides a set of so-called probing functions to extract the specified aspects from a coverage. The extraction of these specified aspects relies on the coverage model as defined in [5]; for example, the WCPS probing function imageCrsDomain(C) delivers the domain extent expressed in Image Coordinate Reference System (CRS) [18] of a coverage with the identifier C.

3   WCS Coverage Ontology

A coverage is formally defined as a function f: $D \rightarrow R$ where D, the coverage's *domain*, represents the spatiotemporal extent in which coverage values can be queried and R, the coverage's *range*, specifies the values which can be associated with coverage locations [5]. A concrete, implementable model of this abstract model is available in the GML 3.2.1 standard [17] where coverages are represented by XML structures defined through XML Schema. This concrete coverage model has been slightly amended by the GML 3.2.1 Application Schema for WCS 2.0 [8], which forms the basis of our discussion here.

In our coverage Ontology, the *AbstractCoverage* is a general concept to define all the shared abstract features of any coverage types. As its subclass, *GridCoverage,* defines raster data. *GridCoverage* is a coverage which has equidistant grid points, but no positioning ("geo reference") in a space-time environment, so that it only can be addressed through its array index coordinates). While *RectifiedGridCoverage* and *ReferenceableGridCoverage*, which are geo rectified or referenced, can be addressed by using spatial-temporal coordinates. The overview of the coverage Ontology is shown in the Tab. 1.

Table 1. Specification-oriented coverage ontology

Abstract Coverage[6]	Domain	Function	Range
GridCoverage	*GridEnvelope*	*{Coverage-* *Map_pingRule,* *GridFuction}*	*RangeSet* ⊔ *RangeType*
RectifiedGridCoverage	*GridEnvelope* ⊔ *OffsetVector* ⊔ *Origin*		
ReferencableGridCoverage	*GridEnvelope* ⊔ *CoordTransform*		

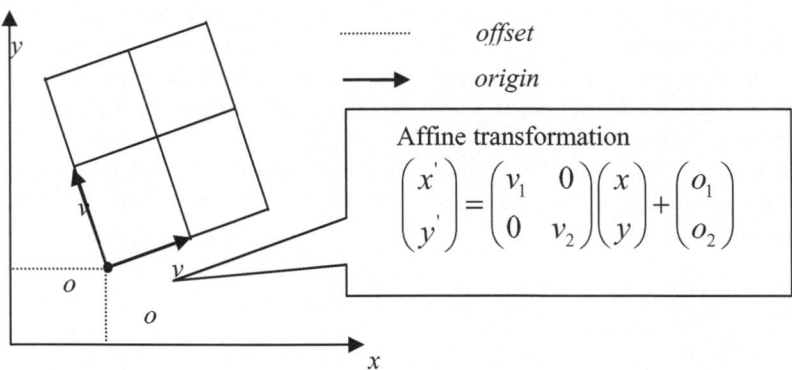

offset

origin

Affine transformation

$$\begin{pmatrix} x' \\ y' \end{pmatrix} = \begin{pmatrix} v_1 & 0 \\ 0 & v_2 \end{pmatrix} \begin{pmatrix} x \\ y \end{pmatrix} + \begin{pmatrix} o_1 \\ o_2 \end{pmatrix}$$

Fig. 3. Geometrical positioning of *RectifiedGridCoverage*

Mathematically, *RectifiedGridCoverage* anchors the array grid to an external spatial-temporal CRS via an affine transformation[7] as described by Fig. 3, while *ReferencableGridCoverage* anchors the grid other than an affine transformation.

The spatio-temporal region, within which the coverage is defined, is described by the coverage *domainSet* [5]. For example, a *GridEnvelope* is used to indicate the *low* and *high* boundary of grid index position, additional *Origin* and *OffsetVector* are used

---

[6] The research is aimed to address the formal description requirements of multi-dimensional raster data. The other ISO coverage type, such as continuous coverage is not addressed in this research.

[7] http://mathworld.wolfram.com/AffineTransformation.html

to indicate the region of *RectifiedGridCoverage*(see Fig.3), and *CoordTransform* for *ReferencableGridCoverage*.

The set of feature attribute values, within the spatio-temporal region, is described by coverage *rangeSet* [5]. However, current GML3.2.1 coverage lacks of detailed implementation on the range information description. WCS2.0 introduces *rangeType*[8] as well to describe its range structure and meaning, including a name, a data type definition and an optional unit of measure (UOM). The range is delivered in different encoding representations [17], including *AbstractScalarValueList* for scalar value list, *ValueArray* for homogeneous arrays of primitive and aggregate values, *DataBlock* for a block of text encoded values similar to a Common Separated Value (CSV) representation, and *File* for arbitrary external encoding. The external encoding data formats, can be a data format with geospatial descriptions, such as GeoTIFF, NetCDF, and HDF5, or a data format without geospatial descriptions, such as PNG, TIFF, JPEG, and GIF.

The coverage *function* [5] maps the *domainSet* to the *rangeSet* of the coverage. The function can be either a *GridFunction* or a *CoverageMappingRule* [17]. A *GridFunction* includes a *startPoint* for the start index position of a point in the grid that is mapped to the first value in the range set and a *sequenceRule* [5] that describes how the grid points are ordered for association to the elements of the sequence values. An *axisOrder* [17] provides the incrementation order of the grid axis, regularly expressed by regular expression "[\+\-][1-9][0-9]*", implying that "+1 +2" means the points in the grid are to be traversed from lowest to highest on the first and second axis. Fig. 4 shows examples of linear scanning in a 2-dimensional grid under different *axisOrders*. A *CoverageMappingRule* provides a formal or informal description of the coverage function, and these descriptions depend on the further requirements on grid sequence methods. Therefore, it will be either an inline string or a remote reference for the mapping descriptions.

When the *function* is omitted for a coverage, its *startPoint* is assumed to be the *low* boundary of the grid, the *sequenceRule* is assumed to be linear, and the *axisOrder* is assumed to be "+1 +2".

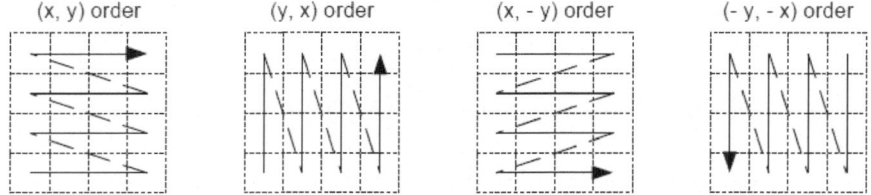

Fig. 4. Examples of linear *sequenceRule* in a 2-dimensional grid [ISO 19123 D.1]

4   Coverage Ontology Implementation

Currently, relevant specifications cannot completely fulfill the requirements of interoperations of heterogeneous geospatial data, and are still under-development or revision

---

[8] Currently, *rangeType* conforms with the DataRecord definition given in SWE Common [OGC 08-094]

for a future geospatial cloud applications. Basically, our coverage Ontology is defined for digesting the OGC WCS coverage and has been developed with the open world assumption (OWA). It means the coverage-related knowledge, that is not included in or inferred from the knowledge explicitly recorded in this paper, will be considered unknown, rather than wrong or false.

The Web Ontology Language[9] (OWL) is a standard-based language for defining ontologies, based on the Resource Description Framework (RDF and RDF Schema (RDFS) by providing additional vocabulary along with a formal semantics. The behind description logic (DL)[19] can provide provides rich express capabilities for our ontology, specifically, the $\mathcal{SHQ(D)}$ which extends $\mathcal{ALC}$ with transitive role, role hierarchy, nominals and data types. Therefore, we chose OWL as our knowledge representation language and Protégé4.0[10] as our development tool.

The coverage ontology defines a set of axioms which describe the constraints of classes and relationships between concepts and concept properties. The instances of the coverage Ontology is interpreted as a set of individuals with a set of property assertions.

By reusing the coverage example in section 1, we instantiate the returned NIR image and visualize it by OntoGraf[11]. The visualization result can be seen in Fig. 5.

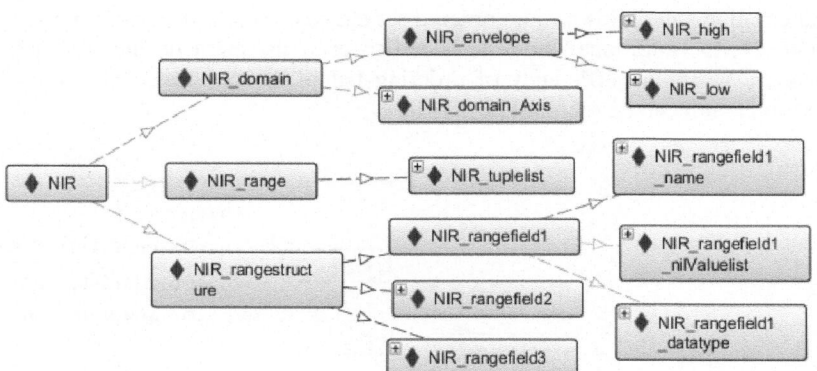

Fig. 5. Visualization of the example WCS coverage ontology

The coverage Ontology defines a key concept, which relies on the ordering list. For example, the coverage boundary *low* and *high* implementations depend on integer list, the *Origin* and *OffsetVector* implementations depend on a double list, and the *AxisOrder* depends on the string pattern implementation. Additionally, the feature attribute *range* relies on the list for different encoding representations.

However, the OWL contains no specific support to ordering support. An approach proposed by [19] was found as a solution to operate the ordering list. We simplified this solution with a recursion pattern, as followings:

$$list = element + list$$

---

[9] http://www.w3.org/2004/OWL
[10] http://protege.stanford.edu/
[11] http://protegewiki.stanford.edu/wiki/OntoGraf

The visualization result can be seen in Fig. 6.

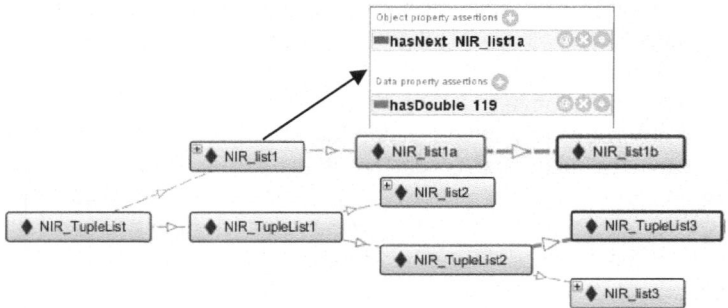

Fig. 6. Visualization of the example coverage's *rangeSet* by ordering list

The response attribute values are represented as a sequential *NIR_TupleListi*, which each one composes of a *NIR_listi* to represent the three band values.

However, practically speaking we found out the solution is computationally expensive and memory consuming when it is applied in the *rangeSet* representation.

An alternative solution is a finite ordered set indexed by non-negative numbers. By this approach, the additional index is added to each list element and the indexing improves the reasoning efficiency of ordering list in the coverage Ontology. The visualization result can be seen in Fig. 7.

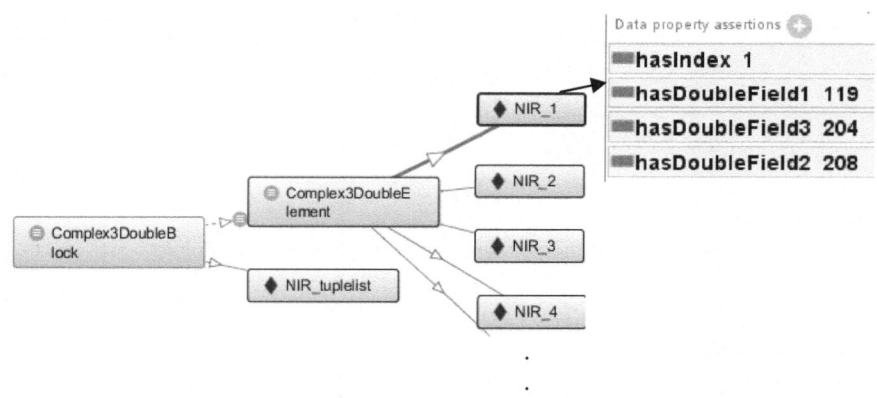

Fig. 7. Visualization of the example coverage's *rangeSet* by ordered set

The response attribute values in *NIR_tuplelist* are represented as a set of complex *NIR_i* elements, which each one composes of an index to indicate the order and three double fields to represent the three band values.

However, this modeling does not ensure that the list is well formed. Further rules (e.g. SWRL rules) are needed to check the integrity of the list representation. For example, the coverage boundary *low* and *high* are constrained by coverage dimension; *rangeSet* is constrained by coverage boundary and range structure.

5 Conclusions and Outlook

Geospatial ontologies are crucial in geospatial data description. Although there are a number of geospatial ontologies, there is still a lack of a suitable coverage ontolgies for WCS coverage services, specifically the WCS2.0 version. Based on the related geo coverage specifications, we modeled the geospatial coverage Ontology. This Ontology can particularly seamlessly describe WCS coverage, and support the OWL reasoning on both metadata and pixel level.

In order to adapt to the dynamic cloud computing environment, it is an evolution process to model such coverage Ontology. It involves ontology enrichment along with adding new concepts, e.g., *ContinuouCoverage*, topology relationship, quality description and so on. It also includes ontology revision, such as the addition or removal of concept mapping.

Acknowledgments. For the work reported in this article we gratefully acknowledge the financial support of the European Space Agency (ESA) through the HMA-FO Online Data Access project and the China Scholarship Council (CSC) through stipends, as well as Earth Science System Research School (ESSReS). The authors would like to thank Katrina Stollmann for fruitful academic discussions.

References

1. Parekh, V., et al.: Ontology based Semantic Metadata for Geoscience Data. In: Proceedings of the International Conference on Information and Knowledge Engineering, IKE 2004, pp. 485–490. CSREA Press, Las Vegas (2004)
2. Jia, Q., Guo, S.Z., Chen, H.Y., Li, N.: Research on Ontology-Based Metadata Model. In: First International Workshop on Database Technology and Applications, pp. 363–366. IEEE press, Wuhan (2009)
3. Mitschick, A., Meißner, K.: Generation and Maintenance of Semantic Metadata for Personal Multimedia Document Management. In: 1st International Conference on Advances in Multimedia, pp. 74–79. IEEE Press, Colmar (2009)
4. Baumann, P. (ed.): WCS 2.0 Overview: Core and Extensions. Number 09-153. OGC (2009)
5. n.n.: Geographic information—coverage geometry and functions. Number 19123:2005. ISO (2005)
6. Evans, J.D. (ed.): Web Coverage Service (WCS), Version 1.0.0. Number 03-065r6. OGC (2003)
7. Whiteside, A., Evans, J.D. (eds.): Web Coverage Service (WCS) Implementation Standard, Version 1.1.2. Number 07-067r5. OGC (2007)
8. Baumann, P. (ed.): GML 3.2 Application Schema for WCS 2.0. Number 19-146. OGC (2009)
9. Morris, C. (ed.): Compliance Test Language (CTL) Best Practice. Number OGC 06-126r2. OGC (2006)
10. Di, L., Zhao, P., Yang, W., et al.: Ontology-driven Automatic Geospatial-Processing Modeling Based on Web-service Chaining. In: Proceedings of the Sixth Annual NASA Earth Science Technology Conference. College Park, MD, USA (2006)

11. Lan, G., Huang, Q.: Ontology-based Method for Geospatial Web Services Discovery. In: Int. 2007 Conference on Intelligent Systems and Knowledge Engineering (2007)
12. Dietze, S., Domingue, J.: Enriching Service Semantics through Conceptual Vector Spaces. In: Workshop: Workshop on Ontology, Conceptualization and Epistemology for Information Systems, Software Engineering and Service Science (ONTOSE 2009), at: The 21st International Conference on Advanced Information Systems (CAiSE 2009), Amsterdam, NL (2009)
13. Gärdenfors, P.: Conceptual Spaces - The Geometry of Thought. MIT Press, Cambridge (2000)
14. Ressler1, J., Dean, M.: Geospatial Ontology Trade Study. In: OIC 2007, Columbia, Maryland, pp. 55–59 (2007)
15. Cox, S., Daisey, P., Lake, R., et al. (eds.): OpenGIS Geography Markup Language (GML) Encoding Standard, Version 3.0. Number 02-023. OGC (2002)
16. Baumann, P. (ed.): OpenGIS Web Coverage Processing Service (WCPS) Language Interface Standard, Number OGC 08-068r2. OGC (2008)
17. Portele, C. (ed.): OpenGIS Geography Markup Language (GML) Encoding Standard, Version 3.2.1. Number 07-036. OGC (2007)
18. Lott, R. (ed.): OGC Abstract Specification Topic 2, Spatial referencing by coordinates, Number 04-046r3. OGC (2004)
19. Baader, F., Calvanese, D., McGuinness, D.L., Nardi, D., Patel-Schneider, P.F.: The Description Logic Handbook: Theory, Implementation, Applications. Cambridge University Press, Cambridge (2003)
20. Drummond, N., Rector, A.L., Stevens, R., Moulton, G., Horridge, M., Wang, H., Seidenberg, J.: Putting OWL in Order: Patterns for Sequences in OWL. In: 2nd OWL Experiences and Directions Workshop, Athens, GA (2006)

Appendix: The DL Definitions

*definition*1

AbstractCoverage $\doteq$ $\forall hasDomainSet.DomainSet$ ⊓= $1hasDomainSet$

⊓$\forall hasFuntion.fuction$⊓≤$1hasFunction$

⊓$\forall hasRangeSet.rangeSet$⊓=$1hasRangeSet$

⊓$\forall hasRangeStructure.rangeType$⊓=$1hasRangeStructure$

$GridCoverage \sqsubseteq AbstractCoverage$

$RectifiedGridCoverage \sqsubseteq AbstractCoverage$⊓$\neg GridCoverage$⊓$\neg ReferencableGridCoverage$

$ReferencableGridCoverage \sqsubseteq AbstractCoverage$⊓$\neg GridCoverage$⊓$\neg RectifiedGridCoverage$

*definition*2

$GridCoverage \doteq \forall hasDomainSet.Grid$⊓=$1hasDomainSet$

⊓$\forall hasFuntion.fuction$⊓≤$1hasFunction$

⊓$\forall hasRangeSet.rangeSet$⊓=$1hasRangeSet$

⊓$\forall hasRangeStructure.rangeType$⊓=$1hasRangeStructure$

*definition*3

$RectifiedGridCoverage \doteq \forall hasDomainSet.RectifiedGrid$⊓=$1hasDomainSet$

⊓$\forall hasFuntion.Fuction$⊓≤$1hasFunction$

⊓$\forall hasRangeSet.RangeSet$=$1hasRangeSet$

⊓$\forall hasRangeStructure.rangeType$⊓=$1hasRangeStructure$

*definition*4

$ReferencableGridCoverage \doteq \forall hasDomainSet.ReferencableGrid$⊓=$1hasDomainSet$

⊓$\forall hasFuntion.fuction$⊓≤$1hasFunction$

⊓$\forall hasRangeSet.rangeSet$=$1hasRangeSet$

⊓$\forall hasRangeStructure.rangeType$⊓=$1hasRangeStructure$

*definition*5

$GridEnvelope \doteq \forall hasLow.Integer$⊓=$1hasLow$⊓$\forall hasHigh.Integer$⊓=$1hasHigh$

*definition*6

$Grid \sqsubseteq DomainSet$

$RectifiedGrid \sqsubseteq DomainSet \sqcap \neg Grid \sqcap \neg ReferencableGrid$

$ReferencableGrid \sqsubseteq DomainSet \sqcap \neg GridCoverageDomain \sqcap \neg RectifiedGridCoverageDomain$

*definition*7

$Grid \doteq DomainSet \sqcap \forall hasGridEnvelope.GridEnvelope \sqcap =1hasGridEnvelope$

*definition*8

$RectifiedGrid \doteq DomainSet \sqcap \forall hasGridEnvelope.GridEnvelope \sqcap =1hasGridEnvelope$

$\sqcap hasOrigin.Origin \sqcap =1hasOrigin$

$\sqcap hasOffsetVector.OffsetVector \sqcap =1hasOffsetVector$

*definition*9

$ReferencableGrid \doteq DomainSet \sqcap \forall hasGridEnvelope.GridEnvelope \sqcap =1hasGridEnvelope$

$\sqcap hasCoordTransform.CoordTransform =1hasCoordTransform$

*definition*10

$AbstractScalarValueList \sqsubseteq RangeSet$

$ValueArray \sqsubseteq RangeSet \sqcap \neg AbstractScalarValueList \sqcap \neg DataBlock \sqcap \neg File$

$DataBlock \sqsubseteq RangeSet \sqcap \neg AbstractScalarValueList \sqcap \neg ValueArray \sqcap \neg File$

$File \sqsubseteq RangeSet \sqcap \neg AbstractScalarValueList \sqcap \neg DataBlock \sqcap \neg ValueArray$

*definition*11

$GridFuction \sqsubseteq Function$

$CoverageMappingRule \sqsubseteq Function \sqcap \neg GridFuction$

*definition*12

$GridFuction \doteq \forall hasStartPoint.StartPoint \sqcap \leq 1hasStartPoint$

$\sqcap \forall hasSequenceRule.SequenceRule \sqcap \leq 1hasSequenceRule$

$\sqcap \forall hasAxisOrder.AxisOrder \sqcap \leq 1hasAxisOrder$

*definition*13

$CoverageMappingRule \doteq (\forall hasRuleDefinition.String \sqcap \leq 1hasRuleDefinition)$

$\sqcup (\forall hasRuleReference.anyURI \sqcap \leq hasRuleReference)$

A Space-Based Interoperability Model

Diego Bernini, Daniela Micucci, and Francesco Tisato

Department of Informatics, Systems and Communication,
University of Milano - Bicocca,
Viale Sarca 336, 20126 Milan, Italy
{diego.bernini,daniela.micucci,francesco.tisato}@disco.unimib.it
http://www.sal.disco.unimib.it

Abstract. Software components may need to reason on thematic information that are usually contextualized in several and different dimensions. A person, for instance, may be physically located in a room; may play a specific role in an organization chart; and may be associated with an RFID tag in a set of identifiers. Moreover, software components may require thematic information which are produced by other software components and, in turn, they may be sources of information. This paper presents an interoperability model based on spatial concepts. The spatial model supports the contextualization of thematic information in different spaces - be they conceptual or physical. Main concepts are spaces, locations and mapping between locations belonging to different spaces. The model constitutes the basis to enable information sharing between software components. From this point of view, software components declare their interest in information from specific spatial locations (subscription contexts) and diffuse information in possibly other specific spatial locations (publication contexts). In a framework reifying the model we propose, software components may retrieve information without knowing who are the other components in the system. Indeed, the model enforces the indirect communication between software components which may rely on different views of the information domain.

Keywords: space-awareness, localized information, interoperability, complex and distributed system.

1 Introduction

Ubiquitous computing, pervasive computing, ambient ecologies, ambient intelligence, smart spaces, responsive environments, and so forth, are nowadays emerging interaction models. Their applications range from automated monitoring and control of homes for safety and comfort in Domotics [1] to Interactive Architecture, Design and Art [2].

Realizing large-scale systems that reify interaction models requires developing software systems that integrate various heterogeneous devices and technologies for sensing different properties of the environment and for providing different kinds of services. Typical input components are motion sensors, localization systems, cameras and vision systems; while common output ones are screens, lights,

M.-A. Sicilia, C. Kop, and F. Sartori (Eds.): ONTOSE 2010, LNBIP 62, pp. 75–89, 2010.

audio synthesizers and general electronic appliances. In such systems interoperability is a key requirement.

A successful architecture should model interoperability so that software components may be not aware about the existence of the other software components. Indeed, such an architecture allows to "indirectly connect" software components even if they are heterogeneous.

The devised interoperability model should be then realized by an underlying framework. To be general, that is, to support any kind of system, such a framework must rely on a generic "communication model" that is, it must not depend on a specific application domain. In other words, the framework should be aware of a few basic concepts that may be considered general enough to be applicable in several application domains. This requires, at least, that the semantics of the information is left to applications. Moreover, the domain of information should be arranged in an appropriate way that, in turn, must be general enough to be applied in several domains.

The paper presents a space-based model supporting interoperability among software components. The model we present aims at identifying the services and the mechanisms that a framework should support to guarantee cooperation in terms of information sharing between software components.

The model exploits space as the metaphor to model the domain of information and derives from space-awareness the interoperability model.

Space-based concepts are suitable to represent both physical spatial models (e.g., geo-referred) and conceptual spatial models (e.g., organization structure). Software components exploit suitable spaces - which are defined according to generic spatial models - to indirectly interact with other software components.

Thematic information is localized in several spaces. Talking about localized information suggests a clean separation between spatial contextualization ("where") and thematic information ("what"), whose meaning depends on software component interpretation beyond its localization. Spaces and localized information constitute the domain of information of the system.

Likewise the semantics of information is left to applications, the semantics of spaces is, in turn, up to applications only. This ensures that the framework reifying the model is generic to support any kind of application domain in which the generic spatial model suffices to model the domain of information.

Obviously, in order to cooperate, software components must share a common view of the domain of information, or, in other terms, they must rely on an ontology of the the domain of information.

Unfortunately, software components usually rely on a view of the domain of information that is subjective (i.e., partial) and, what is worse, they do not rely on the same view.

A mapping is then required to harmonize different subjective views. A mapping enables an information localized by a software component in its subjective view to be accessed by another software component relying on a different subjective view possibly derived by different spatial models.

Finally, the space-based interoperability model must provide the basic space-based concepts enabling a software components both to access the information they need (i.e., they specify a subscription context) and to diffuse the information they produce (i.e., they publish a thematic information within a publication context).

The space model supporting interoperability is built over a revised version presented in [3] and [4]. [3] introduces a common set of space-related concepts that provides applications with a unique view of the spaces. The devised model allows software components to rely on an operational view of the space, which is defined in terms of opaque locations and of movements between them. Actual space model maintains the opaqueness of locations, but discards movements assuming that software components are aware about the structure of the space. [4] presents a space-aware architecture based on the space model described in [3].

The rest of the paper is organized as follows. Section 2 describes spatial concepts that are the basis of the interoperability model described in Section 3. Spatial concepts and the interoperability model are presented by means of UML [5] class diagrams enriched with OCL [6] constraints when required. Section 4 presents some related works. Finally, Section 5 sketches some conclusions and discusses future developments.

2   Spatial Concepts

Space-based concepts are suitable to represent both physical spatial models (e.g., geo-referred) and conceptual spatial models (e.g., organization structure). Software components exploit suitable spaces - which are defined according to generic spatial models - to indirectly interact with other software components.

2.1   Generic Spatial Models

A *generic spatial model* define a space typology. A *space* is an instance of a spatial model and it is a collection of *location*s. The related spatial model specifies how locations are defined.

In a space there cannot be two locations that are equal. Moreover, each location is part of one space only.

Thematic information may be localized in one or more locations belonging to one or more spaces.

Different spatial models may be identified. In this version we deal with finite spaces. The graph spatial model supports the definition of graph spaces whose locations are nodes and edges. The grid spatial model supports the definition of spaces whose locations are arranged in a bi-dimensional grid and are characterized by a pair of indexes. Finally, a name spatial model just supports the definition of name spaces as collections of named locations.

Fig. 1 sketches the UML class diagram modelling generic spatial models.

The abstract class Location reifies a generic location. It is characterized by an attribute - called position - specifying its position in a space.

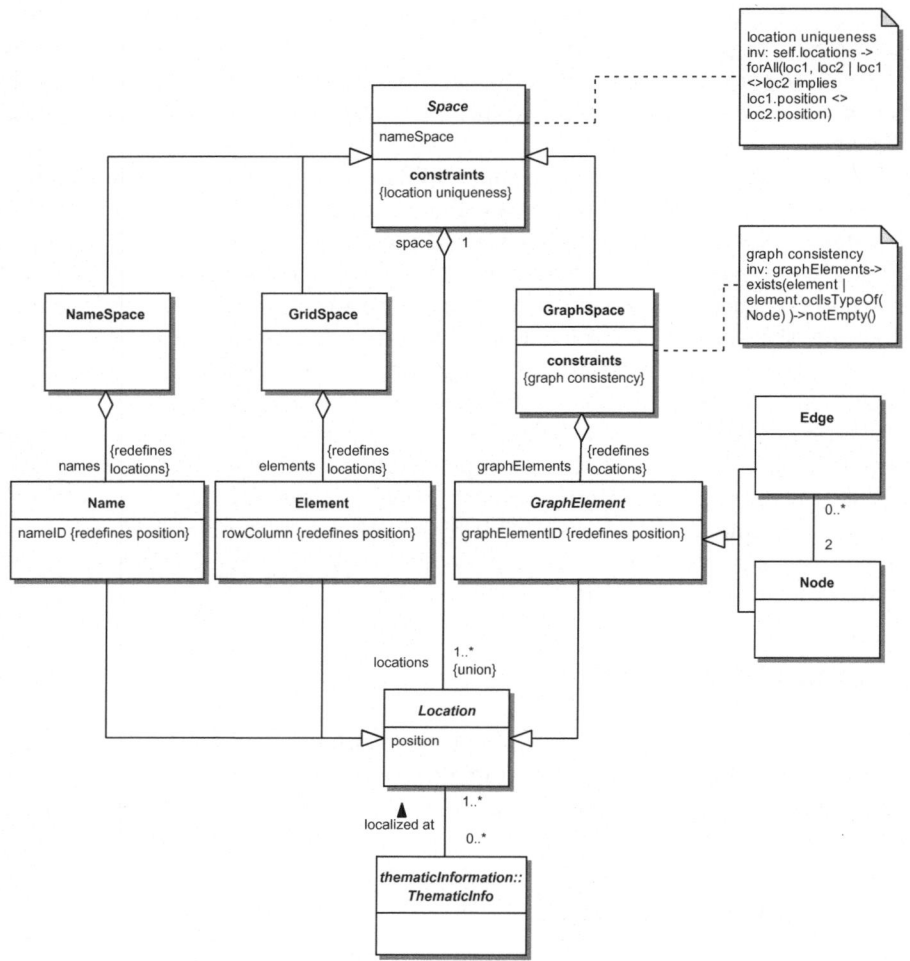

Fig. 1. Spatial Models

The abstract class Space reifies a generic spatial model. The aggregation with the Location class specifies that a space is a collection of locations. In a space there must exist at least one location. This is specified by the 1..* cardinality in the association-end (the one with the role labelled locations) of the aggregation. Moreover, a location belongs to one space only. This is expressed by the 1 cardinality in the association-begin (the one with the role labelled space) of the aggregation. Since aggregations specify a Set type collection (i.e., a collection in which duplicates are not allowed), it does not ensure uniqueness in terms of instances state too. In the specific case, this means that even if two locations belonging to the same space are different instances, they may have the same value for position. To overcome the drawback, we introduce the constraint *location uniqueness*. Obviously, Location is an abstract class, but defining this property at this level allows generalizing the constraint that must hold for each derived class. As we will see, the uniqueness property is fundamental for localizing and sharing thematic information.

From the more general definition of spatial model (Space), we derived the following specific spatial models: GraphSpace (i.e., a space representing a graph), GridSpace (i.e., a space representing a bi-dimensional grid), and NameSpace (i.e., a space representing a collection of names). Obviously, other typologies may be identified.

The derived spatial models redefines both Location and position to accomplish their spatial characteristics.

Concerning with GraphSpace, we introduced the *graph consistency* constraint stating that if a graph is defined by one element only, such element must be a Node.

Finally, ThematicInfo represents any kind of spatially-localized information. An information is spatially-localized when it is bound to one or more locations. Such locations my be part of different spaces.

Generic spatial models are defined once and for all. Their are generic enough to model a set of commonly used spaces and, since are generic, they may be used in several application domains. Indeed, applications using such spatial models should provide them the correct semantics.

Software components rely on spaces that are instances of generic spatial models. Such spaces constitute the *awareness* that a software component has about the overall system (i.e., the domain of information). Such awareness is termed *subjective view* of the domain of information since it may not contain all the defined spaces. Different software components may rely on different subjective spaces. Thus, the intersection between two subjective spaces may be the empty set.

2.2   Space Mappings

One or more locations belonging to a space may be related to one or more locations belonging to a different (another) space. When a relation between two locations exists, then a *binary map* is defined. A binary map is a relation with direction: from a source to a target. If two locations need to be mapped in both directions, then two binary maps must be defined.

Mapping helps in making software components able to share information even if they are not aware of the same spaces, that is, they rely on different subjective views. Suppose to have two spaces (*aSpace* and *bSpace*) and a map between *locA* (source) belonging to *aSpace* and *locB* (target) belonging *to bSpace*. If a software component *s1* is aware of *spaceA* and localizes a thematic information *t1* in *locA*, the existing map between *locA* and *locB* indirectly localizes *t1* in *locB* too. If there is another software component *s2* that is aware of *bSpace* and is interested in thematic information localized in *locB*, it will be able to retrieve *t1*.

This way, software components may rely on spaces they are aware without knowing the spaces (and related spatial models) exploited by the other software components.

Fig. 2 sketches spatial concepts related to mapping.

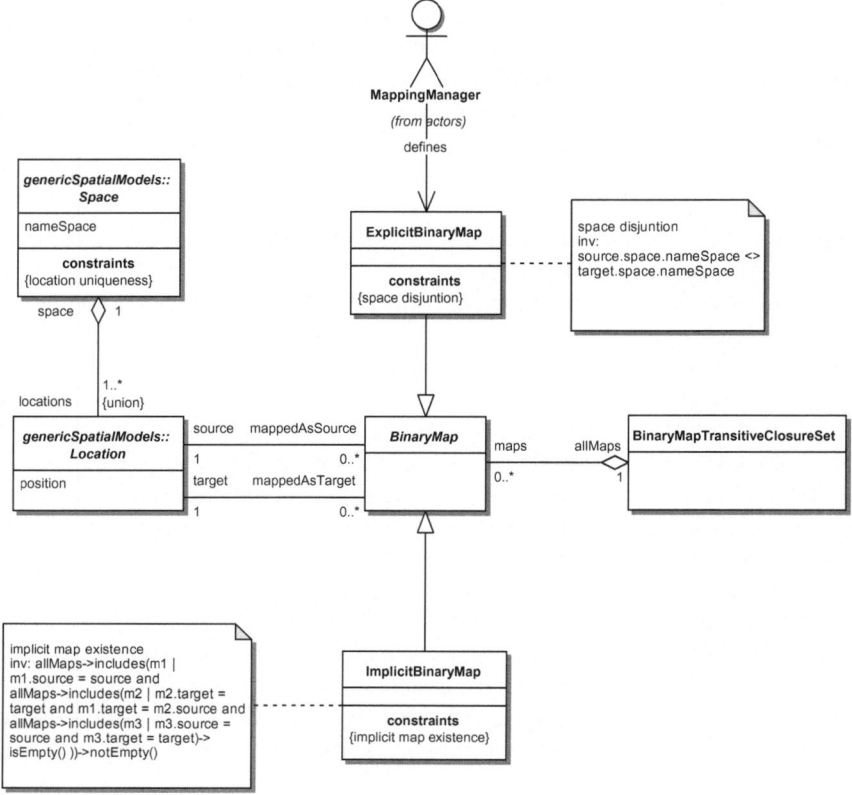

Fig. 2. The Mapping

The `BinaryMap` class specifies a generic mapping. A mapping is a binary relation involving one location acting as `source` and another location acting as `target`. This is explicated by the two associations relating `BinaryMap` and `Location` classes.

`ExplicitBinaryMap` is a kind of binary map that is explicitly defined by associating a source location to a target location. The constraint *space disjunction* states that the source and the target must belong to different spaces.

`ImplicitBinaryMap` is another kind of binary map. It maps a source location to a target one too, but it is implicitly derived from applying the transitive property to the explicit mappings. In particular, it is considered the restricted transitive closure of the explicit mappings. With restricted transitive closure of a mathematical relation R (the set of explicit mappings in our case) we intend the relation T containing all the pairs:

- (a,b) belonging to R
- (a,c) where (a,z) and (z,c) belongs to T for some z and c is not equal to a.

The constraint termed *implicit map existence* bounds the existence of an ImplicitBinaryMap by a set of properties reifying the transitive closure.

Finally, the BinaryMapTransitiveClosureSet maintains all the binary maps.

3   Space-Based Interoperability Model

Spatial concepts presented in the previous section constitute the building blocks of the interoperability model. To share thematic information with other parties, software components localize information in *publication contexts*. Parties interested in localized-information specify *subscription contexts*. A publication context and a subscription context possibly rely on different spaces. A *match* occurs when the contexts are directly or indirectly related due to the existence of at least a binary map involving a location of the publication context acting as source and a location of the subscription context acting as target. When a match occurs, the software component who made the subscription receives the information and its complete spatial contextualization.

3.1   Contexts and Publications

A *context* specifies a set of locations belonging to the same space. A *publication context* is the context used by a software component when sharing a thematic information. After a contextualization, the information will be localized in all the locations specified in the context. On the other side, a *subscription context* is the context used by a software component when specifying the locations in a space that are relevant to it, that is, locations that may have localized thematic information useful to the software component and generated by other software components.

Fig. 3 sketches the classes modelling contexts. The more general Context class specifies a set of locations defined in the same space. It may contain from 1 location only as far as the whole locations in the space.

The constraint *space uniqueness* ensures that all the contained locations belong to the same space.

Two special kinds of Context are defined:

- PublicationContext is the context specified by a software component acting as information source (InformationSource);
- SubscriptionContext is the context specified by a software component (InformationTarget) acting as information sink.

PublicationContext and SubscriptionContext only differ in that the former is used by the software component sharing a information, while the latter is used by the software component to subscribe. Really they are simple contexts.

A software components acting as information source contextualizes thematic information by defining a *publication*, that it the pair (publication context, thematic information). In Fig. 4 Publication models a publication act. The class is in association with 1..* (one or more) PublicationContext and with one ThematicInfo. Publishing an information implies localizing the information in

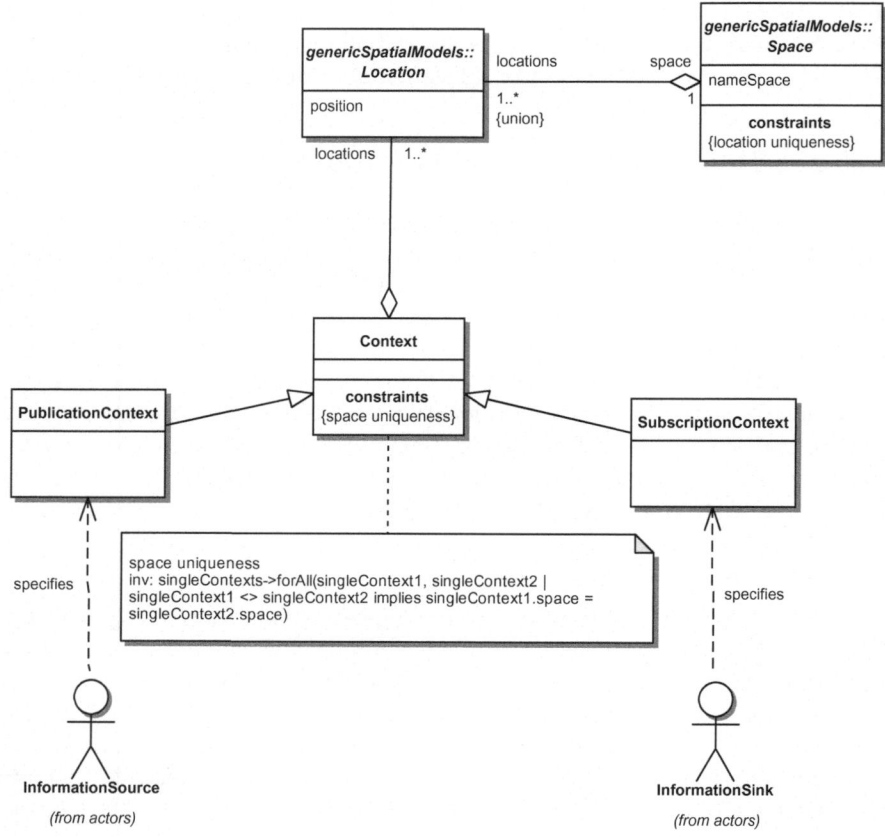

Fig. 3. Contexts

all the locations specified in the publication context and in all the locations belonging to different spaces for which a binary map exists (explicitly or implicitly).

3.2   Matching

Publication context and subscription context possibly rely on different spaces. In any case, information published on a publication context *PC match* a subscription context *SC* if (see Fig. 5):

– *direct match*: the intersection of the sets of locations specified in *SC* and *PC* is not empty, or
– *indirect match*: the set of locations specified in *PC* includes a location *L* which is mapped explicitly or implicitly to a location *L'* belonging to *SC*. Indirect match exploits the restricted transitive closure of the enumerative mappings (as presented in subsection 2.2).

Direct match is modelled by the `DirectMatch` class. The constraint *direct match existence* specifies the condition under which a direct match exists. The condition

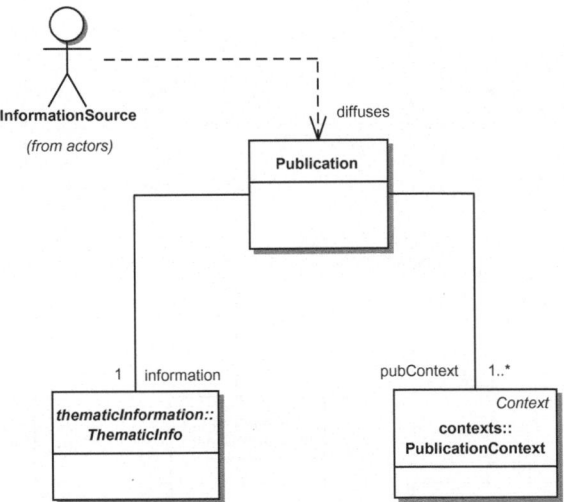

Fig. 4. Publications

is quite trivial: a direct match occurs if publication context and subscription context share a location. If this kind of match occurs, both the software components have respectively published and subscripted in the same space.

Indirect match is modelled by the `IndirectMatch` class which, in turn, has defined the constraint *indirect match existence* that specifies the conditions under which an indirect match exists. This case, the software component who made the subscription has specified a different space from the one used to publish information. The match occurs if there exists at least a location in the publication context that acts as source in a binary map and there exits a location in the subscription context that acts as the target of the binary map. In other words, a (implicit or explicit) map must exist between a location in the publication context and a location in the subscription context.

`Match` class is the superclass of both `DirectMatch` and `IndirectMatch`. It maintains related the `SubscriptionContext` and the `PublicationContext` that have matched (as specified by the two associations with end-roles labelled `subcontext` and `pubContext` respectively).

Note that both the aggregation relating `Space` and `Location` and the constraint defined in `Space` ensure that a publication reaches a subscriber.

3.3 Matched Publications

The result of a match is a *matched publication* that includes the information enriched with the publication contexts where the information was originally published and those which are explicitly or implicitly mapped from them, according to the restricted transitive closure (*context completeness*).

In Fig. 6, a matched publication is modelled by the `MatchedPublication` class. It is in association with the `ThematicInfo` originally published and one

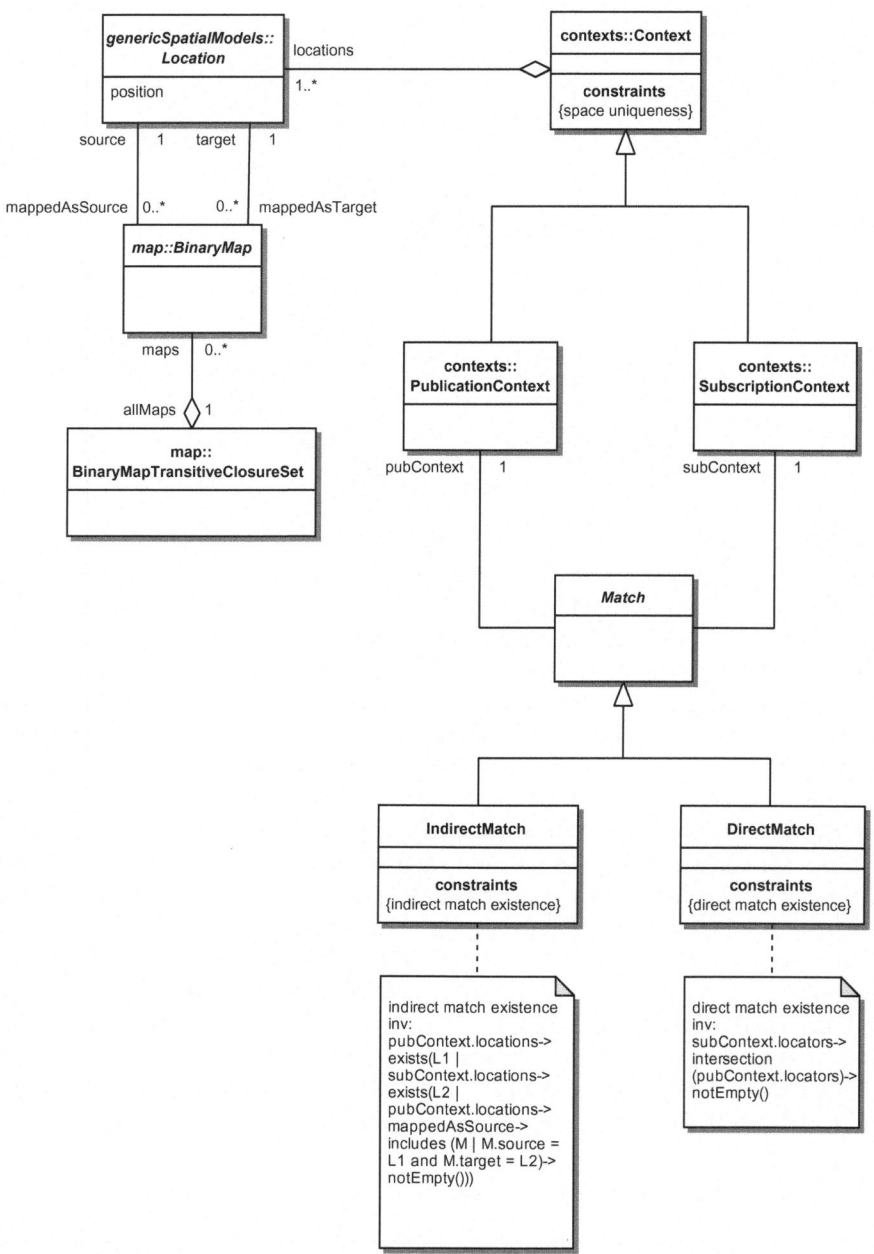

Fig. 5. The match

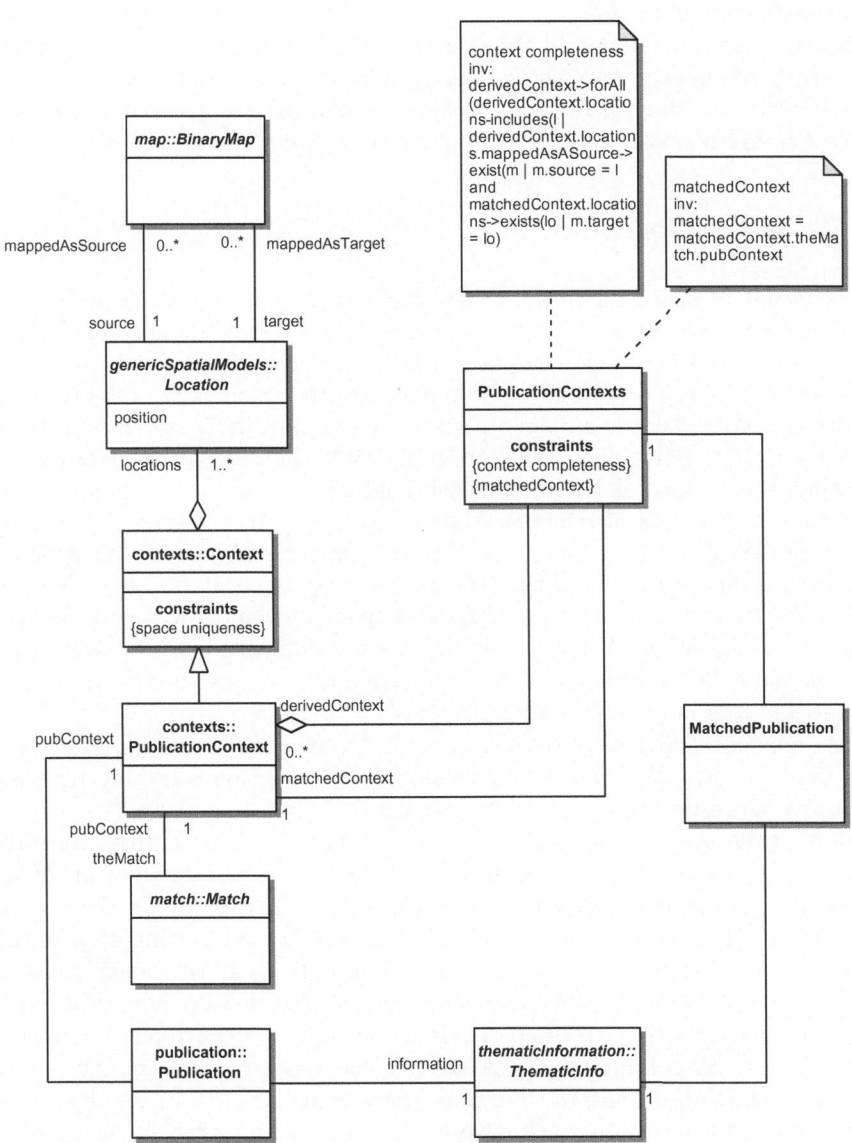

Fig. 6. Matched publication

PublicationContexts. PublicationContexts is a set of PubblicationContext
that contains the original publication context (matchedContext) that matched
the publication against the subscription and possibly a set of other publication
contexts (derivedContext).

derivedContext model all the contexts in which each contained location is
the target in a binary map where a location in matchedContext is its source. In
other words, the derivedContext reifies the context completeness (constraint
context completeness in PublicationContexts class).

4   Related Works

The concept of space has been widely studied in computer science as several
domains (e.g., emergency management systems, video-surveillance, smart spaces,
collaborative and pervasive computing) take advantage from it.

Space models are often based on an ontology that defines the relevant space-
related concepts in a non-ambiguous way. For example, in [7] such a set contains:
how space is modeled (explicitly or implicitly), the way physical objects are
modeled, the spatial relationships which hold for entities located in spaces, and
the concept of frames of reference. The first category is relevant to this paper.
Space modeling can take one of two basic views: the *Newtonian*, in which the
space exists independently of the objects that may be located in it (this view is
also called substantival view [8] or general space [9]), and the *Leibnizian* view,
in which the space exists as a matter of inter-relationships between objects (this
view is also called relational [8] or local space [9]). An exhaustive overview of
spatial concepts may be found in [10].

Different ontologies have been proposed. An exhaustive comparison may be
found in [11] and [12]; whereas [7] provides their evaluation based on the expressiveness with respect to space-related aspects.

Most of the proposed spatial ontologies carefully separate entities from their
location in the space, as claimed in [13], [14] and [7], to obtain what in software
engineering is termed separation of concerns [15]. In this line is the ontology
proposed in [16], as a generalization of [17]. It is an interesting step towards
the separation between entity, space and time. It looks at relationships as first
class objects. Specifically, through relationships, information should be related
to its thematic aspect, to its spatial location and its occurrence in time: the
thematic domain is indirectly associated to the space via the located_at and
occurred_at relations and to time since these relations are enriched by discrete
time stamps. Such an approach ensures flexibility in integrating thematic and
spatial information.

From an software architecture point of view, the approaches proposed to
interaction-based systems differ in how the interactions between components are
achieved. Following [18] we can identify three main kinds of interaction styles.

In *direct interaction* components interact directly through different kinds of
protocols, like message passing and (remote) procedure calls. CORBA [19] and
the Open Service Gateway initiative (OSGi) [20] are popular examples of general

purpose framework supporting direct interactions. Direct communication can be very efficient, however the main lack of this approach is that components should know each other or at least the interfaces of the other components. This can obstacle the integration of new and heterogeneous components.

Shared data spaces are typical mediums to achieve indirect interaction. Components interact through common data structures. These data structures are hosted in some centralized data space (e.g., a traditional LINDA-like tuple space [21]), or they can be fully distributed over different computational nodes. In this way openness to heterogeneous components is promoted, because interaction is based on an agreement on the data structures. Equip [22] is an example of shared data space conceived for building pervasive applications.

According to the *event-based publish/subscribe interaction style*, components can publish events and react to events of interest that are indicated through subscriptions. Subscription patterns and matching rules define the relation among subscriptions and events of interest. This style allows a strong decoupling between components which can ignore the identities of other components or even their existence. Context-based publish subscribe separates events from their contexts: subscriptions are based on the events' contexts, not on the events themselves. [23] proposes a generic model that introduces the concept of "context of relevance" and "context of interest" which are comparable to our model's contexts.

A framework reifying our model will combines context-based publish subscribes and the shared data spaces interaction styles. Components publish information on publication contexts and they receive information specifying subscription contexts trough subscriptions. The matching rules consider only spatial contexts and their mappings. [18] is also based on the combination of these two styles. It allows to explicitly program the matching rules but it does not strongly separate information from its context.

Finally, differently from other works like [24], a framework supporting our model will not focus on spaces representing physical locations only: information can be located in multiple spaces with different semantics, either physical or logical. We claim that this is a key conceptual aspect in realizing interaction-based systems. In fact it promotes fully context-based interactions, according to the definition of context as "any information that can be used to characterize the situation of entities [...]" [25].

5   Conclusion and Ongoing Activities

The paper presented a model for interoperability based on spatial concepts. The space-related concepts devised are general enough to be applied to several application domains. Such concepts require an underlying framework supporting them and providing a set of services that subscribers and publishers may use to diffuse and receive information.

A reasonable framework supporting our model will combine context-based publish/subscribe and the shared data spaces interaction styles. Components publish information on publication contexts and they receive information specifying subscription contexts trough subscriptions. The matching rules consider only spatial contexts and their mappings.

A prototypal implementation of a framework reifying the presented model has been realized. The platform has been called SIS (Space Integration Services) [26], and is being experimented in the context of the project "GAS (Grandi Attrezzature Scientifiche) - Intelligent Building", University of Milano Bicocca. The project aims at realizing systems in which several and heterogeneous acquisition devices provide information to applications like tracking people, localizing specific persons inside the building and so on.

Finally, we are planning to enrich the spatial models with metrics allowing properties like adjacency, distance between locations, paths and the like to be defined.

Acknowledgments. This work was supported in part by MIUR-FIRB Integrated System for Emergency "InSyEme" project under the grant RBIP063BPH.

References

1. Aiello, M., Dustdar, S.: Are our homes ready for services? a domotic infrastructure based on the web service stack. Pervasive Mob. Comput. 4(4), 506–525 (2008)
2. Bullivant, L.: Responsive Environments: architecture, art and design. Victoria and Albert Museum (2006)
3. Tisato, F., Micucci, D., Adorni, M., Cirasa, E.: Architectural abstractions for space awareness. In: Proceedings of the 2nd International Workshop on Ontology, Conceptualization and Epistemology for Software and Systems Engineering (ONTOSE) (2007)
4. Micucci, D., Tisato, F., Adorni, M.: Engineering spatial concepts. The Knowledge Engineering Review 24(Special Issue 01), 77–93 (2009)
5. Group, O.M.: OMG Unified Modeling LanguageTM (OMG UML), Superstructure (February 2009), http://www.omg.org/spec/UML/2.2/Superstructure
6. Group, O.M.: Object Constraint Language (February 2010), http://www.omg.org/spec/OCL/2.2
7. Bateman, J., Farrar, S.: Spatial ontology baseline. Technical Report SFB/TR8 internal report I1-[OntoSpace]:D2, Collaborative Research Center for Spatial Cognition, University of Bremen, Germany (2004)
8. Grenon, P.: Tucking RCC in cyc's ontological bed. In: Proceedings of the 18th International Joint Conference on Artificial intelligence, Acapulco, Mexico, pp. 894–899. Morgan Kaufmann Publishers Inc, San Francisco (2003)
9. Vieu, L.: Spatial representation and reasoning in artificial intelligence. In: Spatial and Temporal Reasoning, pp. 5–41 (1997)
10. Habel, C., Eschenbach, C.: Abstract structures in spatial cognition. In: Freksa, C., Jantzen, M., Valk, R. (eds.) Foundations of Computer Science. LNCS, vol. 1337, pp. 369–378. Springer, Heidelberg (1997)
11. Masolo, C., Borgo, S., Gangemi, A., Guarino, N., Oltramari, A.: Wonderweb deliverabled18, ontology library (final). laboratory for applied ontology. Technical Report D18 (2003)
12. Mascardi, V., Cord, V., Rosso, P.: A comparison of upper ontologies. In: Proceedings of the Conference on Agenti e industria: Applicazioni tecnologiche degli agenti software, WOA 2007 (2007)

13. Parent, C., Spaccapietra, S., Zimnyi, E.: Spatio-temporal conceptual models: data structures + space + time. In: Proceedings of the 7th ACM International Symposium on Advances in Geographic Information Systems, Kansas City, Missouri, United States, pp. 26–33. ACM Press, New York (1999)

14. Mark, D.M., Skupin, A., Smith, B.: Features, objects, and other things: Ontological distinctions in the geographic domain. In: Montello, D.R. (ed.) COSIT 2001. LNCS, vol. 2205, pp. 488–502. Springer, Heidelberg (2001)

15. Parnas, D.L.: On the criteria to be used in decomposing systems into modules. Communications of the ACM 15(12), 1053–1058 (1972)

16. Perry, M., Hakimpour, F., Sheth, A.: Analyzing theme, space, and time: an ontology-based approach. In: Proceedings of the 14th Annual ACM International Symposium on Advances in Geographic Information Systems, Arlington, Virginia, USA, pp. 147–154. ACM, New York (2006)

17. Yuan, M.: Modeling Semantical, Temporal and Spatial Information in Geographic Information Systems. In: Geographic Information Research: Bridging the Atlantic, pp. 334–347. Taylor & Francis, Abington (1996)

18. Mamei, M., Zambonelli, F.: Programming pervasive and mobile computing applications: The tota approach. ACM Trans. Softw. Eng. Methodol. 18(4), 1–56 (2009)

19. Emmerich, W., Kaveh, N.: Component technologies: Java beans, com, corba, rmi, ejb and the corba component model. In: Proceedings of the 24th International Conference on Software Engineering, ICSE 2002, pp. 691-692 (2002)

20. Lee, C., Nordstedt, D., Helal, S.: Enabling smart spaces with osgi. IEEE Pervasive Computing 2(3), 89–94 (2003)

21. Carriero, N., Gelernter, D.: Linda in context. ACM Commun. 32(4), 444–458 (1989)

22. MacColl, I., Millard, D., Randell, C., Steed, A., Brown, B., Benford, S., Chalmers, M., Conroy, R., Dalton, N., Galani, A., Greenhalgh, C., Michaelides, D., Rodden, T., Taylor, I., Weal, M.: Shared visiting in equator city. In: CVE 2002: Proceedings of the 4th International Conference on Collaborative Virtual Environments, pp. 88–94. ACM, New York (2002)

23. Frey, D., Roman, G.: Context-aware publish subscribe in mobile ad hoc networks. In: Murphy, A.L., Vitek, J. (eds.) COORDINATION 2007. LNCS, vol. 4467, pp. 37–55. Springer, Heidelberg (2007)

24. Cugola, G., Margara, A., Migliavacca, M.: Context-aware publish-subscribe: Model, implementation, and evaluation, pp. 875 –881 (July 2009)

25. Dey, A.K.: Understanding and using context. Personal Ubiquitous Comput. 5(1), 4–7 (2001)

26. Bernini, D., Micucci, D., Tisato, F.: Space integration services: a platform for space-aware communication. In: Proceedings of the 2010 International Conference on Wireless Communications and Mobile Computing: Connecting the World Wirelessly. ACM, New York (2010)

Visualising Semantic Coupling among Entities in an OWL Ontology

Juan Garcia, Francisco Garcia, and Roberto Theron

Computer Science Department,
University of Salamanca
{ganajuan,fgarcia,theron}@usal.es

Abstract. An ontology consists of a finite set of entities and relationships among these entities. Relationships in an OWL ontology are given by the object properties, defined as a binary relation between classes in the domain with classes in the range. These relationships define semantic coupling among classes. This paper formally define some metrics to measure semantic coupling among classes in OWL ontologies. Moreover it also describes a visualisation to analyse the proposed metrics using visual analytics techniques. We have implemented a tool to test our metrics with real public ontologies and the results are analysed and discussed.

Keywords: Semantic Coupling, Coupling Metrics, OWL Ontologies, Visual Analytics.

1 Introduction

In general, an ontology describes formally a domain of discourse. Typically, an ontology consists of a finite list of terms and the relationships between these terms. The terms denote important concepts (classes of objects) of the domain. Relationships typically include hierarchies of classes. A hierarchy specifies a class C to be a subclass of another class C if every ob ject in C is also included in C. Apart from subclass relationships, ontologies may include information such as properties, value restrictions, disjoint statements, specifications of logical relationships between ob jects. We focus on OWL ontologies that distinguish between two main categories of properties: Object properties and Datatype properties. Object properties relate classes in the domain with classes in the range while Datatype properties relate classes in the domain with simple data values in the range. Relationships among classes are given by the Object properties so in order to measure them these properties need to be analysed.

Ontologies are represented in some ontology description languages such as Resource Description Framework (RDF), Web Ontology Language (OWL) and Description Logic (DL). OWL is an extension of RDF and a machine-readable language for sharing and reasoning information on the web. It has been recomended as the standard web ontology language. An OWL ontology representation consists of axioms and facts. Axioms are the semantic knowledge defined

M.-A. Sicilia, C. Kop, and F. Sartori (Eds.): ONTOSE 2010, LNBIP 62, pp. 90–106, 2010.
© Springer-Verlag Berlin Heidelberg 2010

by building relationships between classes and properties. Facts represent the individual assertions [8].

Ontologies play an important role to provide shared knowledge models to semantic-driven applications targeted by Semantic Web. Ontology metrics represent an important approach due to they can help to assess and qualify an ontology. From the viewpoint of ontology developers, by assessing quality of ontology, they can automatically recognise areas that might need more work and specify some parts of the ontology that might cause problems. Furthermore metrics are useful in the process of reuse because before using a previously defined ontology would be desirable to evaluate it in order to determine the worthiness of using it. Metrics should always be taken into account to evaluate ontologies both during engineering and application processes.

In the software engineering field, Coupling Between Objects (CBO) has been defined in [1] with two variants. CBO-in that measures the number of classes that depend on the class under consideration and CBO-out that measures the number of classes on which the class under consideration depends. This approach has been taken into account to define our metrics but focused on ontologies.

1.1 Our Contribution

In this paper we formally define the metrics that help to analyse and evaluate coupling between classes in an ontology. These metrics are focused on providing an insight about the importance of the classes according to their relationships and the way they are related. Moreover we also propose a visualisation to analyse coupling using diverse techniques taken from the Visual Analytics field.

This paper is organised as follows: we provided a brief introduction, then we discuss some related work. In the third section we formally define our metrics to measure coupling. In the fourth section we propose a visualisation framework, then we analyse a case study in the fifth section and finally we discuss the conclusions and the future work.

2 Related Work

Diverse ontology metric proposals have been done in the past years; such as [3] that describes some metrics to normalize ontologies and [4][5] that represent a way to rank them. The paper [3] reviews the current state-of-the-art and basically proposes normalization as a pre-process to apply structural metrics. This normalization process consists of five steps: name anonymous classes, name anonymous individuals, classify hierarchically and unify the names, propagate the individuals to the deepest possible classes and finally normalize the object properties. This proposal is focused on content metrics based on Onto-Metric framework and basically they have been proposed to improve ontology behaviour or to fix some mistakes. Papers [4][5] propose some metrics to rank ontologies. Basically this proposal consists of a Java Servlet to process as inputs some keywords introduced by the user. Then the framework searches using

Swoogle[1] engine and retrieves all the URI's representing the ontologies related with these keywords. Then the framework searches on its internal database if these ontologies have been previously analysed and retrieves their information. Finally the framework ranks retrieved ontologies.

Orme et al. [6] proposed a set of coupling metrics for ontology-based systems represented in OWL, these metrics are: the number of external classes (NEC), reference to external classes (REC), and referenced includes (RI). This proposal defines a new type of coupling measurement for system development that defines coupling metrics based on ontology data and its structure. The first proposed metric is NEC, representing the number of distinct external classes defined outside the ontology but used to define new classes and properties in the ontology. The external classes can include standard classes defined as ontology language primitives and user-defined classes from other ontologies. The second metric REC is the number of references to external classes in the ontology. As we described above, NEC is a direct measure of the number of classes in the ontology. REC is a direct measure of the number of fanouts (in this case fanouts are different class hierarchies with external roots) within the ontology resulting from external classes. RI is a direct measure of the number of referenced includes in the ontology. Authors have also proposed some cohesion metrics for ontologies [7]. They proposed a set of ontology cohesion metrics to measure the modular relatedness of OWL ontologies. These metrics are Number of Root Classes (NoR), Number of Leaf Classes (NoL) and Average Depth of Inheritance Tree of all Leaf Nodes (ADIT-LN). Authors define NoR metric as the total number of root classes explicitly defined in the ontology. A root class in an ontology means the class has no semantic super class explicitly defined in the ontology. NoL metric is defined as the number of leaf classes explicitly defined in the ontology. A leaf class in an ontology means the class has no semantic subclass explicitly defined in the ontology. Finally ADIT-LN is defined as the sum of depths of all paths divided by the total number of paths. A depth is the total number of nodes starting from the root node to the leaf node in a path. The total number of paths in an ontology is all distinct paths from each root node to each leaf node if there exists an inheritance path from the root node to the leaf node. And root node is the first level in each path.

Yinglong et al. [8] proposed another set of ontology cohesion metrics to measure the modular relatedness of ontologies in the context of dynamic and changing Web. These metrics have been defined taking into account the cohesion principle from Object Oriented Approach adpated to ontologies. Authors concentrate on measuring inconsistencies in ontologies and fully consider the ontological semantics rather than structure. The metrics they propose are Number of Ontology Partitions (NOP), Number of Minimally Inconsistent Subsets (NMIS) and the Average Value of Axiom Inconsistencies (AVAI). This work also describes the algorithms to compute these metrics and validate the metrics by using validation frameworks. These metrics are focused on assesing the quality of ontologies. Authors define NOP metric as the number of semantical partitions of a knowledge

---

[1] http://swoogle.umbc.edu

base. NMIS is defined as the number of all minimally inconsistent subsets in a knowledge base. This metric is useful to measure the scope of inconsistency impacts of a knowledge base. The third metric AVAI is defined as the ratio of the sum of inconsistency impact values of all axioms and assertions to the cardinality of the knowledge base. Moreover, the article analyses and validates the proposed metrics. Generally speaking, the advantages of these metrics include the possibility of assessing the quality of an consistent ontology.

OntoClean methodology [9], [10] proposes the use of some defined metaproperties. These metaproperties are rigidity, unity, identity and dependency. Authors have borrowed these concepts from their ancient philosophical counterparts. The methodology consists of assigning these metaproperties to the entities in order to provide with a logical and semantic meaning. Applying these metaproperties results on imposing several constraints on the taxonomic structure of an ontology and let to develop a conceptual analysis of the concepts and their validity. Moreover this methodology let to analyse and detect not logically consistent relationships.

YANG et al. [11] proposed metrics from a different point of view. Taking into account the evolution of the ontologies. Authors suggest a metrics suite of complexity, which mainly examine the quantity, ratio and correlativity of concepts and relationships, to evaluate ontologies from the viewpoint of complexity and its evolution. These metrics are divided into two groups: Primitive Metrics and Complexity Metrics. The Primitive metrics include TNOC (Total Numbers of Concepts or Classes), TNOR (Total Number of Relations), TNOP (Total Number of Paths), where a path is defined as a trace that can be taken from a specific particular concept to the most general concept in the ontology. The first Complexity Metric defined is the average relations per concept, that is calculated by dividing TNOR by TNOC. The second metric is the average paths per concept, and is calculated by dividing TNOP by TNOC.

2.1   Tools That Implement Metrics

There are some developed tools that implement diverse metrics. ONTOMETRIC, OntoQA and Protege represent the main available proposals. We consider that OntoQA [12], [13] represents the main proposal about metrics on ontologies. It proposes some Schema Metrics to measure the richness of schema relationships, attributes and schema inheritance. These metrics are focused on evaluating the ontology in general. Another proposed categories are class richness, average population, cohesion, importance of a class, fullness of a class, class inheritance and class relationship richness, connectivity and readability. Class Relationship Richness is defined as the number of relationships that are being used by instances that belong to the class. On the other hand, the Connectivity of a class is defined as the number of instances of other classes that are connected to instances of the selected class. All these metrics are focused on the structure of the ontology.

Currently Protege[2] is the most widely used tool to create or modify an ontology. The metrics are classified into 6 categories. The first one is related with general metrics such as counters for classes, object properties, datatype properties and individuals. The second category is related with class axioms and includes counters for subclass axioms, equivalent classes axioms, disjoint classes axioms, GCI and hidden GCI. The third category includes counters for object properties axioms. These counters are total of sub object properties, equivalent, inverse, disjoint, functional, inverse functional, transitive, symmetric, anti symmetric, reflexive and irreflexive object properties. Furthermore object property domain and range counters are also included. The fourth category is dedicated for datatype properties counters. This category includes total values for sub datatype properties, equivalent, disjoint and functional datatype properties, as well as counters for data properties domain and range. The fifth category is focused on individuals. It defines counters for class assertions, object and datatype property assertions, negative object and negative datatype assertions and same or different individuals axioms. Finally, the last category involves annotation axioms and defines just two metrics, the entity annotation axioms count and the axiom annotation axioms count. All these metrics represent simple counters for the items in the ontology and do not provide any kind of semantic metric.

ONTOMETRIC [14] is a framework proposed to measure the suitability of existing ontologies. This tool was defined to quantify the suitability of ontologies. Authors propose a taxonomy of 160 characteristics, also called multilevel framework of characteristics that provides the outline to be able to choose and to compare existing ontologies. This framework is used as a representation template of the information and starts by defining an analytic hierarchy process. This process involves building a hierarchy tree with the root node being the objective of the problem. The intermediate are the criteria and finally the lowest levels contain the alternatives. Then as the second step, the methodology applies the analytic hierarchy process to decide whether or not to reuse ontologies.

Ontology Metrics [3] is a web-based tool that validates and displays statistics about an OWL ontology, including the expressivity of the language it is written in. This tool calculates the same metrics than Protege. These metrics include counters for classes, properties, individuals, logical axioms, as well as specific counters described above in the Protege section.

2.2 Comparing Metrics

Comparing diverse analysed metrics we consider that OntoQA offers the best set of metrics for analysing the structure and ranking the ontologies according to these metrics. Just Yinglong proposal and OntoClean are clearly focused on the semantics. On the other hand Orme, Yinglong and OntoQA have proposed different metrics to calculate the cohesion. It is important to highlight that they represent three completely different ways to define cohesion. OntoQa defines cohesion as the number of separate connected components of the graph representing the Knowledge Base. In contrast Orme's proposal metrics measure the

---

[2] Protege Ontology Editor http://protege.stanford.edu/

Table 1. Summarises the analysed metrics and compares some interesting properties

Metric	Semantic / Structure	Ranking	Cohesion	Coupling
Vrandecic	*Structure*	*No*	*No*	*No*
Alani	*Structure*	*Yes*	*No*	*No*
Orme	*Structure*	*No*	*Yes*	*Yes*
Yinglong	*Semantic*	*No*	*Yes*	*No*
OntoClean	*Semantic*	*No*	*No*	*No*
Ontometric	*Structure*	*No*	*No*	*No*
Protege	*Structure*	*No*	*No*	*No*
OntoQA	*Structure*	*Yes*	*Yes*	*No*
OntologyMetrics	*Structure*	*No*	*No*	*No*
Yang	*Structure*	*No*	*No*	*No*

modular relatedness of OWL ontologies while Yinglong focuses on measuring ontologies in the context of dynamic and changing web. The metrics proposed by Orme et al. [6] represent the coupling among entities from diverse ontologies. There is another coupling that has not been taken into account: the coupling among entities in the same ontology that provides useful information about the connection among the classes in the same ontology. Sometimes systems use no more than one ontology then the coupling metrics proposed by Orme become completely useless. Finally, the metrics proposed by Yang et al. [11] are intended to reflect the complexity of an ontology during its lifecycle and evolution.

3   Our Metrics

As we said above relationships between classes in an ontology provide us with an insight of the ontology. The direction of a property can be logically considered going from the domain to the range. This direction provides us important information about the role that classes play in the ontology. For instance a class that belongs to the domain of many properties would represent one of the main subjects of the ontology. This is obvious because it implies that this class is being qualified, evaluated or described. In contrast, a class that belongs to the range of one or many properties would represent a qualifier, characteristic or even more important may be used to infer a certain type, and sometimes these classes represent an enumeration of values. It is important to differentiate between both types of classes in an ontology. Furthermore it is also important to distinguish between a property that has the same class belonging to both domain and range. Our metrics have been defined to be the analogous counterpart from Object- Oriented Systems to ontologies. We define CBE (Coupling Between Entities) for ontologies with two possibilities. CBE-out representing the coupling where the class belongs to the domain of the property and CBE-in representing the coupling where the class belongs to the range of the property. Furthermore we also define SC (Self Coupling) for those properties that have the same class belonging to both domain and range of the property. Figure 1 shows a diagram where CBE is illustrated over class A. The same class may play different roles in an ontology, nevertheless almost always there are some of them that play specific roles being either subjects or qualifiers, depending on the side they belong to.

3.1   Extending the Coupling Metrics

Relationships among entities are also inherited from superclasses to subclasses. In consequence, coupling between entities is also inherited. Our previously defined metrics are focused on direct coupling, it refers to the coupling directly defined in the class without considering the coupling defined in the superclasses. Because of that, we extend the metrics to also consider the inherited coupling from the superclasses. We define iCBE-out as the inherited CBE-out metric, representing the CBE-out metric value from all the superclasses of the selected class. In addition, we also define iCBE-in, iCBE-io and iSC as the CBE-in, CBE-io and SC metrics respectively from all the superclasses of the selected class.

We provide a formal definition of all metrics.

Definitions:

1. *Let Θ be an OWL ontology*
2. *Let ϕ be the set of properties $\in \Theta$*
3. *Let C be the set of classes $\in \Theta$*
4. *$\exists\, c \in C$*
5. *$\exists\, \rho \subseteq \phi$*
6. *$\exists\, p \in \rho$, $q \in \rho$ and $p \neq q$*
7. *$\exists\, d \in C$ such as d is subclass of $c(i) \, \forall\, i \in [1, n]$*
8. *Let $\alpha(i)$ be the $CBE - out$ metric value for $c(i)$*
9. *Let $\beta(i)$ be the $CBE - in$ metric value for $c(i)$*
10. *Let $\gamma(i)$ be the $CBE - io$ metric value for $c(i)$*
11. *Let $\delta(i)$ be the SC metric value for $c(i)$*

Metrics:

1. We define CBE-out metric as:

$$if\ c \in domain(p) \, \forall\, p \in \rho\ then\ CBE - out\ =\ |\rho|$$

2. We define CBE-in metric as:

$$if\ c \in range(p) \, \forall\, p \in \rho\ then\ CBE - in\ =\ |\rho|$$

3. We define CBE-io metric as:

$$if\ \exists\, p \in \rho\ and\ q \in \rho\ such\ as\ p\ is\ inverse\ of\ q\ then\ CBE - io\ =\ |\rho|/2$$

4. We define SC (Self-coupling) as:

$$if\ \exists\, c \in domain(p)\ and\ c \in range(p) \, \forall\, p \in \rho\ then\ SC\ =\ |\rho|$$

5. We define iCBE-out metric for class d as:

$$\sum \alpha(i) \, \forall\, i \in [1, n]$$

6. We define iCBE-in metric for class d as:

$$\sum \beta(i) \,\forall\, i \,\in\, [1,n]$$

7. We define iCBE-io metric for class d as:

$$\sum \gamma(i) \,\forall\, i \,\in\, [1,n]$$

8. We define iSC metric for class d as:

$$\sum \delta(i) \,\forall\, i \,\in\, [1,n]$$

9. Finally we define Coupling Between Entities (CBE) as:

$$\text{CBE} = \text{CBE-out} + \text{CBE-in} + \text{CBE-io} + \text{SC} + \text{iCBE-out} + \text{iCBE-in} + \text{iCBE-io} + \text{iSC}$$

The main advantages of our metrics include: the capacity to detect classes that represent the subject of the ontology and classes that qualify, moreover to be able to discern between both. Furthermore metrics tell us information about how coupled classes in the ontology are, resulting in a low or high coupled ontology. We consider that high coupled ontologies would be desirable because low coupling would imply that classes are not related each other except for ISA relationships.

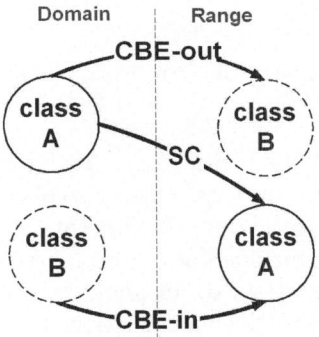

Fig. 1. Shows the CBE-out, CBE-in and SC definitions on class A

Our metrics are semantically defined due to coupling between entities (CBE) involve to define the direction of coupling. This means that semantically speaking CBE-in, CBE-out and SC represent different concepts as explained above in the definition of them. Furthermore changes in CBE values would represent semantic variations not structural. The structure in the ontology is not directly related with our metrics. Opposite to coupling metrics proposed by Orme et al. [6] that relate the external classes, our metrics take into account not just external but internal classes too. External classes refer only to classes defined in other ontologies. Furthermore our proposal is focused on coupling from the point of view of the same coupled classes. We mean that if we take a specific class we represent its own coupling.

4   Our Visualisation Framework

4.1   Framework Architecture, a Visual Analytics Approach

Our framework has been written in Java and uses Jena API to manage OWL ontologies [3]. Jena framework is responsible for loading ontologies. As illustrated on figure 2, our framework queries directly over Jena framework, and builds some data structures to manage the information. This information is processed, managed by the framework and finally visualised. This design was intended to get a framework independent from the API to manage ontologies.

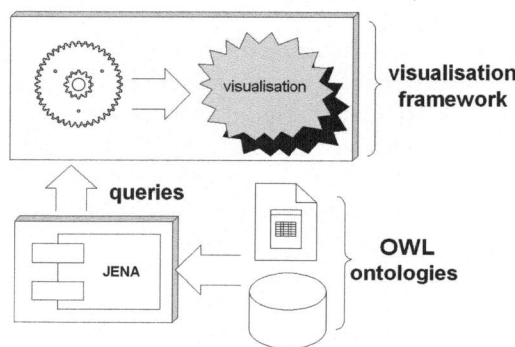

Fig. 2. Shows the framework's architecture

The framework consists on diverse Visual Analytics techniques specialised in covering some aspects of the ontology. These visualisations are interconnected to interact each other. It means that captured events in one visualisation alter the state of other ones. Events include data filtering, or selection of internal items. The term Visual Analytics refers to an analytical reasoning using automated analysis techniques and interactive visualizations to synthesize information and derive insight from massive, dynamic, ambiguous, and often conflicting data. Our framework includes diverse visualisation techniques, to cover most aspects related with ontologies in a visual manner. The visualisation of metrics defines just one of the aspects to be considered, in our framework.

4.2   Visualising Coupling

Our visualisation is based on a radial layout where selected class is located at the centre, meaning that we are focusing from the point of view of the class. All the properties related with this class are queried and displayed in the radial. Then, for each property the domain and range are analysed in order to detect the classes belonging to each one. According to our definition for CBE, this class is coupled if the CBE value is greater than cero. Furthermore this class is

---

[3] http://jena.sourceforge.net/

CBE-in or CBE-out coupled according to the place the class belongs to in the property. Coupling is represented in the radial going from left to right as shown in Fig. 3. The radial layout is divided in two sections, having each one a total circumference value of PI. The left side is used to represent CBE-in by showing the properties and the classes in the domain. The selected class belongs to the range of these properties. CBE-out is represented in the right side of the radial in the same way. All the properties are proportionally distributed within an angle equal to PI. Opposite to CBE-in, the selected class belongs to the domain of all these properties, and is located at the left side.

Figure 3 shows a selected class with a CBE-out value of 6 where each property has the selected class in the domain. In consequence each property can have one or more classes in the range. The first property is labeled with hierarchy and illustrates one class in the range and its own subclasses hierarchy. In this case we are representing 6 pink-coloured subclasses inside the class. The second property labeled with cluster represents three classes in the range of the property in a cluster layout like view. The third property labeled with class represents the simplest case where just one class belongs to the range. Finally the fourth property illustrates the way to indicate the attributes of a property; in this case the property is reflexive and symmetric.

Our tool is also intended to highlight the bad definition of concepts in the ontology. For instance a typical and very common error in ontologies occurs when properties are defined without a specific type in the domain or range or neither domain nor range. We consider this a lack of a semantic content due to each property should have clearly defined the types in the domain and range. We highlight this lack by using a symbol that clearly indicates a non-defined type, as illustrated on fig. 3 in the fifth property.

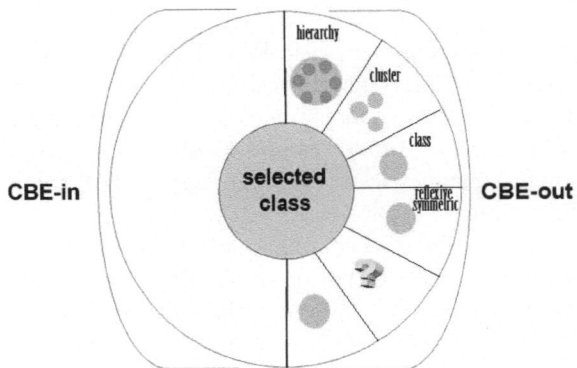

Fig. 3. Shows the general description of our visualisation

4.3   Visualising the Hierarchy and Filtering Data

Hierarchy represents a crucial part of the ontology. We have implemented a treemap visualisation to represent the hierarchy. A treemap is a widely used visual analytics technique proposed by Shneiderman [18]. It is a space-filling visualisation technique that represents large hierarchical data sets via a two-dimensional rectangular map, providing a compact visual representation of complex data spaces through both area and color. The area is related with the internal hierarchy it means the total of subclasses, while the color is related with properties of classes such as transitive, symetric, inverse, functional, etc.

Metrics are represented using another technique called table lens [19]. Table Lens technique has been motivated by the particular nature of tables. This technique is used to represent all the measured metric values and it is basically used to filter data. Criteria to filter data is based on metrics such as cbe, sc or the number of properties. Filtering is very important because when we are analysing coupling we are just interested in coupled classes, and the tool provides a way to filter these classes. Left side on figures 7(a) and 8 show a table lens where a filter on classes has been applied. The classes with a cbe value greater or equal than one have been filtered and descending ordered. This let us to recognise the coupled classes and specifically the most coupled one which in both cases is the class Person.

5   Case Study

We started our case study by searching some public available ontologies to analyse. The easiest way to search for ontologies is by using the Swoogle Semantic Web Search Engine [4]. We searched for ontologies related with the keyword "person", we consider it is the most basic word to search for. After a selection process and discarding those ones bad-defined, we selected five OWL ontologies to work with. Each one are described below.

5.1   SWETO

The first analysed ontology is Semantic Web Technology Evaluation Ontology (SWETO) version 1.4 [5] [16]. This general-purpose ontology was developed in 2004 by the Computer Science Department at the University of Georgia. This SWETO version consists of 114 classes and 13 object properties. Table 1 shows the result of applying our metrics to this ontology and all the classes that have at least 1 coupling value.

The simple analysis of SWETO coupling metrics has shown interesting results. Even having no background information about the ontology, we can clearly deduce the most coupled class also represents the most important one, in this case 'Person' depicted on figure 4(b). This is an obvious result because if this class contains most of the object properties then it represents the main ontology's subject. Furthermore this result can be supported by the fact that all the relationships are in the CBE-out metric which means that this class belongs to the domain in all the object properties. This fact implies these object properties were defined having as main purpose to satisfy some needs for this specific class. On

---

[4] http://swoogle.umbc.edu/
[5] http://knoesis.wright.edu/library/ontologies/sweto/

Table 2. Summarises the proposed coupling metrics in the ontology SWETO

Class	Object properties	CBE-out	CBE-in	CBE-io	SC	CBE
Person	5	5	0	0	0	5
Organization	1	1	3	0	0	4
Publication	1	1	2	0	1	4
Place	0	0	3	0	0	3
AcademicDepartment	0	0	2	0	0	2
Event	1	1	1	0	0	2
Researcher	1	1	0	0	0	1
University	1	1	0	0	0	1
Proffesor	1	1	0	0	0	1
ScientificPublication	1	1	0	0	0	1
Thing	1	1	0	0	0	1
Country	0	0	1	0	0	1
Classification	0	0	1	0	0	1

the other hand, classes that only have CBE-in values such as Place, Academic Department, Country or Classification belong to the range in the properties. It means that individuals of these classes represent all the possible values the properties can take in the range. Moreover these individuals represent qualifiers for other entities. Analysing CBE-io metric we realise that there are no values greater than 0. It means there are no inverse functions declared in the ontology. Moreover there is only one class with self coupling value (Publication); meaning that exists one property which has the same class in the domain and range. This analysis let us to have an insight into the behaviour of the ontology even without previous knowledge background of it. The main purpose is to relate persons with places, organizations or academic departments. Furthermore more specialized classes such as Professor or Researcher are related with Publication class depicted on figure 4(c). We can deduce from this ontology that it shows low coupling between classes. Just 13 out of 114 classes are related, which represents less than 10 percent of the total.

5.2   C2IEDM

The second analysed ontology is C2IEDMTrackCoreOnt.owl [17] downloaded from VIStology corporation website [6] designed to be used in military operational environments. This ontology is an implementation of the Command and Control Information Exchange Data Model (C2IEDM) developed by Multilateral Interoperability Programme (MIP). This is a small ontology, being the most coupled class OBJECT-ITEM-LOCATION which is depicted on figure 5(b). The property object-item-location-bearing-angle has no defined type class in the range as can be seen on the same figure 5(b). Figure 5(c) depicts the coupling for the class REPORTING-DATA where it can be seen that the functional property 'reporting-data-id' has more than one class in the domain, specifically three.

---

[6] http://www.vistology.com/index.html

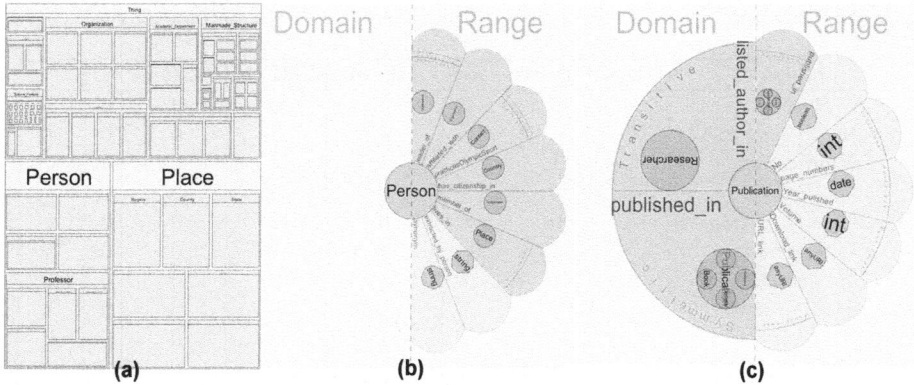

Fig. 4. Fig. 4(a) shows the hierarchy of the ontology represented in a treemap visualisation. Fig. 4(b) shows coupling for class Person and Fig. 4(c) shows coupling for Publication class.

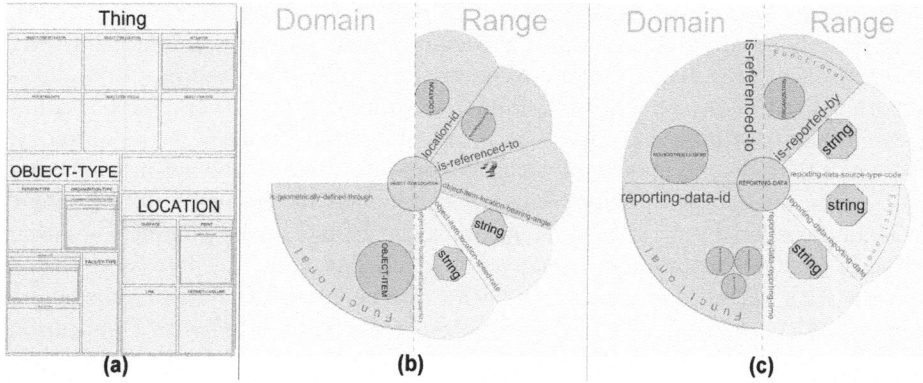

Fig. 5. Fig. 5(a) shows the hierarchy of the ontology represented in a treemap visualisation. Fig. 5(b) shows the most coupled class OBJECT-ITEM-LOCATION. Fig. 5(c) shows the coupling for class REPORTING-DATA.

They are represented as a cluster in the domain of the property. This ontology has just 25 classes and 8 of them with cbe value equal or greater than one, representing 32 percent of coupled classes.

5.3   JC3IEDM3

The ontology JC3IEDM3.1a.owl [17] developed by VIStology corporation is an implementation of the Joint Command, Control and Communication Information Exchange Data Model (JC3IEDM). JC3IEDM is being developed by the NATO-sponsored Multilateral Interoperability Programme (MIP) for the purpose of facilitating the exchange of command, control and communication

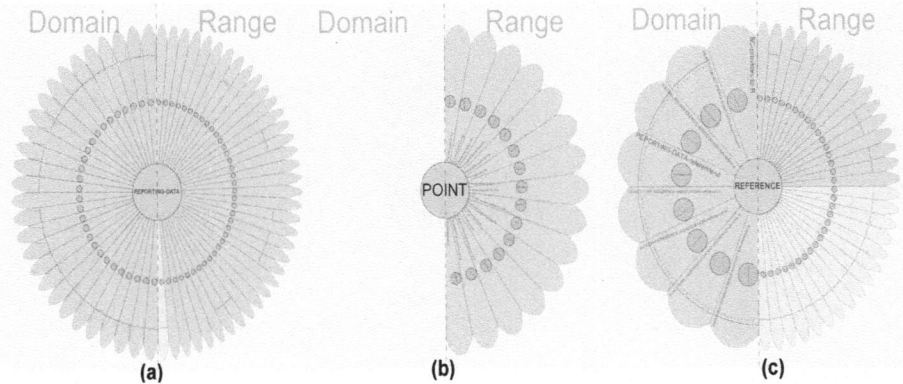

Domain   Range   Domain   Range   Domain   Range

(a)   (b)   (c)

Fig. 6. Fig. 6(a) shows the class REPORTING-DATA which is the most coupled class in the ontology. Fig. 6(b) shows the class Point which is a typical class with CBE-out coupling. Fig. 6(c) shows the class REFERENCE one of the most coupled classes.

information among coalition forces. It represents a modified updated version from C2IEDM. This is a very extensive ontology containing over 7900 elements (OWL classes, properties and their instances).

REFERENCE is shown in the figure 6c. It can be seen that most of the properties are functional, which means that they can have only one unique value for each instance. This OWL ontology was automatically generated from the ERwin data model containing the C3 Information Exchange Data Model. As consequence, this is a well-defined ontology, all properties have been defined with one class in the domain and range, being the most coupled class REPORTING-DATA shown in the figure 6c. This class has a CBE total value of 76 according to 36 for CBE-out, 28 for CBE-in and 12 for CBE-io and 1 datatype. It is a very high coupled ontology in contrast to C2IEDM and SWETO. This ontology is very crowded with 1488 classes and also very coupled. There is no a minimal percentage of coupling for a class, nevertheless high coupling is always desirable in contrast to low coupling.

5.4   Portal

The ontology portal.owl [7] taken from ontoware server is a general purpose related with some aspects of technology and academics. We emphasise on figure 7(a) the data filtering according to cbe metric value. Analysis is focused on coupling among classes, so the first step is to filter classes to only keep the coupled ones, this is done using the table lens visualisation. Then all the filtered classes are descending ordered according to cbe value to stablish coupling levels for each one. The result is illustrated on figure 7(a) where it can be depicted just the filtered classes and coupling for class Person. In contrast, figure 7(b) depicts the coupling for the class Generic-Agent which as can be clearly seen has cbe-in

---

[7] http://ontoware.org/swrc/portal.owl

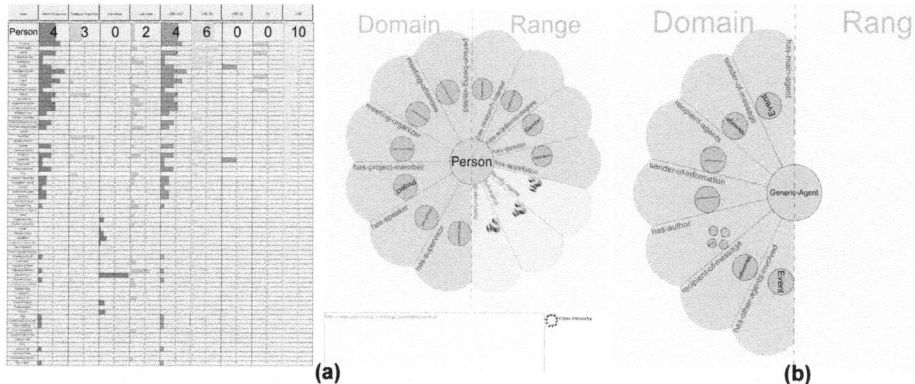

Fig. 7. Fig. 7(a) shows the table lens with the coupled classes filtered, and selected the most coupled class Person. Fig. 7(b) shows the class Generic-Agent which has a value for cbe-in metric of 7.

class	Object Properties	Datatype Properties	CBE-OUT	CBE-IN	SC	CBE
Person	14	13	14	9	3	26
Organization	8	2	8	7	3	18
Event	6	2	6	6	2	14
Facility	7	2	7	2	0	9
Location	1	0	1	8	0	9
Terrorist_Group	6	1	6	1	1	8
TravelEvent	5	2	5	1	1	7
Vehicle	4	1	4	1	0	5
Ownership Transfer	3	1	3	1	0	4
Terrorist	1	0	1	2	0	3
Contact	1	3	1	1	0	2
Arrest	2	0	2	0	0	2
Document	0	0	0	1	0	1
Country	0	0	0	1	0	1
Terroristincident	0	0	0	1	0	1
Terrorist_cell	0	0	0	1	0	1

Fig. 8. Fig. 8 shows coupled classes in the ontology filtered by the metric cbe in a table lens, and the coupling of the class Person, that as can be seen is the most coupled class in the ontology

coupling value of 7. This class is an example of a class with only cbe-in coupling. This ontology has 168 classes and coupling percentage of almost 55 percent which is consider acceptable.

5.5   Terrorism

The ontology terrorOnt.owl [8] published by the mindswap group was also used to analyse coupling. This ontology is very coupled due to 16 out of 30 classes have cbe values equal or greater than one, representing 53 percent of coupled classes. In contrast there are many properties with no definitions as can be seen in figure 8 remarked with an interrogation sign. In fact all the datatype properties

---

[8] http://www.mindswap.org/2004/terrorOnt.owl

have no defined a specific type. We consider this fact as a lack of information and a bad defined ontology. A weakly typed ontology is easier to become inconsistent with the data. Data inconsistencies are not desirable due to they could affect either syntactically or semantically to the ontology.

6   Conclusions and Future Work

We have formally proposed some metrics to measure coupling among classes in OWL ontologies. These metrics are focused on semantic coupling that as we have shown it is important to be considered. Our proposals are based on the widely used CBO (Coupling Between Objects) metrics taken from the Object Oriented Approach, but modified to be applied to OWL ontologies. To illustrate our metrics and our visualisation, we analysed diverse ontologies based on a search related with the subject Person. As it would be expected the class Person in all these ontologies is either the most or one of the most coupled classes. On the other hand, we developed a visualisation that clearly represents our metrics and highlights some aspects such as lack of definitions. We have illustrated and described our visualisation with the analysed ontologies to support the analysis process of coupling. The future work includes more proposal of metrics and new visualisations of these metrics, as well as the integration of this visualisation in a whole visualisation framework for ontoologies.

References

1. Chidamber, S., Kemerer, C.: A Metrics suite for object Oriented Design. IEEE Transactions on Software Engineering 20(6), 476–493 (1994)
2. Harrison, R., Counsell, S., Nithi, R.: Coupling Metrics for Object-Oriented Design. In: Proceedings of the 5th International Symposium on Software Metrics. IEEE Computer Society, Los Alamitos (1998)
3. Vrandecic, D., Sure, Y.: How to Design Better Ontology Metrics. In: Franconi, E., Kifer, M., May, W. (eds.) ESWC 2007. LNCS, vol. 4519, pp. 311–325. Springer, Heidelberg (2007)
4. Alani, H., Brewster, C., Shadbolt, N.: Ranking Ontologies with AKTiveRank. In: Cruz, I., Decker, S., Allemang, D., Preist, C., Schwabe, D., Mika, P., Uschold, M., Aroyo, L.M. (eds.) ISWC 2006. LNCS, vol. 4273, pp. 1–15. Springer, Heidelberg (2006)
5. Alani, H., Brewster, C.: Metrics for Ranking Ontologies. In: 4th Int. EON Workshop, 15th Int. World Wide Web Conference (2006)
6. Orme, A., Yao, H., Etzkorn, L.: Coupling Metrics for Ontology-Based Systems. IEEE Software, 102–108 (2006)
7. Yao, H., Orme, A., Etzkorn, L.: Cohesion Metrics for Ontology Design and Application. Journal of Computer Science 1(1), 107–113 (2005)
8. Y. Ma, B. Jin, Y. Feng, Semantic oriented ontology cohesion metrics for ontology-based systems. The Journal of Systems and Software (2009)
9. Guarino, N., Welty, C.: An Overview of OntoClean. In: The Handbook on Ontologies, pp. 151–172. Springer, Berlin (2004)

10. Guarino, N., Welty, C.: Evaluating Ontological Decisions with OntoClean. Communications of the ACM, 61–65 (2002)
11. Yang, Z., Zhang, D., Ye, C.: Evaluation Metrics for Ontology Complexity and Evolution Analysis. In: IEEE International Conference on e-Business Engineering (ICEBE 2006) (2006)
12. Tartir, S., Arpinar, B., Moore, M., Sheth, A., Aleman-meza, B.: OntoQA: Metric-based ontology quality analysis. In: CiteSeerX - Scientific Literature Digital Library and Search Engine (2005)
13. Tartir, S., Arpinar, B.: Ontology Evaluation and Ranking using OntoQA. In: Proceedings of the International Conference on Semantic Computing (2007)
14. Lozano-Tello, A., Gomez-Perez, A.: ONTOMETRIC: A Method to Choose the Appropiate Ontology. Journal of Database Management (2004)
15. Antoniou, G., van Harmelen, F.: A Semantic Web Primer, 2nd edn. The MIT Press, Cambridge (2008)
16. Aleman-meza, B., Halaschek, C., Sheth, A., Arpinar, B., Sannapareddy, G.: SWETO: Large-Scale Semantic Web Testbed. In: 16th International Conference on Software Engineering and Knowledge Engineering (2004)
17. Carlton, B., Farmer, G., Scrudder, R.: A C2IEDM Based Approach to C4I and Simulation Initialization and Synchronization. In: The Interservice/Industry Training, Simulation and Education Conference, I/ITSEC (2003)
18. Shneiderman, B.: Tree visualization with treemaps: a 2-d space-filling approach. ACM Transactions on Graphics 11(1), 92–99 (1992)
19. Rao, R., Card, S.: The Table Lens: Merging Graphical and Symbolic Representations in an Interactive Focus+Context Visualization for Tabular Information. In: Proceedings of the ACM SIGCHI Conference on Human Factors in Computing Systems, Boston, MA (1994)

Query Expansion for the Legal Domain: A Case Study from the JUMAS Project

Fabio Sartori and Matteo Palmonari

Department of Computer Science, Systems and Communication (DISCo)
University of Milan - Bicocca
viale Sarca, 336
20126 - Milan, Italy
Tel.: +39 02 64487913, Fax: +39 02 64487839
{sartori,palmonari}@disco.unimib.it

Abstract. This paper presents an ongoing research on the comparison of ontological query expansion methods. Query Expansion is a technique that aims to enhance the results of a search by adding terms to the search query; today, it is a very important research topic in the semantic web and information retrieval areas. Although many efforts have been made from the theoretical point of view to implement effective and general methods for expanding queries, based on both statistical and ontological approaches, the practical applicability of them is nowadays restricted to few and very specific domains. The aim of this paper is the definition of a platform for the implementation of a subset of such methods, in order to make comparisons among them and try to define how and when use ontological QE. This work is part of JUMAS, a research project funded by European Community where query expansion is used to support the retrieval of significant information from audio–video transcriptions in the legal domain.

Keywords: Ontological Query Expansion.

1 Introduction

The legal domain has been of interest to Artificial Intelligence (AI) for many years. A number of studies in AI and Law have been produced, which are based on ontological assumptions drawn from legal theory.

For instance, Allen and Saxon [1] have developed a language for legal relations representations in which they have translated the Hofheldian approach to law[1] into about forty relations. Mamfelt [2] proposed a framework where Hart's primary and secondary rules[2] were divided into meta–levels of logic programming. Valente and Breuker [3] have formalized legal knowledge in the ON–LINE system mainly taking into account concepts expressed by Kelsen and Hart.

---

[1] See e.g. http://www.yale.edu/lawweb/jbalkin/articles/hohfeldiansemiotics.pdf.
[2] See e.g. http://legaltheorylexicon.blogspot.com/2004/06/legal-theory-lexicon-039-primary-and.html.

M.-A. Sicilia, C. Kop, and F. Sartori (Eds.): ONTOSE 2010, LNBIP 62, pp. 107–122, 2010.

In literature, it is possible to identify many legal ontologies that have been used in practice, like LLD (*Language for Legal Discourse*) [4], *NORMA*, [5] [6], FOLaw (*Functional Ontology of Law*), FBO (*Frame-Based Ontology of Law*) [7] and LRI (*Core Legal Ontology*) [8]. Moreover, legal ontologies have been widely used in the recent past to support the the formalization of legal knowledge and create useful tools. For example, they have found application in many projects founded by the European Commission (EC), like CLIME [9], e–Power [10], e–COURT [11]. These projects are mainly devoted to disambiguate legal jargon except the CLIME one, in which also the legal problem solving strategy is partially implemented.

The purpose of this work is the description of a part of the JUMAS system, a research project funded by EC under the 7th Frame Programme[3], where ontologies are exploited to build a complete knowledge management system for legal operators (e.g. judges, prosecutors, witnesses).

A Query Expansion (QE) Platform based on a thesaurus of legal terms has been designed and implemented to allow operators to browse process transcriptions and audio–video data acquired from courtrooms. QE is a technique that aims to enhance the results of a search by adding terms to the search query. It is useful because it can deal with the inherent ambiguity of natural language, indeed every language has problems of synonymy (more terms for a concept) and polysemy (more concepts for a term) that cause a decay of performance: the search engine doesn't return relevant documents that are present in the domain (low recall) and returns documents that are not relevant (low precision). Query expansion aims to increase the number of relevant documents retrieved.

There are two main approaches to accomplish this task [12]: probabilistic query expansion and ontological query expansion. The first is based on statistic data that indicates the frequency of terms in a collection of supposed relevant documents, or the frequency of co-occurence of terms. The second is based on knowledge models, in particular ontologies, in which the method search for the terms that have to be added to the query.

Although probabilistic query expansion is the dominant approach, it has shown limits in different fields and tasks: Carpineto et al. [13] highlight how this approach weights the terms on the basis of their relevance within the text rather than the real benefits for the user; moreover, it has been pointed out [14][15] that probabilistic methods are very influenced by the corpus of documents and their relevance to the query.

On the contrary, ontological approaches are less developed and studied, but they virtually have a lot of undiscovered possibilities to semantically improve queries: being *corpus-independent*, they are more precise than probabilistic methods in the text disambiguation within a given domain. Moreover, they are particularly suitable to treat short queries. Anyway [16] [17], ontological methods have some important drawbacks: ontologies are typically difficult to create and maintain in order to guarantee the necessary level of precision to avoid the decrease of performance. The so called *query drift* (i.e. the choice of an expansion direction that is

---

[3] Grant agreement nr. FP7-214306.

out of user scope) phenomenon is more probable with ontological approaches than probabilistic ones.

Our work has been initially focused on the comparison of ontological query expansion methods in an analytic way. Then, we implemented a generic testing platform that allows to easily create, test and compare methods with different ontologies and on different domains.

The platform has been finally adopted in the context of the JUMAS project, where a thesaurus of legal terms has been used as the source ontology for query expansion. The results of QE in JUMAS are exploited from other modules of the system, in particular the audio and video summarization ones.

The paper is organized as follows: Section 2 briefly introduces the context and the aims of the JUMAS project; Section 3 concerns a brief review of literature about query expansion and ontological methods for making it as well as the design and implementation issues we took into account for developing a QE platform for JUMAS. An example of platform application to a thesaurus developed for the JUMAS project is briefly introduced in Section 5, where some preliminary considerations about the effectiveness of our platform are also presented. Finally, conclusions and future work are briefly pointed out in Section 6.

2   The JUMAS Project

Recent technological advances in multimedia production, storage and distribution have moved to digitize the traditional analogical archives creating large digital libraries. This will increase the need of tools for content analysis, information extraction and retrieval of multimedia objects in their native form in order to make easier both the access and the management of multimedia archives. In the last years huge advances have been done in the context of text document processing and several researchers have been working for finding more efficient algorithms for retrieval and information extraction from textual sources.

On the other hand starting from the 80s Audio&Video have been attracting the attention of an increasing number of researchers working on segmentation, clustering and topic identification in Multimedia Document. Using an automatic speech recognition system to transcribe captured speech would leverage its potential value as an information source by making it available for use in the same way as written documents. Capturing the information that people exchange in meetings, during telephone conversations, and in public settings like trial processes and council meetings, could provide access to knowledge whose preservation is of crucial importance.

The experience with applying several documents-based tasks to multimedia document indicates that there is potential for success in this endeavor. In particular, in order to apply traditional retrieval methods to spoken document, the current solution is to produce a manual verbatim transcription performing then the effective consultation process on the generated text. In contrast, the system proposed in this project provides an automatic fusion and integration of audio, video and text sources where high-quality automatic transcription is provided by continuous semantic feedback between the media and text analysis components.

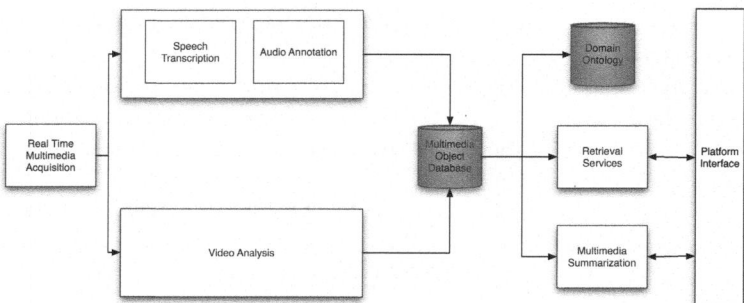

Fig. 1. The Architecture of the JUMAS System

JUMAS contribution (see Figure 1) is focused on supporting the workflow management and the semantic interpretation of recorded audio-video streams by developing new models and techniques for representing and automatically extracting the embedded semantics derived from multiple data sources. JUMAS will be used for collecting, sharing, annotating and retrieving information from multimedia data streams typical of video-recorded administrative and public debates.

The most important goal of the JUMAS system is to collect, enrich and share multimedia document annotated with embedded semantic minimizing manual transcription activity. These complex activities will be performed in order to assist the user with information extraction, text mining and retrieval tools to improve information production, exploitation and interpretation. Following these objectives the key functionalities of the proposed system are:

- Automatic Transcription: Today the bottleneck of the consultation process is the production of text associated to the stream audio/video, carried out by manual transcriptions. Automatic processes of information transcription are necessary and helpful for the end-users during the consultation phases.
- Semantic Annotation: The exploitation of knowledge is spread across information in different media. Using a fusion of information derived from audio transcription and video analysis can compensate eventually corrupted sources, define more fine grained annotation concepts, allow user-friendly browsing, etc. Video annotation (assigning semantic values to scene events) is based on the segmented objects and events, considering a given scene geometry and the possible rules of the legal process. Annotation is a high level process where visual information of the previous feature extraction steps are connected to the textual (from speech) and scene (geometry, position, motion) information. The annotation also needs a learning environment to register the situation of the detected objects.
- Retrieval Services: Currently the process of audio/video segments retrieval needs the manual consultation of the entire tracks on which it has been recorded part of a specific spoken document. Today the identification of a particular position on multimedia stream, with the aim to look at/to listen specific declarations, participations, testimonies, etc..., is possible only

remembering the temporal instant in which events happened. For this reason, the proposed system based on an automatic transcription and semantic annotation components, will allow the construction of a flexible retrieval environment not only based on simple textual queries, but on wide and complex concepts. In order to define an integrated platform for cross-modal access to audio, video recordings and their automatic transcript, models capable to perform semantic multimedia indexing and retrieval will be developed.

The subject of this paper is the description of the domain ontology part of the JUMAS architecture. As shown in Figure 1 this a module that works on the transcription produced by audio and video summarization to support the retrieval methods implemented to guide operators in finding useful information and knowledge used in the past.

3 Query Expansion: State of the Art and Our Approach

In the analysis of literature we first explored the various definition of query expansion[18][19][20][21] and we tried to merge them to obtain a possible common definition that contains the main characteristic of each vision. Indeed, there are several different definitions because the problem of query expansion has been approached by different ways and different points of view. However the goals and basic mechanisms of expansion are common: to improve the effectiveness of a search, that is finding more relevant documents and less irrelevant documents, by adding new terms to the original search query.

We can consider query expansion as a system that accepts in input a set of words Q returning a new set Q' as the union between Q the set of expanded words E:

$$Q \implies \boxed{\text{QEXP}} \implies Q' = Q \cup E$$

Words belonging to E are functions of a subset of Q, i.e. each element of E has been obtained starting from an element of Q.

$$E = \{ \, \omega_e \, : \, \omega_e \, \in f(\, W_e \subseteq Q \,), W_e \subseteq Q \, \}$$

More or less, all the existing approaches perform query expansion on the basis of one and only one word of Q:

$$E = \{ \, \omega_e \, : \, \omega_e \, \in g(\, \omega_i \in Q \,), w_i \in Q \, \}$$

The general model of QE can be further developed according to the following constraints:

- the Q and Q' set can be *ordered* or *not ordered*. In the first case, the order according to which the different words are arranged must also be considered;

- the Q' set can be a collection of pairs (w, p), where w is the word to expand and p is a *weight* related to it. This kind of output is useful when the result of query expansion must be returned to a research engine accepting weighted terms in input. The output would become a set Q'' as follows:

$$Q'' = \{ \ (\omega, p) \ : \ \omega \in Q', \ p \in \{0, 1\} \ \}$$

- the output can be the result of a rewriting of Q' according a given rule r. For example, if the research engine supports operators like $\wedge(AND)$ e $\vee(OR)$, we could obtain a rewriting similar to the following one:

$$(\ \omega_1 \ \vee \ \omega_{1,1} \ \vee \ \omega_{1,2} \ \vee \ ... \ ) \ \wedge \ (\ \omega_2 \ \vee \ \omega_{2,1} \ \vee \ \omega_{2,2} \ \vee \ ... \ ) \ \wedge \ ...$$

where $\omega_{i,e}$ are all the expanded terms of the word ω_i.

The first step in the design and implementation of a QE platform for the JUMAS project was a literature review to find the most suitable ones for our scope. As briefly introduced above, QE can be made exploiting both statistical and ontological methods.

Ontological methods are mainly based on the adoption of *thesauri* as the source ontology, like e.g. in the approach (i.e. *Voorhees* in the following) defined by Voorhees [14], where synonyms and any other kinds of term are added to the query linking them directly to the original term. The ONKI method [12] allows the user to select interactively by means of a thesaurus the concepts to search for. Then, it expands automatically the keywords exploiting the same thesaurus. The method is also interesting because it is *multi–ontology*: the *Finnish Collaborative Holistic Ontology (KOKO)* is used for expanding the concepts and the *Finnish Spatio-temporal Ontology (SAPO)* for expanding the places; Alani et al. [22][23] developed an approach (i.e *ATJ* in the following) which expands a query on every direction within the ontology, assigning different weights according to the nature of the followed relationship; Navigli&Velardi [16] defined two methods for QE: in the first one, ontologies are used to extract the concept descriptions. The similarity between two concepts is then evaluated on the basis of the similarity value between their descriptions. The second method is based on the creation of semantic nets of candidate concepts starting from a given ontology, to chose in a second step the terms according to how much such nets overlap. Finally, in [24] an approach to QE (i.e. *HO* in the following) is described that considers the sequences of links through which the terms are bounded to the query terms, taking especially care of terms whose links satisfy given patterns.

Moreover, there exist hybrid systems that exploit ontologies during one or more expansion phases: the method by Andreou [25] has a first step in which an expansion based on probabilistic methods is done, and a second one during which an ontology is used to accomplish a revision of terms, getting better results; the approach proposed by Xhu et al. [18] exploits the *Latent Semantic Indexing* technique, comparing *local* and *global* expansion methods. Here, ontologies allow weighting the terms; Calegari and Pasi [26] exploited a local fuzzy ontology to keep trace of past searches made by the user, with the aim to expand searches with the terms that are most frequently inserted in the same query.

Among these methods, it has been decided to implement three of them: **Voorhees, ATJ** and **HO**. In addition, the platform includes **Ancestor**, an approach that calculates the distance between the meanings of two concepts in terms of their distance from a common parent in a tree–like structure.

4   Towards a Platform for QE in JUMAS: Implementation

In the second step, we implemented a generic platform for testing query expansion, and also the previously selected methods. We first defined requirements and motivations for the platform, then we discussed all the implementation choices made during the process. One of the most important choice concerned the decision of which type of ontology to use: we decided to use a *thesaurus*, a restriction of ontologies expressly defined for lexical networks of terms. Next, we'll describe the architecture of the platform, that has been implemented in *Java*. In the implementation process we paid attention to fulfill the requirements and provide the platform with the necessary characteristics: *generality, expandability, modularity* and *uniformity*. The platform has been exploited to codify the four methods introduced above.

4.1   Type of Ontologies: Thesauri

Thesauri are structured vocabularies where relationships among terms are specified. They can be considered as a subclass of ontologies, since they represent only a part of the knowledge involved and their power of expression is limited [27]. Anyway, their main features are compatible with most of the ontological methods for QE available at the moment.

There exist two *ISO* standards for the definition of thesauri, the *ISO2788* for single–language thesauri and *ISO5968* for multi–language thesauri, which define the possible relationships among the terms of a thesaurus:

USE / UF (Use For) are two relationships for solving synonymy problems; the *USE* relationships specifies that the term considered is linked to another one that would be preferable (i.e. its synonym), while the *UF* relationship is the inverse of USE. These relationships generate networks are *synonyms clusters* which are be referred to as *synsets* within *WordNet*[4], probably the most known English thesaurus;

BT (Broader Term) is a relationship used for specifying more generic terms. Its inverse is the *NT (Narrower Term)*. relationship. BT and NT allows the definition of hierarchical structures among the terms and the synonym clusters;

RT (Related Term): is a relationship which describes a generic association between two terms. This association is neither USE / UF nor BT / NT.

Moreover, the two standards define the following property:

SN (Scope Note): is used to bind a term and its textual description, with the aim to make not ambiguous the usage of such term.

---

[4] http://wordnet.princeton.edu/

The relationships above are sufficient to create a network of terms which can be very useful in the QE process: for this reason, many approaches are based on WordNet. Moreover, thesauri are simpler to implement and maintain than ontologies and they have no significant drawbacks with respect to the QE approaches we have chosen to implement. For this reasons, it has been decided to design the platform for QE on the basis of thesauri, paying attention to an opportune strategy for adapting it to ontologies adoption in the future.

4.2   Definition of the Ontology Representation Language: SKOS

The initial idea to exploit *OWL (Ontology Web language* [5] for the ontology representation has been modified with the restriction to thesauri. For this reason, it has been chosen to withdraw to *SKOS* (Simple Knowledge Organization System)[6] a formal language that is going to become the standard de facto for thesauri representation.

As the OWL language, SKOS is based on *RDF*: this is very important from the adaptability of our platform to more general ontologies in the future. As *RDF*, *SKOS* is a language for the definition of graphs (in this case graphs of concepts) by means of 3–ples ⟨*subject, predicate, object*⟩. The *predicate* represents the relationship between the *subject* and the *object* .

The elements of the graph are the *concepts* expressed by the terms, which belong to a specific class named *skos:Concept*. The whole graph is described by the *skos:conceptScheme* class.

The kinds of relationships (i.e. the *predicates*) and properties fulfill very well the standards previously described; in fact:

- *skos:prefLabel* and *skos:altLabel* allow modeling the synonymy: every concept is described by a *prefLabel*, which is the preferred term to express that concept and a sequence of alternative terms named *altLabel*, which can be considered synonyms. In this way, an opportune *synset*is defined;
- *skos:broader* and *skos:narrower* represent the *BT (Broader Term)* and *NT (Narrower Term)* relationships;
- *skos:related* represents the *RT (Related Term)* relationship;
- *skos:scopeNote* is a representation of the Scope Note property.

Moreover, *SKOS* introduces other relationships and properties: for example, the*skos:definition* property is exploited to give a precise definition of a term.

4.3   Platform Architecture

Figure 2 shows a sketch of the platform architecture, which is divided into three main blocks responsible for the different functionalities:

- the **Query Expansion Testing Interface** implements generic functions to interact with the user;

---

[5] http://www.w3.org
[6] http://www.w3.org/2004/02/skos/

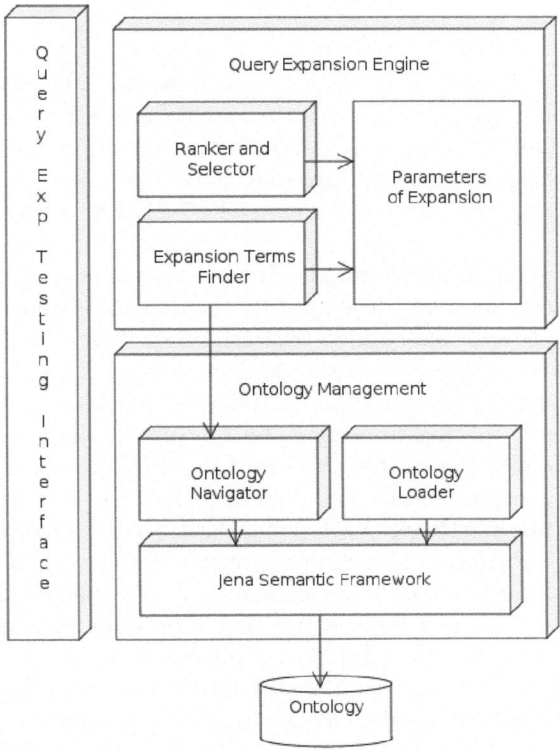

Fig. 2. The Architecture of the QE Platform

- the **Query Expansion Engine** implements the engine for the expansion, which is the specific query expansion method chosen among the four approaches introduced above. This component is made of an *Expansion Terms Finder* (ETF) that looks for the closest terms to the subject of QE and a *Ranker and Selector* that focuses on the following expansion phases, weighting the terms returned by ETF and adding the most significant ones to the QE output set;
- the **Ontology Management** allow managing the ontologies by means of Jena, a semantic framework that provides the system with many tools to treat ontologies and RDF language.

    Moreover, also an *Ontology Loader* and an *Ontology Navigator* are supplied: the first component allows the system to load ontologies from files or other sources, the second one allows searching within the ontology the terms to add to the candidate set by means of SPARQL queries.

The platform has been designed to be an effective and flexible tool to test the different methods, to modify their parameters and to combine sets of methods for deriving new approaches to QE.

5   A Case Study: Expanding Legal Terms in the JUMAS Context

In this section we present the results of the collaboration between the Research Centre on Complex Systems and Artificial Intelligence (CSAI) of the University of Milan-Bicocca and Project Automation in the context of the JUMAS project (Judicial Management by Digital Libraries Semantics), co-funded by the European Community (grant agreement number FP7-214306) within the 7th Frame Programme.

The aim of the collaboration was the development of a legal ontology for supporting the retrieval methods developed by the JUMAS Consortium to extract useful information from audio-video transcriptions of legal acts and processes. In this sense, it was decided to design and implement a software platform for the ontological query expansion (QE) of Italian and Polish legal terms, the target judicial systems taken into account by the project. The section illustrates different steps through which this platform has been developed.

The query expansion module (see Figure 3) is a web service, realized with the JAX-WS 2 (Java API for XML Web Services) technology, which is part of the Java EE 5 platform. The chosen semantic framework is Jena , an open source Java framework for building Semantic Web applications grown out of work with the HP Semantic Web. It provides a programmatic environment for OWL ontologies and includes a rule-based inference engine. Jena provides persistent storage of ontologies in relational databases, through RDBMS back–end adapters. It is possible at runtime to download the ontology, edit the ontology with and external tool (e.g. Protègè) and reload it on the repository. The query expansion engine is the main component of the query module. It is composed of two sub-modules: the Ontology Explorer and the Ranker. The aim of the Ontology Explorer is, starting from a given term, explore the ontology graph and search the terms the are related. The output of the Ontology Explorer is a graph, that is a sub-graph of the ontology. The size of the graph depends on the searched term, the max size of the sub-graph is configurable. The ranker takes as an argument the sub-graph and produces a weighted list of related terms.

In order to expand the query, it is necessary to find in the thesaurus terms that are related to the users query. Usually specific kinds of relations are tested ("synonyms", "hyponyms", "hypernyms", "meronyms", etc).

In order to allow the query module to expand the query with related terms, the Query Expansion Web Service is employed. This Web Service has one method (getRelatedWords) that accepts one word, searches the word in the ontology and returns a list of related weighted words. The words are weighted according to the "semantic distance" to the original word. The number of retrieved results depends on the specific word: the list will be longer in case of words related to many terms, it could be empty otherwise.

The implemented system is composed of several logic modules, as shown in Figure 4. The main module is the Ontology Manager. Its aim is to act as an ontology repository, allowing query and modification of the ontology. The Query Expansion Web Service invokes the ontology manager for retrieving the word

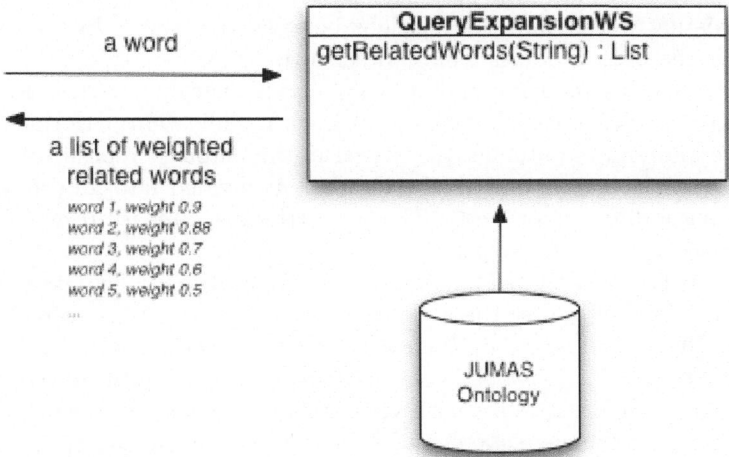

Fig. 3. An example of QE

to expand and calculate the similarity between the words. The web service can be invoked by external services and by the Query Expansion GUI. This GUI allows to the user to test the query expansion module before the integration with the other modules. Another GUI is implemented: the Ontology Management

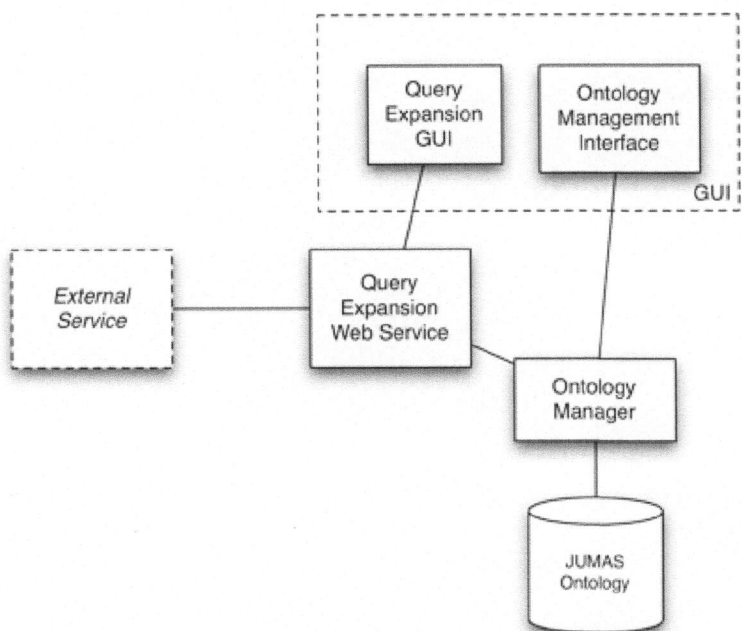

Fig. 4. Query Expansion Modules of the JUMAS system

Interface. It allows to navigate and edit the ontology, allowing create new word, deleting existing words, and the relations between the words. In the following paragraphs, the main modules will be described.

The query editing interface allows to modify the vocabulary, (see Figure 5), adding and removing terms and relations. Each modification performed by the user on the ontology is automatically saved in the ontology repository, used by the query expansion component. The interface is divided into four areas, each one regarding a different property. The properties are *Broader term, Narrower term, Related term* and *Synonym*.

In the figure the Italian word *cassaforte* (i.e. *strongbox* in English) is shown. The strongbox is a kind of box, so the word *contenitore* (i.e. *box*) it is a broad term of cassaforte. The related terms are *baule* (i.e. *trunk*), *cassa* (i.e. *till*), *combinazione* (i.e. *combination lock*), *grimaldello* (i.e. *lock picking*), and *serratura* (i.e. *lock*).

Synonyms are different words with very similar meanings. In the example the synonyms are *forziere* (i.e. *casket*) and *scrigno* (i.e. *treasure chest*).

To add a relation from the current term to another one, it is sufficient to write the term in one of the four text–fields and press the related button (e.g. to write a synonyms click the *Add synonym* button will be chosen). If the term is already in the ontology, a new relation between the two terms is added. In the term is not in it, it is automatically created. The interface displays the current relations. By clicking on the *delete* link near each relation, it is possible to remove the relation

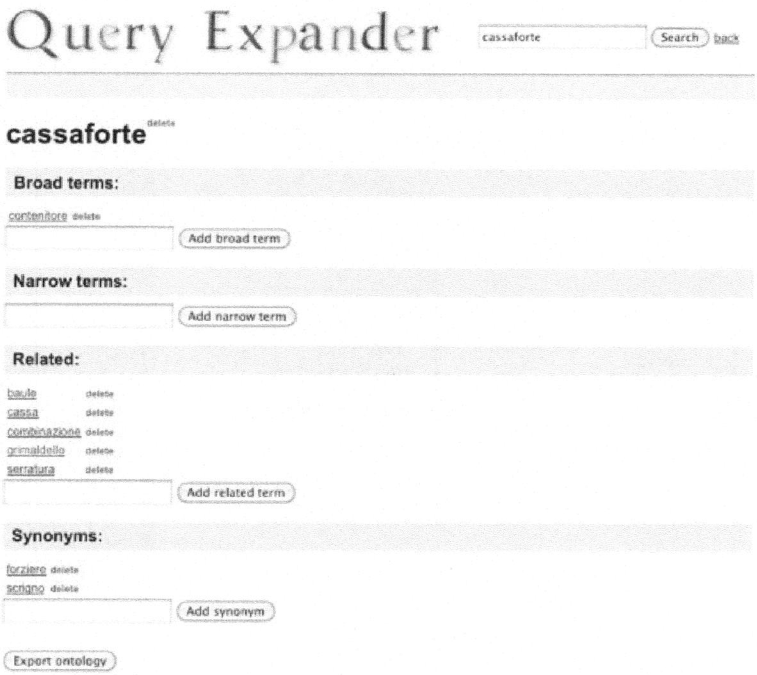

Fig. 5. A screenshot of the Ontology Management Interface

between the two words. When a word is removed from the ontology (by means of the *delete* link near the word name), all its relations are automatically deleted. Thanks to this interfaces the user can also export the ontology into an OWL file, clicking on the *Export Ontology* button.

An opportune GUI (see Figure 6) allows the user to test the query expansion module. It is very simple: when a user inserts a term, the page containing the expanded terms is generated. From the resulting page it is possible to navigate through the result clicking on the words. For each result it is presented the score (i.e. the level of similarity), the relation followed and the terms visited. For example, the similarity between *cassaforte* and *portagioielli* is 0.5; *cassaforte* is a synonymous of *scrigno* and *scrigno* is a synonymous of *portagioielli*. By clicking on the words, the user can finally access the editor interface. The similarity degree depends on the properties which are navigated. The weight of the properties can be changed through the configuration interface, accessible by clicking the *config* link. Through this interface it is possible to configure several parameters of the query expansion method, in particular:

Fig. 6. Query Expansion GUI

- the max distance of the retrieved words;
- the weight for the different properties;
- the weight of the single word/multi words;
- the threshold;
- the max length of the multi-word results.

6 Conclusions

Ontological query expansion is a field in which a lot of improvements are theoretically possible. In this work we tried to set up an environment for testing and discovering potentiality of expansion through ontologies: we created a platform that allows to easily implement and analytically compare different methods and we started tests and comparisons to evaluate the usefulness of methods and techniques. The obtained results demonstrated that the platform works and can be useful to the goals for which it has been implemented. Moreover the results showed the possible scenarios in which the four methods implemented could obtain the best performances. We concluded our work by considering possible future developments in both the extension of the platform, the concrete applications and the researches that could be started from the results obtained.

Future work consists in the further development of the platform: to this aim, the first step is the evolution of the analyzed thesaurus of the current version towards a real and complete ontology: the exploitation of more complex relationships and properties should theoretically bring us to better results in QE, but the current development of research in this field is not supported by adequate practical advances.

In this sense, the platform has been tested in the context of the JUMAS project (*Judicial Management by Digital Libraries Semantics*), co–funded by the European Community (grant agreement number FP7-214306) in the context of the 7th Frame Programme. The platform will be used in JUMAS to implement a query expansion interface for users in the legal domain (e.g. judges, witnesses and so on) in order to help them to find significant audio–video transcriptions.

References

1. Allen, L.E., Saxon, C.S.: Achieving fluency in modernized and formalized hohfeld: Puzzles and games for the legal relations language. In: ICAIL, pp. 19–28 (1997)
2. Hamfelt, A.: Formalizing multiple interpretation of legal knowledge. Artif. Intell. Law 3(4), 221–265 (1995)
3. Valente, A., Breuker, J.: On-line: An architecture for modelling legal information. In: ICAIL, pp. 307–315 (1995)
4. McCarty, L.T.: A language for legal discourse i: Basic features. In: ICAIL, pp. 180–189 (1989)
5. Stamper, R.K.: The role of semantics in legal expert systems and legal reasoning. Ratio Juris 4(2), 219–244 (1991)

6. Breuker, J., Winkels, R.: Taking ontological commitments seriously: Folaw, a functional core ontology of legal knowledge. In: Hérin, D., Zighed, D.A. (eds.) EGC. Extraction des Connaissances et Apprentissage, vol. 1, pp. 9–25. Hermes Science Publications (2002)

7. Kralingen, R.W.V.: Frame-Based Conceptual Models of Statute Law. Kluwer Law Intl., Dordrecht (1995)

8. Breuker, J., Hoekstra, R.: Epistemology and ontology in core ontologies: Folaw and lri-core, two core ontologies for law. In: Proceedings of the EKAW 2004 Workshop on Core Ontologies in Ontology Engineering, Northamptonshire, UK, pp. 15–27 (2004)

9. Winkels, R., Boer, E., Hoekstra, R.: Clime: lessons learned in legal information serving. In: Proceedings of the European Conference on Artificial Intelligence (ECAI 2002) (2002)

10. van Engers, T.M., Vanlerberghe, R.A.W.: The power-light version: Improving legal quality under time pressure. In: Traunmüller, R., Lenk, K. (eds.) EGOV 2002. LNCS, vol. 2456, pp. 75–83. Springer, Heidelberg (2002)

11. Breuker, J.: The construction and use of ontologies of criminal law in the ecourt european project. In: Golaczynski, V. (ed.) Proceedings of Means of Electronic Communication in Court Administration (2003)

12. Tuominen, J., Kauppinen, T., Viljanen, K., Hyvnen, E.: Ontology-based query expansion widget for information retrieval. In: Proceedings of the 5th Workshop on Scripting and Development for the Semantic Web (SFSW 2009), 6th European Semantic Web Conference (ESWC 2009) (May 31-June 4, 2009)

13. Carpineto, C., de Mori, R., Romano, G., Bigi, B.: An information-theoretic approach to automatic query expansion. ACM Trans. Inf. Syst. 19(1), 1–27 (2001)

14. Voorhees, E.M.: Query expansion using lexical-semantic relations. In: SIGIR 1994: Proceedings of the 17th Annual International ACM SIGIR Conference on Research and Development in Information Retrieval, pp. 61–69. Springer, New York (1994)

15. Ruthven, I., Tombros, A., Jose, J.M.: A study on the use of summaries and summary-based query expansion for a question-answering task (2001)

16. Navigli, R., Velardi, P.: An analysis of ontology-based query expansion strategies. In: Proc. of Workshop on Adaptive Text Extraction and Mining (ATEM 2003), in the 14th European Conference on Machine Learning (ECML 2003), pp. 42–49 (2003)

17. Durão, F.A., Vanderlei, T.A., Almeida, E.S., de Meira, L.S.R.: Applying a semantic layer in a source code search tool. In: SAC 2008, pp. 1151–1157. ACM, New York (2008)

18. Xu, X., Zhu, W., Zhang, X., Hu, X., Yeol Song, I.: A comparison of local analysis, global analysis and ontology-based query expansion strategies for bio-medical literature search (2006)

19. Bhogal, J., Macfarlane, A., Smith, P.: A review of ontology based query expansion. Inf. Process. Manage. 43(4), 866–886 (2007)

20. Delort, J.Y.: A user-centered approach for evaluating query expansion methods. In: WI 2005: Proceedings of the 2005 IEEE/WIC/ACM International Conference on Web Intelligence, Washington, DC, USA, pp. 586–589. IEEE Computer Society, Los Alamitos (2005)

21. Manning, C.D., Raghavan, P., Schütze, H.: Introduction to Information Retrieval. Cambridge University Press, Cambridge (July 2008)

22. Tudhope, D., Alani, H., Jones, C.: Augmenting thesaurus relationships: Possibilities for retrieval. Journal of Digital Information 1, 15 (2001)

122   F. Sartori and M. Palmonari

23. Alani, H., Jones, C., Tudhope, D.: Associative and spatial relationships in
thesaurus-based retrieval. In: Borbinha, J.L., Baker, T. (eds.) ECDL 2000. LNCS,
vol. 1923, pp. 45–58. Springer, Heidelberg (2000)
24. Hirst, G., St-Onge, D.: Lexical chains as representations of context for the detection
and correction of malapropisms (1997)
25. Andreou, A.: Ontologies and query expansion. Master's thesis, School of Informatics, University of Edinburgh (2005)
26. Calegari, S., Pasi, G.: Personalized ontology-based query expansion. In:
IEEE/WIC/ACM International Conference on Web Intelligence and Intelligent
Agent Technology, vol. 3, pp. 256–259 (2008)
27. Wielinga, B.J., Schreiber, A.T., Wielemaker, J., Sandberg, J.A.C.: From thesaurus
to ontology. In: K-CAP 2001: Proceedings of the 1st International Conference on
Knowledge Capture, pp. 194–201. ACM, New York (2001)

A Mereology-Based Ontology for Services Science: Example of an e-health Service Modelling

Florie Bugeaud[1,2] and Eddie Soulier[1]

[1] University of Technology of Troyes – ICD/Tech-CICO FRE CNRS 2848,
12 rue Marie Curie – BP2060, 10010 Troyes Cedex, France
{florie.bugeaud,eddie.soulier}@utt.fr
[2] Orange Labs – RD/BIZZ/BUC/RTS,
38-40 rue du General Leclerc, 92794 Issy-Les-Moulineaux, France
florie.bugeaud@orange-ftgroup.com

Abstract. This paper presents an ontological approach to formalize the concept of service upstream of the innovative process of telecommunication operators. These operators try to propose innovative solutions to meet their customers' expectations and to ensure their market position. We pursue the discussion of the SSME community and propose to conceive the service as a dynamic phenomenon: the "Service System". Traditional ontologies seem inadequate to represent it, so we introduce a new primitive (dynamic entities) based on the Mereology and the General Process Theory. A semi-formal method has been created through the import of key documents, the extraction of candidate-terms, the generation of an actions network (Galois lattice) and the construction of a mereological ontology. This method and its supporting tool OntoStoria[2] are currently tested within the process of opportunities research of a French telecom operator in order to promote the collaboration, sharing of knowledge and creativity of its innovators network.

Keywords: Services Science, Ontology, Mereology, Service System, Innovation.

1 Introduction: Innovation and Services Systems

The telecommunication operators have to identify and develop more and more innovative solutions. They try to meet a highly competitive context and the deep change of their customers' role and expectations [1]. But the evolution of ICT (Information and Communication Technologies) has led to important economic and social changes. It has significantly transformed the way of designing and delivering services. Moreover, these operators find in their value networks the skills and resources that are sometimes lacking in-house. But these networks also change their borders. Our work is interested in the upstream stage of the services innovation cycle of such an operator. Generally, telecom operators implement a design process which includes a step of opportunities research. During this step, their communities of innovators (i.e. innovation actors) have to interact in order to describe the service situation of the targeted customer / segment and then try to imagine some ideas of new IT or telecom services that fit the target lacks or expectations. In order to describe, evaluate and mature a

M.-A. Sicilia, C. Kop, and F. Sartori (Eds.): ONTOSE 2010, LNBIP 62, pp. 123–134, 2010.
© Springer-Verlag Berlin Heidelberg 2010

situation, they implement a design reasoning related to a complex and collaborative practice in which they share and co-create knowledge [1][3]. But the implementation of this reasoning remains difficult because of the distributed and inter-professional (marketing, usage, ergonomics, and engineering) nature of their network, the lack of a structured approach and the inadequacy of the supporting tools. However the core problems are linked to the complexity of the concept of "service" that remains poorly understood and the the lack of interest for the notion of experience. The innovators meet some difficulties to imagine and represent the phenomenon of the service experience. And the customers meet some difficulties to determine the offered experience. One objective of our work is to address these difficulties by providing an integrated framework and a shared representation. This framework support their communication, collaboration and creativity upstream of the design cycle. The knowledge engineering provides some interesting elements. It facilitates the extraction, the annotation and the structuring of knowledge.

This article focuses on the conceptual representation of a service based on the information and knowledge which are available upstream of the innovation cycle. This requires a description of the concept of service at a business and more abstract level than the one we usually find in the literature (i.e. reusable technical functionality). We worked on the service theories and classifications (socio-economic, organizational, marketing and technology approaches that are rarely integrated) [2][3] and on the discussions of SSME (Services Science Management and Engineering, a multidisciplinary approach, initiated by IBM and several universities). Based on their proposal, we conceive the service as a "Service System" [4][5]. The Service System is an artefact, the object of a co-production between a client and a supplier. But it is also a dynamic configuration linked to the combination of heterogeneous entities. These entities form "a service" at a given moment and in a given situation. In other words, it is a dynamic and performative phenomenon related to a customer's help request to a supplier to transform a reality or a property. Then the question is: how to represent these kinds of informational collections of processes or procedural entities [6] which express a particular phenomenon (i.e. an experience)?

An important point of our work is related to the criticism of the substantiality principle which is the basis of all traditional ontologies. These ontologies use static and located entities and they consider the dynamics of these entities only as properties or secondary categories. We therefore propose a formal model, a construction method and a tool to explain and implement the information and knowledge surrounding the Service System that the innovators are studying. Indeed, we do not try to articulate the innovators' points of view. We propose them a more high level view of the overall service situation they have to study. It allows them to identify some tracks of new services by the modelling and simulation of dynamic situations.

This paper is organized as follows. Section 2 presents the arguments in favour of a new generation of ontology and the emergence of the proposed knowledge model to represent Services Systems. Section 3 describes OntoStoria[2]: a design and construction method of mereological ontologies, and its web-based tool. Section 4 gives the results of our first experiment within the e-health domain (i.e. modelling of the remote monitoring of diabetics patients). Section 5 concludes and points some perspectives.

2 Modelling of Dynamic Phenomena

2.1 Inadequacy of the Substance Epistemology

The service is often considered as a hierarchy of core services and peripheral services. The ontological representation of a Service System can be considered in order to help the telecom innovators to better conceptualize a customer's service situation as a dynamic phenomenon or a configuration of heterogeneous entities in a specific space-time. However, the traditional ontologies seem inadequate regarding the nature of the Service System. Ontology is the study of categories of things that exist or may exist in some domain [7]. Domain ontologies are based on an epistemology of the substance which expresses the being / thing / object in a nominal and static way. Even if some existing ontologies use events or processes as first class entities, domain ontologies describe the systems they study through the concept of object, the admission of the identity and object permanence principles, the possible consolidation into abstract classes and the instantiation as a redefinition of the object by the properties of the class. A process is only considered as *"the particular performance of a human activity, such as a particular running or reading, or, the particular occurrence of a 'subjectless', 'absolute', or 'pure process' : a snowing or thundering in a particular spatiotemporal region"* [8][9]. This substantial principle does not fit the dynamic and experiential nature of the Service System (collection of processes / dynamic entities). Moreover, the documents, that are used by telecom innovators to describe the services situations and interactions they address, are structured in a verbal form.

The representation of the "acting" service or the experience is therefore linked to the computation of the dimensions that impact its conceptualization as a process or a combination of parts in a given moment. Its elements can be considered as episodes or service tracks. We make the hypothesis that the reality is a continuous flow where "things" are processes. Their mode of existence is their activity mode and not their supposed universal substance. So we consider an ontological alternative based on dynamic categories rather than on abstract classes and static concepts. The role of ontologies in Information Systems seems to become central [10]. Domain ontologies provide some strategic improvements in terms of knowledge management (information research, knowledge sharing, etc.) [11]. However, in order to adopt a dynamic view answering the question of the service experience representation, we have studied the field of processes ontologies and mereological principles. Indeed we make a new hypothesis: the mereological "part-whole" relations allow getting the dynamic and systemic dimensions of a Service System when some innovation actors try to describe and understand it to imagine and propose some innovative solutions that will be adapted to precise spatio-temporal experiences.

2.2 Emergence of Process Ontologies

A new generation of ontologies seems to emerge: the processes ontology [6]. The conceptualization of dynamic categories is becoming possible thanks to a process-oriented metaphysics. It can be realized in a conventional way through aspectualities or in a less traditional way through an alternative theory to the paradigm of the substance [8]. According to our previous hypothesis, it is necessary to identify dynamic entities based on the mode of their activity and the kind of associated control (nature of the participants in the process / activity) rather than on objects (their properties, identity, information structure, etc.). It does not disprove the need for a knowledge theory of the area. But this knowledge will be expressed as dynamic categories rather than static categories. This implies to reverse the usually adopted perspective: from static entities to "development" / "progress" whose spatio-temporal structure and arrangement are complex. We use the basic principles of the Mereology and the General Process Theory to consider the modelling of dynamic categories and their associated situations. Indeed, a scientific track is to consider the "part_of" relationship rather than the traditional "is_a" relationship.

2.3   Contribution of the Mereology

The Mereology comes from philosophy. It is based on the formal ontological study of the "part-whole" relationship [13]. The semantic relation "part_of" (called "meronymy") represents a hierarchical and partitive relationship (e.g. the roof of a house). The main principles of the Mereology are the transitivity, non-reflexivity and anti-symmetry. The main kinds of meronymic relations can be established by the combination of three basic properties:

- Configuration: the parts support, or not, a structural or functional relationship with another individual or with the whole,
- Homeomery: the parts are, or are not, the same as the whole (same nature, same properties, etc.),
- Separability: the parts can, or can not, be separated from the whole (without denaturing the whole's identity).

Winston, Chaffin and Herrmann have identified, in 1987, six kinds of relationships (some of them are challenged by other authors): component-object, member-collection, portion-mass, material-object, phase-activity, area-zone [14]. Here we can note that some of them are more suited than others for the modelling of Services Systems: phase-activity ("script") and element-object (a service is an artefact and it is the object of a co-production). Some predicates have also been defined to describe these meronymic relationships: proper part, direct part, overlap, underlap, etc. Moreover, these relationships give rise to operations between entities such as sum, product or extension that can affect the parts of a whole.

2.4   Contribution of the General Process Theory

J. Seibt investigates for an ontological theory of emergence (i.e. conceptual claim based on empirical phenomena) [8]. She proposes a mereological extension which is non-standard and non-transitive. It is called the "General Process Theory" (GPT). This ontological framework for processes uses a new ontological category which is dynamic, concrete, non-particular (i.e. located in multiple and uncountable ways) and non-universal: the "general process". When processes interact or "interfere", they modify the representation of the complex process they form. In general, every verbal predication can be conceived as an activity in a general process, and may play different inferential roles depending on the context. GPT is based on:

- The mereological signature: homeomery and anhomeomery,
- A non-transitive "part-whole" relationship and some levels of partition (corresponding to the levels in the hierarchical tree and useful to identify and refer to entities / processes according to their position in a given partition)
- The principles of interference, mereological sum and product, spatio-temporal location.

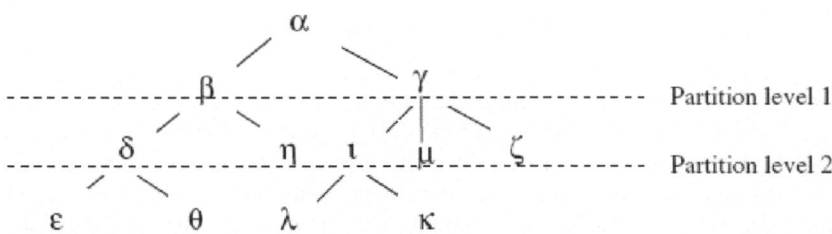

Fig. 1. Schematic representation of a mereological ontology in GPT [8]

The GPT non-transitivity principle changes the way of connecting some parts into a whole. A consequence is that the GPT reduces the number of possible relationships to the non-overlap and overlap. Another consequence is related to the operations of sum and product that can only be extended to the first partition level. Then any arbitrary amount of general processes can be created and any amount of general processes is itself a general process. Moreover, the "part_of" relationship does not necessarily involve a spatial or temporal inclusion. Processes can be arbitrarily dispersed in space and time. The GPT uses the definition of mereological properties, the analysis of mode of occurrence, the pattern classification of homeomery and the analysis of dynamic parameters in order to characterize each entity (see 3.1). It can thus answers the need of identifying the dynamic entities, their mode of activity, the nature of participants and the interactions between entities (causal, temporal, etc.). These framework helps us to capture the systemic and the dynamic dimensions of a targeted Service System (thanks to the definition and the representation of the "part-whole" relations and the interference/interactions between the processual entities of this Service System), then to imagine the possible scenarios / configurations and the service experiences to finally imagine adapted solutions.

3 OntoStoria[2]: Method and Tool

3.1 Methodology to Define and Build a Service System Mereological Ontology

We use the capabilities that are offered by the Mereology and the GPT to provide an adapted description of the Service System concept. The proposed method is based on a semi-formal semantic description of dynamic categories (see figure 2) (note that an ongoing work is related to the study of existing methodology for ontology engineering in order to improve and implement our proposition):

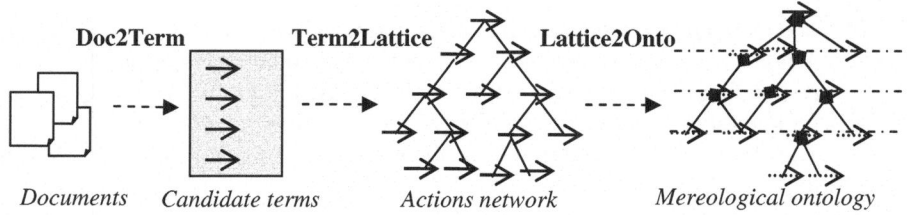

Fig. 2. The OntoStoria² method

The first step (*Doc2Term*) concerns the extraction of key terms from the documents which are available upstream of the design cycle of telecom operators (see 3.2 for the mechanisms). The constitution of a corpus of documents about the studied Service System is an important step. These documents contain stabilized knowledge coming from previous studies, information of the market, specific documentation of the studied domain (e.g. e-heath), etc. The extraction of key terms helps formalizing the elements that were previously informal. Moreover, the innovators, who participate in the co-construction of the Service System representation, can modify the resulting key terms structure (i.e. delete some terms or adding their own knowledge). The following steps are completely transparent for the user (until the display of the result).

The second step (*Term2Lattice*) is linked to the hypothesis that we all are accustomed to the paradigm of the substance (see 2.1). Therefore, we need to move from the conceptual space to a dynamic space [7][8]. Saillot, Poitrenaud and others authors consider that when we think about an object, we must grasp not only the semantic dimension but also the pragmatic dimension [19]. There is a direct relationship between objects and activities. This can be used to go beyond the mental habituation we introduced. It provides a direct access to the processes world and therefore to the pragmatic. The Galois lattices are helpful to represent hierarchical networks of categories (i.e. semantic networks of actions). They use this basic combination between actions (procedural knowledge) and objects (declarative knowledge). For us, the benefit of such a network is to structure the key terms from *Doc2Term*, and then to consider a processual perspective. The Galois lattice generation is based on the following rules:

- The triplet (O, A, I): a set of objects O, a set of attributes A (i.e. actions which are applicable to the objects) and the binary relations I between O and A (Rule 1: $I \subseteq OxA$).
- Two "Galois connections": An intension of Oz (Rule 2.1: $f(Oz)=An$, i.e. all the subsets of A with which the objects of Oz have a common binary relation) and Oj extension of As (Rule 2.2: $f(As)=Oj$, i.e. all the subsets of O with which the actions of As have a common binary relationship).
- The reciprocity of the Galois connections: Oi is the extension of Ai and Ai is the intention of Oi (Rule 3: $g(Ai)=Oi$ and $f(Oi)=Ai$). Then (Oi, Ai) is a "concept".
- The order relation: the set of concepts is ordered thanks to the inferiority (denoted $\leq$) and the inclusion (denoted $\subseteq$) relations (Rule 4: $(Oi,Ai) \leq (On,An)$ if $Oi \subseteq An$ or $Ai \subseteq An$).

We have created four algorithms based on these rules in order to transform the entities extracted from the upstream documents into an actions network (see 3.2).

The resulting actions network helps us to identify "candidate processes". Then, the next step (*Lattice2Onto*) determines the ontological links between thse entities (i.e. the candidate processes) and builds a complete representation. Here we use some mereological conditions and criteria which have been proposed by the General Process Theory [8]. The process typology is based on the:

- Classical criteria: dynamicity, unboundedness, distributivity, homeomerity,
- Mode of occurrence criteria: completeness, resumability, recurrence,
- Mereological criteria: homomerity and automerity pattern (according to spatial and temporal occurrence),
- GPT Classification criteria:

    • Participant structure (according to number and type of causal agents and patients),
    • Dynamic constitution (according to process architecture, e.g. sequences, forks, joints, cycles, etc.),
    • Dynamic shape (according to their trajectories, verbal aspects),
    • Dynamic context (according to its influence on the generative environment of the process).

Thanks to these criteria, we obtain several kinds of entities' profiles: activity, event, thing, substance and quality. In the case of Services Systems, the activity and event profiles seem relevant. We then look at the relationships between these entities, the number of partition levels (i.e. levels in the tree) and the kinds of involved dynamics. Three main characteristics have to be taken into account:

- Profile of each entity,
- Homeomy ("like-partedness") and automery ("self-partedness") degrees,
- Type of relationship: non-overlap or overlap,
- Type of operations: sum, product, cause.

The discovery of part-whole relationships leads to build a mereological ontology. This framework allows the emergence of various types of dynamics (sequential, co-occurring, causal) when it is applied to a particular field. The final ontology is thus very useful to represent the possible dynamic configurations of a Service System.

3.2 Proposition of a Web-Based Design Studio

We are implementing a Services Systems Design Studio based on the previous method. It is a web-based tool associated with a database server (see figure 3), a design space (to create or open project), a toolbox and a collaborative space. It can be used in an asynchronous way (through the remote and inter-professional network of innovators) or in a direct access (an innovator or a group of innovators during a brainstorming). It uses the traditional mechanisms of social networks for the asynchronous access: profiles, tags, etc. In both cases, the first step is related to the initialization of the theme / topic by an innovator or a group of innovators that either received a specific request for a specific service situation (e.g. a demand coming from the direction), or think that a study of this service situation may lead to the discovery of new telecom services. Various mechanisms are then implemented (see below).

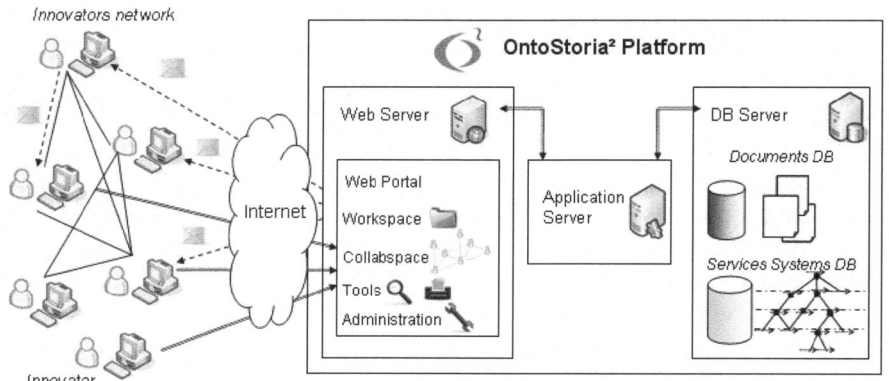

Fig. 3. Global architecture of the web-based studio OntoStoria²

The Natural Language Processing (NLP) and Text Mining propose some mechanisms to create indexes or build ontologies from texts. The extraction of key terms from marketing or R&D documents requires the definition of an analysis framework and some rules for the procedure of terms research and extraction [15]. Here, the "candidate terms" are the key objects and actions of the studied Service System. The main steps of *Doc2Term* (see figure 2) are:

- Locating and cutting phrases / terms [16],
- Identifying relationships / correspondences between them,
- Identifying and eliminating redundancies and synonyms,
- Extracting and displaying terms in a list-like structure.

This list is then provided to the innovators (considered as human analysts [15]) who participate in the Service System study. They may remove a term they consider improper, add a missing term and validate the selection of "candidate terms". Based on the triplets objects/actions/relationships, the four algorithms (related to the Galois Lattice rules, page 6) create a hierarchical representation (*Term2Lattice*):

- Rule 1: determining the possible sets of actions and sets of objects,
- Rules 2.1 and 2.2: researching the objects / actions pairs,
- Rule 3: identifying the objects / actions pairs which are concepts,
- Rule 4: classifying the concepts thanks to the actions order relation (because we are here interested in the actions: $(Oi, Ai) \leq (On, An)$ if $Ai \subseteq An$).

The actions network is then generated. Its conversion into a mereological ontology (*Lattice2Onto*) requires two main steps:

- Describing the entities profiles (activity or event) (see 3.1 for the typology),
- Identifying the part-whole relationships between processes (sum, product, etc.) and characterize their nature.

The resulting list of entities profiles and interferences as well as the focus of interference (i.e. the macro-process / phenomenon / main dynamic we want to study) allow us to fit all processes and determine the number of partition levels in the graph. We obtain a complete description of everything that can intervene in the procedural universe of the studied Service System.

4 Experiment on e-health Service System

We applied the proposed method and calculations to an e-health Service System: the remote monitoring of diabetics patients. It is supported by a telecom solution (PDA + Internet) and has been the object of several experiments a few years ago [17]. But we have discovered that, during these experiments, the telecom innovators that have worked on the diabetics monitoring description (in order to imagine some technical solutions to support it) met some coordination difficulties and did not converge towards a consensual representation. It is thus a good example and we have decided to position ourselves "as innovators" during an opportunities research process and to test our proposition (a more complete evaluation with a "real" group of innovators is currently under preparation). We used different kinds of documents as input: sales brochures, press articles and conferences presentations. The key objects and actions of the remote monitoring of diabetics have been extracted from this corpus. As the result was sizeable, we only treated a sample in this first experiment:

-    Objects: medical advice, consultation, evolution prevention, constraints, events, emotions, weekly remote monitoring, blood sugar level balance, consulting at the doctor's office, self-monitoring rhythm,
-    Actions: sending the data, advocating a change in treatment, recognizing a feeling of faintness, receiving a medical advice, adding some information, using lancing, visualizing the results, calculating the blood glucose rate, planning the meals for the week, making an injection.

The four "Galois-lattice-based" algorithms have been applied to the sample triplets.

To avoid overloading this paper, the figure 4 proposes a reduced view of the resulting actions network. We have removed the objects and actions redundancy in each node in order to highlight their specificity. The inheritance and inclusion mechanisms can help to rebuild their extensions and intensions.

According to Saillot *et al.*, the cognitive complexity is the measure of quantitative parameters in the graph [18]. If we analyze the figure 4, we find 8 categories (nodes), 8 relations (arcs), 4 levels of abstraction (maximum number of class on a line), 2 categories that have only one immediate neighbour, and 6 categories that have more than one immediate neighbour. Moreover, the "superordinate category" (i.e. whose source is remote and which has an important extension / number of objects) is the node at the top (its main action is "advocate a change in treatment"). It corresponds to the main representation of remote monitoring of diabetics in people's mind. The "subordinate categories" (i.e. whose sources are close and which have an important intension / number of actions) are the two nodes at the bottom (their main actions are: "use a lancing device" and "recognize a feeling of faintness"). They are probably a later representation of the disease monitoring in people's mind.

Then, we have applied the mereological ontology construction steps to our case. The profile of each process of the sample has been identified thanks to the process typology and the part-whole relations have been detected. For example:

-    "visualizing the results" meets the criteria of the activity profile,
-    "adding some information" meets the criteria of the activity profile,
-    "sending the data" meets the criteria of the event profile,

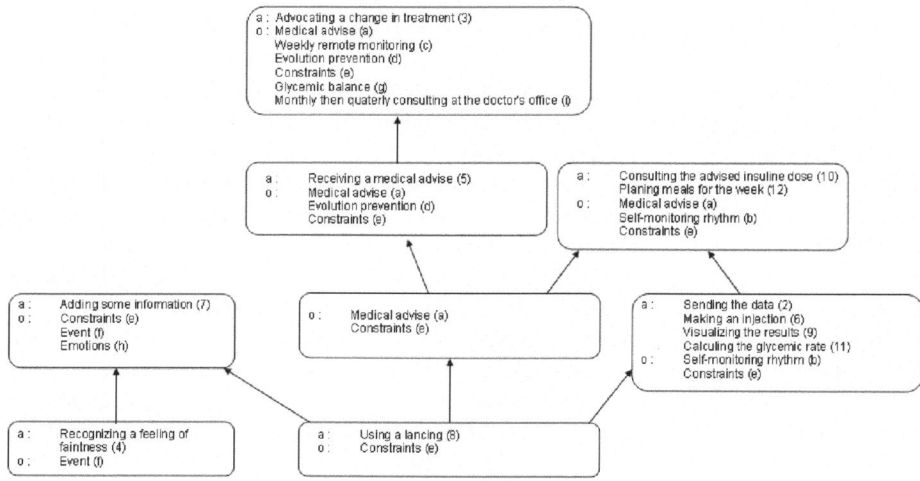

Fig. 4. Actions network on the sample

- the interference between "visualizing the results" and "sending the data" is a part-whole relationship,
- the interference between "adding some information" and "sending the data" is a part-whole relationship, etc.

Once all processes and interferences have been qualified, their dependencies help us to generate the ontological model (see figure 5 on the original sample).

In this first model, the interference focus corresponds to the process of "Diabetes remote-monitoring" and there are three levels in the partition. A more complete view is under construction. It will take into account and show the other interactions between entities (e.g. functional, causal, etc.) at the same partition level. This is a key

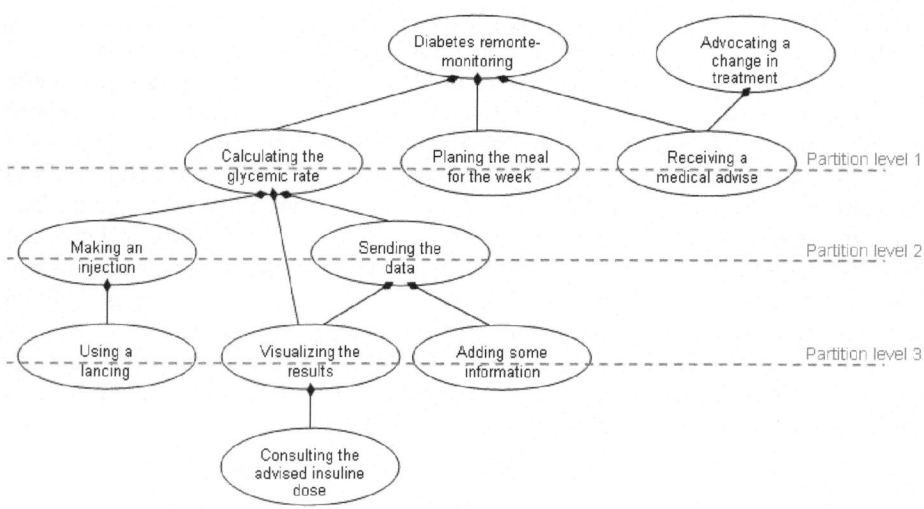

Fig. 5. Mereological ontology on the sample

point that will help us to consolidate the discovery of the possible scenarios / configurations and therefore experiences in a specific service situation. Indeed, it will help the innovators, during the opportunities research step, to not only better conceptualize and understand the addressed service situation as a dynamic configuration of heterogeneous entities in a specific spatio-temporal region, but also to identify new ideas of telecom or IT services to answer the situation's lacks or customer's expectations (e.g. a classical voice server for the monitoring of older diabetics patients who are familiar with the PDA and web technologies).

5 Discussion

This paper is concerned with "what does" or "how interacts" what we talk about and the mereological relationships between the associated processes. We adopt a critical position against the paradigm of the substance and we pursue the discussions about processes ontologies. We propose the construction of mereological ontologies by categorizing each entity and each interference between these entities. Their part-whole relationships and their dynamics animate this procedural universe through all the possible scenarios. It therefore aims at supporting the telecoms innovators' collaboration and creativity through a shared representation of the services situations.

One of the main perspectives of our work concerns the complete experimentation of the method and algorithms on the remote monitoring of diabetic patients (this paper presents a sample) and on other Services Systems in order to verify the suitability of the GPT and OntoStoria[2] framework as well as the rest of the platform. Ongoing works are related to the comparison of existing initiatives in the field of events or processes ontologies (even if they are based on the paradigm of the substance) with our proposition and on the existing methodologies for ontology engineering. Another perspective is related to the representation of the mereological ontologies. There are still very few mereological representations. Some works about the mereotopology [19][20] propose a representation based on a logical description of the SEP triplets. These triplets are typically used to emulate the property of transitivity in the general theory. The GPT proposes a "part-whole tree" which is organized according to different levels of partition [8]. Our work is closer to the GPT proposal which does not use the property of transitivity in the decomposition of a whole into parts and does use the concept of interference as a key point. Therefore, the representation as a "part-whole tree" seems more appropriate. But in the context of telecom innovation, this kind of model can be hardly understood by some professions. It now seems necessary to consider the creation of more suited views for both innovators and customers (in both cases, we can imagine a kind of structure of dynamic trajectories in the mental space, one being related to the design of an offer and the other to an experience).

To conclude, this work is included in a more global approach. This approach describes and simulates Services Systems upstream of the innovation cycle of telecom operators. The proposed steps, in this paper, are part of a unique phase of cognitive representation of Services Systems. Other phases complete it: behavioral representation, computation of the service experience, simulation / animation, validation and detection of ideas of new services (that can be transferred towards the design and development phases of the innovation cycle). This approach and its main mechanisms have been or will be the object of other publications.

References

1. Bugeaud, F., Soulier, E.: Raisonnement de conception de services à l'aide d'un réseau social. In: 20èmes Journées Francophones D'Ingénierie des Connaissances (IC 2009), Hammamet, Tunisie (2009)
2. Tannery, F.: Le management stratégique des services: synthèse bibliographique et repérage des questions génériques. Finance Contrôle Stratégie 4(2), 215–259 (2001)
3. Bugeaud, F., Soulier, E.: Services Systems to Leverage Innovators' Knowledge: the Telecoms Industry Case. In: 10th IFIP Working Conference on Virtual Enterprises (PROVE 2009), Thessaloniki, October 07-09 (2009)
4. Spohrer, J., Maglio, P., Bailey, J., Gruhl, D.: Steps Toward a Science of Service Systems. IEEE Computer 40(1), 71–77 (2007)
5. Weigand, H., Johannesson, P., Andersson, B., Bergholtz, M.: Value-based Service Modeling and Design: Toward Unified View of Services. In: van Eck, P., Gordijn, J., Wieringa, R. (eds.) CAiSE 2009. LNCS, vol. 5565, pp. 410–424. Springer, Heidelberg (2009)
6. Soulier, E.: Storytelling, Plateformes Sociales et Ontologies de Processus pour la simulation du Mouvement. Habilitation à Diriger Des Recherches (2009)
7. Sowa, J.F.: Building, Sharing, and Merging Ontologies (2001)(unpublished paper)
8. Seibt, J.: Forms of Emergent interaction in General Process Theory. Synthese 166, 479–512 (2009)
9. Seibt, J.: Free process theory: Towards a typology of occurrings. Axiomathes 14, 23–55 (2004)
10. Guarino, N.: Formal Ontology and Information Systems. In: International Conference on Formal Ontology in Information Systems (FOIS 1998), Trento, Italy (1998)
11. Gandon, F.: Ontology Engineering: A Survey and a Return on Experience, INRIA Report no. 4396 (2002)
12. DAML-S Coalition: Ankolekar, A., Burstein, M., Hobbs, J.R., Lassila., Martin, D., McIlraith, S.A., Narayanan, S., Paolucci, M., Payne, T., Sycara, K., Zeng, H.: DAML-S: Semantic Markup ForWeb Services. In: Semantic Web Working Symposium (2001)
13. Varzi, A.C.: Standford Encyclopedia of Philosophy Mereology (2003 and 2009), http://plato.stanford.edu/entries/mereology/
14. Winston, M.E., Chaffin, R., Herrmann, D.: A Taxonomy of Part-Whole Relations. Cognitive Science 11(4) (1987)
15. Aussenac-Gilles, N., Bourigault, D., Teulier, R.: Analyse comparative de corpus: cas de l'ingénierie des connaissances. In: 14èmes Journées Francophones d'Ingénierie des Connaissances (IC 2003), Laval (2003)
16. Bourigault, D.: Conception et exploitation d'un logiciel d'extraction de termes: problèmes théoriques et méthodologiques. In: Clas, A., Thoiron, P., Béjoint, H. (eds.) AUPELF-UREF, Montréal, Traduction, Lyon. 4èmes Journées scientifiques du réseau thématique Lexicologie, Terminologie, pp. 137–145 (1996)
17. Franc, S., Dardari, D., Boucherie, B., Riveline, J.P., Biedzinski, M., Petit, C., Requeda, E., Leurent, P., Varroud-Vial, M., Hochberg, G., Charpentier, G.: Diabeo: an innovative Telemedicine system for the follow-up of type 1 diabetic patients. In: DTM, San Francisco (2009)
18. Saillot, I., Patou-Mathis, M., Richard, J.F., Sander, E., Poitrenaud, S.: Modéliser les activités cognitives des Hommes au Paléolithique. Math. & Sci. Hum. (159), 55–72 (2002)
19. Varzi, A.C.: Parts, wholes, and part-whole relations: the prospects of mereotopology. Data and Knowledge Engineering 20, 259–286 (1996)
20. Schulz, S., Hahn, U.: Mereotopological Reasoning about Parts and (W) Holes in Bio-Ontologiest. In: Conference FOIS 2001, Ogunquit, Maine, USA, pp. 210–221 (2001)

On Using the REA Enterprise Ontology as a Foundation for Service System Representations

Miguel-Angel Sicilia[1] and Manuel Mora[2]

[1] Computer Science Dept., University of Alcalá
Ctra. Barcelona km. 33.6 – 28871 Alcalá de Henares (Madrid), Spain
msicilia@uah.es
[2] Department of Information Systems, Autonomous University of Aguascalientes,
Aguascalientes, Mexico, 20000
mmora@securenym.net

Abstract. The complexity of service systems has raised interest in developing ontologies that contribute to the conceptual clarification of value co-creation activities and that eventually serve as knowledge representations for systems exploiting reasoning and inference on those ontologies for various practical purposes. The Resource-Event-Agent (REA) enterprise ontology shares similar aims even though it addresses the more generic domain of economic phenomena as modeled by interchange events between agents. In consequence, the REA ontology appears as a good candidate to serve as a framework for a module dealing with an event based account of service provision that could be part of a broader service system ontology. This paper reports a preliminary analysis of the applicability of the REA enterprise ontology to the service domain, according to its formulation by Geerts and McCarthy [14] [15]. Service provision can be modeled as a kind of REA *transfer*, and the selling of a service that will be provided in the future can be modeled by associating the selling with the *commitment* to provide the service associated with the transfer. Different kind of *resources* can be used to model intangibles that are put into action during the service encounter itself, and a separate event structure can be used to model the service encounter. The paper sketches a preliminary refinement of the REA ontology to explicitly account for these aspects.

Keywords: services, service systems, service science, ontology, REA enterprise ontology.

1 Introduction

Service Science, Management and Engineering (SSME) is an emerging interdisciplinary academic and professional discipline, focusing on the design and management of co-generative service systems [8]. As services are pervasive as the "front stage" in economic activities of any kind [22], the role of software systems adequately supporting services is critical in approaches to services enabled by Information Technology (IT) infrastructure. This is in addition becoming more important with the widespread use of the Internet for e-commerce and other activities based on the Web [7], [11].

M.-A. Sicilia, C. Kop, and F. Sartori (Eds.): ONTOSE 2010, LNBIP 62, pp. 135–147, 2010.

The nature of services had raised interest in the development of knowledge models able to capture the inherent complexity of service systems. The approach to knowledge modeling known as *ontology engineering* appears as a promising vehicle for that task as shared ontologies aim at avoiding conceptual ambiguities, promoting re-utilization and standardization, and serving as building blocks for more complex automated-reasoning systems [6], [16]. Some specific ontology initiatives have been reported to date that address the specificities of services, with *OntoServSys* ([21], to appear) as the one described in more detail and the unique to date that explicitly and at the same time exhaustively addresses all the key theoretical elements of SSME as an emerging discipline. Other relevant previous works are the reports from Ferrario and Guarino [12] and Ferrario, Guarino and Fernández-Barrera [13].

However, to the best of our knowledge there are no existing reports that attempt to evaluate existing ontologies as candidate building blocks to be reused for service ontologies. Among these existing previous models, the evolution of the Resource-Event-Action (REA) framework [19] into a full ontology appears to be an important precedent for modeling services, as it is accounting for value transfer in economic phenomena, which is also the key element in service from the business perspective. However, most examples found in REA-related research are related to good selling, and the specific elements of services are not dealt with explicitly (although in principle they are not excluded from the scope of the REA model).

More concretely, we consider here the REA Enterprise Information System (REA-EIS or REA enterprise) ontology, which is an evolution of the REA model for transaction processing of economic phenomena in a shared data environment [14], [15]. The REA-EIS neither provides an explicit service orientation nor includes a differentiation of services from selling of goods that has a clear reflection in the resulting models. This has leaded us to examine its applicability for modeling service systems and to look for necessary extensions or refinements that could be needed for that particular purpose. This paper reports on a preliminary exploration of the REA-EIS as described by Geerts and McCarthy [14] [15], and suggests extensions or refinements to integrate the sound conceptual backbone of REA with the specificities of service systems. It should be noted that there is an ongoing development of a new version of the REA ontology called REA2[1] that has not been fully considered here, but that might result in differences that also affect the extensions and refinements described hereinafter.

The rest of this paper is structured as follows. Section 2 briefly sketches the different views on service ontologies that can be found in previous work and discusses our focus in this paper. Then, Section 3 reviews the main elements of the REA enterprise ontology pointing out to elements requiring conceptual classification, extension or further specification to meet the needs of service systems modeling. Finally, conclusions and outlook are provided in Section 4.

2   The Different Views in Service-Related Ontologies

Engineering an ontology for services poses a significant challenge as the concept of service is understood differently depending on the discipline or application area. Alter [1]

---

[1] The REAv2-WIKI can be reached through this Web page:
http://www.managementinformatics.ugent.be/

has analyzed this disparity comparing the views of marketing, operations and computer science, resulting in three models: work system, value chain and lifecycle. In a different direction, the European project OBELIX[2] described an RDF service ontology in its deliverable D6.1 titled "Service ontology specification". That model divided the ontology in three viewpoints: service value (the customer perspective), service offering (the supplier perspective) and service process (how the service is actually performed). Ferrario and Guarino [12] emphasize commitment of agents to provide the service, and elaborate with examples of public service, which entails a different perspective from other services in which value transfer is not mediated by taxation but it is explicit in a transfer of value. They clearly differentiate commitment, service bundling, acquisition, process and value exchange as interrelated but distinct kinds of service activities.

This plurality of views, aspects or models points out to the need of having a collection of ontologies covering different viewpoints rather than a single, larger ontology. In addition to these aspects, there are existing product and service classifications as eClassOWL [17] that serve as intensional catalogues of types of services (i.e. different service *contents*). However, in its current version, eClassOWL is a "product or service" ontology that merges products and services in the same taxonomy, as reflected for example in concepts as ProductOrService, ActualProductOrServiceInstance.

The term service is also used in the domain of Information Technology to refer to a concrete way of structuring distributed software systems. Service-Oriented Architecture (SOA) is an architectural style that supports service orientation, i.e. structuring software interfaces as distributed services that can be invoked remotely to obtain some effect or output data for some given input data. Obviously, these "software services" are not necessarily related to services in the economic sense, considered as value co-production activities. However, SOA has promoted a particular paradigm of structuring computer-based systems that fits well services as a human activity, and it has even fostered the business model of "Software as a service" (SaaS), in which a provider licenses an application to customers for use as a service on demand [5]. Also, the Open Group has recently released a draft for a SOA ontology expressed in OWL-DL[3], which could eventually be reused to match general service ontologies to software service ontologies. We should highlight that we are not dealing here with software service ontologies, so in the discussion below service is referring to events involving humans (directly or indirectly).

OntoServSys ([21], to appear) provides a comprehensive account of service concerns, based on an analysis of the literature regarding SSME. Among many other aspects, it covers actual service interaction including actors, resources and events. These form the basis of the operational model of any service system ontology, as *service encounters* are the target of design and management that can be considered to conform the core conceptual structure. That part of the ontology has a precedent in the REA framework [19], which provided a model strongly rooted in accounting and economic theory and addressed the issue of what phenomena should be captured in an enterprise system in general.

As mentioned above, services are considered essentially as commitments by Ferrario and Guarino [12]. This is connected also with the concept of commitment in the

---

[2] http://cordis.europa.eu/fetch?CALLER=PROJ_ICT&ACTION=D&CAT=PROJ&RCN=61165
[3] http://www.opengroup.org/projects/soa-ontolo gy/

REA model, and there are several links between REA-EIS elements and the general framework of Ferrario and Guarino. These authors have proposed a general ontological foundation for the notion of service, which in turn is based on the notion of commitment. Their definition of service as *"A service is present at a time T and location L iff, at time T, an agent is explicitly committed to guarantee the execution of some type of action at location L, on the occurrence of a certain triggering event, in the interest of another agent and upon prior agreement, in a certain way."* . This notion of service is related to a possibility of action, not the real "service encounter", and other authors refer to this notion as "service offering". The notion of commitment appears in the REA-EIS ontology, but the central element in REA models is the transfer of value. Even though the transfer is considered in Ferrario and Guarino framework [12] as part of "Service value exchange", that part of the model is not described to the level of detail that can be found in REA. In consequence, it seems reasonable that REA models can be combined with other service areas but still reused as a mature model.

In this paper, we are examining the position of the REA model which is rooted on accountancy and as such, focuses on value transfer. However, the theoretical standpoint of any ontology of services requires some basic ontological commitments that characterize services as opposed to goods. We approach services here as *events* (similarly to Ferrario and Guarino), but focusing on service as *"value co-creation through inter-action"*. That notion can be integrated with good production and selling using theoretical economic frameworks. For example, let's take praxeology – the "science of human action" according to [20] – as a departure foundation. Then, we can consider the axiom that humans engage in conscious actions toward chosen goals as they have values (not necessarily rational) and they believe to have the technological knowledge that certain means will achieve his desired ends. In consequence, agents purposefully produce offerings and are served by the offerings of other agents that they select to achieve their aims. This can be combined with the axiom that means employed are scarce in relation to desired ends, and we end up with reflecting on the means to fulfill needs, and how humans organize themselves in production processes to help others in that fulfilling. This leads to the following categorization:

- Production and provision as *two separated actions*. This is the case of good selling, in which production is organized to produce tangible goods that are eventually stocked and later subject to selling. That last selling step could be considered a service also, but restricted to facilitating the transfer of the tangible item previously produced.
- Production and provision when *combined in the same, inseparable course of action*. This is the case of services, in which the value is created at request of the customer, with some degree of interaction with him and not necessarily involving any transfer of ownership.

In both cases, it is possible that the transfer of value is done in different arrangements, e.g. advanced payment or delayed payment. Both kind of combinations (production and service) can also be bundled together in complex ways. Combined production and provision seems to be the main aspect of service definition, so that value transfer is done in interaction with the customer. It should be noted that interaction does not necessarily mean face-to-face or physical interaction (as in services provided through the Web), and that there is not a need that interactions of customers and providers are not necessarily synchronous in time (as in the services of a private detective agency, in which they act on behalf of the customer).

These are the main elements considered as essential aspects of services here:

- *Inseparability.* Events cannot be inventoried, as they are created and consumed at the same time.
- *Intangibility.* As services are events, we cannot possess events (even thus we can own they results).
- *Perishability.* It is also a consequence of considering services as events. The lifespan of the service is that of the event itself, while in goods, these can be persistent in time.

These characteristics will be revisited in the following discussion as a test to the account of service presented. Heterogeneity and personalization are also usually mentioned as distinguishing characteristics of services from goods. However, this is not a clear distinction, as goods production has evolved in some cases to reach high levels of personalization, as it is common in "mass customization" approaches [9].

The REA model and its subsequent refinements intend to cover value transfer phenomena. In consequence, it is apparent that it should be able to cover service provision as interaction events. It should be noted this does not exhaust all the aspects identified previously by Mora et al. [21] and Ferrario and Guarino [12], but touches the key aspect of modeling the value transfer event structure.

3   The REA Ontology and Service Representation

The REA (*Resource-Event-Agent*) enterprise ontology is a core framework for transaction processing of economic phenomena in a shared data environment [14] [15]. As such, it is obviously of potential usefulness as a model for service interaction. However, there is a need to carefully analyze the ontology to assess if the specifics of service interactions are explicitly captured or specializations of some concepts or relationships are required.

Services represent the "front stage" of virtually any kind of business [22], when interaction with the customer takes place. Such interaction is sustained in many cases by some complex "back stage" machinery, however such back stage mechanisms are out of scope of our present effort.

In what follows, the main elements of the REA model are discussed in the aspects that are directly relevant to services. It should be noted that the good/services sector separation is nowadays considered largely artificial, so that a good model should account for a model of interaction in which both can be represented together.

Economic Events and Resource Exchange and Use

The REA model is organized around (composite) Events[4] in which Agents participate. Concretely, the definition of EconomicEvent in the OWL version of the REA

---

[4] In what follows, ontology elements are in Courier font, to differentiate them easily when reading the text.

ontology[5] is as follows: *"Represent either an increment or a decrement in the value of economic resources that are under control of the enterprise"*. Concretely, there are "increment" economic events, and "decrement" economic events, which are related to each other via the predicate `duality` that "keeps track of which resources were exchanged for which others". In principle, this same distinction can be applied to services. The increments are related to receipt of money or other kind of resource, and the decrements in the case of good selling are the transfer of the tangible good (so, the model has the perspective of the provider). In the case of services, decrements are related to the capability of the provider to do service, e.g. when a service is being provided by a masseur to a customer, it cannot be simultaneously provided to other. This fits well with the notion of considering opportunity costs as a kind of economic resource. However, this also requires a very broad notion of "resources". For example, in OpenCyc[6] we can find the predicate:

```
(resourceAvailable AGENT RESOURCE)
```

Which means that AGENT has access to the object RESOURCE in such a way that AGENT could make some immediate use of RESOURCE in any type of action which required it. Resources are considered as instances of the OpenCyc concept SomethingExisting, which includes tangible things (as persons or machines) but also some intangibles as agreements or obligations. Resource unavailability for the time of the service (in the sense that cannot be used for other customer at the same time) is a way to model the outflow of the service providing part. This would require a ternary relation as for example (resourceAvailable AGENT RESOURCE TIMEINTERVAL), or defining an additional concept representing time bound usage of resources as a specific kind of resource, e.g. the usage of an infrared sauna (an economic resource) for 15 minutes at some given time. This is a consequence of the intangibility of services, as what is transferred is the work of some resources for some time.

This in OWL could be expressed as a constraint on a TemporalUseOf EconomicResource concept in the form:

```
EconomicResource and temporalConstraint some TimeInterval.
```

However, this would entail some change in the model so that unavailability is temporally marked, and it is not clear that this matches the current semantics of REA that appear to be related to transfer of possession (but the formal OWL definitions are not precluding that matching). This would have the benefit to connect to models of availability management which are common in the practice of service planning.

The EconomicAgents relate to EconomicEvents via participate relations. They contribute EconomicResources they own to the event, which results in a "stock-flow", including an "inflow" and an "outflow". These elements are in principle applicable to service provision, provided that the stock flows include intangible elements. For example, in consultancy the output stock can be considered to be

---

[5] http://www.managementinformatics.ugent.be/REAontology/OWLdoc/

[6] OpenCyc is the open source version of the Cyc Knowledge Base (Lenat, 1995), which contains over one hundred thousands atomic terms, and is provided with an associated efficient inference engine.

the increase in know-how in the customer (a kind of intangible). The concept of `EconomicAgent` in REA needs not any extension in service transactions, and the distinction between "outside agents" (customers) and "inside agents" (employees) remains valid, as the accountability elements are equally valid (but not of specific relevance to model the service encounter). Nonetheless, the two specialized kinds of participations of agents are `provide` and `receive` and they relate an `EconomicAgent` to an `EconomicEvent`. This is somewhat limiting as it is not linking agents to resources in the context of events, i.e. it is not modeling ternary relationships. Such level of detail is needed to account for example for user-providing resources. For example, in consulting services, both the customer and the provider are usually providing some economic resources as valuable information or know-how, and there is a need to distinguish that different actors provide different resources to the same event. This should be accomplished in some way, and providing an extended service event structure (as described below) appears a good option to avoid changing the participation model in REA directly.

Resource Types

Even though the REA model seems to be valid for modeling resource exchange in services, the heterogeneity and special nature of resources in services deserve the elaboration of a detailed categorization of economic resources beyond the generic definition now available as "a thing that is scarce and has utility for economic agents and is something users of business applications want to plan, monitor and control". From the consideration of service as a kind of transfer described above, the next step is reviewing the different aspects that have been proposed in the literature to differentiate service from good transfer, and exercise REA modeling, eventually identifying *resource types* that are relevant enough in service to deserve separate representation. A particularly important subset of these resources is competencies, which can be defined as measurable capabilities required in performing some concrete work situations [10], but also physical elements that are not transferred but play a role in the service experience should be represented, e.g. facilities. Things as ontologies of competencies or even representations of social capital [4] could be used to characterize resources in a broad way, including intellectual capital. There are organizational theories that are relevant to resource classification and emphasize the role of some particular classes of resources given some contingent features as scarcity or non-substitutability. The Resource-based view of the firm (RBV) is a particularly interesting theory [3] that should be considered given that it explains organizational features based on the notion of resource. The current OWL version of the REA ontology is providing an `EconomicResourceType` concept accounting for a reification of types of resources that could be used as an alternative to define a terminology of resource types at the instance level. However, a detailed account of the typology of resources is needed for the REA to be more applicable in practice, avoiding the re-definition of kinds of resources that are recurring.

Kinds of Exchanges

The REA model considers a basic structure of events with two salient characteristics: events can be composite, and there is a relation of duality in the events, representing the two sides (producer-consumer) of the event. In REA, there are two types of inter-changes: *transformations* and *transfers*. Transformations "create value through changes in form or substance" and "we either *use* or *consume* a resource to produce another", while transfers "create market value in a market transaction with outside parties". This is described in the model with the following sentence: "*A transfer fulfills a contract while a transformation fulfills a schedule*".

Transfers are basically targeted to model the transfer of ownership, which is closely connected with selling goods. Transformations are targeted to change, but they are mainly targeted to "back stage" transformations.

One possible option for modeling services is considering them a *kind of transfer*. In principle, there is nothing in the model that prevents us to do so:

1. The model does not preclude the provision of resources from the role of the customer, which is typical of many kinds of service encounters.
2. The model does not mandate that any physical good is necessarily part of the stock flow. What is transferred can be realized as an intangible, including elements aimed at producing some kind of satisfaction (e.g. in the case of a leisure service).

However, according to its definition, a transfer should model the transfer of value, so that for the models to be complete, there is a need to specify all the value creating steps, which are *ocurrents* bound in time [2], this is a requirement related to the insepa-rability of services from their actual provision. Figure 1 shows an example of a frag-ment of an interchange[7] where a typical REA dual purchase event is modeled with some added elements of service in a flight are also included[8] (in the dashed rectangle). It should be noted that these additional events are not in this case related to the sale event itself, but they are realizing the event. In the case of good transfer, the *use* stock flow is in many cases sufficient to represent the value transfer, but this is not the case in service. One option for this additional modeling is connecting outflow resources of type `ServiceCommitment` to the events realizing the service itself. Commitments in REA are defined as "a promise or obligation of economic agents to perform an eco-nomic event in the future". In consequence, a modification of transfers in REA can be done so that the buy of the service is modeled in the usual way with two events paired by a `duality` relation, but the outgoing stockflow is substituted by a `ServiceCom-mitment` that can be further described and that is described by the previous event.

However, this might be considered to be in contradiction with the necessity of pair-ing inflows and outflows stated by Geerts and McCarthy. Nonetheless, the alternative of having the commitment itself as outflow is not appropriate as commitments are not transferring by themselves the possession or temporal usage of resources. This separa-tion of the event of buying the service from the service provision is convenient to model most service encounters, which are typically first agreed and later provided.

---

[7] It should be noted that the diagrams represent only fragments, abstracting many details for the sake of clarity.

[8] The notation used for the example is adapted from the original paper of Geerts and McCarthy (2000). Filled ovals are instances, and links between them are property instances with prop-erty names on top of them. Instance names and the concepts they belong are referenced as `instanceName:ConceptName`. This notation has been selected for ease of comparison with the diagrams in the previously mentioned REA paper.

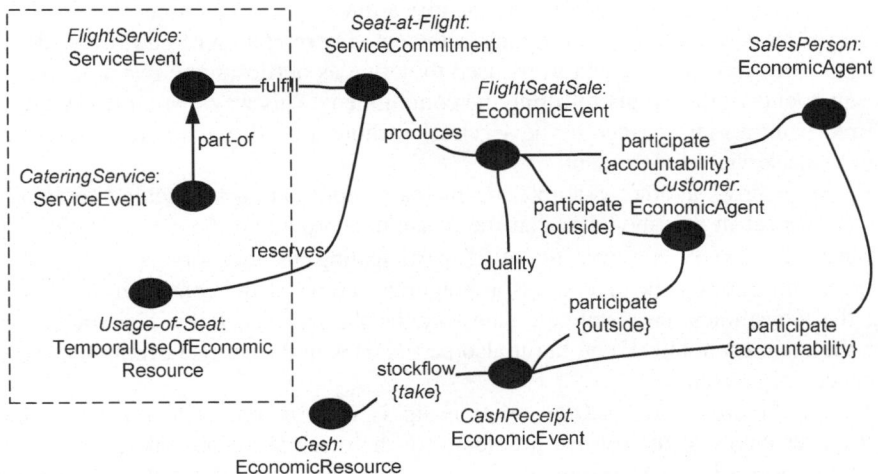

Fig. 1. An example REA representation of the sale of a flight seat

A ServiceEvent is a kind of Event but not an EconomicEvent, as it is not re-quired to have a paired, dual event. However, the connection to a commitment allows tracing the original economic event to all the service events that are fulfilling the commitment produced by the former. This separation and use of the commitment as an intermediate entity allows for a flexible modeling of service events structures. ServiceEvents can be found as a concept in OpenCyc, defined as "event in which one or more agents (related to the event via the predicate providerOfSer-vice) do something for one or more other agents (related to the event via the predi-cate recipientOfService". A relevant OpenCyc subclass is ServiceProduct, representing services done for payment. This definition captures the idea of "doing something for somebody" that need not necessarily be modeled together with the transfer of value itself (both can be considered two different levels of ontological concern).

Figure 1 is also showing how the commitment reserves some economic resource (in this case is a temporal usage of a resource, i.e. the seat, labeled as Usage-of-Seat). The use of intangibles in service and their eventual transfer requires some additional extensions. The actual flight service could be composed of some sub-services, using an standard part-of relationship. Following the above provide dis-cussion on the output of services, the resources reserved can be used to infer the out-put flow of resources committed. This can be achieved in a straightforward way with SWRL[9] rules as the following:

```
ServiceCommitment(?sc) and DecrementEconomicEvent(?e)
and produces(?e, ?sc) and EconomicResource(?r)
and reserves(?sc, ?r)
-> outflow(?e, ?r)
```

---

[9] http://www.w3.org/Submission/SWRL/

However, as described above, this identification of resources used temporally as outflows can be considering conflicting with some interpretation of outflows in REA. In other direction, other rules can be used to define as outflows any resource used in the sub-events of the events fulfilling the commitment. This way, the outflows can be inferred from resource usage in the services, without a need to explicitly connecting them to the service commitment.

Figure 2 shows another example, in this case representing a coaching service. A relevant aspect in that model is that the *consultant* providing the service is both an instance of `EconomicAgent` (as it is participating in the service), but also a `EconomicResource` (actually, it is a temporal lending of the consultant to the service that constitutes the resource). This way, he/she has also links of participations with the main economic event, but it also participates in the service event themselves as a necessary resource.

Also in Figure 2, the *linkage* relationship is used to represent the key value-creating resources of the service providers (in the original model linkage is used to express relations between resources also), e.g. the know-how about the focus of the consultancy service. These resources are *required* in some of the events conforming the actual service provision. Further, these resources become outflows for the interchange of subtype `creates`, expressing that the know-how is not given (thus disappearing internally) but it is "copied" or reproduced (in this case, as the know-how is transferred to the customer). A common theme in service science is considering service as co-production of value, which in terms of the model entails that the customer role is also providing input flows to the transaction. This can be represented in a similar way with *linkage*s and requirements for some of the activities that are part of the service.

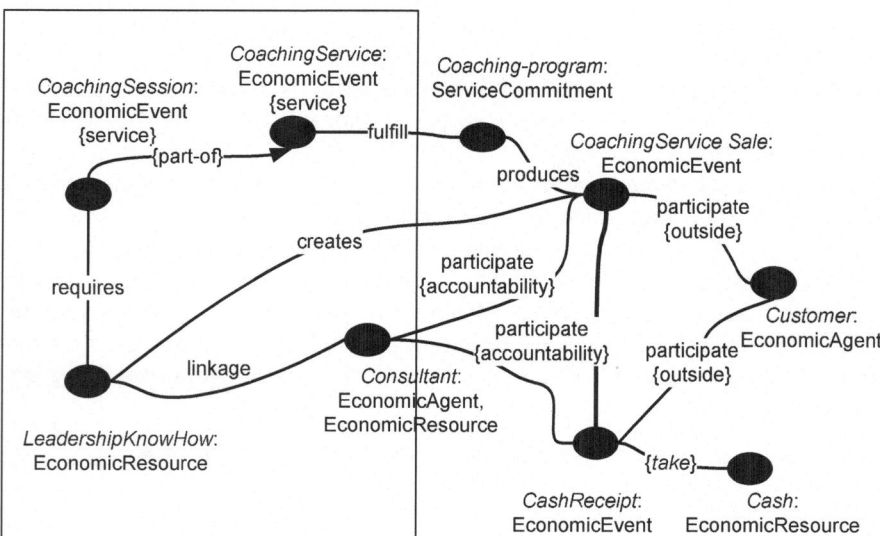

Fig. 2. An example REA representation of the sale and provision of a coaching service

Customer-provided resources are also typically part of service encounters. Following the example in Figure 2, a "business analysis" done by the customer as part of the process of consultancy could be considered a kind of `EconomicResource`. This example raises the concern if that resource could be associated to the inflow or the outflow of the service, as the analysis (the document) is done applying effort from the side of the customer, so it is providing something in, but it is done also with assistance of the consultant, so that it is not clearly an inflow or outflow. This example is a consequence of the intangibility of services, so that it is difficult to assess the direction of the flow of value in some cases. That "value directionality" paradox requires a much thorough analysis and a clarification of the notion of value transfer, beyond the duality of increment/decrement of value that has been introduced in the OWL version of the REA ontology.

4 Conclusions and Outlook

Services have been approached from different perspectives in previous research about service ontologies, emphasizing different aspects of services. In any case, service system ontologies require a sound modeling account of the interchange occurring in service encounters, which is the essential economic event addressed by design, management and measurement. The REA model addresses the dual structure of these events and the main elements necessary for their modeling, but requires some refinement to adequately support the conceptual structure of services in a explicit way. These refinements include the central notion of considering the temporal transfer of a resource to serve a specific customer as a kind of `outflow` that is not resulting in a transfer of ownership. This is consistent with opportunity costs as a consideration of resources, but it would require some changes in the ontology to represent the flow of available resources as services are being delivered. Other additions include a detailed model of the resources provided by different actors to the same event and the use of commitments to model the reserve of economic resources that are providing the service, separating in that way service buy from service provision. In general, the REA ontology appears as an appropriate point of departure for service systems ontology, as it is representing value transfer appropriately and has the potential of accommodating the specifics of services, but cannot be reused "as is" as there are several conceptual issues that remain unclear.

The analysis provided here is provisional, and it would require extensive evaluation by contrasting service theories and models, and by developing complex service provision case studies, that would be subject to future work. In any case, the analysis provides a point of departure for reusing the REA model in the SSME domain by correcting, extending or modifying the main aspects described above.

Further work is needed in developing a complete extension of the REA enterprise ontology for services, or perhaps developing some guidelines and links to other ontologies that complement what the REA is offering as an abstract model for value exchange. Also, future work should address how software services can be integrated with the account of services provided here.

References

1. Alter, S.: Service system fundamentals: Work system, value chain and life cycle. IBM Systems Journal 47(1), 71–85 (2008)
2. Arp, R., Smith, B.: Function, role, and disposition in basic formal ontology. In: Proceedings of the 11th Annual BioOntologies Meeting (2008)
3. Barney, J.B.: Firm resources and sustained competitive advantage. Journal of Management 17, 99–120 (1991)
4. Burt, R.: The Social Capital of Structural Holes. In: Guillén, M.F. (ed.) The New Economic Sociology: Developments in an Emerging Field, pp. 148–190. Russell Sage Foundation, New York (2002)
5. Buxmann, P., Hess, T., Lehmann, S.: Software as a Service. Wirtschaftsinfor-Matik 50(6), 500–503 (2008)
6. Chandrasekaran, B., Josephson, J., Benjamins, R.: What are ontologies, and why do we need them. IEEE Intelligent Systems 14(1), 20–26 (1999)
7. Chen, J.S., Tsou, H.T.: Information technology adoption for service innovation practices and competitive advantage: the case of financial firms. Information Research 12(3), Paper 314 (2007)
8. Chesbrough, H., Spohrer, J.: A research manifesto for services science. Communications of the ACM 49(7), 35–40 (2006)
9. Da Silveira, G., Borenstein, D., Fogliatto, F.S.: Mass customization: Literature review and research directions. International Journal of Production Economics 72(1), 1–13 (2001)
10. Dzinkowski, R.: The measurement and management of intellectual capital: An introduction. Management Accounting 78(2), 32–36 (2000)
11. Feigenbaum, J., Parkes, D.C., Pennock, D.M.: Computational challenges in e-commerce. Communications of the ACM 52(1), 70–74 (2009)
12. Ferrario, R., Guarino, N.: Towards an Ontological Foundation for Services Science. In: Domingue, J., Fensel, D., Traverso, P. (eds.) FIS 2008. LNCS, vol. 5468, pp. 152–169. Springer, Heidelberg (2009)
13. Ferrario, R., Guarino, N., Fernández Barrera, M.E.: Towards an Ontological Foundation for Services Science: the Legal Perspective. In: Sartor, G., Casanovas, P., Biasiotti, M., Fernandez Barrera, M. (eds.) Approaches to Legal Ontologies, Springer, Heidelberg (2009)
14. Geerts, G., McCarthy, W.E.: An Accounting Object Infrastructure For Knowledge-Based Enterprise Models. IEEE Intelligent Systems & Their Applications (July/August 1999), 89–94 (2000)
15. Geerts, G.L., McCarthy, W.E.: The Ontological Foundation of REA Enterprise Information Systems. Paper presented at the American Accounting Association Conference Philadelphia, PA (2000), https://www.msu.edu/user/mccarth4/Alabama.doc [retrieved online November 15, 2009]
16. Gruber, T.: The Role of Common Ontology in Achieving Sharable, Reusable Knowledge Bases. In: Allen, J.A., Fikes, R., Sandewall, E. (eds.) Proceedings of the Second International Conference on Principles of Knowledge Representation and Reasoning, pp. 601–602. Morgan Kaufmann, Cambridge (1991)
17. Hepp, M.: Products and Services Ontologies: A Methodology for Deriving OWL Ontologies from Industrial Categorization Standards. International Journal on Semantic Web & Information Systems 2(1), 72–99 (2006)
18. Lenat, D.: Cyc: A large-scale investment in knowledge infrastructure. Communications of the ACM 38(11), 33–38 (1995)

19. McCarthy, W.: The REA Accounting Model: A Generalized Framework for Accounting Systems in a Shared Data Environment. The Accounting Review, 554–578 (1982)
20. von Mises, L.: Human Action: A Treatise on Economics, 3rd edn. Henry Regnery, Chicago (1966)
21. Mora, M., Raisinghani, M., Gelman, O., Sicilia, M.A.: Onto-ServSys: a Service System Ontology. In: Demirkan, H., Spohrer, J., Krishna, V. (eds.) The Science of Service Systems/Service Systems Implementation. Service Science: Research and Innova-tions (SSRI) Series. Springer, Heidelberg (to appear)
22. Teboul, J.: Service is Front Stage: Positioning Services for Value Advantage. Insead Business Press, Palgrave Macmillan (2006)

Author Index

Lecture Notes in Computer Science 5425

Commenced Publication in 1973
Founding and Former Series Editors:
Gerhard Goos, Juris Hartmanis, and Jan van Leeuwen

Eitan Altman Augustin Chaintreau (Eds.)

Network Control and Optimization

Second EuroFGI Workshop, NET-COOP 2008
Paris, France, September 8-10, 2008
Revised Selected Papers

 Springer

Volume Editors

Eitan Altman
INRIA
2004 Route des Lucioles, 06902 Sophia-Antipolis CEDEX, France
E-mail: eitan.altman@sophia.inria.fr

Augustin Chaintreau
Thomson
46 quai Alphonse le Gallo, 92648 Boulogne CEDEX, France
E-mail: augustin.chaintreau@thomson.net

Library of Congress Control Number: Applied for

CR Subject Classification (1998): C.2.4, F.2, D.2, D.1.3, H.4

LNCS Sublibrary: SL 5 – Computer Communication Networks
and Telecommunications

ISSN   0302-9743
ISBN-10   3-642-00392-3 Springer Berlin Heidelberg New York
ISBN-13   978-3-642-00392-9 Springer Berlin Heidelberg New York

springer.com

© Springer-Verlag Berlin Heidelberg 2009
Printed in Germany

Typesetting: Camera-ready by author, data conversion by Scientific Publishing Services, Chennai, India
Printed on acid-free paper   SPIN: 12620258   06/3180   5 4 3 2 1 0

Preface

We are pleased to present the proceedings of the Second Workshop on Network Control and Optimization (NET-COOP) that took place during September 8-10, 2008, in Paris, France, sponsored by the EuroFGI Network of Excellence.

Thanks to the generous support of EuroFGI, we were able to combine contributed sessions with an outstanding list of invited plenary speakers: Thomas Bonald, Vivek S. Borkar, Pierre Fraigniaud, Ayavaldi J. Ganesh, Takis Konstantopoulos, Alexandre Proutière, R. Srikant, Sacha Stolyar, Laurent Viennot, Milan Vojnovic, Damon Wischik.

The workshop received 27 submissions which underwent a thorough review process. The Program Committee selected 13 of these as contributed papers. The proceedings include in addition two invited papers in connection with two of the plenary talks.

Continuing a young tradition, the workshop aims at developing research on control and optimization of the Internet, ranging from performance evaluation and optimization of general stochastic networks to more specific targets such as lower-layer functionalities in mobile networks, routing for computational grids, game theoretic approaches to access control, cooperation, competition and adversary capacities in diverse environments.

November 2008   Eitan Altman
                                                                     Augustin Chaintreau

Organization

NET-COOP 2008 was co-organized by Thomson and TELECOM SudParis, France

Organizing Committee

General Chair: Laurent Massoulié (Thomson, France)
General Co-chair: Tijani Chahed (TELECOM SudParis, France)
Program Co-chairs: Eitan Altman (INRIA, France) and Augustin
                         Chaintreau (Thomson, France)
Web Chair: Nelson Vicuna (Avignon University, France)

Program Committee

Ivo Adan, TU/e
Panayotis Antoniadis, U. Paris 6
Konstantin Avratchenkov, INRIA
Urtzi Ayesta, CNRS
Tamer Basar, UIUC
Randall Berry, Northwestern
Thomas Bonald, OrangeLabs
Vivek S. Borkar, TIFR
Onno Boxma, TU Eindhoven
Costas Courcoubetis, AUEB
Bruno Gaujal, INRIA
Moshe Haviv, HUJI
Nidhi Hedge, OrangeLabs
Mikael Johansson, KTH
Hisao Kameda, U. Tsukuba
Peter Key, Microsoft Res.
Anurag Kumar, IISc
Nikolaos Laoutaris, Telefonica
Marc Lelarge, INRIA-ENS
Steven Low, CIT
D. Manjunath, IIT-Mumbai

Ravi Mazumdar, U. Waterloo
Pietro Michiardi, Eurecom
Giovanni Neglia, INRIA
José Niño-Mora, U. Carlos III
   de Madrid
Fernando Paganini, U. ORT
Pascale Primet, ENS-Lyon
Alexandre Proutière, Microsoft Res.
Guy Pujolle, U. Paris 6
Jacques Resing, TU Eindhoven
Ulrich Rieder, U. Ulm
Nahum Shimkin, Technion Haifa
George Stamoulis, AUEB
Nicolas Stier, Columbia
Leandros Tassiulas, U. Thessaly
Corinne Touati, INRIA
Don Towsley, UMASS
Darryl Veitch, U. Melbourne
Jorma Virtamo, HUT
Milan Vojnovic, Microsoft Res.
Bert Zwart, GeorgiaTech

Sponsoring Institutions

Euro-NF
INRIA
Thomson

Table of Contents

TCP and Congestion Control

Wireless Networks

A Comparison of Bilateral and Multilateral Exchanges for Peer-Assisted Content Distribution

Christina Aperjis, Michael J. Freedman, and Ramesh Johari

Abstract. Peer-assisted content distribution matches user demand for content with available supply at other peers in the network. Inspired by this supply-and-demand interpretation of the nature of content sharing, we employ *price theory* to study peer-assisted content distribution. In this approach, the market-clearing prices are those which exactly align supply and demand, and the system is studied through the characterization of price equilibria. We rigorously analyze the efficiency and robustness gains that are enabled by price-based multilateral exchange. We show that multilateral exchanges satisfy several desirable efficiency and robustness properties that bilateral exchanges do not, *e.g.*, equilibria in bilateral exchange may fail to exist, be inefficient if they do exist, and fail to remain robust to collusive deviations even if they are Pareto efficient. Further, we show that an equilibrium in bilateral exchange corresponds to a multilateral exchange equilibrium if and only if it is robust to deviations by coalitions of users.

1 Introduction

Peer-to-peer systems have been wildly successful as a disruptive technology for content distribution. Varying accounts place peer-to-peer (P2P) traffic as comprising anywhere between 35% and 90% of "all" Internet traffic [1]. Early P2P systems did not provide any incentives for participation, leading to extensive freeloading [2, 3]. The P2P community responded with mechanisms to prevent freeloading by incentivizing sharing on a *bilateral barter* basis, as used by BitTorrent [4] and its variants [5, 6], where peers can achieve better download performance from peers to which they are simultaneously uploading.

While BitTorrent's usage numbers are certainly impressive, it can only perform bilateral barter by matching up well-suited pairs of nodes that have disjoint subsets of a file (or, more generally, files), and it is often hard to find good reciprocation with bilateral barter alone. Furthermore, potential "free-riding" attacks have been observed [7, 8, 9, 5], and altruistic uploading often turns out to be critical for providing continued content availability [10].

Another alternative is to use *market-based multilateral exchange* to match user demand for content to available supply at other peers in the system. This approach uses virtual currency and assigns a budget to each peer, which decreases when downloading and increases when uploading. Monetary incentives in a virtual currency have been previously proposed to incentivize uploading in P2P systems [11, 12, 13, 14]. In this paper, we compare bilateral and multilateral exchanges for peer-assisted content distribution.

We provide a formal comparison of P2P system designs with bilateral barter, such as BitTorrent, and a market-based exchange of content enabled by a price mechanism to match supply and demand. We start in Section §2 with a fundamental abstraction

E. Altman and A. Chaintreau (Eds.): NET-COOP 2008, LNCS 5425, pp. 1–8, 2009.

of content exchange in systems with bilateral barter: *exchange ratios*. The exchange ratio from one peer to another gives the download rate received per unit upload rate. Exchange ratios are a useful formal tool because they directly allow us to compare bilateral P2P systems with price-based multilateral P2P systems.

In §3 and §4, we compare bilateral and multilateral P2P systems through the allocations that arise at equilibria. In particular, we show that a multilateral price-based exchange scheme satisfies a number of desirable properties lacking in bilateral exchange, *e.g.*, equilibria in bilateral exchange may fail to exist, be inefficient if they do exist, and fail to remain robust to collusive deviations even if they exist and are efficient. We show that with an additional technical condition, a bilateral equilibrium corresponds to a multilateral equilibrium if and only if it is robust to deviations by coalitions of users.

2   Exchange Ratios in Bilateral Protocols

The BitTorrent protocol and its variants enable exchange on a *bilateral* basis between peers: a peer i uploads to peer j if and only if peer j uploads to peer i in return. While such protocols are traditionally studied solely through the rates that peers obtain, in this section we provide an interpretation of these protocols through *exchange ratios*. As exchange ratios can be interpreted in terms of prices, these ratios will allow us to compare bilateral and multilateral P2P systems in the following section.

Let r_{ij} denote the rate sent from peer i to peer j in an instantiation of a BitTorrent swarm. We define the *exchange ratio* between peer i and peer j as the ratio $\gamma_{ij} = r_{ji}/r_{ij}$; this is the download rate received by i from j, per unit of rate uploaded to j. By definition, $\gamma_{ij} = 1/\gamma_{ji}$. Clearly, a rational peer i would prefer to download from peers with which he has higher exchange ratios.

The exchange ratio has a natural interpretation in terms of prices. An equivalent story emerges if we assume that peers charge each other for content in a common monetary unit, but that all transactions are *settlement-free*, *i.e.*, no money ever changes hands. In this case, if peer i charged peer j a price p_{ij} per unit rate, the exchange of content between peers i and j must satisfy $p_{ij}r_{ij} = p_{ji}r_{ji}$. Note that the preceding condition thus shows the exchange ratio is equivalent to the ratio of bilateral prices: $\gamma_{ij} = p_{ij}/p_{ji}$ (as long as the prices and rates are nonzero). The rates achieved by the BitTorrent and BitTyrant [5] protocols can be naturally modeled through exchange ratios [15].

The preceding discussion highlights the fact that the rates in a bilateral P2P system can be interpreted via exchange ratios. Thus far we have assumed that *transfer rates* are given, and exchange ratios are computed from these rates. In the next section, we turn this relationship around: we explicitly consider an abstraction of bilateral P2P systems where peers react to given exchange ratios, and compare the resulting outcomes to price-based multilateral exchange.

3   Bilateral and Multilateral Equilibria

Motivated by the discussion in the preceding section, this section rigorously analyzes the efficiency properties of price-based bilateral and multilateral mechanisms. Assuming that peers explicitly react to exchange ratios or prices, we compare the schemes through their resulting price equilibria.

In the formal model we consider, a set of peers N shares a set of files F. Peer i has a subset of the files $F_i \subseteq F$, and is interested in downloading files in $T_i \subseteq F - F_i$. We use

Bilateral Peer Optimization:	Multilateral Peer Optimization:
maximize $V_i(\mathsf{d}_i)$	maximize $V_i(\mathsf{d}_i)$
subject to $d_{if} = \sum_j r_{jif}$ for all f	subject to $d_{if} = \sum_j r_{jif}$ for all f
$r_{ijf} = 0$ if $f \notin F_i$	$r_{ijf} = 0$ if $f \notin F_i$
$\sum_{j,f} r_{ijf} \leq B_i$	$\sum_{j,f} r_{ijf} \leq B_i$
$\sum_f r_{jif} = \gamma_{ij} \sum_f r_{ijf}$ for all j	$\sum_{j,f} p_j r_{jif} = p_i \sum_{j,f} r_{ijf}$
$r \geq 0.$	$r \geq 0.$

Fig. 1. Optimization problems for price-based exchange

r_{ijf} to denote the rate at which user i uploads file f to user j. We then let $d_{if} = \sum_j r_{jif}$ be the total rate at which user i downloads file f. We use sans serif to denote vectors, e.g., $\mathsf{d}_i = (d_{if}, f \in T_i)$ is the vector of download rates for user i. We measure the desirability of a download vector to peer i by a *utility function* $V_i(\mathsf{d}_i)$ that is nondecreasing in every d_{if} for $f \in T_i$. We ignore any resource constraints within the network; we assume that transfers are only constrained by the upload capacities of peers. The upload capacity of peer i is denoted B_i.

We start by considering peers' behavior in bilateral schemes, given a vector of exchange ratios (γ_{ij}). Peer i solves the bilateral optimization problem given in Figure 1. Note that we allow peers to bilaterally exchange content over multiple files, as the more general design, even though this is not typically supported by swarming systems like BitTorrent. This more general design makes it possible to explicitly identify the relative demand for files and reward peers that share more popular content.

By contrast, in a *multilateral price-based exchange*, the system maintains one price per peer, and peers optimize with respect to these prices. In a slight abuse of notation, we denote the price of a peer i by p_i. Figure 1 also gives the peer optimization problem in multilateral price-based exchange. Note that the first three constraints (giving download rates, ensuring peers only upload files they possess, and meeting the upload capacity constraint) are identical to the bilateral peer optimization. While the bilateral exchange implicitly requires peer i to download only from those peers to whom he uploads, no such constraint is imposed on multilateral exchanges: peer i accrues capital for uploading, and he can spend this capital however he wishes for downloading.

For bilateral (resp., multilateral) exchange, an *equilibrium* is a combination of a rate allocation vector and an exchange ratio vector (resp., price vector) such that all peers have solved their corresponding optimization problems. In this case, the exchange ratios (resp., prices) have exactly aligned supply and demand: for any i, j, f, the transfer rate r_{ijf} is simultaneously an optimal choice for both the uploader i and downloader j.

Definition 1. *The rate allocation* r^* *and the exchange ratios* $(\gamma_{ij}^*, i, j \in N)$ *with* $\gamma_{ij}^* > 0$ *for all* $i, j \in N$ *constitute a **bilateral equilibrium** if for each peer* i, r^* *solves the Bilateral Peer Optimization problem given exchange ratios* $(\gamma_{ij}^*, j \in N)$.

Definition 2. *The rate allocation* r^* *and the peer prices* $(p_i^*, i \in N)$ *with* $p_i^* > 0$ *for all* $i \in N$ *constitute a **multilateral equilibrium** if for each peer* j, r^* *solves the Multilateral Peer Optimization problem given prices* $(p_i^*, i \in N)$.

This latter is the traditional notion of competitive equilibrium in economics [16]. A multilateral equilibrium can be shown to exist under general conditions in our setting [14].

Moreover, the corresponding allocation is Pareto efficient, *i.e.*, there is no way to increase the utility of some peer without decreasing the utility of some other peer. A bilateral equilibrium, on the other hand, does not always exist, and, even when it exists, the allocation may not be (Pareto) efficient as the following examples illustrate.

Example 1. Consider a system with n peers and n files, for $n > 2$. Each peer i has file f_i and wants $f_{(i \bmod n)+1}$. With these utilities, no bilateral exchange can satisfy all peers, and a bilateral equilibrium does not exist.

Example 2. Consider a system with peers $\{1,2,3\}$ and files $\{f_1, f_2, f_3\}$. Peer i has file f_i and wants the other two files. The peer's utilities are, $V_1(d_{13}, d_{12}) = \ln(d_{13}) + 9\ln(d_{12})$, $V_2(d_{21}, d_{23}) = \ln(d_{21}) + 9\ln(d_{23})$, and $V_3(d_{32}, d_{31}) = \ln(d_{32}) + 9\ln(d_{31})$, where d_{ij} is the rate at which peer i downloads file f_j. The unique bilateral equilibrium is inefficient, because each peer is allocated a smaller rate of the file it values more.

These observations are intuitive: after all, exchange is far more restricted in a bilateral equilibrium than in a multilateral equilibrium. In the next section, we will focus on determining conditions under which a bilateral equilibrium yields a multilateral equilibrium.

We conclude this section by justifying our choice of pricing per peer instead of pricing per file. In the P2P setting we are considering, the two pricing schemes are equivalent in terms of equilibria, since the resource that is being priced is the upload capacity of a peer. A peer with multiple files will only upload his most "expensive" files at equilibrium. We chose to price per peer for simplicity. In the bilateral setting, pricing per file would require to have an exchange ratio $\gamma_{ij,fg}$ for each pair of files f, g that peers i, j can exchange, while pricing per peer only requires one exchange ratio for each pair of peers.

4   Robustness to Collusive Deviations

In this section we demonstrate that a bilateral equilibrium may not be robust to collusive deviations and show that a bilateral equilibrium corresponds to a multilateral equilibrium if and only if it is robust to deviations by coalitions of users. The following is a key step in establishing the relationship between bilateral and multilateral equilibrium. For clarity, all proofs are in the Appendix.

Proposition 1. *Consider a bilateral equilibrium with exchange ratios γ_{ij} for every pair of peers i, j. If there exist prices p_i for all $i \in N$ such that $\gamma_{ij} = p_i/p_j$ for all $i, j \in N$, then the bilateral equilibrium allocation is also a multilateral equilibrium allocation.*

This proposition is quite revealing: it shows that if exchange ratios are "fair," in the sense that they yield a unique price per peer, then the bilateral equilibrium allocation is also a multilateral equilibrium allocation, and thus is efficient.

We have already seen that a bilateral equilibrium need not exist and need not be Pareto efficient when it exists, whereas multilateral equilibria exist under general conditions and are Pareto efficient; thus, the two concepts are not equivalent. We now show that even an efficient bilateral equilibrium does not necessarily yield one price per peer, and thus is not always equivalent to a multilateral equilibrium.

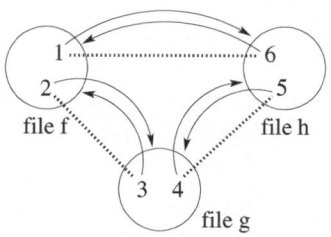

Fig. 2. Bilateral equilibrium for Ex.3. Peers $\{1,2\}$ have file f, peers $\{3,4\}$ have file g, and peers $\{5,6\}$ have file h. Solid arrows are drawn from a peer to its desired file, *e.g.*, 1 and 4 want h. Heavy dotted lines are between peers bartering at the unique bilateral equilibrium.

Example 3. There are 6 peers ($\{1,2,3,4,5,6\}$) and 3 files ($\{f,g,h\}$) in the system, with file allocation and demand as shown in Figure 2. The upload capacities of peers are $B_1 = 2$, $B_j = 1, \forall j \neq 1$. At the unique bilateral equilibrium, the following pairs exchange: $\{1,6\}$, $\{2,3\}$ and $\{4,5\}$, and the allocation is Pareto efficient. Thus for these pairs, the equilibrium exchange ratios must be $\gamma_{16} = 1/2$, $\gamma_{32} = 1$ and $\gamma_{54} = 1$.

The optimality conditions in the bilateral equilibrium must ensure that peer 1 does not wish to download from peer 5 instead of peer 6, which implies that we must have $\gamma_{15} \leq \gamma_{16} = 1/2$. Similarly, we must have $\gamma_{53} \leq \gamma_{54} = 1$, and $\gamma_{31} \leq \gamma_{32} = 1$. Note that we thus have $\gamma_{15}\gamma_{53}\gamma_{31} \leq 1/2$. However, this implies there do not exist prices per peer p_i such that $\gamma_{ij} = p_i/p_j$, since such a price vector would imply $\gamma_{15}\gamma_{53}\gamma_{31} = 1$. Thus the bilateral equilibrium cannot be a multilateral equilibrium.

Given the equilibrium exchange ratios of Example 3, peers $\{1,3,5\}$ can benefit by deviating together. By choosing upload rates $r'_{13} = 1/3, r'_{35} = 1/4, r'_{51} = 1/5$, while reducing upload rates to their original trading partners accordingly, each peer in $\{1,3,5\}$ obtains a download rate strictly larger than 1 (the download rate each of these peers gets at the bilateral equilibrium). For example, user 1 obtains a total download rate of $1/5$ (from user 5) plus $5/6$ (from user 6, who in turn gets $r'_{16} = 5/3$), which results in a rate greater than 1.

Inspired by this observation, we show next that if a bilateral equilibrium is robust to deviations by a coalition of peers, and if each peer is only uploading one file, then it corresponds to a multilateral equilibrium. We formalize this result adapting the notion of the *core* [16] to bilateral exchange. An allocation has the core property with respect to given exchange ratios if no coalition of peers can strictly improve the utility of all its members by bartering with peers outside the coalition, subject to the given exchange ratios. Inside the coalition, peers do not need to follow the exchange ratios, and they may allocate rates in any way subject to bandwidth constraints.

Definition 3. *Given exchange ratios* $\gamma = (\gamma_{ij}, i, j \in N)$, *an allocation* r *is feasible for a set of peers S with respect to* γ *if:*

(i) $r_{ijf} = 0$ *iff* $f \notin F_i$;
(ii) $\sum_{j,f} r_{ijf} \leq B_i$ *for all* $i \in S$;
(iii) $\sum_{i \in S} \sum_f r_{jif} = \sum_{i \in S} \gamma_{ij} \sum_f r_{ijf}$, *for all* $j \notin S$.

The first condition ensures that all peers only upload files they have. The second condition ensures that peers in S do not exceed their upload constraints. The third ensures that exchanges between the coalition S and each peer outside S take place at the given exchange ratios.

Definition 4. *Given fixed exchange ratios* γ, *a coalition* S *blocks an allocation* r^* *with respect to* γ *if there exists a feasible allocation* r *for* S *with respect to* γ *such that* $V_i(\sum_j r_{jif}, f \in T_i) > V_i(\sum_j r^*_{jif}, f \in T_i)$ *for all* $i \in S$.

Definition 5. *The allocation* r *has* the core property *with respect to exchange ratios* γ *if it can not be blocked by any coalition of peers.*

We note that the usual definition of the core in microeconomics [16] does not allow exchange with agents outside the coalition. Our definition of the core is distinct and more appropriate to model collusion in a bilateral exchange setting, as it depends on the exchange ratios.

We first show that the core property is satisfied by any multilateral equilibrium. This is a standard result from microeconomic theory [16]. However, our result is more general, since our core definition allows a coalition to exchange with peers outside the coalition, and thus there are more feasible allocations which may potentially block the multilateral equilibrium allocation.

Proposition 2. *Any multilateral equilibrium allocation has the core property with respect to the equilibrium exchange ratios* $\gamma_{ij} = p_i/p_j$.

We conclude that a bilateral equilibrium that does not have the core property can not correspond to a multilateral equilibrium. We next show that, when each peer is uploading one file, a bilateral equilibrium with the core property is a multilateral equilibrium. The insight is similar to Example 3: it can be shown that if no price vector exists such that $\gamma_{ij} = p_i/p_j$, then there must exist users $i_1, i_2, ..., i_k$ such that $\prod_{i=1}^{k} \gamma_{i,(i \bmod k)+1} < 1$. In that case, there is a coalition of k peers that can block the allocation.

Proposition 3. *Suppose* $|F_i| = 1$ *for all* $i \in N$. *If a bilateral equilibrium allocation* r^* *with exchange ratios* γ *such that* $\sum_j r^*_{jif} > 0$ *for all* $i \in N, f \in T_i$ *has the core property, then it is also a multilateral equilibrium allocation.*

A corollary of Proposition 3 is that if a bilateral equilibrium has the core property, then its allocation is Pareto efficient. Proposition 3 requires that $|F_i| = 1$ for all $i \in N$. The result holds more generally if each peer is uploading a unique file at the bilateral equilibrium (peers may have more files). Whether it holds for the general case where peers upload multiple files at the bilateral equilibrium remains an open problem.

5   Conclusions

This paper analyzes the efficiency and robustness gains that are enabled by price-based multilateral exchange. We identify the condition that a bilateral equilibrium needs to satisfy in order to correspond to a multilateral equilibrium. These results help clarify the tradeoffs inherent in choosing between bilateral and multilateral exchanges: simplicity in the former, and efficiency and robustness gains in the latter.

Our novel theoretical results provide insight into the gap between bilateral and multilateral exchange. Even though the two exchanges are compared theoretically in terms of equilibria in this paper, it is possible to design a system that practically realizes the benefits of multilateral exchange. In particular, since it is hard to know the equilibrium prices in advance, peers can update their prices according to supply and demand. A system for currency-backed content exchange is presented in [15].

References

[1] Bangeman, E.: P2P responsible for as much as 90 percent of all 'Net traffic. ArsTechnica (September 3, 2007)

[2] Adar, E., Huberman, B.: Free riding on Gnutella. First Monday 5(10) (2000)

[3] Hughes, D., Coulson, G., Walkerdine, J.: Free riding on Gnutella revisited: The bell tolls? IEEE Distributed Systems Online 6(6) (2005)

[4] Cohen, B.: Incentives build robustness in BitTorrent. In: Proc. Workshop on Economics of Peer-to-Peer Systems (2003)

[5] Piatek, M., Isdal, T., Anderson, T., Krishnamurthy, A., Venkataramani, A.: Do incentives build robustness in BitTorrent? In: Proc. Symposium on Networked Systems Design and Implementation (2007)

[6] Wu, F., Zhang, L.: Proportional response dynamics leads to market equilibrium. In: Proc. Symposium on Theory of Computing (2007)

[7] Jun, S., Ahamad, M.: Incentives in BitTorrent induce free riding. In: Proc. Workshop on the Economics of Information Security (2005)

[8] Locher, T., Moor, P., Schmid, S., Wattenhofer, R.: Free riding in BitTorrent is cheap. In: Proc. HotNets (2006)

[9] Sirivianos, M., Park, J.H., Chen, R., Yang, X.: Free-riding in BitTorrent networks with the large view exploit. In: Proc. International Workshop on Peer-to-Peer Systems (2007)

[10] Guo, L., Chen, S., Xiao, Z., Tan, E., Ding, X., Zhang, X.: Measurements, analysis, and modeling of BitTorrent-like systems. In: Proc. Internet Measurement Conference (2005)

[11] Gupta, M., Judge, P., Ammar, M.: A reputation system for peer-to-peer networks. In: Proc. Workshop on Network and Operating System Support for Digital Audio and Video (2003)

[12] Vishnumurthy, V., Chandrakumar, S., Sirer, E.G.: KARMA: A secure economic framework for P2P resource sharing. In: Proc. Workshop on the Economics of Information Security (2003)

[13] Sirivianos, M., Park, J.H., Yang, X., Jarecki, S.: Dandelion: Cooperative content distribution with robust incentives. In: Proc. USENIX Technical Conference (2007)

[14] Aperjis, C., Johari, R.: A peer-to-peer system as an exchange economy. In: Proc. GameNets (2006)

[15] Aperjis, C., Freedman, M.J., Johari, R.: The role of prices in peer-assisted content distribution. Technical report

[16] Mas-Colell, A., Whinston, M.D., Green, J.R.: Microeconomic Theory. Oxford University Press, Oxford (1995)

A Proofs

Proof of Proposition 1: Substituting $\gamma_{ij} = p_i/p_j$ in the fourth set of constraints of the Bilateral Peer Optimization problem, we get the constraints $p_j \sum_f r_{jif} = p_i \sum_f r_{ijf}$ for all j. The Multilateral Peer Optimization problem has a larger feasible region; however, the two optimization problem have the same optimal value. In particular, if r is feasible for the Multilateral Optimization problem of peer i, then we can construct r̄ such that (i) r̄ is feasible for the Bilateral Optimization problem of peer i, and (ii) r̄ gives the same utility as r to user i. For example, we can achieve this by setting $\bar{r}_{jif} = r_{jif}$ for all j, f and then choosing $\bar{r}_{ijf}$ for each j such that $\sum_f \bar{r}_{ijf} = (p_j/p_i) \sum_f \bar{r}_{jif}$. This shows that an optimal solution for the Bilateral Peer Optimization problem is also optimal for the Multilateral Peer Optimization problem, and concludes the proof. ∎

Proof of Proposition 2: Consider a competitive equilibrium and suppose that there exists a coalition S that blocks it and let r be the corresponding rate allocation. Then by Definition 4 and the Multilateral Optimization problem, $\sum_{j,f} p_j \cdot r_{jif} > p_i \cdot B_i, \forall i \in S$. Summing over all $i \in S$, $\sum_{i \in S} \sum_{j \in S} p_j \cdot \sum_f r_{jif} + \sum_{i \in S} \sum_{j \notin S} p_j \cdot \sum_f r_{jif} > \sum_{i \in S} p_i \cdot B_i$. Since $\gamma_{ij} = p_i/p_j$, condition (iii) of Definition 3 becomes $p_j \cdot \sum_{i \in S} \sum_f r_{jif} = \sum_{i \in S} p_i \cdot \sum_f r_{ijf}$ for all $i \in S$, $j \notin S$. Combining the two conditions and rearranging, $\sum_{i \in S} p_i \sum_{j,f} r_{ijf} > \sum_{i \in S} p_i \cdot B_i$, which contradicts condition (ii) of Definition 3.   ∎

Proof of Proposition 3: We first show that the exchange ratios in a bilateral equilibrium only depend on the files being exchanged, not on the peers' identities. Suppose that $f \in F_{i_1}$, $f \in F_{i_2}$, $g \in F_{j_1}$ and $g \in F_{j_2}$ and at the bilateral equilibrium, peers i_1 and j_1 exchange f and g, and i_2 and j_2 exchange f and g. Then,

$$\gamma_{i_1,j_1} \geq \gamma_{i_1,j_2} ; \; \gamma_{j_1,i_1} \geq \gamma_{j_1,i_2} ; \; \gamma_{i_2,j_2} \geq \gamma_{i_2,j_1} ; \; \gamma_{j_2,i_2} \geq \gamma_{j_2,i_1},$$

since i_1 exchanges with j_1 at equilibrium, not j_2; j_1 exchanges with i_1, not i_2; etc. Combining these inequalities with the fact $\gamma_{ij} = 1/\gamma_{ji}$, we conclude that $\gamma_{i_1,j_1} = \gamma_{i_1,j_2} = \gamma_{i_2,j_1} = \gamma_{i_2,j_2}$. When there is exchange between files f and g in a bilateral equilibrium we define γ_{fg} to be the unique value of the exchange ratio between files f and g.

We define the *bilateral equilibrium exchange graph* to have a node for every file, and an edge between two files if those files are exchanged at the bilateral equilibrium. Suppose that for every cycle $f_1, f_2, ..., f_k, f_1$ in the bilateral equilibrium exchange graph, we have $\prod_{i=1}^{k} \gamma_{f_i, f_{i+1}} = 1$.[1] Then we get a unique price for each file in the following way. We start from a file (say f_1) whose price we set equal to 1 and then take a minimum spanning tree of the graph. We move along the edges of this tree and set prices for other files, so that the exchange ratios are satisfied. In this way we get prices p_f for each file f. Since the optimization problem of peer i with $f \in F_i$ is not affected by γ_{fg} if $g \notin T_i$, we can derive prices per peer by setting $p_i = p_f$ for $f \in F_i$ which do not change the optimal rate allocations for peers. Thus, by Proposition 1, the bilateral equilibrium allocation is also a multilateral equilibrium allocation.

To complete the proof, it suffices to show that if there is a cycle $f_1, f_2, ..., f_k, f_1$ in the bilateral equilibrium exchange graph with $\prod_{i=1}^{k} \gamma_{f_i, f_{i+1}} < 1$, then there is a coalition that blocks the bilateral equilibrium allocation. Let i be some peer that uploads file f_i, and downloads file f_{i+1} at the bilateral equilibrium. It can be shown that the coalition $S = \{1, ..., k\}$ blocks the bilateral equilibrium allocation by demonstrating that there is a way to increase the rates $r_{i,i-1,f_i}$ for $i = 1, ..., k$ so that the utilities of all peers in S strictly increase. Due to space limitations, here we only sketch the proof for the case that $f_{i-1} \notin T_i$ for all $i \in S$. We provide the complete proof in [15].

If $f_{i-1} \notin T_i$ for all $i \in S$, then at the bilateral equilibrium $r^*_{i,i-1,f_i} = 0$ for all $i \in S$. By sending $r_{i,i-1,f_i}$ to peer $i-1$, peer i reduces the rate he gets from outside S by $\gamma_{f_i,f_{i+1}} \cdot r_{i,i-1,f_i}$. So, the coalition increases i's utility if and only if the rate he receives from S, i.e., $r_{i+1,i,f_{i+1}}$, is greater than $\gamma_{f_i,f_{i+1}} \cdot r_{i,i-1,f_i}$. To show that S blocks r^*, it suffices to find $r_{i+1,i,f_{i+1}} \leq B_{i+1}$, such that $r_{i+1,i,f_{i+1}} > \gamma_{f_i,f_{i+1}} \cdot r_{i,i-1,f_i}$, for all $i \in S$. This is possible because $\prod_i \gamma_{f_i,f_{i+1}} < 1$. In particular, we can choose small $\delta, \varepsilon > 0$, and set: $r_{1,k,f_1} = \delta$, $r_{i+1,i,f_{i+1}} = \gamma_{f_i,f_{i+1}} r_{i,i-1,f_i} + \varepsilon$, for all $i \in S$.   ∎

---

[1] We denote by f_{i+1} and f_{i-1} the files after and before file f_i with respect to the cycle $f_1, f_2, ..., f_k, f_1$.

Auctions for Resource Allocation in Overlay Networks

Pablo Belzarena[1], Andrés Ferragut[1,2], and Fernando Paganini[2]

[1] Universidad de la República
[2] Universidad ORT
Montevideo, Uruguay

Abstract. The paper studies the problem of allocating bandwidth resources of a Service Overlay Network, to optimize revenue. Clients bid for network capacity in periodically held auctions, under the condition that resources allocated in an auction are reserved for the entire duration of the connection, not subject to future contention. This makes the optimal allocation coupled over time, which we formulate as a Markov Decision Process (MDP). Studying first the single resource case, we develop a receding horizon approximation to the optimal MDP policy, using current revenue and the expected revenue in the next step to make bandwidth assignments. A second approximation is then found, suitable for generalization to the network case, where bids for different routes compete for shared resources. In that case we develop a distributed implementation of the auction, and demonstrate its performance through simulations.

1 Introduction

In recent years, many types of "overlay" networks have been proposed for the Internet. These overlays include content delivery networks, peer-to-peer file sharing, some voice-over-IP services, and testbed networks such as PlanetLab. A particular architecture called Service Overlay Network (SON) [6] has been proposed to deploy value-added Internet services with end-to-end quality of service (QoS). The basic components of the SON architecture are service gateways located in domain boundaries, and a network of tunnels acquired from the underlying domains with guaranteed bandwidth. Through this overlay, a client with good local connectivity in one domain can secure a high QoS connection with a remote domain. The overlay operator invests in the infrastructure and leased bandwidth to offer high-value services, for instance through distributed content servers; a profitable sale of this capacity is thus essential. In this paper we study an access control policy based on auctions for this purpose, where users bid for a service connection and the network gives access to the best bids to maximize its payoff, subject to the QoS constraints for the admitted clients.

Resource sharing policies based on auctions have been analyzed by different previous works [7],[5],[8],[10],[3]. One main difference in our approach is that we impose the condition that once bandwidth has been allocated in an auction, the successful bidder is guaranteed to hold it for the duration of his/her connection. Previous work on auctions allows future bidders to compete with incumbent

E. Altman and A. Chaintreau (Eds.): NET-COOP 2008, LNCS 5425, pp. 9–16, 2009.

ones, albeit given the latter some advantage. Our application scenario does not allow this: consider selling video-on-demand content about 100 minutes long, in auctions every 5 minutes. A consumer will not purchase the service if he/she faces the risk of losing the connection close to the end of the movie.

Reserving bandwidth over multiple auctions means that the operator must assume the risk of future bids. Optimizing revenue with this risk becomes a stochastic dynamic optimization problem, that we formulate as a Markov decision process (MDP) [1,9]. The optimization involves a tradeoff between the revenue of the current auction, and the expected value of bids the operator will miss in future auctions if it runs out of resources. In Section 2 we analyze the above problem in the case of a single link, and develop a series of approximations to the optimal policy. The aim of our approximations is to allow a distributed implementation of the policy over an arbitrary network topology, where bids are received at the edge for end-to-end services, and the network optimizes the overall revenue. This is described in Section 3, and the method is evaluated by simulation. Conclusions given in Section 4.

2   Auctions for One Link

In this section we consider auctions for one access link. We make a few simplifying assumptions: all consumers bid for the same amount (unit) of bandwidth, and the link has capacity for C such connections. Bids are collected for a period of time T, and an auction is held; we assume for simplicity that the number N of bids is given, and bids are drawn from a known probability distribution. We denote by $b_k^{(1)} \geq b_k^{(2)} \geq \cdots \geq b_k^{(N)}$ the ordered bids in decreasing order that participate in the auction at time kT. The bids are for the entire duration of the service, and this is a first-price auction: the admitted users will pay their bid.

Let a_k represent the number of admitted connections in auction k. The revenue from this auction is then

$$U_{b_k}(a_k) := \sum_{i=1}^{a_k} b_k^{(i)}. \tag{1}$$

The function $U_b(a)$ is defined above for integer values of a; it is also convenient to extend it to a function of $a \in \mathbb{R}$, by linear interpolation. The latter function is increasing and concave in a. We also define $\overline{U}(a) = E[U_b(a)]$, where the expectation is over the distribution of the bids b; i.e., we replace the current bids in (1) by their expectation. This is also increasing, piecewise linear and concave.

We will model the connection durations as independent exponential random variables, of mean $1/\mu$. Therefore at the end of the period T each connection has probability $p := e^{-\mu T}$ of remaining active for the following period. While in practice one would have more deterministic information of the service duration, the above allows for a Markovian treatment of the allocation problem.

Let x_k denote the number of connections active at $t = kT^-$, i.e. before the k-th auction. The system admits a_k new connections, $0 \leq a_k \leq C - x_k$, taking the total to $x_k + a_k$. By the next auction period, $t = (k+1)T^-$, the number of active connections x_{k+1} follows then a binomial distribution with parameters

$x_k + a_k$ and p. Specifically, $P[x_{k+1} = i|x_k, a_k] = \binom{x_k+a_k}{i}p^i(1-p)^{x_k+a_k-i}$. We are ready to state our design objective.

Optimal revenue problem: Maximize $\lim_n \frac{1}{n}\sum_{k=0}^{n-1} E[U_{b_k}(a_k)]$.

Here the expectation is over two sources of randomness: the vector of bids b_k and the departure process. The constraints are $0 \leq a_k \leq C - x_k$ where x_k follows the binomial transition dynamics defined above. We can also consider the discounted version: Maximize $\sum_{k=0}^{\infty} \rho^k E[U_{b_k}(a_k)]$, where $0 < \rho < 1$.

Both of these are Markov Decision Processes (MDPs) [2,9]. The *state* at time k is $s_k = (x_k, b_k)$, i.e. the current occupation and the incoming bids. Based on this state, the *action* $a_k = a(s_k)$ decides how many bids to accept. Solving the MDP requires finding the *policy* $a(s)$ that results in a minimum cost. In the discounted case $\rho < 1$, this policy satisfies the Bellman equation

$$V^*(x_0, b) = \max_{a \in \mathcal{A}_s} \{U_b(a) + \rho E[V^*(x_1, b')]\}, \qquad (2)$$

where V^* is the value function and the expectation is taken over the binomial distribution of $x_1|(x_0, a)$ and the distribution of the next bid b'. The state-dependent constraints are $\mathcal{A}_s = \{0 \leq a \leq C - x_0\}$. For $\rho = 1$, V^* satisfying (2) is no longer the optimal cost, but (2) still characterizes the optimal action $a(s)$.

It is in general difficult to solve the Bellman equation; a commonly used strategy is the *value iteration* $V_{m+1}(x_0, b) := \max_{a \in \mathcal{A}_s}\{U_b(a) + \rho E[V_m(x_1, b')]\}$; starting with an arbitrary $V_0(s)$, $V_m(s)$ converges to $V^*(s)$, and the corresponding maximizing action converges to the optimal action [2].

Receding horizon approximation. We will use initial steps of the value iteration to approximate the optimal policy. Starting from $V_0 \equiv 0$, we have

$$V_1(x_0, b) = \max_{a \leq C - x_0} U_b(a) = U_b(C - x_0). \qquad (3)$$

This first step gives the "myopic" policy $a = C - x_0$, that sells all available capacity disregarding the future. To improve on it, we take a second step in the value iteration:

$$\begin{aligned} V_2(x_0, b) &= \max_{a \leq C - x_0} \{U_b(a) + \rho E[V_1(x_1, b')]\} \\ &= \max_{a \leq C - x_0} \{U_b(a) + \rho E[U_{b'}(C - x_1)]\} \\ &= \max_{a \leq C - x_0} \{U_b(a) + \rho E_{x_1}\overline{U}(C - x_1)]\}. \end{aligned} \qquad (4)$$

In (4), the expectation over the random bid b' is included in $\overline{U}$ defined above; the remaining expectation is over $x_1 \sim \text{Bin}(x_0 + a, p)$. The policy (4) can be given a *receding horizon* interpretation: the decision considers the current revenue plus the expected revenue of looking one step ahead, assuming all available capacity will be sold off at that time. This decision is then applied recursively; thus the future is taken into account at a limited level of complexity.

The first term in (4) increases with a. To characterize the second, we rewrite it as follows. Consider the function $W(i) = \overline{U}(C) - \overline{U}(C-i)$, piecewise linear and

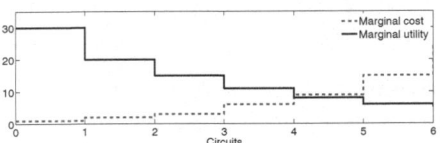

Fig. 1. Marginal utility versus marginal cost

convex in i. Indeed, the increments $W(i+1) - W(i) = E[b^{(C-i)}]$, (expectation of the $(C-i)$-th largest offer) are increasing in i. Now define $\overline{W}(x) = E[W(x_1)]$, where $x_1 \sim \text{Bin}(x, p)$, again linearly interpolated for non-integer x. The next statement follows from a stochastic comparison argument, omitted for brevity.

Proposition 1. $\overline{W}(x)$ *is increasing and convex in* x.

With this notation, our one-step ahead optimization can be rewritten as

$$\max_{a \le C - x_0} U_b(a) - \rho\overline{W}(x_0 + a), \tag{5}$$

a convex optimization problem. In it, $\overline{W}(x_0 + a)$ plays the role of a *cost function* that makes the decision at the current time "internalize" the impact on future decisions. $\overline{W}(x_0 + a)$ measures the expected loss of revenue in the auction at time T from having left $x_0 + a$ occupied circuits at time $t = 0^+$.

It is now straightforward to determine the optimal policy $a(x_0, b)$. To optimize over a we plot the derivatives of $U_b(a)$ and $\rho\overline{W}(x_0 + a)$ (marginal utilities and costs) and look for a crossing point. This is depicted in Figure 1. The marginal utilities are just the current bids in decreasing order. The marginal costs represent the value of leaving one more free circuit for the next auction.

The increasing marginal costs $\overline{w}_i = \rho(\overline{W}(i) - \overline{W}(i-1))$ act as successive thresholds for accepting bids. The acceptance policy is the value a such that for $i = x_0 + a$ we have $b^{(1)} \ge b^{(2)} \ge \cdots \ge b^{(a)} \ge \overline{w}_i > b^{(a+1)}$. In words: to accept a bids, the *lowest* one must exceed $\overline{w}_i$ for $i = x_0 + a$. To accept one more, we require a *more demanding* threshold $\overline{w}_{i+1}$ on this (smaller) bid[1].

From the binomial distributions $j_1 \sim \text{Bin}(i, p)$, $j_2 \sim \text{Bin}(i-1, p)$ and some combinatorics we obtain for the thresholds the expression

$$\overline{w}_i = \rho[E(W(j_1)) - E(W(j_2))] = \rho \, p \sum_{l=0}^{i-1} E(b^{(C-l)})\binom{i-1}{l}p^l(1-p)^{i-1-l}. \tag{6}$$

Based on knowledge of ρ, p, and the distribution of bids, this expression could be calculated offline and used for carrying out auctions with the policy (4).

Examples: We evaluate the previous results in a few simple cases (for $\rho = 1$).

For $C = 1$, there is a single link cost $\overline{w}_1 = pE(b^{(1)})$, that acts as an admission threshold for bids received when the circuit becomes empty. For instance in the case of N bids, uniformly distributed in $[0, b_{max}]$, we have $\overline{w}_1 = p\frac{N}{N+1}b_{max}$.

---

[1] Since b's are random, the curves of Fig. 1 will generically cross at a single point.

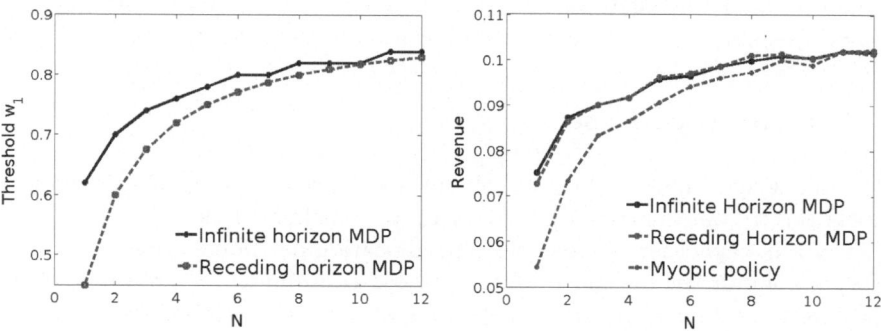

Fig. 2. Optimal MDP, receding horizon and myopic policies. $C = 1$, $p = 0.1$.

If the link has capacity $C = 2$, there are two marginal costs: $\overline{w}_1 = pE(b^{(2)})$ for occupying the first connection, and $\overline{w}_2 = p(E(b^{(2)})(1 - p) + E(b^{(1)})p)$ for occupying the second. Again, for uniform in $[0, b_{max}]$ bids this becomes

$$\overline{w}_1 = p\,\frac{N - 1}{N + 1}\,b_{max}; \qquad \overline{w}_2 = p\,\frac{(N - 1)(1 - p) + Np}{N + 1}\,b_{max}.$$

We now compare by simulations our receding horizon policy with the optimal infinite-horizon MDP, in the case of one circuit ($C = 1$). In this simple case, the latter is also a threshold policy on the bids, but the optimal threshold does not have a simple formula; we computed it numerically through the value iteration algorithm from [4]. On the left in Figure 2 we show the acceptance thresholds for both policies: we see the infinite horizon threshold is more demanding. On the right we show the average utility obtained empirically by simulation of these two policies. Results are very similar. Therefore, in this case we have managed to extract almost the optimal utility just be looking one-step ahead with the policy. On the other hand, if we apply the myopic policy that always fills the link, the right-hand side plot shows there is a clear loss in utility.

A further approximation. Our ultimate goal is to perform an auction over a general network, where bids appear at different routes and are coupled by scarce resources at links. The stochastic calculations involved in (6) appear difficult to generalize, so we adopt a second approximation, replacing the function $\overline{W}(x)$ in (5) by something easier to compute. Namely, define $\phi(x) = W(E[x_1])$ for $x_1 \sim \text{Bin}(x, p)$. Since $W(\cdot)$ is convex, this underestimates the one-step cost from before, $\phi(x) \leq \overline{W}(x)$. Nevertheless, if C is large the binomial distribution will be concentrated around its mean and the error is moderate. In return, we have the simple expression $\phi(x) = W(px) = \overline{U}(C) - \overline{U}(C - px)$. This is still piecewise linear and convex, but easier to compute. The second approximation to the optimal policy is given by $\max_{a \leq C - x_0} U_b(a) - \rho\phi(x_0 + a)$.

Equivalently, we can rewrite the above as the convex program

$$\max\ U_b(a) + \rho\overline{U}(z),$$
$$\text{subject to}\quad x_0 + a \leq C, \quad p(x_0 + a) + z \leq C. \tag{7}$$

At the optimum, the slack variable z will satisfy the constraint with equality, i.e. $z = C - p(x_0 + a)$ is the expected allocation in the next interval.

3   The Network Case

In the following, l indexes the network links, r the routes across the network. R denotes the routing matrix, $R_{lr} = 1$ iff route r includes link l. $c = (c_l)$ is the vector of link capacities. We describe the allocation decision at time $t = 0$.

Define column vectors x_0, a, and z, whose coordinates per route r denote respectively the rate x_0^r from previous occupation, the rate allocation a^r at the current auction, and the expected allocation z^r in the following auction $(t = T)$. We also define the piecewise linear utility $U_{b^r}(a^r)$ based on current bids (1), and the utility $\overline{U}_r(z^r)$ based on expected bids. Let $p^r = e^{-\mu^r T}$ be the probability that a connection active at $t = 0$ will remain active at $t = T$; $P = \mathrm{diag}(p^r)$ is the corresponding diagonal matrix. Thus, $P(a + x_0)$ is the expected input rate vector at $t = T^-$. The network generalization of (7) is

$$\max \sum_r \left[U_{b^r}(a^r) + \rho \overline{U}_r(z^r) \right],$$

$$\text{subject to} \quad R(a + x_0) \le c; \qquad RP(a + x_0) + Rz \le c. \qquad (8)$$

This optimization can also be rewritten as one for the current allocation a with a convex cost function $\phi(x_0 + a)$ that represents the optimization in z. However, here the cost function would be coupled over the network. A better way to solve (8) is by duality. Consider the Lagrangian $L(a, z, \alpha, \beta)$ given by

$$L = \sum_r \left[U_{b^r}(a^r) + \rho \overline{U}_r(z^r) \right] + \alpha^T (c - R(a + x_0)) + \beta^T (c - Rz - RP(a + x_0))$$

$$= \sum_r [U_{b^r}(a^r) - (q^r + p^r v^r)a^r] + [\rho \overline{U}_r(z^r) - v^r z^r] + \alpha^T (c - Rx_0) + \beta^T (c - RPx_0).$$

Here, α and β are the vectors of Lagrange multipliers (prices) for each of the two constraints, and we have defined the aggregate prices per route $q = R^T \alpha$, $v = R^T \beta$. We can solve the convex program through a dual, gradient projection algorithm similar to those used in the congestion control literature [11], but with additional prices. The algorithm takes the following form (in continuous time):

$$a^r = \arg\max_{a^r}[U_{b^r}(a^r) - (q^r + p^r v^r)a^r]; \qquad \dot{\alpha} = [R(a + x_0) - c]_\alpha^+;$$

$$z^r = \arg\max_{z^r}[\rho \overline{U}_r(z^r) - v^r z^r]; \qquad \dot{\beta} = [RP(a + x_0) + Rz - c]_\beta^+.$$

An important difference with the congestion control case is that here the algorithm should take place in the *control plane* prior to the allocation of resources. Despite this difference, we can still obtain a *distributed* computation by message passing between the network links, and a broker entity at the ingress node of route r. The maximization for a^r amounts simply to comparing the bids with

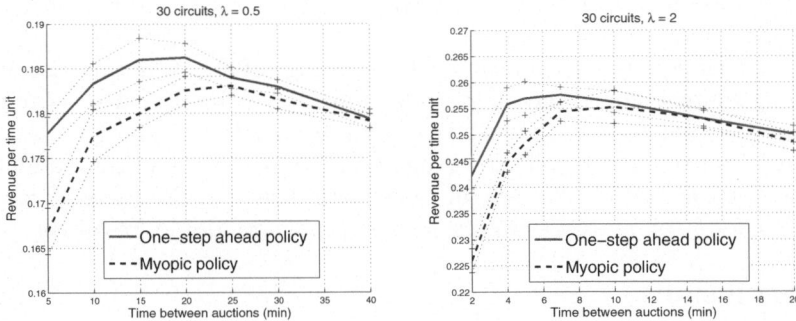

Fig. 3. One link situation: 30 circuits, offer arrival rate $\lambda = 0.5$ (left) and $\lambda = 2$ (right). Dotted lines are 5% confidence intervals.

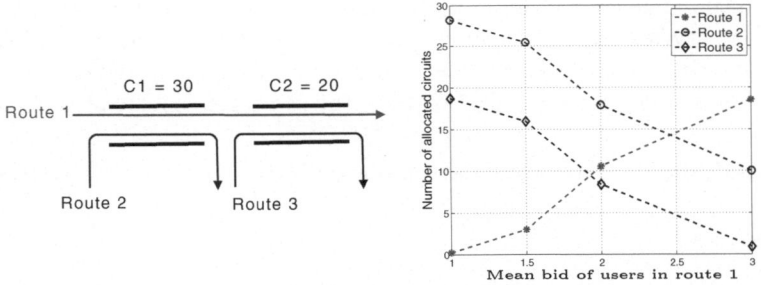

Fig. 4. Linear network, allocation as a function of the mean bid $\bar{b}$ of route 1

the threshold price $q^r + p^r v^r$. Solving for z^r involves the expected bids, and the price v^r/ρ. We must allow time after closing the auction for this distributed algorithm to settle on an allocation vector a.

It is useful to compare this algorithm with an implementation of the myopic policy which optimizes the first term in (8); the latter would involve only the variables a, α, but a very similar overhead in terms of message passing.

Simulations. To evaluate the proposed algorithm we present some simulation studies, carried out on a flow-level simulator we developed in Java.

First, we compare the one-step ahead policy (7) with the myopic one (3) in a single link case, with $C = 30$ circuits. Auctions take place every T minutes, and bids arrive periodically with fixed intensity λ, totalling $N = \lambda T$ bids per auction. Bids are independent and uniformly distributed in $[0, 1]$; rejected bids are discarded. Job duration is $exp(\mu)$ with $1/\mu = 100$ minutes.

We simulate both policies and compare the respective revenues, for several values of T which is a critical design parameter: enlarging T will allow more bids per auction, hence better ones, but decrease the auction rate. Results are shown in Fig. 3 for two different values of λ. In both cases, the one-step ahead policy outperforms the myopic one, as expected; and as remarked before, the gain is achieved with minor extra overhead.

Our second study uses the linear network topology of Fig. 4. In this case, users in the long route 1 should pay more to be allocated a circuit, since it occupies two links. We used $N = 10$ uniform bids with mean 1 for the short routes, and with mean $\bar{b}$ for route 1. Fig. 4 shows the mean number of connections admitted by the auction algorithm, for several values of $\bar{b}$. If $\bar{b} = 1$, the users in route 1 starve, but for $\bar{b} \approx 2$ all routes receive a comparable fraction of resources.

4   Conclusions

In this work we proposed an auction mechanism to assign resources in overlay networks. We formulated the problem of maximizing operator revenue, and found near-optimal policies that can be computed via convex optimization, and allow a distributed implementation over a network. In future work we will study some natural extensions: random numbers of bids per auction, bidding for heterogeneous services which consume different amounts of bandwidth, learning an unknown distribution of bids over time, and multiple-step extensions to the receding horizon policy. We will also study the strategic aspects of the auction.

Acknowledgment. This work was supported by a grant from PDT-Uruguay.

References

1. Altman, E.: Applications of Markov Decision Processes in Communication Networks: a Survey. In: Feinberg, E., Shwartz, A. (eds.) Markov Decision Processes, Models, Methods, Directions, and Open Problems, pp. 488–536. Kluwer, Dordrecht (2001)
2. Bertsekas, D.P.: Dynamic Programming: Deterministic and Stochastic Models. Prentice-Hall, Englewood Cliffs (1987)
3. Dramitinos, M., Stamoulis, G.D., Courcoubetis, C.: An auction mechanism for allocating the bandwidth of networks to their users. Computer Networks 51 (2007)
4. Chads, I., Cros, M.-J., Garcia, F., Sabbadin, R.: Markov Decision Process Toolbox for MATLAB,
   http://www.inra.fr/internet/Departements/MIA/T//MDPtoolbox/
5. Dramitinos, M., Stamoulis, G., Courcoubetis, C.: Auction-based resource reservation in 2.5/3G Networks. Mobile Networks and Apps. 9, 557–566 (2004)
6. Duan, Z., Zhang, Z.-L., Hou, Y.T.: Service Overlay Networks: SLAs, QoS and Bandwidth Provisioning. IEEE/ACM Trans. on Networking, 870–883 (2003)
7. Lazar, A.A., Semret, N.: Design and Analysis of the Progressive Second Price auction for Network Bandwidth Sharing. Telecommunications Systems (2000)
8. Maillé, P., Tuffin, B.: Pricing the internet with multibid auctions. IEEE/ACM Trans. Netw. 14(5), 992–1004 (2006)
9. Puterman, M.L.: Markov Decision Processes. Wiley, New Jersey (2005)
10. Reichl, P., Wrzaczek, S.: Equilibrium Market Prices for Multi-Period Auctions of Internet Resources. In: MMB 2004, pp. 25–34 (2004)
11. Srikant, R.: The Mathematics of Internet Congestion Control. Birkhäuser, Basel (2004)

Marketing in a Random Network

Hamed Amini[1], Moez Draief[2], and Marc Lelarge[1]

[1] INRIA & ENS, Paris
[2] Imperial College, London

Abstract. Viral marketing takes advantage of preexisting social networks among customers to achieve large changes in behaviour. Models of influence spread have been studied in a number of domains, including the effect of "word of mouth" in the promotion of new products or the diffusion of technologies. A social network can be represented by a graph where the nodes are individuals and the edges indicate a form of social relationship. The flow of influence through this network can be thought of as an increasing process of active nodes: as individuals become aware of new technologies, they have the potential to pass them on to their neighbours. The goal of marketing is to trigger a large cascade of adoptions. In this paper, we develop a mathematical model that allows to analyze the dynamics of the cascading sequence of nodes switching to the new technology. To this end we describe a continuous-time and a discrete-time models and analyse the proportion of nodes that adopt the new technology over time.

Keywords: Models of contagion, random graphs.

1 Introduction

With consumers showing increasing resistance to traditional forms of advertising, marketers have turned to alternate strategies like *viral marketing*. Viral marketing exploits existing social networks by encouraging customers to share product information with their friends. Social networks are graphs in which nodes represent individuals and edges represent relations between them. To illustrate viral marketing, consider a company that wishes to promote its new instant messenger (IM) system [10]. A promising way would be through popular social network such as Myspace: by convincing several persons to adopt the new IM system, the company can obtain an effective marketing campaign and diffuse the new system over the network.

If we assume that "convincing" a person to "spread" the new technology costs money, then a natural problem is to detect the influential members of the network who can trigger a cascade of influence in the most effective way [2], [7]. In this work, we consider a slightly different problem: the marketer has no knowledge of the social network. Hence he will not be able to detect the most influential individuals and his only solution is to "convince" a fraction of the total population. However, the marketer can still use the structure of the underlying network by targeting the neighbours of the adopters. There are a number of

E. Altman and A. Chaintreau (Eds.): NET-COOP 2008, LNCS 5425, pp. 17–25, 2009.
© Springer-Verlag Berlin Heidelberg 2009

incentive programs around this idea: each time an individual chooses the new technology, he is given the opportunity to send e-mail to friends with a special offer; if the friend goes on to buy it, each of the individuals receives a small cash bonus.

In this paper, we develop a mathematical model that allows to analyze the dynamics of the cascading sequence of nodes switching to the new technology. To this end we describe a continuous-time and a discrete-time models and analyze the proportion of nodes that adopt the new technology over time. In the continuous setting we derive a general bound for the proportion of new adopters in terms global graph properties, namely the spectral radius and the minimum degree. In the discrete setting we show that the proportion of new adapters is the solution of a fixed point equation. To this end we examine the case of regular trees, and prove that our approach carries over to random regular graphs. We extend our model to the general threshold model [7] and to sparse random graphs. We conclude by presenting a framework that enables the control of the marketing policy and discuss other possible applications.

2   Model

We consider a set of n agents represented by an undirected graph structure $G = (V, E)$ accounting for their interaction. For $i, j \in V$, we write $i \sim j$ if $(i, j) \in E$ and we say that agents i and j are neighbours. As in [14], we consider binary models where each agent may choose between two possible strategies that we denote by A and B. Let us introduce a game-theoretic diffusion model proposed by Morris [12]: Whenever two neighbours in the graph opt for strategy A they receive a payoff q_A, if they both choose B they receive a payoff q_B, and they receive nothing if they choose opposite strategies. The payoff of an agent corresponds to the sum of its payoffs with each of its neighbours.

Initially all nodes play A except for a small number of nodes that are forced to adopt strategy B. The nodes that started with strategy A will subsequently apply best-response updates. More precisely, these nodes will be repeatedly applying the following rule: switch to B if enough of your neighbours have already adopted B. There can be a cascading sequence of nodes switching to B such that a network-wide equilibrium is reached in the limit. This equilibrium may involve uniformity with all nodes adopting B or it may involve coexistence, with the nodes partitioned into a set adopting B and a set sticking to A.

The state of agent i is represented by X_i; $X_i = 0$ if player i plays strategy A and $X_i = 1$ otherwise. Hence $\sum_{j \sim i} X_j$ is the number of neighbours of i playing strategy B and $\sum_{j \sim i}(1 - X_j)$ is the number of neighbors of i playing strategy A.

We now describe the economic model for the agents. Recall that the payoff for a $A - A$ edge is q_A, for a $B - B$ edge is q_B and for a $A - B$ edge is 0. We assume that if an agent chooses A, his payoff is just the sum of the payoffs obtained on each of his incident edges but if he chooses B, his payoff is the sum of these payoffs increased by an amount $u \geq 0$ plus a bonus of $r \geq 0$. Now the total payoff for an agent is given by

$$S_i^A = q_A \sum_{j \sim i} (1 - X_j) \quad \text{for strategy } A,$$

$$S_i^B = r + (q_B + u) \sum_{j \sim i} X_j \quad \text{for strategy } B. \tag{1}$$

We consider that q_A and q_B are fixed and correspond to the level of performance of the technologies A and B.

By (1), we have $S_i^B \leq S_i^A$ iff

$$r + (q_B + u) \sum_{j \sim i} X_j \leq q_A \sum_{j \sim i} (1 - X_j) \quad \Leftrightarrow \quad \sum_{j \sim i} X_j \leq \theta(d_i), \tag{2}$$

with $\theta(d) := \frac{q_A d - r}{q_A + q_B + u}$ and d_i is the degree (number of neighbours) of i. We now explain the dynamics of our model for the spread of strategy B in the network as time t evolves. We consider a fixed network G (not evolving in time) and let all agents play A for $t < 0$. At time $t = 0$, some agents are forced to strategy B. These agents will always play strategy B, hence the dynamics described below does not apply to these initially forced agents. We encode the initial population forced to strategy B by a vector χ, where $\chi_i = 1$ if agent i is forced to B and $\chi_i = 0$ otherwise. We will assume that the vector $\chi = (\chi_i)_{i \in V}$ is a sequence of i.i.d. Bernoulli random variables with parameter α.

3   Continuous-Time Dynamic

We first consider the following continuous version of the contagion model. Assume that each non infected node i updates its state at rate 1 and it holds on to strategy A if (2) is satisfied and switches to B if $\sum_{j \sim i} X_j(t) > \theta(d_i)$. The state at time t is represented by a vector $X(t)$. Denote by A the adjacency matrix of the graph G and let $\lambda_1(A)$ the spectral radius of A, namely, its largest eigenvalue and by d_{min} the minimum degree of graph G. In addition we will assume that the graph is connected so that $d_{min} \geq 1$ and $\lambda_1(A)$ has multiplicity one. Therefore we have, $X_i(0) = \chi_i$, for all $i \in V$, and

$$X_i : 0 \to 1 \quad \text{at rate } \mathbb{1} \left(\sum_j A_{ij} X_j(t) > \theta(d_i) \right).$$

Note that $\mathbb{1} \left(\sum_j A_{ij} X_j(t) > \theta(d_i) \right) \leq \frac{\sum_j A_{ij} X_j(t)}{\theta(d_i)}$. We now consider the continuous time Markov process $Z(t) = (Z_i(t))_{i \in V}$, with $Z(0) = X(0)$, and transition rate:

$$Z_i : k \to k + 1 \quad \text{at rate } \frac{\sum_{j=1}^n A_{ij} Z_j(t)}{\theta(d_{min})},$$

standard coupling arguments yield $X(t) \leq_{st} Z(t)$ for all $t \geq 0$, where $X \leq_{st} Z$ denotes that Z stochastically dominates X. This implies that $\sum_{i=1}^n \mathbb{E}(X_i(t)) \leq \sum_{i=1}^n \mathbb{E}(Z_i(t))$. Moreover, the transition rates of the process Z are such that

$$\frac{d\mathbb{E}[Z(t)]}{dt} = \frac{A}{\theta(d_{min})}\mathbb{E}[Z(t)],$$

Hence

$$\mathbb{E}[Z(t)] = e^{\frac{t}{\theta(d_{min})}A}\,\mathbb{E}[Z(0)]. \tag{3}$$

Using Cauchy-Schwartz inequality, we obtain that $\sum_{i=1}^{n}\mathbb{E}(Z_i(t)) \leq \|\mathbb{E}(Z(t))\|_2\|1\|_2$. Combining this with (3), we have that

Theorem 1. *Let $\beta(t)$ be the proportion of nodes that opted for strategy B by time t. Then*

$$\beta(t) := \frac{\sum_{i=1}^{n}\mathbb{E}(X_i(t))}{n} \leq \alpha e^{\frac{\lambda_1(A)}{\theta(d_{min})}t}.$$

Moreover if the G is a regular graph with degree Δ, then, using the spectral decomposition of the matrix $e^{\frac{t}{\theta(\Delta)}A}$, we have that

$$\beta(t) \leq \frac{\alpha}{\Delta}e^{\frac{\Delta}{\theta(\Delta)}t}$$

The above result states that the number of nodes that have adopted B increases at most exponentially in time and that the speed is given by $\frac{\lambda_1(A)}{\theta(d_{min})}$. Similar results have been found in [4] in the case of the Susceptible-Infected-Susceptible (SIS) epidemic.

As a matter of example for Erdös-Rényi graphs $G(n,p)$ with parameters n and p in the regime $\log(n) << np$, Theorem 1 yields $\beta(t) \leq \alpha e^{\frac{np}{\theta(np)}t}$ with high probability.

In the next section, we describe a discrete-time version of our contagion model for which we derive more accurate results for the proportion of B-adopters and illustrate the coexistence of the two strategies.

4   Discrete-Time Dynamic

The state of the network at time t is described by the vector $(X_i(t))_{i\in V}$, $t \in \mathbb{N}$. We have $X_i(0) = \chi_i$ and $X_i(t) \geq \chi_i$. Then at each time step $t \geq 1$, each agent applies the best-response update: if $S_i^B > S_i^A$ then he chooses B and if not then he chooses A. It is readily seen that

$$1 - X_i(t+1) = (1 - \chi_i)\mathbb{1}\left(S_i^B(t) \leq S_i^A(t)\right). \tag{4}$$

4.1   Diffusion Process on the Infinite Regular Tree

Let $T(\Delta)$ be an infinite Δ-regular tree with nodes $\emptyset, 1, 2, \ldots$, with a fixed root $\emptyset$. For a node i, we denote by $\mathrm{gen}(i) \in \mathbb{N}$ the generation of i, i.e. the length of the minimal path from $\emptyset$ to i. Also we denote $i \to j$ if i belongs to the children of j, i.e. $\mathrm{gen}(i) = \mathrm{gen}(j) + 1$ and j is on the minimal path from $\emptyset$ to i. For an edge (i, j) with $i \to j$, we denote by $T_{i \to j}$ the sub-tree of T with root i obtained by the deletion of edge (i, j) from T.

For a given vector χ, we say that node $i \neq \emptyset$ is infected from $T_{i \to j}$ if the node i switches to B in $T_{i \to j} \bigcup \{(i, j)\}$ with the same vector χ for $T_{i \to j}$ and the strategy A for j. We denote by $Y_i(t)$ the corresponding indicator function with value 1 if i is infected from $T_{i \to j}$ at time t and 0 otherwise.

Proposition 1. *We have*

$$1 - X_\emptyset(t+1) = (1 - \chi_\emptyset)\mathbb{1}\left(\sum_{i \sim \emptyset} Y_i(t) \le \theta(\Delta)\right). \tag{5}$$

The representation (5) is crucial to our analysis. In fact, thanks to the tree structure, the random variables $(Y_i(t), i \sim \emptyset)$ are independent of each other and identically distributed. More precisely, a simple induction shows that (4) becomes, for $i \neq \emptyset$:

$$1 - Y_i(t+1) = (1 - \chi_i)\mathbb{1}\left(\sum_{j \to i} Y_j(t) \le \theta(\Delta)\right). \tag{6}$$

Note that (6) allows to compute all the $Y_i(t)$ recursively, starting with $Y_i(0) = \chi_i$. It is then easy to compute their distribution from (6). We summarize this result in the next proposition.

Proposition 2. *For t fixed, the sequence $(Y_i(t), i \sim \emptyset)$ is a sequence of i.i.d. Bernoulli random variables with parameter $h(t)$ given by $h(0) = \alpha$ and, for $t \ge 0$,*

$$h(t+1) = \mathbb{P}(Y_i(t+1) = 1) = 1 - (1-\alpha)g_{\Delta-1,\theta(\Delta)}(h(t)),$$

where $g_{k,s}(x) = \mathbb{P}(Bin(k,x) \le s)$. $Bin(k,x)$ corresponds to the binomial distribution with parameters k and x.

Combining Propositions 1 and 2, we obtain that

Theorem 2. *$X_\emptyset(t)$ is a Bernoulli random variable with parameter $\tilde{h}(t)$ given by*

$$\mathbb{P}(X_\emptyset(t+1) = 1) = \tilde{h}(t+1) = 1 - (1-\alpha)g_{\Delta,\theta(\Delta)}(h(t)). \tag{7}$$

Moreover let h^* the smallest solution of the following fixed point equation

$$h = 1 - (1-\alpha)g_{\Delta-1,\theta(\Delta)}(h). \tag{8}$$

Suppose $0 \le \theta(\Delta) < \Delta - 2$. There exists $\alpha_{crit} < 1$ such that for all $\alpha > \alpha_{crit}$, the fixed point equation (8) has a unique solution $h^* = 1$ and for all $\alpha < \alpha_{crit}$ it has three solutions $h^* < h^{**} < h^{***} = 1$.

4.2   Random Regular Graphs

We now come back to the process $(X_i^{(n)}(t))_{i \in V}$ on $G_\Delta^{(n)}$, a random Δ−regular graph, satisfying (4). Given $d \geq 1$, let $N(i, d, G_\Delta^{(n)})$ be the set of vertices of $G_\Delta^{(n)}$ that are at a distance at most d from $i \in G_\Delta^{(n)}$. A depth-d Δ-regular tree $T(\Delta, d)$ is the restriction of $T(\Delta)$ to nodes i with $\text{gen}(i) \leq d$. A simple induction on t shows that $X_i^{(n)}(t)$ is determined by the $\{\chi_j, j \in N(i, t, G_\Delta^{(n)})\}$. Using the following convergence [6]: for any fixed $d \geq 1$, we have as n tends to infinity $N(0, d, G_\Delta^n) \xrightarrow{d} T(\Delta, d)$, we have $X_0^{(n)}(t) \xrightarrow{d} X_\varnothing(t)$ as n tends to infinity. Therefore the process defined on the tree in Section 4.1 is a good approximation of the real process. Hence,

Proposition 3. *For any fixed $t \geq 0$, we have*

$$\lim_{n \to \infty} \mathbb{E}\left[X_i^{(n)}(t)\right] = \tilde{h}(t) \tag{9}$$

where $\tilde{h}(t)$ is defined in (7).

Let $\beta^{(n)}(t)$ be the proportion of agents choosing B at time t: $\beta^{(n)}(t) = \sum_i X_i^{(n)}(t)/n$. We have as $n \to \infty$,

$$\mathbb{E}\left[\beta^{(n)}(t)\right] = \mathbb{E}\left[X_i^{(n)}(t)\right] \to \tilde{h}(t). \tag{10}$$

The final proportion of agents choosing B is $\beta^{(n)} = \lim_{t \to \infty} \beta^{(n)}(t)$.

Proposition 4. *We have*

$$\lim_{n \to \infty} \mathbb{E}\left[\beta^{(n)}\right] = \tilde{h}, \tag{11}$$

in particular, for $\alpha \geq \alpha_{crit}$, we have

$$\lim_{n \to \infty} \mathbb{E}\left[\beta^{(n)}\right] = 1. \tag{12}$$

The interchange of limits in t and n needs a proper mathematical proof. This has been done in [1] and our statement follows from their Theorem 1. For Δ-regular graphs, bootstrap percolation is equivalent to our model. It is noticed in [1] that the critical value on the Δ-regular random graph turns out to be the same as that on the Δ-tree, although the proof goes along a quite different route.

4.3   Extensions: Random Networks and Linear Threshold Model

The study of games on networks has attracted a lot of attention during the recent year. We refer to [3] for the description of a general framework and references to the economic literature. An attractive way to model the social network consists in using a mean field approach to study the random network. The main advantage of this approach is its simplicity. A random network is characterized by its connectivity distribution: the fraction of agents in the population with d neighbors is described by the degree distribution $P(d)$. Such a model is analyzed in [5], where the dynamic of the diffusion process is also considered.

In this section, we show how our approach extends to random networks and to the linear the linear threshold model (see [9], [8] for a rigorous proof). Let us assume that the graph $G^{(n)}$ is defined via its degree sequence $(D_i)_{i \in V}$ which is i.i.d. distributed according to D. Such graphs can be generated using the configuration model [13]. Let $L_n = \sum_{k=1}^{n} D_k$, where $L_n/2$ is the number of edges in the graph. The underlying tree rooted at node i can be described by a branching process with the offspring distribution of the root given by D_i. Besides the subsequent generations have offspring distribution

$$ p_j^{(n)} = \sum_{k=1}^{n} \mathbb{1}\,(D_k = j + 1)\,\frac{D_k}{L_n}\,. $$

If the degree sequence is such that $\mathbb{E}[D^2]$ is finite then, by the strong law of large numbers

$$ \lim_{n \to \infty} p_j^{(n)} = \frac{(j+1)\mathbb{P}(D_1 = j+1)}{\mathbb{E}D}\,, \quad a.s. $$

Let $\tilde{P}(j) = \frac{jP(j)}{\sum_j jP(j)}$ be the (asymptotic) probability that an edge points to a node with degree j. Then for any fixed d, the neighbourhood of radius d about node 0, $N(0, d, G^{(n)})$ converges in distribution as n tends to infinity to a depth-d a Galton-Watson tree with a root which has offspring distribution P and all other nodes have offspring distribution P^* given by $P^*(j-1) = \tilde{P}(j)$ for all $j \geq 1$. Thus the associated fixed point equation is:

$$ h^* = 1 - (1 - \alpha) \sum_j P^*(j) g_{j, \theta(j+1)}(h^*), \tag{13} $$

and we have $\lim_{t \to \infty} \beta(t) = \tilde{h}$ given by

$$ \tilde{h} = 1 - (1 - \alpha) \sum_j P(j) g_{j, \theta(j)}(h^*). \tag{14} $$

As a matter of example, for Erdős-Rényi graphs, the fixed point equation associated with our model is given by (13) and (14) with $P(j) = P^*(j) = e^{-\lambda}\frac{\lambda^j}{j!}$.

Besides the methods developed in this paper are not restricted to this particular model. We consider the general threshold model [7]. We have a non-negative random weight W_{ij} on each edge, indicating the influence that i exerts on j. We consider the symmetric case where $W_{ij} = W_{ji}$ and we assume W_{ij} are i.i.d with distribution function W. Each node i has an arbitrary function f_i defined on subsets of its neighbours set N_i: for any set of neighbours $X \subseteq N_i$, there is a value $f_i(X)$ between 0 and 1 which is monotone in the sense that if $X \subseteq Y$, then $f_i(X) \leq f_i(Y)$. This node chooses a threshold θ_i at random from $[0, 1]$ and at time step $t + 1$ it becomes active, it plays B, if its set of currently active neighbours $N_i^B(t)$ satisfies $f_i(N_i^B(t)) > \theta_i$.

5 Conclusion and Future Work

In this paper we presented two models of marketing wherein individuals, represented by a graph structure, receive payoffs to entice them to adopt a strategy that is different from their initial choice. To this end we initially force a small proportion of nodes to opt for the new strategy and then use an economic model that accounts for the cascading dynamic of adoption. We analyze the evolution of the proportion of agents that switch to the new strategy over time. First, the implications of our results concern marketing strategies in online social networks. More precisely, let $\alpha = \frac{\sum_i X_i}{n}$ be the proportion of forced agents and let $M_1(\alpha)$ the price incurred to force the initial agents. Typically if there is a fixed cost per agent, say c, we could take $M_1(\alpha) = c\alpha$. Let $\beta(t)$ be the proportion of agents choosing B at time t: $\beta(t) = \frac{\sum_i X_i(t)}{n}$. We have $\gamma(t) = \beta(t) - \alpha \geq 0$ which corresponds to the proportion of agents choosing B without being initially forced. We denote by $M_2(\gamma(t))$ the price incurred by the rebates until time t. We typically take $M_2(\gamma) = r\gamma$. Let $\delta(t)$ be the proportion of edges $B - B$ at time t. We denote by $M_3(\delta(t))$ the price incurred by the marketing of edges until time t. We typically take $M_3(\delta) = u\delta$. Hence the total price of the marketing strategy at time t is given by $M(t) = M_1(\alpha) + M_2(\gamma(t)) + M_3(\delta(t))$. One can compute the quantities $\gamma(t)$ and $\delta(t)$ in function of α, r and u. This opens the possibilities of doing an optimal control of the marketing policy.

Finally we remark that the marketing problem that we considered in this paper is just one application of our method. Our approach can indeed be adapted to the analysis of the dissemination of new versions of existing protocols, voting protocols through simple majority rules, i.e., $\theta(d) = \frac{d}{2}$ and distributed digital preservation systems [11].

References

1. Balogh, J., Pittel, B.G.: Bootstrap percolation on the random regular graph. Random Structures Algorithms 30(1-2), 257–286 (2007)
2. Domingos, P., Richardson, M.: Mining the network value of customers. In: KDD 2001: Proceedings of the seventh ACM SIGKDD international conference on Knowledge discovery and data mining, pp. 57–66. ACM Press, New York (2001)
3. Galeotti, A., Goyal, S., Jackson, M.O., Vega-Redondo, F., Yariv, L.: Network games (2007)
4. Ganesh, A., Massoulié, L., Towsley, D.: The effect of network topology on the spread of epidemics. In: Proceedings IEEE Infocom (2005)
5. Jackson, M.O., Yariv, L.: Diffusion of behavior and equilibrium properties in network games. American Economic Review (Papers and Proceedings) 97(2), 92–98 (2007)
6. Janson, S., Łuczak, T., Rucinski, A.: Random graphs. Wiley-Interscience Series in Discrete Mathematics and Optimization. Wiley Interscience, New York (2000)
7. Kleinberg, J.: Cascading behavior in networks: Algorithmic and economic issues. In: Nisan, N., Roughgarden, T., Tardos, E., Vazirani, V. (eds.) Algorithmic Game Theory. Cambridge University Press, Cambridge (2007)

8. Lelarge, M.: Diffusion and cascading behavior in random networks (in preparation)
9. Lelarge, M.: Diffusion of innovations on random networks: Understanding the chasm. In: Papadimitriou, C.H., Zhang, S. (eds.) WINE 2008. LNCS, vol. 5385, pp. 178–185. Springer, Heidelberg (2008)
10. Mahajan, V., Muller, E., Bass, F.M.: New product diffusion models in marketing: A review and directions for research. Journal of Marketing 54(1), 1–26 (1990)
11. Maniatis, P., Roussopoulos, M., Giuli, T., Rosenthal, D.S.H., Baker, M.: The lockss peer-to-peer digital preservation system. ACM Transactions on Computer Systems 23 (2005)
12. Morris, S.: Contagion. Rev. Econom. Stud. 67(1), 57–78 (2000)
13. van der Hofstad, R.: Random graphs and complex networks (2008), http://www.win.tue.nl/~rhofstad/NotesRGCN2008.pdf
14. Watts, D.: A simple model of global cascades on random networks. Proceedings of the National Academy of Science 99, 5766–5771 (2002)

A Stochastic Epidemiological Model and a Deterministic Limit for BitTorrent-Like Peer-to-Peer File-Sharing Networks

George Kesidis[1,*], Takis Konstantopoulos[2,**], and Perla Sousi[3]

[1] CSE and EE Departments, Pennsylvania State University,
University Park, PA 16802, USA
gik2@psu.edu
[2] School of Mathematical & Computer Sciences and the Maxwell Institute for
Mathematical Sciences, Heriot-Watt University, Edinburgh EH14 4AS, UK
takis@ma.hw.ac.uk
[3] Statistical Laboratory, Centre for Mathematical Sciences, University of Cambridge,
Wilberforce Road, Cambridge CB3 0WB, UK
P.Sousi@statslab.cam.ac.uk

Abstract. We propose a stochastic model for a file-sharing peer-to-peer network which resembles the popular BitTorrent system: large files are split into chunks and a peer can download or swap from another peer only one chunk at a time. We exhibit the fluid and diffusion limits of a scaled Markov model of this system and look at possible uses of them to draw practical conclusions.

1 Introduction

Peer-to-peer (p2p) activity continues to represent a very significant fraction of overall Internet traffic, 44% by one recent account [4]. BitTorrent [1,2,8,21,18,9,19] is a widely deployed p2p file-sharing network which has recently played a significant role in the network neutrality debate. Under BitTorrent, peers join "swarms" (or "torrents") where each swarm corresponds to a specific data object (file). The process of finding the peers in a given swarm to connect to is typically facilitated through a centralised "tracker". Recently, a trackerless BitTorrent client has been introduced that uses distributed hashing for query resolution [16].

For file sharing, a peer is typically uploads upload pieces ("chunks") of the file to other peers in the swarm while downloading his/her missing chunks from them. This chunk swapping constitutes a transaction-by-transaction incentive for peers to cooperate (i.e., trading rather than simply download) to disseminate data objects. Large files may be segmented into several hundred chunks, all of which the peers of the corresponding warm must collect, and in the process disseminate their own chunks before they can reconstitute the desired file and possibly leave the file's swarm.

---

* Supported by an NSF grant.
** Corresponding author; supported by an EPSRC grant.

E. Altman and A. Chaintreau (Eds.): NET-COOP 2008, LNCS 5425, pp. 26–36, 2009.

In addition to the framework in which data objects are segmented into chunks to promote cooperation through swapping, there is a system whereby the rate at which chunks are uploaded is assessed for any given transaction, and peers that allocate inadequate bandwidth for uploading may be "choked" [14,17]. Choking may also be applied to peers who, by employing multiple identities (sybils), abuse BitTorrent's system of allowing newly arrived peers to a swarm to just download a few chunks (as they clearly cannot trade what they simply do not as yet possess). BitTorrent can also rehabilitate peers by (optimistically) unchoking them. In the following, we do not directly consider upload bandwidth and related choking issues.

In this paper, we motivate a deterministic epidemiological model of file dissemination for peer-to-peer file-sharing networks that employ BitTorrent-like incentives, a generalisation of that given in [10,11]. Our model is different from those explored in [15,21,18] for BitTorrent, and we compute different quantities of interest. Our epidemiological framework, similar to that we used for the spread of multi-stage worms [12], could also be adapted for network coding systems. In [9], the authors propose a "fluid" model of a single torrent/swarm (as we do in the following) and fit it to (transient) data drawn from aggregate swarms. The connection to branching process models [21,8] is simply that ours only tracks the number of active peers who possess or demand the file under consideration, i.e., a single swarm. Though our model is significantly simpler than that of prior work, it is derived directly from an intuitive transaction-by-transaction Markov process modelling file-dissemination of the p2p network and its numerical solutions clearly demonstrate the effectiveness of the aforementioned incentives. A basic assumption in the following is that peers do not distribute bogus files (or file chunks) [20].

2   The Stochastic Model

A file is represented as a set F of size n, the elements of which are called chunks. Consider a large networked "swarm" of N nodes called peers. Each peer possesses a certain (possibly empty) subset A of F. As time goes by, this peer interacts with other peers, the goal being to enlarge his set A until, eventually, the peer manages to collect all n chunks of F. The interaction between peers can either be a download or a swap; in both cases, chunks are being copied from peer to peer and are assumed never lost. A peer will stay in the network as long as he does not possess all chunks. After collecting everything, sooner or later a peer departs or switches off. By splitting the desired file into many chunks we give incentives to the peers to remain active in the swarm for long time during which other peers will take advantage of their possessions.

2.1   Possible Interactions

We here describe how two peers, labelled A, B, interact. The following types of interactions are possible:

1. **Download:** Peer A downloads a chunk i from B. This is possible only if A is a strict subset of B. If $i \in B$ then, after the downloading A becomes $A' = A \cup \{i\}$ and but B remains B because it since it gains nothing from A. Denote this interaction by: $(A \leftarrow B) \rightsquigarrow (A', B)$. The symbol on the left is supposed to show the type of interaction and the labels before it, while the symbol on the right shows the labels after the interaction.

2. **Swap:** Peer A swaps with peer B. In other words, A gets a chunk j from B and B gets a chunk i from A. It is required that j is not an element of A and i not an element of B. We denote this interaction by $(A \leftrightarrows B) \rightsquigarrow (A', B')$, where $A' = A \cup \{j\}$, $B' = B \cup \{i\}$. We thus need $A \setminus B \neq \varnothing$ and $B \setminus A \neq \varnothing$.

2.2 Notation

The set of all combinations of n chunks, which partition F, is denoted by $\mathscr{P}(F)$, where $|\mathscr{P}(F)| = 2^n$ and the empty set is included. We write $A \subset B$ (respectively, $A \subsetneqq B$) when A is a subset (respectively, strict subset) of B. We (unconventionally) write

$$A \sqsubset A' \text{ when } A \subset A' \text{ and } |A' - A| = 1.$$

If $A \cap B = \varnothing$, we use $A + B$ instead of $A \cup B$; if $B = \{b\}$ is a singleton, we often write $A + b$ instead of $A + \{b\}$. If $A \subset B$ we use $B - A$ instead of $B \setminus A$. We say that

$$A \text{ relates to } B \text{ (and write } A \sim B) \text{ when } A \subset B \text{ or } B \subset A;$$

if this is not the case, we write $A \nsim B$. Note that $A \nsim B$ if and only if two peers labelled A, B can swap chunks. The space of functions (vectors) from $\mathscr{P}(F)$ into $\mathbb{Z}_+$ is denoted by $\mathbb{Z}_+^{\mathscr{P}(F)}$. The stochastic model will take values in this space. The deterministic model will evolve in $\mathbb{R}_+^{\mathscr{P}(F)}$. We let $e_A \in \mathbb{Z}_+^{\mathscr{P}(F)}$ be the vector with coordinates

$$e_A^B := \mathbf{1}(A = B), \quad B \in \mathscr{P}(F).$$

For $x \in \mathbb{Z}_+^{\mathscr{P}(F)}$ or $\mathbb{R}_+^{\mathscr{P}(F)}$ we let $|x| := \sum_{A \in \mathscr{P}(F)} |x^A|$.

2.3 Defining the Rates of Individual Interactions

We follow the logic of stochastic modelling of chemical reactions or epidemics and assume that the chance of a particular interaction occurring in a short interval of time is proportional to the number of ways of selecting the peers needed for this interaction [13]. Accordingly, the interaction rates *must* be given by the formulae described below.

Consider first finding the rate of a download $A \leftarrow B$, where $A \subsetneqq B$, when the state of the system is $x \in \mathbb{Z}_+^{\mathscr{P}(F)}$. There are x^A peers labelled A and x^B labelled B. We can choose them in $x^A x^B$ ways. Thus the rate of a download $A \leftarrow B$ that results into A getting *some* chunk from B should be proportional to $x^A x^B$. However, we are interested in the rate of the *specific* interaction $(A \leftarrow B) \rightsquigarrow (A', B)$, that turns A into a specific set A' differing from A by one single chunk

$(A \sqsubset A')$; there are $|B - A|$ chunks that A can download from B; the chance that picking one of them is $1/|B - A|$. Thus we have:

$$(DR) \quad \begin{cases} \text{the rate of the download } (A \leftarrow B) \rightsquigarrow (A', B) \text{ equals } \beta x^A \dfrac{x^B}{|B - A|}, \\ \text{as long as } A \sqsubset A' \subset B, \end{cases}$$

where $\beta > 0$.

Consider next a swap $A \leftrightarrows B$ and assume the state is x. Picking two peers labelled A and B (provided that $A \not\sim B$) from the population is done in $x^A x^B$ ways. Thus the rate of a swap $A \leftrightarrows B$ is proportional to $x^A x^B$. So if we *fix* two chunks $i \in A \setminus B, j \in B \setminus A$ and specify that $A' = A + j, B' = B + i$, then the chance of picking i from $A \setminus B$ and j from $B \setminus A$ is $1/|A \setminus B||B \setminus A|$. Thus,

$$(SR) \quad \begin{cases} \text{the rate of the swap } (A \leftrightarrows B) \rightsquigarrow (A', B') \text{ equals } \gamma \dfrac{x^A x^B}{|A \setminus B||B \setminus A|}, \\ \text{a long as } A \sqsubset A', \quad B \sqsubset B', \quad A' - A \subset B, \quad B' - B \subset A, \end{cases}$$

where $\gamma > 0$.

2.4 Deriving the Markov Chain Rates

Having defined the rates of each individual interaction we can easily define rates $q(x, y)$ of a Markov chain in continuous time and state space $\mathbb{Z}_+^{\mathscr{P}(F)}$ as follows.

Define functions $\lambda_{A,A'}, \mu_{A,B} : \mathbb{R}^{\mathscr{P}(F)} \to \mathbb{R}$ by:

$$\lambda_{A,A'}(x) := \left[\beta x^A \sum_{C : C \supset A'} \frac{x^C}{|C - A|} \right] \mathbf{1}(A \sqsubset A') \tag{1a}$$

$$\mu_{A,B}(x) := \gamma \frac{x^A x^B}{|A \setminus B||B \setminus A|} \mathbf{1}(A \not\sim B). \tag{1b}$$

Consider also constants $\delta \geq 0$ and $\alpha^A \geq 0$ for $A \in \mathscr{P}(F)$, i.e., $\alpha \in \mathbb{R}_+^{\mathscr{P}(F)}$. The transition rates of the closed conservative Markov chain are given by:

$$q(x, y) := \begin{cases} \lambda_{A,A'}(x), & \text{if } y = x - e_A + e_{A'} \\ \mu_{A,B}(x), & \text{if } \begin{cases} y = x - e_A - e_B + e_{A'} + e_{B'} \\ A \sqsubset A', B \sqsubset B', A' - A \subset B, B' - B \subset A, \end{cases} \\ \alpha^A & \text{if } y = x + e_A \\ \delta x^F & \text{if } y = x - e_F \\ 0, & \text{for any other value of } y \neq x, \end{cases} \tag{2}$$

where x ranges in $\mathbb{Z}_+^{\mathscr{P}(F)}$.

A little justification of the first two cases is needed: that $q(x, x - e_A - e_B + e_{A'} + e_{B'}) = \mu_{A,B}(x)$ is straightforward. It corresponds to a swap, which is only possible when $A \sqsubset A', B \sqsubset B', A' - A \subset B, B' - B \subset A$. The swap rate was defined by (SR). To see that $q(x, x - e_A + e_{A'}) = \lambda_{A,A'}(x)$ we observe that a peer labelled A can change its label to $A' \sqsupset A$ by downloading a chunk from some set C that contains A', so we sum the rates (DR) over all these possible individual interactions to obtain the first line in (2). We can think of having Poisson process of arrivals of new peers at rate $|\alpha|$, and that each arriving peer is labelled A with probability $\alpha^A / |\alpha|$. Peers can depart, by definition, only when they are labelled F and it takes an exponentially distributed amount of time (with mean $1/\delta$) for a departure to occur. Thus, $q(x, x - e_F) = \delta x^F$. We shall let $\mathbf{Q}$ denote the generator of the chain, i.e. $\mathbf{Q}f(x) = \sum_y (f(y) - f(x))q(x,y)$, when f is an appropriate functional of the state space.

Definition 1 (BITTORRENT$[x_0, n, \alpha, \beta, \gamma, \delta]$). *Given* $x_0 \in \mathbb{Z}_+^{\mathscr{P}(F)}$ *(initial configuration),* $n = |F| \in \mathbb{N}$ *(number of chunks),* $\alpha \in \mathbb{R}_+^{\mathscr{P}(F)}$ *(arrival rates),* $\beta > 0$ *(download rate),* $\gamma \geq 0$ *(swap rate),* $\delta \geq 0$ *(departure rate) we let* BITTORRENT$[x_0, n, \alpha, \beta, \gamma, \delta]$ *be a Markov chain* $(X_t, t \geq 0)$ *with transition rates* (2) *and* $X_0 = x_0$. *We say that the chain (network) is* <u>open</u> *if* $\alpha^A > 0$ *for at least one* A *and* $\delta > 0$; *it is* <u>closed</u> *if* $\alpha^A = 0$ *for all* A; *it is* <u>conservative</u> *if it is closed and* $\delta = 0$; *it is* <u>dissipative</u> *if it is closed and* $\delta > 0$.

In a conservative network, we have $q(x,y) = 0$ if $|y| \neq |x|$ and so $|X_t| = |X_0|$ for all $t \geq 0$. Here, the actual state space is the simplex $\{x \in \mathbb{Z}_+^{\mathscr{P}(F)} : |x| = N\}$, where $N = |X_0|$. It is easy to see that the state e_F is reachable from any other state, but all rates out of e_F are zero. Hence a conservative network has e_F as a single absorbing state.

In a dissipative network, we have $|X_t| \leq |X_0|$ for all $t \geq 0$. Here the state space is $\{x \in \mathbb{Z}_+^{\mathscr{P}(F)} : |x| \leq N\}$, where $N = |X_0|$. It can be seen that a dissipative network has many absorbing points.

In an open network, there are no absorbing points. On the other hand, one may wonder if certain components can escape to infinity. This is not the case:

Lemma 1. *If* $\alpha^F > 0$ *then the open* BITTORRENT$[x, n, \beta, \gamma, \alpha, \delta]$ *is positive recurrent Markov chain.*

Proof. (sketch) If $\alpha^F > 0$, $\delta > 0$ the Markov chain is irreducible. The remainder of the proof is based on a the construction of a simple Lyapunov function: $V(x) := |x|$, for which it can be shown that there is a bounded set of states K such that $\sup_{x \notin K}(\mathbf{Q}V)(x) < 0$. Perhaps the easiest way to see this is by appealing to the stability of the corresponding ODE limit; see Theorem 1 below and [7]. □

3 Macroscopic Description: Fluid Limit and Diffusion Approximation

Analysing the Markov chain in its original form is complicated. We thus resort to a first-order approximation by an ordinary differential equation (ODE). Let $v(x)$ be the vector field on $\mathbb{R}_+^{\mathscr{P}(F)}$ with components $v^A(x)$ defined by

$$v^A(x) = \alpha^A - x^A\big(\beta\varphi_d^A(x) + \gamma\varphi_s^A(x)\big)$$

$$+ \beta \sum_{B:A\subset B} \frac{\psi_d^A(x)x^B}{1 + |B\setminus A|} + \gamma \sum_{B:A\not\subset B} \frac{\psi_s^{A,B}(x)x^B}{1 + |B\setminus A|} - \delta x^F \mathbf{1}(A = F), \quad (3)$$

where

$$\varphi_d^A(x) := \sum_{B\supset A} x^B, \quad \varphi_s^A(x) := \sum_{B\not\supset A} x^B$$

$$\psi_d^A(x) := \sum_{a\in A} x^{A-a}, \quad \psi_s^{A,B}(x) := \sum_{a\in A\cap B} x^{A-a} \quad (4)$$

Consider the differential equation

$$\dot{x} = v(x) \text{ with initial condition } x_0. \quad (5)$$

Consider the sequence of stochastic models $\texttt{BITTORRENT}[X_{N,0}, n, N\alpha, \frac{\beta}{N}, \frac{\gamma}{N}, \delta]$ for $N \in \mathbb{N}$ and let $X_{N,t}$ be the corresponding jump Markov chain.

Theorem 1. *There is a has a unique smooth (analytic) solution to (5), denoted by x_t for $t \geq 0$. Also, if there is an $x_0 \in \mathbb{R}_+^{\mathscr{P}(F)}$ such that $X_{N,0}/N \to x_0$ as $N \to \infty$, then for any $T, \varepsilon > 0$,*

$$\lim_{N\to\infty} P\big(\sup_{0\leq t\leq T} |N^{-1}X_{N,t} - x_t| > \varepsilon\big) = 0.$$

Proof. See [11].

Next, let

$$Y_{N,t} := \sqrt{N}(X_{N,t}/N - x_t).$$

For each $y \in \mathbb{Z}_+^{\mathscr{P}(F)}$ let W_y be a standard one-dimensional Brownian motion; suppose that these Brownian motions are independent over y. Define the (time-inhomogeneous) Gaussian diffusion process Y by

$$dY(t) = \sum_y (y - x_t)\sqrt{q(x_t, x_t + y)}dW_y(t) + Dv(x_t)Y(t)dt,$$

where $Dv(x)$ is the matrix of partial derivatives of $v(x)$. Due to the form the rates (2), the first sum ranges over finitely many y and so only finitely many Brownian motions are needed.

Theorem 2. *If $\sqrt{N}(X_{N,t}/N - x_0) \to 0$ as $N \to \infty$, where $x_0 \in \mathbb{R}_+^{\mathscr{P}(F)}$, then the law of Y_N (as a sequence of probability measures in $D[0,\infty)$ with the topology of uniform convergence on compacta) converges weakly to the law of Y.*

Proof. We refer to [13] for the relevant arguments.

4   Examples

Suppose that F consists of $n = 2$ chunks. The limiting ODE is easily found to be:

$$\dot{x}^{\varnothing} = \alpha^{\varnothing} - \beta x^{\varnothing}(x^1 + x^2 + x^{12})$$
$$\dot{x}^1 = \alpha^1 - x^1(\beta x^{12} + \gamma x^2) + \beta x^{\varnothing}(x^1 + \tfrac{1}{2}x^{12})$$
$$\dot{x}^2 = \alpha^2 - x^2(\beta x^{12} + \gamma x^1) + \beta x^{\varnothing}(x^2 + \tfrac{1}{2}x^{12})$$
$$\dot{x}^{12} = \alpha^{12} + \beta(x^1 + x^2)x^{12} + 2\gamma x^1 x^2 - \delta x^{12}.$$

We look at its behaviour in three cases. To make things easier, assume that $\gamma = 0$.

4.1   Closed Conservative System: $\alpha^1 = \alpha^2 = \alpha^{12} = 0, \delta = 0$

Letting $x = x^{\varnothing}, u = x^1 + x^2, w = x^{12}$, assuming that $x + u + w = 1$, and eliminating the variable w we obtain

$$\dot{x} = -\beta x(1 - x)$$
$$\dot{u} = \beta u^2 - \beta u(1 - x) + \beta x(1 - x).$$

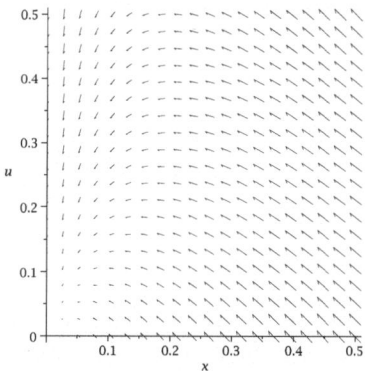

Fig. 1. Typical vector field plot for a closed conservative BitTorrent model

The vector field in the $x - u$ plane is depicted in Figure 1. The unique equilibrium point $x = 0, u = 0$ corresponds to $w = 1$, i.e. everybody possesses the full file. By solving the equation in x, substituting into the equation for u, we find the explicit solution

$$w_t = \frac{x_0 + (1 - x_0)e^{\beta t}}{x_0 + (1 - x_0)e^{\beta t} + x_0\beta t + (1 - w_0)w_0^{-1}},$$

from which one can estimate the time required for w to reach an ε-neighbourhood of the equilibrium, which can be turned into an estimate for the original stochastic system.

4.2   Closed Dissipative System: $\alpha^1 = \alpha^2 = \alpha^{12} = 0, \delta > 0$

With $x = x^\varnothing, u = x^1 + x^2, w = x^{12}$ as before, change the time variable to $s = \beta t$, let $\rho = \delta/\beta$, and write x' for dx/ds, to obtain:

$$x' = -x(u + w)$$
$$u' = -uw + x(u + w)$$
$$w' = uw - \rho w.$$

Assume $x_0 + u_0 + w_0 = 1$, so that $x_t + u_t + w_t < 1$ for all $t > 0$. We cannot eliminate the variable w now since there is no obvious conserved quantity, but we can study the equilibria of the system. It is easily seen that the only equilibria are of the form $(0, u, 0)$ which are unstable if $u > \rho$ and stable if $u < \rho$. In terms of the original variables, the stable equilibria are $(x^\varnothing, x^1, x^2, x^{12}) = (0, x^1, x^2, 0)$, $0 \le x^1 + x^2 < \rho$. This is as expected: since there is no swapping ($\gamma = 0$), the system eventually settles to a situation where there are peers with label 1 and peers with label 2. Had γ been positive, x^1, x^2 could not have simultaneously been positive in equilibrium.

4.3   Open System: $\alpha^1 = \alpha^2 = 0, \alpha^{12} = \lambda > 0, \delta > 0$

Choosing variables appropriately, we have

$$x' = -x(u + w)$$
$$u' = -uw + x(u + w)$$
$$w' = \lambda + uw - \rho w.$$

The system eventually settles to the unique stable equilibrium $(x, u, w) = (0, 0, \lambda/\rho)$. It is easily seen that the eigenvalues of the differential of the vector field at this point are $-\lambda/\rho$ and $-\rho$ (the first one has algebraic multiplicity 1 but geometric multiplicity 2), and so there is no possibility of spiralling.

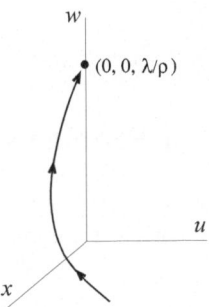

Fig. 2. Trajectory for open system

5   Performance Improvement in Presence of BitTorrent Incentives

To split or not to split? The answer is yes, but not always. We can address this question by looking at the behaviour of the ℓ_1-norm $|x^*|$ of the unique equilibrium point of an open system as the number of chunks (dimension) increases.

As an example, consider a situation where peers possessing nothing arrive at rate λ, download at rate β and depart at rate δ once they have the full file. This is described by

$$\dot{x}^{\varnothing} = \lambda - \beta x^{\varnothing} x^1$$
$$\dot{x}^1 = \beta x^{\varnothing} x^1 - \delta x^1.$$

The globally attracting stable equilibrium is given by $x^* = (\delta/\beta, \ \lambda/\delta)$.

Suppose now that we split into $n = 2$ chunks. Peers arrive and depart at the same rates but download at a rate $\widetilde{\beta} \geq \beta$ and swap at rate $\widetilde{\gamma}$. The new equilibrium is easily found to be

$$\widetilde{x}^* = \left(\frac{\delta}{\widetilde{\beta}} \left(\frac{\delta}{\lambda} u + 1 \right)^{-1}, \ \frac{u}{2}, \ \frac{u}{2}, \ \frac{\lambda}{\delta} \right),$$

where u is the positive number which solves

$$q(u) := u^2 + \frac{2\widetilde{\beta}\lambda}{\widetilde{\gamma}\delta} u - \frac{2\lambda}{\widetilde{\gamma}} = 0. \tag{6}$$

The following is shown in [11]:

Lemma 2

1. $\widetilde{x}^{*\varnothing} < x^{*\varnothing}$.
2. $|x^*| > |\widetilde{x}^*|$ if and only if $u < \widetilde{u}$, where $\widetilde{u}$ is the unique positive number which satisfies

$$\widetilde{q}(\widetilde{u}) := \widetilde{u}^2 - \left(\frac{\delta}{\beta} - \frac{\lambda}{\delta} \right)\widetilde{u} - \left(\frac{\lambda}{\beta} - \frac{\lambda}{\widetilde{\beta}} \right). \tag{7}$$

Furthermore, there exists a $\lambda_0 > 0$ such that for all $\lambda < \lambda_0$ (7) holds.

6   Conclusions and Open Problems

We proposed a stochastic model of a BitTorrent-like network and showed the existence of an ODE limit, along with a diffusion approximation. Several simulations [10] test the suitability of the model. Proofs of some of the results presented in this paper can be found in [11]. One can look at the ODE limit and, more specifically, its equilibria in order to obtain crude information about the stationary distribution of the original model. This requires proving a certain robustness result, as explained in [11, Sec. 5]. Rates of convergence to the ODE limit is another interesting open problem. Its solution requires estimating bounds on the vector field and its derivative. A criticism of the model is that the ODE lives in a high-dimensional space. One can reduce the dimension under some symmetry assumptions on the initial state and the parameters of the model [11, Sec. 7]. Another drawback is the Markovian assumption requires that times between transactions are exponential; this is clearly violated in practise (download times are typically heavy-tailed random variables). A quick fix of this problem is to represent the Markov process on a probability space supporting i.i.d. Poisson processes and then replace these by more general renewal processes.

References

1. BitTorrent, http://www.bittorrent.com
2. Cohen, B.: Incentives Build Robustness in BitTorrent. In: Workshop on Economics of Peer-to-Peer Systems, Berkeley, CA, USA (May 2003)
3. Daley, D.J., Gani, J.: Epidemic Modeling, an Introduction. Cambridge University Press, Cambridge (1999)
4. DC Info (Distributed Systems Newsletter) vol. XXII(8), June 30 (2008), http://www.dcia.info/news/#Newsletters
5. Ethier, S.N., Kurtz, T.G.: Markov Processes: Characterization and Convergence. Wiley, New York (1986)
6. Darling, R.W.R., Norris, J.R.: Differential equation approximations for Markov chains. Probability Surveys 5, 37–79 (2008)
7. Foss, S., Konstantopoulos, T.: An overview of some stochastic stability methods. Journal of the Operations Research Society of Japan 47, 275–303 (2004)
8. Ge, Z., Figueiredo, D.R., Jaiswal, S., Kurose, J., Towsley, D.: Modeling peer-to-peer file sharing systems. In: Proc. IEEE INFOCOM, San Francisco (April 2004)
9. Guo, L., Chen, S., Xiao, Z., Tan, E., Ding, X., Zhang, X.: Measurements, modeling and analysis of BitTorrent-like systems. In: Proc. Internet Measurement Conference (IMC) (October 2005)
10. Kesidis, G., Jin, Y., Mortazavi, B., Konstantopoulos, T.: An epidemiological model for file-sharing with BitTorrent-like incentives. In: Proc. IEEE GLOBECOM (November 2006)
11. Kesidis, G., Konstantopoulos, T., Sousi, P.: A stochastic epidemiological model and a deterministic limit for BitTorrent-like peer-to-peer file-sharing networks (November 2008), http://arxiv.org/abs/0811.1003
12. Kesidis, G., Vojnovic, M., Hamadeh, I., Jin, Y., Jiwasurat, S.: A Model of the Spread of Randomly Scanning Internet Worms that Saturate Access Links. In: ACM TOMACS (May 2008)
13. Kurtz, T.: Approximation of Population Processes. SIAM, Philadelphia (1981)
14. Legout, A., Liogkas, N., Kohler, E., Zhang, L.: Clustering and sharing incentives in BitTorrent systems. ACM SIGMETRICS Performance Evaluation Review 35(1) (June 2007)
15. Massoulié, L., Vojnovic, M.: Coupon replication systems. In: Proc. ACM SIGMETRICS, Banff, Alberta, Canada (2005)
16. Maymounkov, P., Mazieres, D.: Kademlia: a peer-to-peer information system based on the XOR metric. In: Proc. IPTPS, Cambridge, MA, USA (March 2002)
17. Mortazavi, B., Kesidis, G.: A peer-to-peer content-distribution game with a reputation-based incentive mechanism. In: Proc. IEEE Workshop on Information Theory and its Applications (ITA), UC San Diego (February 2006)

18. Qiu, D., Srikant, R.: Modeling and performance analysis of BitTorrent-like peer-to-peer networks. In: Proc. ACM SIGCOMM, Portland, Oregon (2004)
19. Turner, B.: Generalizing BitTorrent: how to build data exchange markets (and profit from them!) (January 2005),
    http://www.fractalscape.org/GeneralizingBitTorrent.htm
20. Walsh, K., Sirer, E.G.: Fighting peer-to-peer SPAM and decoys with object reputation. In: Proc. Workshop on Economics of Peer-to-Peer Systems (p2pecon), Philadelphia, PA (August 2005)
21. Yang, X., de Veciana, G.: Service capacity of peer to peer networks. In: Proc. IEEE INFOCOM, San Francisco (2004)

Ant Colony Optimization Algorithms for Shortest Path Problems

Sudha Rani Kolavali and Shalabh Bhatnagar*

Indian Institute of Science, Computer Science and Automation, Bangalore
sudha@csa.iisc.ernet.in, shalabh@csa.iisc.ernet.in

Abstract. We propose four variants of a recently proposed multi-timescale algorithm in [1] for ant colony optimization and study their application on a multi-stage shortest path problem. We study the performance of the various algorithms in this framework. We observe that one of the variants consistently outperforms the algorithm in [1].

Keywords: Ant colony optimization, stochastic approximation, multi-stage shortest path problem.

1 Introduction

Over the last two decades, ant colony optimization (ACO) has emerged as a leading metaheuristic method for the solution of combinatorial optimization (CO) problems. The ACO metaheuristic has been successfully applied in various application domains such as traveling salesman problem (TSP), sequential ordering problem, the quadratic assignment problem etc., see [2]. A detailed survey of the theoretical aspects of ACO can be found in [3]. Certain convergence proofs of ACO algorithms can be found in [4], [5] and [6]. It is shown that ACO algorithms in general suffer from first order deception in the same way as genetic algorithms. Search techniques and evolutionary algorithms applied to CO problems can sometimes be guided away from potentially good zones of the search space. Such harmful bias can be introduced by the choice of problem representation, choice of operators and by the algorithm itself, see [7].

In [8], the relationship between ACO and stochastic gradient descent is studied. It is shown that some empirical ACO algorithms approximate stochastic gradient descent in the space of pheromones. A stable implementation of gradient based reinforcement learning that belongs to the framework of ACO algorithms is proposed there. In [9], an algorithm for routing in mobile ad hoc networks is presented.

In [1], an ACO algorithm in the framework of multi-timescale stochastic approximation is presented and its convergence analysed in detail using the ordinary differential equation (ODE) approach. The algorithm in [1] has two components – a pheromone update scheme and an agent learning scheme. These two components are viewed as coupled stochastic approximation recursions.

* Supported through Grant No.SR/S3/EECE/011/2007 from Department of Science and Technology, Government of India.

E. Altman and A. Chaintreau (Eds.): NET-COOP 2008, LNCS 5425, pp. 37–44, 2009.
© Springer-Verlag Berlin Heidelberg 2009

We present in this paper four variants of the algorithm proposed in [1] and study the performance of all algorithms on the multi-stage shortest path problem. In two of the variants, we adapt the Q-learning algorithm from the reinforcement learning literature to the ACO framework and study their performance as well. One of the variants that we propose shows the best performance overall and performs consistently better than the MAF-ACO algorithm of [1].

The rest of the paper is organized as follows: Section 2 describes the MAF-ACO model and algorithm of [1] that we implement for performance comparisons with our other algorithms. Section 3 describes the multi-stage shortest path problem on which the algorithms are applied. Section 4 presents our proposed algorithms. In Section 5, we briefly sketch the convergence of the proposed schemes. Section 6 describes the experimental results on the multi-stage shortest path problem. Finally, Section 7 presents the concluding remarks.

2   The Multi-agent Foraging – ACO Algorithm [1]

The foraging model is inspired by the foraging phenomenon observed in nature wherein a colony of ants cooperatively discovers a shortest path between the nest and the food source. Consider a two-node network containing a source node (S) and a destination node (D) and with $d \geq 2$ paths between the two nodes. Let L_i denote the length of the edge i and we assume that each L_i is a positive integer. Each edge i is assumed to consist of m_i stages of unit length (e.g., if $L_i = 10$, then it is a concatenation of 10 stages of unit length and each $m_i = 10$). Each ant traverses one stage at a time. Associated with each edge i are two parameters – the pheromone trail parameter T_i and an agent learning parameter X_i. The agent learning parameter is suitably normalized to obtain the probability of selection of that path by an ant. A theoretical justification for the presence of the agent learning parameter is given in [1].

Let M denote the total number of artificial ants in the system. Initially at time $t=0$, all ants are at node S. Whenever an ant, k, is at node S at time t, it probabilistically chooses one of the edges i to traverse at time $t+1$. Each ant traverses one stage at a time. At every stage, ant k decides to wait with probability p or move ahead with probability $1 - p$, for some small p. Thus, a random delay is introduced in the traversal of each ant. Once an ant, k, reaches the destination node, D, by traversing through edge i, the pheromone value T_i associated with edge i is updated by a constant amount. The ant also instantaneously returns to the source node, S, and is ready to begin a new trip.

The overall algorithm [1] consists of two coupled recursions – a pheromone update scheme and an agent learning scheme. Let $a(t)$, $t \geq 0$ be decreasing step-sizes that satisfy

$$\sum_t a(t) = \infty \text{ and } \sum_t a(t)^2 < \infty. \tag{1}$$

Let $\rho \in (0,1)$ be a constant pheromone decay rate. We denote by $T_i(t)$ and $X_i(t)$, the pheromone strength parameter and the agent learning parameter, respectively, at time t on path i, $i = 1, ..., d$. Let Q be the constant quantum of pheromone deposited by an agent once it has traversed any path. Also, let $R_i(t)$ be the number of agents who have finished traversing path i at time t. The algorithm of [1] is as follows: For $i = 1, \ldots, d$, we have

$$T_i(t+1) = (1 - \rho)T_i(t) + \rho Q R_i(t) \tag{2}$$

$$X_i(t+1) = X_i(t) + a(t)X_i(t)T_i(t+1). \tag{3}$$

In (2), $(1 - \rho)T_i(t)$ accounts for the evaporation of pheromone previously deposited along path i, while $\rho Q R_i(t)$ reinforces the pheromone strength when $R_i(t)$ agents pass through path i at time t. $X_i(t)$ $(t \geq 0)$ in (3) denotes the utility associated with path i as learned by the agents after t time steps. The learning parameter update is then suitably normalized to obtain the probability of path selection by ants. Thus, the probability $P_i(t)$ of an ant selecting path i at time t is given by

$$P_i(t) = \frac{X_i(t)}{\sum_{j=1}^{d} X_j(t)}. \tag{4}$$

Thus a path with a higher utility is selected with a higher probability. Due to the decreasing step sizes $a(t)$, the agent learning scheme runs on a slower time scale as compared to the pheromone update scheme. The step-size schedule also decides the trade off between the exploration and exploitation.

Next, we describe how the MAF-ACO algorithm is applied to the foraging model. Initially all pheromone values are set to zero, i.e., $T_i(0) = 0 \ \forall \ i$. The initial values of the agent learning parameters are identically set equal to a small positive constant, i.e., $X_i(0) = c, \forall \ i$. Given a sufficient number of agents, initially at least one agent goes out on every possible path. Each agent after completion of its journey on a path from source to destination, immediately begins a fresh journey on a new path chosen according to the current values of the path selection probabilities given by (4). Thus the same fixed number of M agents circulate in the system.

At some discrete time instant $t > 0$, starting from $t = 0$, with a very high probability, the agents who traversed the shortest path complete the trip before the agents who chose other longer paths. After completion of the trip they deposit a quantum of pheromone on the corresponding path whose index is say k. Thus $T_k(t) > 0$ while $T_j(t) = 0$ for $j \neq k$. This implies that $X_k(t)$ gets a positive increment while all other $X_j(t)$, $j \neq k$, values remain the same. As a result, the probability $P_k(t)$, of agents choosing path k at time $t + 1$ is greater than the probabilities on the other paths. It is shown in [1] that initial bias builds up towards the shortest path k, that in turn drives the algorithm to converge to it.

3   Multi-stage Shortest Path Problem

Consider the graph representation of a generic multi-stage shortest path problem with K stages. Each stage k is denoted by S_k. Stage S_0 contains a single source node S and stage S_{K+1} has a single destination node D. For simplicity, we assume that each node in stage S_k is connected to every node in stage S_{k+1} for $0 \leq k \leq K - 1$ by a unique edge. There is a unique edge (S,i) between the source node S and every node $i \in S_1$. Similarly there is a unique edge (j,D) between every node $j \in S_K$ and the destination node D. Let L_{ij} denote the length of the edge (i,j). The objective is to find the shortest path between S and D.

At any discrete time instant t, for any $0 \leq k \leq K$, $i \in S_k$ and $j \in S_{k+1}$, let $T_{ij}^k(t)$ denote the pheromone trail associated with edge (i,j) and let $X_{ij}^k(t)$ denote the agent learning parameter associated with edge (i,j). The probability with which any ant chooses to move from node i to node j at time t is given by:

$$P_{ij}^k(t) = \frac{X_{ij}^k(t)}{\sum_{l \in N_i} X_{il}^k(t)} \text{ if } j \in N_i, \tag{5}$$

and is 0 otherwise. Here N_i denotes the set of successor states to state i, i.e., the set of nodes j such that there exists an edge (i,j).

The pheromone update scheme and agent learning scheme for the MAF-ACO applied to the multi-stage shortest path problem are as follows.

$$T_{ij}^k(t+1) = (1-\rho)T_{ij}^k(t) + \rho Q R_{ij}^k(t) \tag{6}$$

$$X_{ij}^k(t+1) = X_{ij}^k(t) + a(t)X_{ij}^k(t)T_{ij}^k(t+1) \tag{7}$$

In (6), $R_{ij}^k(t)$ denotes the number of ants who have completed a trip between S and D at time t and have traversed the edge (i,j) in stage k.

4   Our Algorithms

We present here our variants of the ACO algorithm in [1] and subsequently investigate, via simulation, their performance in relation to the above algorithm. We observe that a slight variation made to the pheromone update scheme in the MAF-ACO algorithm improves its overall performance. We now propose variants to the algorithm (6)-(7) of [1].

Variant A: The pheromone update scheme specified in (6) is used as is. However, the agent learning scheme is now modified to

$$X_{ij}^k(t+1) = X_{ij}^k(t)(1 + a(t)\frac{T_{ij}^k(t+1)}{\sum_{(i,l) \in N_i} T_{il}^k(t+1)}). \tag{8}$$

The idea here is to use normalized pheromone strengths in the learning update instead of the pheromone strengths themselves. The equation has been modified to include the weight contributed by the $(i,j)^{th}$ edge as compared to that of other outgoing edges $(i,l) \in N_i$.

Variant B: The Pheromone update scheme is modified here as

$$T_{ij}^k(t+1) = (1-\rho)T_{ij}^k(t) + \frac{\rho Q R_{ij}(t)}{L_{ij}}. \tag{9}$$

The agent learning scheme specified in (7) is retained here. In (9), we incorporate the fact that the strength of the pheromone deposited by ants along a link must depend on its length in an inverse fashion. Thus, larger the length of a link, lower would be the pheromone strength along the link and vice-versa. As we observe in our experiments, this variant performs the best amongst all variants that we study, and performs better than the algorithm in [1].

Variant C: The Pheromone update scheme is modified as in (9). We however use the self-adaptive Q-routing algorithm [10] for parameter learning. The Q-routing algorithm is primarily the Q-learning algorithm, applied for finding the shortest path in routing applications, that is popular in the reinforcement learning literature. We associate with each node a learning parameter instead of the agent learning parameter for each edge. Let $Q_{id}(t)$ denote the learning parameter that a node i estimates for the ant to reach the destination D at time t. Each ant at each node takes a decision based on the learning parameter Q associated with its neighbor nodes. In particular, the probability of choosing node j for an ant at node i is given by

$$P_{ij}(t) = \frac{Q_{jd}(t)}{\Sigma_{(i,l)\in N_i} Q_{ld}(t)}. \tag{10}$$

Once the next node is decided based on the above probability, the value of the learning parameter Q associated with node i is updated as per the standard Q-learning algorithm (below)

$$Q_{id}(t+1) = Q_{id}(t) + \eta(T_{ij}(t) + Q_{jd}(t) - Q_{id}(t)), \tag{11}$$

where η is a "learning rate" parameter and $T_{ij}(t)$ denotes the pheromone strength associated with edge (i,j) at time t. The idea here is to use Q-values $Q_{ij}(t)$ to update the probabilities of choosing paths instead of the learning rate parameter $X_{ij}(t)$. Thus a path with a higher Q-value has a higher probability of selection.

Variant D: Both the pheromone update and the agent learning schemes are as in Variant C here. The probabilities $P_{ij}(t)$, however, are selected according to

$$P_{ij}(t) = \frac{T_{ij}(t) + Q_{jd}(t)}{\Sigma_{(i,l)\in N_i}(T_{il}(t) + Q_{ld}(t))}, \tag{12}$$

in place of (10). Note that $(T_{ij}(t) + Q_{jd}(t))$ is an estimate of the value of the edge (i,j) chosen at node i at time t. Thus, while in Variant C, we use the Q-value of the 'next' state as the learning parameter for obtaining the path selection probabilities, in Variant D, we use the value of the 'current' state by summing the single-stage reward (note that the pheromone update now serves as the single-stage reward) and the Q-value of the 'next' state, for the same. Thus, in Variant D, the edge with the maximum value has the highest probability of being picked.

5   A Sketch of Convergence

The analysis follows along the lines of [1]. Hence, only a brief sketch is presented. We consider Variant B first. From (5), upon simplification, one obtains the following recursion for $P_{ij}^k(n)$:

$$P_{ij}^k(n+1) = P_{ij}^k(n) + a(n)P_{ij}^k(n)(T_{ij}^k(n+1) - \sum_{l \in N_i} P_{il}^k(n)T_{il}^k(n+1))(1 - O(a(n))).$$

(13)

The above can be seen to be an Euler discretization (see [1]) of the following ODE:

$$\dot{P}_{ij}^k = P_{ij}^k(f_{ij}^k(P) - \sum_{l \in N_i} f_{il}^k(P)P_{il}^k),$$

(14)

where $f_{ij}^k(P) = E_s[T_{ij}^k(n)]$ is the stationary expectation for the pheromone values. For the iterates as in (9), one can obtain in a similar manner as Lemma 2 of [1] that

$$f_{ij}^k(P) = \frac{P_{ij}^k QM}{L_{ij} \sum_{l \in N_i}(m_l + 1)P_{il}^k}.$$

Let S_{N_i} denote the N_i-dimensional simplex

$$S_{N_i} = \{q_i = (q_{i1}, \ldots, q_{i|N_i|}) \in \mathcal{R}^{N_i} \mid q_{il} \geq 0 \ \forall l \in N_i \text{ and } \sum_{l \in N_i} q_{il} = 1\}.$$

Functions $f_{ij}^k(\cdot)$ are Lipschitz continuous on S_{N_i}, hence (14) is well posed. One can now show as in Lemma 4 of [1] that $(1, 0, \ldots, 0)$ is an asymptotically stable equilibrium for the ODE (14) with domain of attraction $\mathcal{D} = \{x \in S_{N_i} \mid x_1 > x_j, j \neq 1\}$. A similar result as Theorem 1 of [1] then shows that once iteration (13) enters $\mathcal{D}$, it asymptotically converges to the above point with a probability that increases asymptotically (with the iteration index) to one. The convergence for Variant A can be shown in a similar manner.

For Variants C and D, note that boundedness of iterates for the Q-learning recursion is not guaranteed. For purposes of showing convergence of the Q-learning recursion, one can reset iterates as soon as they go outside a unit ball. As we see in our experiments, we do not require the modified procedure suggested above. Since we work only with probabilities (in order to compute the optimal paths), the corresponding recursion for the probabilities remains bounded and one can indeed show that using both – Variants C and D, $P_{ij}(t)$ will converge to one for the edge (i, j) that has the maximum Q-value.

6   Experimental Results

In this section, we report the simulation results using our algorithms and the MAF-ACO algorithm of [1], and compare their performance. The multi-stage shortest path model on which the various algorithms have been applied is shown in Fig. 1. In our simulations, we ran each algorithm for a sufficiently long time and the shortest path found in each execution of each algorithm was recorded. We treat each execution of each algorithm as a *trial*. 100 independent *trials* of each algorithm are run and the number of times the algorithm converged to the shortest path was observed. The performance has been summarized for $M \in \{32, 64, 128, 256\}$ ants. The agent learning parameter and pheromone value associated to each edge are set initially to 1 and 0 respectively. The learning parameter η is set to 0.5. The quantity of pheromone Q is initially set to 1.

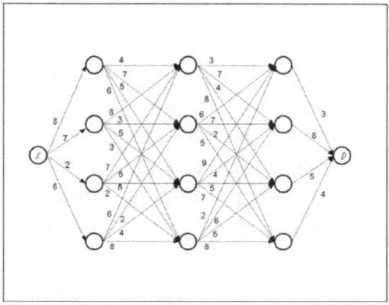

Fig. 1. The directed graph for the multi-stage shortest path problem simulation

The value of ρ was not found to be critical in the experiments and hence was set to 0.1 for all the trials (Table 2). We however also present results (Table 1) of experiments using the original MAF-ACO algorithm and our Variant B for different values of ρ. In the agent learning scheme, the initial value of the step-size was set to $a(0) = 0.9$ and it was updated every 10 iterations by applying the rule: $a(10n) = \frac{a(0)}{n}$ and $a(10n + k) = a(10n)$ for $1 \leq k \leq 10$. This can be seen to satisfy the step-size requirement (1). The choice of ρ plays a significant role in the performance of traditional ACO algorithms. Our algorithms and the MAF-ACO algorithm, however, are quite tolerant to variations in the value of ρ. This can be attributed to the presence of the agent learning scheme which introduces an extra averaging step. It has been observed that in most cases with all the algorithms, where the solution did not converge to the optimal solution, it has converged to the next best solution.

Table 1. The % of correct solutions found by MAF-ACO and Variant B for various values of evaporation rate (ρ) and number of agents (M)

ρ	MAF-ACO				Variant B			
	Number of agents M				Number of agents M			
	32	64	128	256	32	64	128	256
0.1	55	80	95	100	65	88	99	100
0.5	55	88	99	100	67	93	100	100
0.7	57	90	99	100	70	95	100	100

Table 2. The % of correct solutions found by all algorithms for $\rho = 0.1$

	Number of agents M			
	32	64	128	256
MAF-ACO	55	80	95	100
Variant A	53	80	97	100
Variant B	65	88	99	100
Variant C	43	75	89	100
Variant D	56	82	95	100

7   Conclusions

We developed four variants of the recently developed MAF-ACO algorithm and studied their performance on a multi-stage shortest path problem. In three of our variants, we take into account the fact that the increment on the strength of the pheromone update depends inversely as the length of the path. Our Variant B that combines the above with the same learning parameter update as the original MAF-ACO algorithm of [1] is seen to perform the best overall. As future work, we shall study routing applications by considering a network of queues and study the effect of congestion there. We shall also develop ACO algorithms for constrained optimization under inequality constraints involving quality of service (QoS) guarantees.

References

1. Borkar, V.S., Das, D.: A novel ACO algorithm for optimization via reinforcement and initial bias. Swarm Intelligence, special issue on Ant Colony Optimization (to appear, 2008)
2. Dorigo, M., Stutzle, T.: Ant Colony Optimization. MIT Press, Cambridge (2004)
3. Dorigo, M., Blum, C.: Ant colony optimization theory: A survey. TCS: Theoretical Computer Science 345 (2005)
4. Gutjahr, W.J.: A graph-based ant system and its convergence. Future Generation Comp. Syst. 16(8), 873–888 (2000)
5. Stutzle, T., Dorigo, M.: A short convergence proof for a class of ant colony optimization algorithms. IEEE-EC 6, 358–365 (2002)
6. Merkle, D., Middendorf, M.: Modeling the dynamics of ant colony optimization. Evolutionary Computation 10(3), 235–262 (2002)
7. Blum, C., Dorigo, M.: Search bias in ant colony optimization: on the role of competition-balanced systems. IEEE Trans. Evolutionary Computation 9(2), 159–174 (2005)
8. Meuleau, N., Dorigo, M.: Ant colony optimization and stochastic gradient descent. Artificial Life 8(2), 103–121 (2002)
9. Di Caro, G.A., Ducatelle, F., Gambardella, L.M.: AntHocNet: An ant-based hybrid routing algorithm for mobile ad hoc networks. In: Yao, X., Burke, E.K., Lozano, J.A., Smith, J., Merelo-Guervós, J.J., Bullinaria, J.A., Rowe, J.E., Tiňo, P., Kabán, A., Schwefel, H.-P. (eds.) PPSN 2004. LNCS, vol. 3242, pp. 461–470. Springer, Heidelberg (2004)
10. Ghassemlooy, Z., Tekiner, F., Srikanth, T.R.: Comparison of the q-routing and shortest path routing algorithms. In: Proc. of the 5th Annual Postgraduate Symp. on the Convergence of Telecommunications, Networking and Broadcasting (2004)

MPLS Online Routing Optimization Using Prediction

Abutaleb Abdelmohdi Turky and Andreas Mitschele-Thiel

Integrated HW/SW Systems Group, Ilmenau University of Technology
98693 Ilmenau, Germany
{abutaleb-abdelmohdi.turky,mitsch}@tu-ilmenau.de

Abstract. This paper presents an efficient enhancement to the online routing algorithms for the computation of Labeled Switching Paths (LSPs) in Multiprotocol Label Switching (MPLS) based networks. To achieve that, an adaptive predictor is used to predict the future link loads. Then the predicted values are incorporated in the link weights formula. Our contribution is to propose a new idea that depends on the knowledge of the future link loads to achieve a routing that can be done much more efficiently. According to the non-linear nature of traffic, we use a Feed Forward Neural Network (FFNN) to build an accurate traffic predictor that is able to capture the actual traffic behaviour. We study two performance parameters: the rejection ratio and the percentage of accepted bandwidth in different load conditions. Our proposed algorithm in general, reduces the rejection ratio of requests and achieves higher throughput when compared to CSPF and WSP algorithms.

Keywords: MPLS, traffic engineering, routing, neural network.

1 Introduction

The growth of the Internet requires complexity level of network management techniques such as Traffic Engineering (TE) in order to provide the demanded quality of service (QoS). Traffic engineering targets to optimize the performance goals such as delay minimization, throughput maximization and it aims to optimize the resource utilization. The extensions of routing protocols are proposed to modify these protocols for traffic engineering includes connectionless routing protocols such as Open Shortest Path First (OSPF) and the more recently deployed MPLS protocol.

In MPLS networks [1], the packets are assigned with labels at the ingress router and these labels are used to forward the packets according to specific LSPs. Service providers can use LSPs to implement Virtual Private Networks (VPNs) or to satisfy other QoS agreements. There is another signalling protocol such as Recourse Reservation Protocol (RSVP-TE) [2] or Label Distribution Protocol [3] (LDP) that used to setup the paths. In other words, the route of LSPs is explicitly defined between the ingress and egress routers. With the explicit routing of LSPs in MPLS technology, the service providers have an important feature to be able to engineer how their traffic will be routed, and have the ability to improve the network utilization, by minimizing the LSPs rejection ratio when the network is overloaded.

The efficiency of TE schemes mainly depends on route optimization. Routing algorithms [4] can be classified to static or dynamic according to the nature of

E. Altman and A. Chaintreau (Eds.): NET-COOP 2008, LNCS 5425, pp. 45–52, 2009.

information used for selecting LSP routes. Static algorithms depend on fixed information which does not change with time; dynamic algorithms use the current state of the network. Also, routing algorithms can be executed either online or offline according to when the computation is done. In online routing algorithms path requests are attended to one by one request. This paper is focused on dynamic online routing.

In this paper, we introduce a new idea to enhance the routing performance by using FFNN to build an accurate predictor that is able to predict the actual traffic behaviour. Then we use it to predict the future load in every network links and incorporate this value in link weights formula. The remainder of this paper is organized as follows: Section 2 overviews the related work. Section 3 demonstrates the predicting of future load-based routing algorithm. Section 4 discusses the performance evaluation. The future work and our conclusions are presented in section 5.

2 Related Works

The Shortest Path First (SPF) algorithm is the most commonly used algorithm within MPLS Domains. In SPF, the path that contains least number of links between the source and destination pair is selected. Although SPF is trying to minimize resource occupation, it leads to congestions in some network links and causes unbalancing in resource utilization. R. A. Guerin [5] introduced a modification to the shortest path algorithm, called Widest Shortest Path (WSP), which is based on the computation of the shortest paths in the first stage and if there is more than one of those shortest paths, it chooses the one with maximum bandwidth.

E. Crawley [6] proposed the Constraint Shortest Path First (CSPF) protocol to overcome the problem of load balancing in OSPF which modifies the link cost to reflect the current resource availability. The cost of links is inversely proportional to the residual link capacities. Since all previous algorithms choose the LSPs without considering the future LSPs requests, the related performance dose not achieve the best result in maximizing network utilization or request acceptance rate.

An example of advanced routing algorithm is Minimum Interference Routing Algorithm (MIRA) [7]. The idea of MIRA is to prevent routing over links that may interfere with another path requests in the future. The algorithm picks up the minimum interference path for a given LSP that maximizes the minimum max-flow between all other ingress-egress pairs. The computations of MIRA routing are taking long time and MIRA does not work as expected for some network scenarios.

R. Boutaba [8] introduced a dynamic online routing algorithm (DORA) that compute the path potential value (PPV) array associated with a source-destination pair in the first step. PPV is used to avoid routing over links that have high potential to be part of any other paths. Then the algorithm incorporates PPV value with residual link bandwidth to form a weight value for each link that is used to compute a weight-optimized network path. DORA offers better performance than MIRA and WSP algorithms. Additionally computations used in DORA are less expensive.

E. Einhorn and A. Mitschele-Thiel [9] introduced Reinforcement Learning for Traffic-Engineering (RLTE) algorithm. This work presents a novel distributed and self-organized QoS routing approach that is based on reinforcement learning.

3 Predicting of Future Load-Based Routing Algorithm

This section provides a detailed description of Predicting of Future Load-based Routing algorithm (PFLR).Firstly; we want to describe the idea behind design of PFLR. We believe that in any routing algorithm which depend on residual bandwidth in network links in order to choose LSPs: consideration of the future load value will optimize the routing performance more effectively. Therefore, we propose to build an accurate traffic predictor that will be able to predict the actual traffic behaviour.

The future links load depends on many parameters such as network topology, network load condition (inter-arrival rate and holding time of the requests in the network) and the behaviour of selected routing algorithm. Artificial Neural network (ANN) offers prediction capability with different types of network traffic and has ability to learn on line to be adaptive. With experimental results [10], ANN approach can accurately predict a complicated network traffic pattern efficiently.

The operation of PFLR is divided into two stages. The first stage is the prediction of the future available BW on every link after specific period of time WS (Window Size). The operation of predictions should be made decentralized for example; a specific node is responsible for the prediction operations in specific part of the network to acquire fast prediction and to distribute the complexity of prediction.

In the second stage, the predicted value of future load and current residual bandwidth of each link are combined together in specific formula to represent the link weight. The formula is controlled by a parameter called α which represent the prediction weight. Finally, we run the already   selected algorithm to compute a weight-optimized path without any change in its behaviour .In other words, we do not change the routing algorithm that is already running in the network, we just modify the links weights while taking in our consideration the future load. Thus our proposed algorithm has the capability to run with any routing algorithm depend on residual bandwidth in its computations such as WSP, CSFP and DORA.

3.1 PFLR Algorithm

Input:
   The network topology and all residual link capacities.
   The LSPs requests between the different ingress-egress pairs.
Output:
   Routed paths through the network.
Algorithm:
   1.   Predict the future available bandwidth in all links in the network after a specified period of time WS.
   2.   Repeat the following steps until the time of WS has elapsed.
      2.1 Construct the link weight using the following equation:

$$W=(1-\alpha)*(1/\text{current available BW})+\alpha*(1/\text{predicted available BW}) \quad (1)$$

      Where α = (prediction weight)
      2.2 Complete the normal routing algorithm without changing anything.
   3.   Repeat the previous steps and so on.

4   Performance Evaluation

In this section, we will demonstrate the set of experiments used to evaluate the performance of PFLR and will discuss the results. All experiment scenarios are implemented using Visual Basic and Neural Network toolbox in MATLAB [11]. We will test PFLR performance and compare it with WSP and CSPF algorithm. Two parameters performance are studied: first is the rejection ratio of LSPs requests and second is the percentage of accepted BW in two different network load conditions.

Also we want to prove our earlier stated hypothesis of consideration of the future load in routing decision in order to enhance the routing performance. Therefore in every scenario we shall compare two routing algorithms with two different types of future information. The first type is the actual value of link loads after a specific period of time. In this case, we assume that the information of future values related to arrival time, the source and destination nodes and the required capacity of the next LSPs are already known. In other words, we shall run the selected algorithm for routing the next requests in the WS period. Then we take the value of link loads at the end of the WS period (as future info.). Then we return back again to the start of WS period in order to combine this value with the current BW value. The second type is the predicted link load that fully depends on the history of traffic in a particular link and does not know any thing about the future (the real case of network routing).

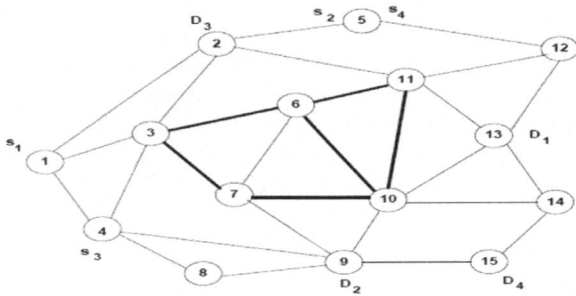

Fig. 1. MIRA network topology

Our experiment is done on MIRA network that is shown in Fig. 1. The thicker links have a capacity of 4800 capacity unit while the thinner links have a capacity of 1200 capacity unit. Fig. 1 shows the location of four different source–destination pairs that are identified by (S1, D1), (S2, D2), (S3, D3), and (S4, D4). The capacities of requested paths are randomly distributed among 10-40 capacity units. We examine the performance for two different network load conditions. The first network load condition is a moderate load condition: when the arrival of requests follows a Poisson distribution with mean $\lambda = 32.5$ requests per time-unit and the holding time of request is based on an Exponential distribution with mean $\mu = 10$ time-units. The second is heavy load condition: when the inter arrival of path requests λ is equal to 35 requests per time-unit and the holding time of request μ is equal to 10 time-units.

The structure of FFNN is shown in Fig. 2. FFNN consists of three layers: The input layer contains 16 neurons that are connected directly to the last 16 traffic sample. The hidden layer consists of 20 neurons and only one neuron in the output which gives the predicted value of link load after WS. The Levenberg-Marquardt training algorithm is used because it is the fastest and most accurate one in our case. FFNN is designed to be adaptive. It takes the previous thousand of traffic samples and train on it to achieve the best predictor design. Then FFNN is used to predict the future link load during the next hundred traffic samples and then it will trains again on the previous thousand of traffic samples and so on.

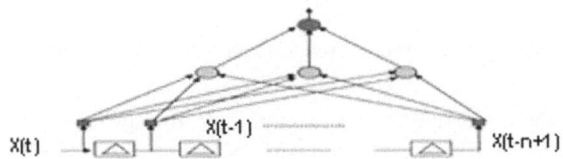

Fig. 2. Feed Forward Neural Network architecture

The optimal values of α and WS depend on the behaviour of routing algorithm and the load condition. In every scenario, we search for the optimal values of α and WS by trying different values of α (range from 0 to 1) and WS (range from 5 to 9). In case of the actual value of link loads, α and WS take different values related to every scenario. In case of the predicted value of link loads, we found the fewest rejection ratio at α=0.1 and WS=8 in all PFLR scenarios. Table 1 show the rejection ratio of 2000 requests (in CSPF with PFLR) for the moderate load condition scenario only with different combination of α and WS.

Table 1. The rejection ratio of requests for different combination of α and WS parameters

α	WS=5	W =6	WS=7	WS=8	WS=9
0.0	1,257	1,257	1,257	1,257	1,257
0.1	1,170	1,234	1,277	**1,166**	1,275
0.2	1,328	1,203	1,186	1,198	1,395

4.1 Moderate Load Condition Scenario

Fig. 3 shows the rejection ratio of requests for the moderate load condition. Based on Fig. 3, WSP_FUT (WSP with actual future load at α=1.0 and WS=6.) rejects approximately 8.68% less requests than WSP, followed by WSP_PFLR (WSP with Prediction at α=0.1 and WS=8.) that rejects approximately 8.51% less requests than WSP. Also CSPF_FUT (at α=0.095 and WS=8.) rejects approximately 6.42% requests less than CSPF, followed by CSPF_PFLR (at α=0.1 and WS=8.) that rejects approximately 4.45% less requests than CSPF.

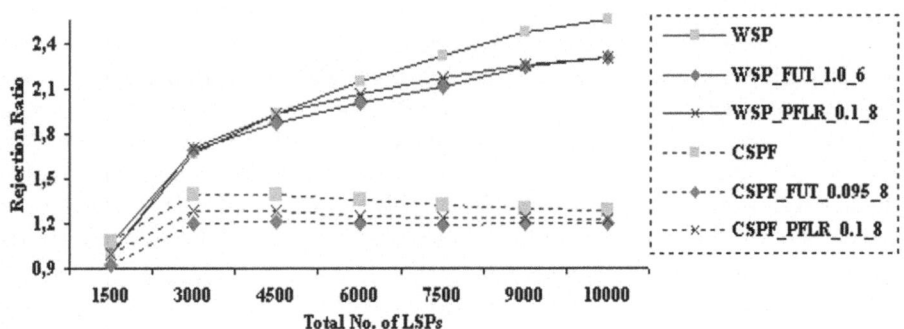

Fig. 3. The rejection ratio of requests for the moderate load condition

Fig. 4 shows the percentage of accepted BW for the moderate load condition. Based on Fig. 4, WSP_PFLR (at $\alpha=0.1$ and WS=8) accepts 0.38% more bandwidth than WSP, followed by WSP_FUT (at $\alpha=1.0$ and WS=6) that accepts 0.35% more bandwidth than WSP. Also CSPF_FUT (at $\alpha=0.095$ and WZ=8.) accepts 0.10% more bandwidth than CSPF, followed by CSPF_PFLR (at $\alpha=0.1$ and WS=8.) accepts 0.06% more bandwidth than CSPF.

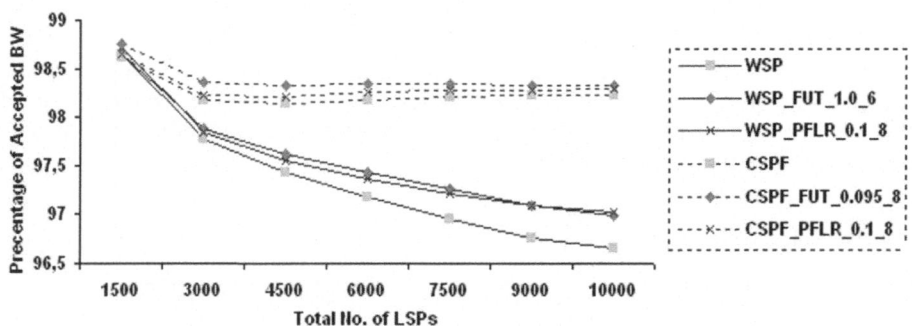

Fig. 4. The percentage of accepted BW for the moderate load condition

4.2 Heavy Load Condition Scenario

Fig. 5 shows the rejection ratio of requests for the heavy load condition. Based on the Fig. 5, WSP_FUT (at $\alpha=1.0$ and WS=6.) rejects approximately 4.45% less requests than WSP, followed by WSP_PFLR (at $\alpha=0.1$ and WS=8.) that rejects approximately 2.58% less requests than WSP. Also CSPF_PFLR (at $\alpha=0.1$ and WS=8) rejects approximately 6.77% less requests than CSPF, followed by CSPF_FUT (at $\alpha=0.205$ and WS=8) that rejects approximately 2.87% less requests than CSPF.

Fig. 6 shows the percentage of accepted BW for the heavy load condition. Based on Fig. 6, WSP_FUT (at $\alpha=1.0$ and WS=8.) accepts 0.29% more bandwidth than WSP, followed by WSP_PFLR (at $\alpha=0.1$ and WS=8.) that accepts 0.13% more bandwidth than WSP. Also CSPF_PFLR (at $\alpha=0.1$ and WZ=8.) accepts 0.57% more

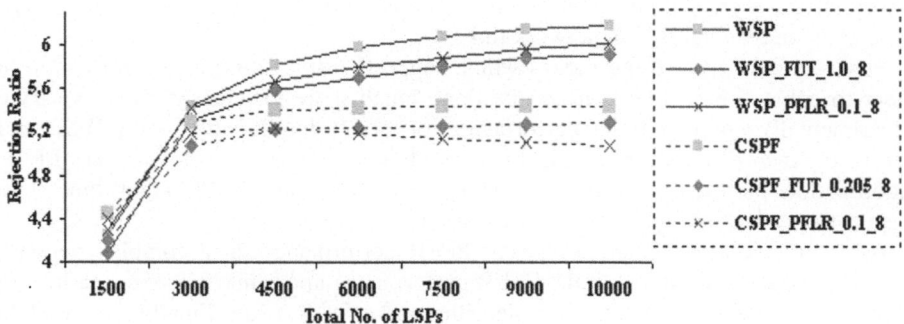

Fig. 5. The rejection ratio of requests for the heavy load condition

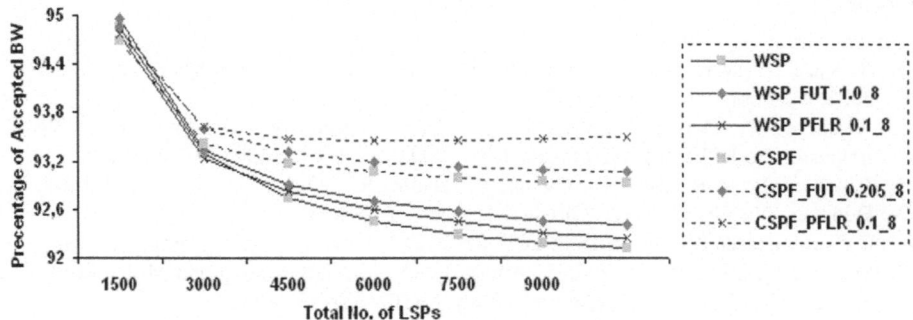

Fig. 6. The percentage of accepted BW for the heavy load condition

bandwidth than CSPF, followed by CSPF_FUT (at α=0.205 and WZ=8.) that accepts 0.13% more bandwidth than CSPF.

4.3 Complexity Analysis of PFLR

PFLR algorithm requires additional commotional time to achieve enhanced routing performance. This time consists of two parts, the training time of predictors and the prediction time. As we say before, the predictors are distributed on the nodes. This means every node will responsible for (E/V) operation where E is the number of links and V is the number of nodes. The training operation happens only one time every specific period RP (Retrain Period). The predation also happens every WS period. Thus, the training requires O ((E Tt) / (V RP)) where Tt is the training time of one predictor and the prediction requires O ((E Pt) / (V WS)) where Pt is the prediction time of one predictor. The prediction is computationally inexpensive which is equal to 0.006 sec. But the training requires more time which is equal to 0.078 sec.

5 Conclusion and Future Work

In this paper, we have proposed a new TE algorithm named PFLR that can efficiently enhance the dynamic on line routing algorithms in MPLS-based networks. This algorithm can work with any other online routing algorithms that have computations depending on residual BW in network links.

First, we have proved our theory which suggests using future load information in order to achieve a routing that can be done much more efficiently. Then we have experimentally compared the performance of PFLR modification with WSP and CSPF in two different network load conditions and have shown that PFLR modification performs considerably better than WSP and CSPF algorithms with respect to two performance comparison criteria.

As future work, we plan to test the PFLR performance on a complex network topology. Also we need to test the PFLR performance upon link failure scenario. We need to compare PFLR with other algorithms like DORA too. Finally, we want to focus on decentralized routing algorithms such as any local optimization algorithms.

References

1. Rosen, E., Viswanathan, A., Callon, R.: Multiprotocol Label Switching Architecture. RFC 3031, Network Working Group (2001)
2. Awduche, D., Berger, L., Gan, D., Li, T., Srinivasan, V., Swallow, G.: RSVPTE: Extensions to RSVP for LSP tunnels. RFC 3209, Network Working Group (2001)
3. Jamoussi, B., Andersson, L., Callon, R., Dantu, R., Wu, L., Doolan, P., Worster, T., Feldman, N., Fredette, A., Girish, M., Gray, E., Heinanen, J., Kilty, T., Malis, A.: Constraint based LSP setup using LDP. RFC 3212, Network Working Group (2000)
4. Marzo, J.L., Calle, E., Scoglio, C., Anjah, T.: QoS Online Routing and MPLS Multilevel Protection: A Survey. IEEE Commun. Mag. 41(10), 126–132 (2003)
5. Guerin, R., Orda, A., Williams, D.: QoS routing mechanisms and OSPF extensions. In: IEEE Global Telecommunication, pp. 1903–1908. IEEE Press, Phoenix (1997)
6. Crawley, E., Nair, R., Jajagopalan, B., Sandick, H.: A Framework for QoS-based Routing in the Internet. RFC 2386, Network Working Group (1998)
7. Kar, K., Kodialam, M., Lakshman, T.V.: Minimum Interference Routing of Bandwidth Guaranteed Tunnels with MPLS Traffic Engineering Applications. IEEE J. Selected Areas in Comm. 18(12), 2566–2579 (2000)
8. Boutaba, R., Szeto, W., Iraqi, Y.: DORA: Efficient Routing for MPLS Traffic Engineering. J. Net. and Sys. Man. 10(3), 309–325 (2002)
9. Einhorn, E., Mitschele-Thiel, A.: RLTE: Reinforcement Learning for Traffic-Engineering. In: 2nd International Conference on Autonomous Infrastructure, Man. and Sec., Bremen (2008)
10. Eswaradass, A., Sun, X.H., Wu, M.: Network Bandwidth Predictor (NBP): A System for Online Network performance Forecasting. In: Sixth IEEE International Symposium on Cluster Computing and the Grid, pp. 265–268. IEEE Computer Society, Singapore (2006)
11. Neural Network Toolbox, MATLAP V.7,
    http://www.mathworks.com/products/neuralnet

On the Identifiability of Link Service Curves from End-Host Measurements

Amr Rizk and Markus Fidler*

Multimedia Communications Lab
TU Darmstadt, Germany
{amr.rizk,markus.fidler}@kom.tu-darmstadt.de

Abstract. We estimate service curves of network internal links from end-host measurements of probing traffic. Our approach belongs to the field of network tomography, which deals with the fundamental challenge of identifiability in a priori under-determined network equation systems. As opposed to recent methods that estimate sole quantities, such as delay and bandwidth, we characterize links using the more generic concept of service curve that comprises various derived quantities including the ones mentioned above. Key to our solution is the Legendre-Fenchel transform that achieves additivity of link service curves. Our measurement results reveal that the burstiness of cross traffic flows, which has significant impact on the shape of leftover service curves, can be attributed to individual links. Using the network calculus we show fundamental limits of certain tomography approaches regarding the identification of propagation delays as well as regarding the resolution of post-narrow links.

1 Introduction

Internet service providers largely keep performance measures of their infrastructure confidential. Taking measurements only at end-hosts, network tomography considered here seeks to break results obtained for network paths down to characteristics even of individual links. Per-link metrics including loss, delay, or available bandwidth are vital for numerous applications, such as network monitoring, fault detection, service level agreement verification, and for improving services [3]. For completeness we mention that network tomography can also be applied to synthesize path characteristics from link results, e.g. for origin-destination traffic matrix estimation, a problem which we do not address here.

In this work we seek to identify link service curves from end-host measurements. The notion of service curve and the network calculus provide a general framework for modeling and analysis of transmission systems that goes significantly beyond single performance metrics such as delay or available bandwidth that are primarily used in network tomography today. At the same time service curves facilitate deriving these metrics easily.

---

* This work was funded by the German Research Foundation (DFG) under an Emmy Noether grant.

The network calculus [2,10] is a min-plus system theory for queuing systems that dates back to the seminal works in [4,14]. A system is said to offer a (lower) service curve $S(t)$ to a cumulative traffic arrival flow $A(t)$ if the departures $D(t)$ satisfy $D(t) \geq A \otimes S(t)$ where $\otimes$ denotes the min-plus convolution defined as $A \otimes S(t) = \inf_{\tau} \{A(\tau) + S(t - \tau)\}$. Here the arrivals $A(t)$ and departures $D(t)$ are the cumulative number of bits entering respectively leaving the system in the time interval $[0, t)$. The service curve $S(t)$ specifies the (minimal) service guarantee over a time interval of duration t. If the system is linear under the min-plus algebra, e.g. a constant rate link or a leaky-bucket traffic regulator, it has an exact service curve $S(t)$ leading to departures given by $D(t) = A \otimes S(t)$. Performance bounds, e.g. for backlog and delay, follow easily from these definitions. Furthermore, whole network paths consisting of tandem systems $S_1, S_2, \ldots S_N$ can be convolved to an end-to-end service curve $S_{e2e}(t) = S_1 \otimes S_2 \otimes \cdots \otimes S_N(t)$. The inverse problem, that is identification of a system's service curve from readings of its arrivals and departures, is solved in [12,13]. Related approaches use max-plus algebra to model and identify discrete event systems, see [11] and references therein.

The remainder of this paper is structured as follows. In Sect. 2 we briefly review network tomography and phrase it in a canonical form. In Sect. 3 we show how the Legendre aka Fenchel transform converts the task of per-link service curve inference into this form. We adapt two particular network tomography methods to service curve identification. We report experimental results in Sect. 4 where we show the benefits of the service curve approach as well as fundamental limits of certain tomography methods. We present brief conclusions in Sect. 5.

2   Related Work on Network Tomography

Given an N-vector of additive link[1] metrics $\mathbf{L}$, e.g. delays, and an $M \times N$-routing matrix $\mathbf{R}$ the M-vector of path metrics $\mathbf{P}$ follows by matrix multiplication as:

$$\mathbf{P} = \mathbf{R} \cdot \mathbf{L} \qquad (1)$$

Note that (1) depicts a very general relationship where $\mathbf{P}$ and $\mathbf{L}$ can describe different metrics, such as delay, loss, or even service curves, if the matrix multiplication in (1) is adapted accordingly.

Network tomography is concerned with the inference of link metrics from path measurements. Given[2] $\mathbf{R}$ the task is an inversion problem, i.e. solving (1) for $\mathbf{L}$. For many realistic networks the number of distinct path measurements that can be taken between end-hosts is smaller than the number of links in the network resulting in an under-determined system, i.e. $M < N$ such that (1) can not be simply inverted. Moreover, there exist basic topologies, e.g. a star, where $M \geq N$ but $\mathbf{R}$ is not invertible due to linear dependencies. We discuss two active probing solutions to these challenges. For a broader overview see e.g. [3].

---

[1] We use unidirectional links and do not make any assumptions of symmetry.

[2] Inference of routing can be based on e.g `traceroute` but is not part of this work.

In [16] multicast-based probing methods for per-link delay inference are developed. The correlation of multicast path measurements provides additional information that is used to solve the otherwise under-determined system (1) for **L**. As a simple example consider three links with labels $1, 2, 3$ that span a tree topology. A probe traverses link 1 and is multicast on link 2 and link 3 afterwards. The probe provides information on paths $\langle 1, 2 \rangle$ and $\langle 1, 3 \rangle$ that are correlated owing to link 1. Using probabilistic methods this correlation is key to inferring the characteristics of link 1 and subsequently of links 2 and 3.

While (1) is defined for additive metrics, e.g. delay, it can be easily extended to multiplicative metrics, such as the probability of successful packet transmission respectively of packet loss. Taking the logarithm of a multiplicative metric yields an additive one such that (1) is recovered. It is shown in [1], that the logarithm transform can ease the multicast-based inference of loss, which is indeed a multiplicative metric.

A different technique called tailgating is proposed in [9] to estimate link bandwidths. It is implemented in a tool called `nettimer`. The approach is also used by `STAB` [17] and adopted in related works [7,15]. Tailgating uses probe packets of alternating size. Large "tailgated" packets are each followed by a very small "tailgating" packet. The large packets are set up by the time-to-live or hop-limit field (TTL) to exit the path after a defined link, causing small packets to queue behind them only up to that part of the path. From there on it is assumed that the small packets travel without queuing to the sink. Hence, the small packets carry information on the first part of the path in their time spacing. This is used to infer the bandwidth only of the first part of the path. Given N links in series labeled $1, 2, \ldots, N$ tailgating can approximate $M = N$ path measurements for the paths $\langle 1 \rangle, \langle 1, 2 \rangle, \ldots, \langle 1, 2, \ldots, N \rangle$ so that (1) is invertible.

Related are bandwidth estimation methods, such as `pathchar`, `clink`, `pchar`, `pathneck`, and `bfind`, that use `ICMP TTL` exceeded messages. These are sent back to the source from the point where the TTL expires. Like tailgating some of these methods send large packets to induce congestion that is measured using small packets. However, here the TTL of the small packets and not the large packets is configured to expire after a certain link to create feedback to the source.

Bandwidth is a metric that uses the minimum, i.e. the bandwidth of a path is determined by the narrow link that is the link with the minimal bandwidth. This results in a modification of (1) where addition is replaced by minimum. As opposed to addition there exists, however, no inverse operation for the minimum. This causes fundamental difficulties regarding the inversion of (1) that are reflected in the inability of current techniques to resolve post-narrow links.

Regarding our target of inferring per-link service curves, denoted **L**, from measured path service curves, denoted **P**, we conclude that a transform that maps min-plus convolution to addition (similar to the logarithm transform that maps multiplication to addition) achieves the canonical form (1). This form facilitates application of various tomography algorithms such as the ones described above. In Sect. 3 we show how the Legendre-transform can be effectively used to this end.

3   Inference of Link Service Curves

In this section we develop methods for inference of link service curves from path measurements. We formulate the problem in min-plus algebra and transform the equation system to obtain the canonical form (1) that can be solved by known tomography algorithms. We adapt two inference methods to our task.

The maximum virtual backlog $B_{\max} = \sup_t \{A(t) - D(t)\}$ is the maximum amount of data contained by a system at any time. Note that virtual backlog comprises bits that are queued, e.g. caused by fluctuating burstiness of the cross traffic, as well as bits that are in transmission. For constant rate probes $A(t) = rt$ at a lossless min-plus linear system, i.e. with an exact service curve $S(t)$,

$$B_{\max}(r) = \sup_t \{rt - S(t)\} =: \mathcal{L}_S(r) \qquad (2)$$

holds, where $\mathcal{L}_S$ is the Legendre transform of the service curve $S(t)$ [4,5,12,13].

An important property of the Legendre transform is that twofold application $\mathcal{L}\mathcal{L}_S$ returns the convex hull of S, i.e. the largest convex function that is smaller than S. Thus, we generally have $\mathcal{L}\mathcal{L}_S \leq S$ and $\mathcal{L}\mathcal{L}_S = S$ if S is convex.

The properties of the Legendre transform are used in [12,13] to establish a measurement method. Using constant rate probes $A(t) = rt$ at increasing rates r, referred to as a rate scan, the backlog is determined from measurements of $A(t)$ and $D(t)$. Once an estimate $\tilde{B}_{\max}(r)$ is quantified the Legendre transform reveals a service curve estimate $\tilde{S}(t) = \mathcal{L}_{\tilde{B}_{\max}}(t)$ of a min-plus linear system.

Furthermore, the Legendre transform turns the min-plus convolution into a sum, i.e. $\mathcal{L}(S_1 \otimes S_2)(r) = \mathcal{L}_{S_1}(r) + \mathcal{L}_{S_2}(r)$. We use this property to recast the task of per-link service curve identification in standard form according to (1), such that the methods from network tomography can be applied to it.

Using service curves $S(t)$ as a metric for links $\mathbf{L}$ and paths $\mathbf{P}$ gives us an equation system similar to (1) where links are, however, concatenated to paths by min-plus convolution, e.g. $S_{P_1}(t) = S_{L_1} \otimes S_{L_2} \otimes \dots$. Such systems are difficult to analyze since there exists no inverse operation for the min-plus convolution[3]. Transforming the whole system into the Legendre domain, however, turns all service curves into backlog curves and all min-plus convolutions into sums, e.g. $B_{\max,P_1}(r) = B_{\max,L_1} + B_{\max,L_2} + \dots$. Hence, we obtain an additive metric that converts the problem into the exact form (1) where $\mathbf{L}$ and $\mathbf{P}$ are vectors of backlog curves for links and paths respectively. Eventually, reapplying the Legendre transform recovers the equivalent service curves.

In summary, we propose a method that comprises the following steps:

1. Perform rate scans between end-hosts to measure per-path backlog curves
2. Infer per-link backlog curves by inversion of (1) that can be under-determined
3. Convert the backlog curves to service curves using the Legendre transform

---

[3] Contradictory to its name, the min-plus de-convolution is **not** an exact inverse of the convolution [12]. Yet, the two operations obey a certain duality [10]. Given an equation system of min-plus convolution statements, we note that by clever expansion of these equations the duality allows deriving **bounds** on the system's solution.

These steps can be conducted using well-known tomography methods, such as multicasting or tailgating, which are detailed in the following subsections.

3.1 Multicast-Based Inference

Multicast-based inference methods, e.g. [1,16], use the correlation of multicast probes to solve otherwise under-determined tomography problems. The algorithm in [16] can infer per-link delay distributions from path delay measurements. Since backlog, like delay, is an additive metric it is straightforward to adapt the algorithm to infer backlog distributions instead.

We estimate per-path backlog distributions for a set of probing rates and execute the algorithm from [16] for each of the rates to infer per-link backlog distributions that are parameterized by the rate. Finally, we determine maximum backlogs and apply the Legendre transform to estimate the service curves.

A precondition for the inference algorithm in [16] is that delay distributions have a non-zero mass at zero. For this reason constant delays, such as propagation delays, cannot be analyzed and measurement data have to be adjusted accordingly. The same limitation applies in our case when inferring backlog distributions where a constant delay, translates to a constant virtual backlog.

For large probing rates that cause overload the backlog of an ideal lossless system becomes infinity. In this case it is not generally possible to apportion all backlogs to individual links. It is conservative to set indeterminable backlogs to an upper bound respectively to infinity. With the order reversing property of the Legendre transform $\mathcal{L}_{\tilde{B}}(t) \leq \mathcal{L}_B(t)$ if $\tilde{B}(r) \geq B(r)$ resulting service curve estimates $\tilde{S}(t) = \mathcal{L}_{\tilde{B}}(t)$ are valid lower service curves, i.e. $\tilde{S}(t) \leq S(t)$.

We simulated the multicast-based inference method from Sect. 3.1 in Matlab using a fluid flow model [18]. The validation produced results of mixed accuracy. The employed inference algorithm from [16] is analytically exact. It assumes, however, that the correlation of multicast probes stems from joint links in the multicast tree only. While the probes are transmitted independently on all other links, it takes a large number of experiments to obtain sufficiently clean data. This effect is also noted in [16]. Compared to single packet probes in [16] we use rate scans that cause a multiple of probing traffic, thus making the method less practicable in our case. Due to space restrictions we omit showing our results.

3.2 Tailgating

Fix some TTL to mark a hop on a given path and denote $S_u = S_1 \otimes \cdots \otimes S_{\text{TTL}}$ and $S_d = S_{\text{TTL}+1} \otimes \cdots \otimes S_N$ the service curve of the sub-path upstream respectively downstream of hop TTL. We will show how close tailgating measurements can approximate S_u and S_d.

Let $T_d = \max\{t \geq 0 : S_d(t) = 0\}$. We decompose $S_d(t) = \delta_{T_d}(t) \otimes S_d'(t)$ with the delay function $\delta_{T_d}(t) = 0$ for $t \leq T_d$ and $\delta_{T_d}(t) = \infty$ otherwise and a service curve $S_d'(t) = S_d(t + T_d)$. Note that $S_d'(t) > 0$ for all $t > 0$ and $S'(0) = 0$.

Denote A_u, A_d the probing arrivals of the sub-path upstream respectively downstream of hop TTL and D_u, D_d the respective departures. If data are not discarded we have $A_d = D_u$ and the end-to-end service curve is $S_{e2e}(t) = S_u \otimes S_d(t)$ so that

$$S_{e2e}(t) = S_u \otimes \delta_{T_d} \otimes S'_d(t). \qquad (3)$$

In case of tailgating we have $A_d = D_u/c$ where $c \gg 1$ since the large tailgated packets are discarded after hop TTL. The receiver uses the small tailgating packets to extrapolate the tailgated packets, i.e. it re-scales the departures D_d by c. Assuming exact service curves we have $D_d(t) = A_d \otimes S_d(t)$. It follows by insertion that $cD_d(t) = c(D_u/c \otimes \delta_{T_d} \otimes S'_d(t))$. Substitution of $D_u(t) = A_u \otimes S_u(t)$ and employing the concept of data scaling from [6] we derive $cD_d(t) = A_u \otimes S_u \otimes \delta_{T_d} \otimes cS'_d(t)$. Hence, the tailgating service curve is $S_{tg}(t) = S_u \otimes \delta_{T_d} \otimes cS'_d(t)$ and for large c

$$S_{tg}(t) \xrightarrow[c \to \infty]{} S_u \otimes \delta_{T_d}(t) \qquad (4)$$

since $cS'_d(t) \to \delta_0(t)$ where $\delta_0(t)$ is the neutral element of min-plus convolution.

Using tailgated rate scans with a large packet size ratio (in practice $c \approx 20$) we measure $B_{\max,e2e}(r)$ and $B_{\max,tg}(r)$ at the respective TTL. For min-plus linear systems the backlog curves are the Legendre transforms $\mathcal{L}_{S_{e2e}}(r)$ and $\mathcal{L}_{S_{tg}}(r)$. Backwards transform of $\mathcal{L}_{S_{e2e}}(r)$ and $\mathcal{L}_{S_{tg}}(r)$ by reapplying the Legendre transform reveals estimates of $S_{e2e}(t)$ and $S_{tg}(t)$ respectively, while backwards transform of the difference $\mathcal{L}_{S_{e2e}}(r) - \mathcal{L}_{S_{tg}}(r) = \mathcal{L}_{S'_d}(r)$ yields an estimate of $S'_d(t)$. The resulting estimates $S_{tg}(t) = S_u(t - T_d)$ and $S'_d(t) = S_d(t + T_d)$ are time-shifted versions of $S_u(t)$ and $S_d(t)$. Even an ideal tailgating scheme cannot determine the time-shift T_d. This restriction[4] is mirrored by the multicast-based method, see Sect. 3.1.

For certain large rates the end-to-end as well as the tailgating measurement will indicate overload. In this case the difference $\mathcal{L}_{S_{e2e}}(r) - \mathcal{L}_{S_{tg}}(r)$ evaluates to $\infty - \infty$ such that $\mathcal{L}_{S'_d}(r)$ cannot be estimated for these rates. This ambiguity confirms a fundamental limitation regarding the resolution of post-narrow links. As mentioned for the multicast method in Sect. 3.1, indeterminable backlog values can be set to infinity to estimate a lower service curve nevertheless.

4   Validation in Emulab Experiments

We implemented the tailgating method developed in Sect. 3.2 as an extension of the `rude/crude` packet sender and receiver (`rude.sourceforge.net`). We validated the method on the Emulab testbed (`www.emulab.org`) using the topology given in Fig. 1. All links have a capacity of 100 Mbps and a latency of 4 ms. We use two types of cross traffic, constant bit rate (CBR) of 50 and exponential (EXP) of an average rate of 70 Mbps using the D-ITG traffic generator (`www.grid.unina.it/software/ITG/`) leaving 50 respectively 30 Mbps unused. We report two experiments where A) the CBR cross traffic is mapped to link 2 and the EXP to link 3 and B) EXP to link 2 and CBR to link 3 such that link 3 becomes a post-narrow link. All except the small tailgating packets have a size of 1000 Byte, including 28 Byte UDP/IP header and 18 Byte MAC header.

---

[4] RTTs of TTL exceeded messages provide a known approach for symmetric paths.

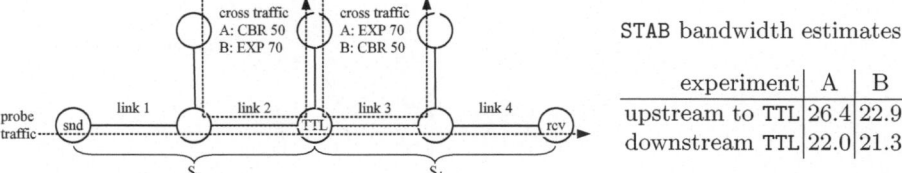

STAB bandwidth estimates

experiment	A	B
upstream to TTL	26.4	22.9
downstream TTL	22.0	21.3

Fig. 1. Topology used for tailgating experiments. The available bandwidths upstream and downstream of TTL are $(50, 30)$ Mbps in experiment A and $(30, 50)$ Mbps in experiment B respectively. The table shows bandwidth estimates from STAB measurements.

Probes, referred to as a rate scan, are CBR packet trains consisting of 400 packets each, sent at rates $5, 10, \ldots, 80$ Mbps. Multiplexing of cross and probing traffic takes place at FIFO schedulers. If not in an overloaded state FIFO systems can be modeled as min-plus linear [13] (a precondition of our method) whereas they become non-linear in case of overload. We use the overload test from [8] to stop the rate scan once overload is detected and set all backlog estimates at subsequent higher rates to infinity.

Fig. 2 shows derivatives of the service curves S_u and S_d upstream and downstream of hop TTL. We display the mean and 0.95 confidence intervals of 100 estimates. Curves labeled "monitor at TTL" and "probe sender at TTL" use a probe monitor respectively sender at hop TTL. These are reference service curves for "tailgating" which assumes no cooperation of hop TTL beyond discarding packets whose TTL expires. Estimates of S_d labeled "inferred" use measurements of the end-to-end path and the path upstream but not downstream of TTL.

Comparing S_u for 50 Mbps CBR cross traffic in Fig. 2(a) with 70 Mbps EXP cross traffic in Fig. 2(c) shows that the long-term rate of S_u converges (within the limits of the probing granularity of 5 Mbps) towards the unused bandwidth of 50 respectively 30 Mbps. Corresponding average available bandwidth estimates of STAB are shown in Fig. 1. Beyond this single value, the service curves show a region of convergence that is dictated by the cross traffic distribution. The burstiness of EXP compared to CBR causes slower convergence where the long-term rate of EXP is achieved only after a relevant time span. Comparing Fig. 2(a) to Fig. 2(b) one can clearly observe the difference in convergence speed that is due to higher burstiness of the cross traffic on link 3 compared to link 2.

Moreover, it can be seen that service is provided only after a certain latency that corresponds to the propagation delay of 4 ms per link. As shown in Sect. 3.2 the tailgating method cannot resolve these delays. Hence, the tailgating estimates of S_u are shifted to the right by $T_d = 8$ ms, which is the delay downstream of hop TTL, see Fig. 2(a) and 2(c). Accordingly, the estimates of S_d are shifted to the left by the same amount, see Fig. 2(b) and 2(d). This restriction is a fundamental limitation of tailgating as shown in Sect. 3.2. Apart from this time-shift the tailgating estimates in Fig. 2(a), 2(b), and 2(c) match the reference service curves accurately. In contrast the inferred S_d in Fig. 2(d) significantly underestimate the reference estimate generated with a probe sender at hop TTL. This effect reflects a general limitation regarding the resolution of post-narrow links, see also Sect. 3.2.

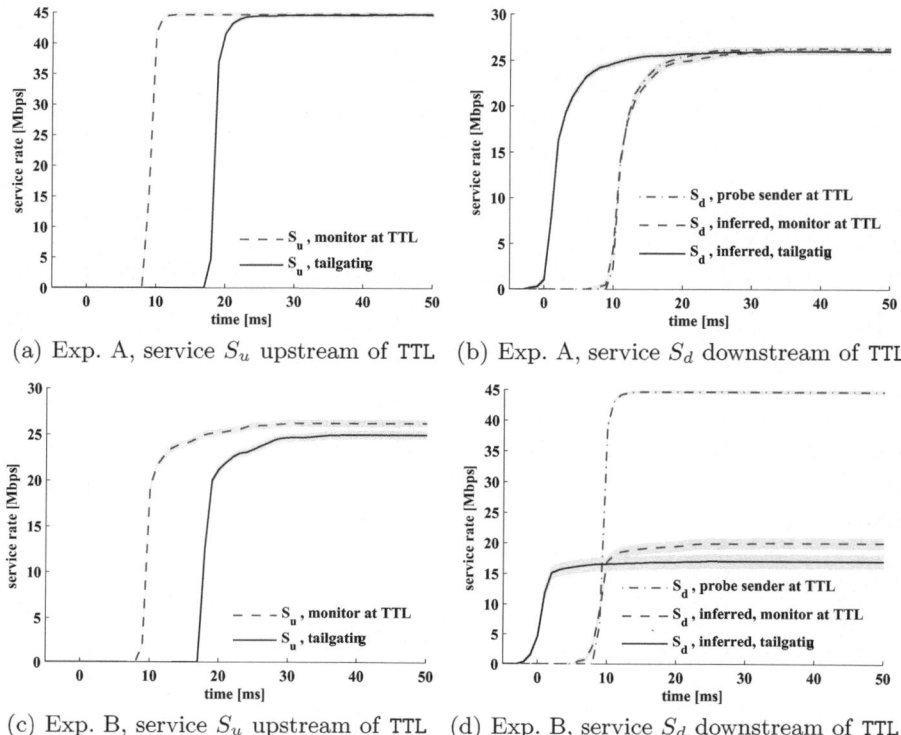

(a) Exp. A, service S_u upstream of TTL (b) Exp. A, service S_d downstream of TTL

(c) Exp. B, service S_u upstream of TTL (d) Exp. B, service S_d downstream of TTL

Fig. 2. Per-link service curve estimates. Tailgating can successfully attribute the short-term service convergence caused by the burstiness of cross traffic as well as the long-term available bandwidth to individual links. The measurements confirm the results in Sect. 3.2 that tailgating cannot identify propagation delays and post-narrow links (d).

As an additional reference theory provides a leftover service curve model, see e.g. [10], that can be easily applied to CBR cross-traffic. The theoretical leftover service curve is of the latency rate type $S(t) = R \cdot \max\{0, t-T\}$ where in our case a rate $R = 50$ Mbps and a latency $T = 8$ ms applies. Regarding Fig. 2(a) the service curve estimate with monitor at TTL matches closely, whereas the service curve from tailgating is a time-shifted version as discussed above.

5   Conclusions

We showed how per-link service curves can be inferred from path measurements. Our work builds on a known duality between service curves and backlogs that is established by the Legendre transform. Backlogs are an additive link metric and owing to this property known tomography approaches like multicast probing and tailgating can be effectively adapted for per-link service curve inference. Our measurement results show that estimated service curves provide a higher level of detail compared to available bandwidths where the shape of the service curves reflects the burstiness of cross traffic. The evaluation confirms that our method can attribute these characteristics to individual links.

References

1. Caceres, R., Duffield, N.G., Horowitz, J., Towsley, D.: Multicast-based inference of network-internal loss characteristics. IEEE Trans. Inform. Theory 45(7), 2462–2480 (1999)
2. Chang, C.-S.: Performance Guarantees in Communication Networks. Springer, Heidelberg (2000)
3. Coates, M., Hero, A., Nowak, R., Yu, B.: Internet tomography. IEEE Signal Processing Magazine 19(3), 47–65 (2002)
4. Cruz, R.L.: A calculus for network delay, Part I and Part II. IEEE Trans. Inform. Theory 37(1), 114–141 (1991)
5. Fidler, M., Recker, S.: Conjugate network calculus: A dual approach applying the legendre transform. Computer Networks 50(8), 1026–1039 (2006)
6. Fidler, M., Schmitt, J.B.: On the way to a distributed systems calculus: A network calculus with data scaling. In: ACM SIGMETRICS, June 2006, pp. 287–298 (2006)
7. Harfoush, K., Bestavros, A., Byers, J.: Measuring bottleneck bandwidth of targeted path segments. In: IEEE INFOCOM, April 2003, pp. 2079–2089 (2003)
8. Jain, M., Dovrolis, C.: End-to-end available bandwidth: Measurement methodology, dynamics, and relation with TCP throughput. IEEE/ACM Trans. Networking 11(4), 537–549 (2003)
9. Lai, K., Baker, M.: Measuring link bandwidths using a deterministic model of packet delay. In: ACM SIGCOMM, October 2000, pp. 283–294 (2000)
10. Le Boudec, J.-Y., Thiran, P.: Network Calculus A Theory of Deterministic Queuing Systems for the Internet. Springer, Heidelberg (2001)
11. Lhommeau, M., Hardouin, L., Ferrier, J.-L., Ouerghi, I.: Interval analysis in dioid: Application to robust open-loop control for timed event graphs. In: CDC - ECC 2005, December 2005, pp. 7744–7749 (2005)
12. Liebeherr, J., Fidler, M., Valaee, S.: Min-plus system interpretation of bandwidth estimation. In: Proc. IEEE INFOCOM (May 2007)
13. Liebeherr, J., Fidler, M., Valaee, S.: A system theoretic approach to bandwidth estimation. Technical Report arXiv:0801.0455v1 (January 2008)
14. Parekh, A.K., Gallager, R.G.: A generalized processor sharing approach to flow control in integrated services networks: The single-node case. IEEE/ACM Trans. Networking 1(3), 344–357 (1993)
15. Pasztor, A., Veitch, D.: Active probing using packet quartets. In: ACM IMC, November 2002, pp. 293–305 (2002)
16. Presti, F.L., Duffield, N., Horowitz, J., Towsley, D.: Multicast-based inference of network-internal delay distributions. IEEE/ACM Trans. Networking 10(6), 761–775 (2002)
17. Ribeiro, V., Riedi, R., Baraniuk, R.: Locating available bandwidth bottlenecks. IEEE Internet Computing 8(5), 34–41 (2004)
18. Rizk, A.: Network tomography using min-plus system theory. Master's thesis, TU Darmstadt (March 2008)

Opportunistic Transmission over Randomly Varying Channels

Vivek S. Borkar*

School of Technology and Computer Science,
Tata Institute of Fundamental Research,
Homi Bhabha Road, Mumbai 400005, India
borkar@tifr.res.in

Abstract. This article briefly surveys a connected body work of the author and his collaborators on opportunistic transmission over a randomly varying channel. Both single user and multi-user scenarios are considered and a reinforcement learning based scheme proposed for both, with provable convergence properties.

Keywords: Randomly varying channels, opportunistic transmission, Markov decision processes, structural properties, reinforcement learning.

1 Introduction

Transmission across randomly varying channels calls for opportunistic schemes which transmit more when the channel is favorable and less when it is not, while queuing the packets as needed to facilitate this. Clearly, queuing leads to delay whereas transmission across a channel at a given rate involves power consumption that increases when the channel degrades. This implies a trade-off between power consumption and delay. This problem was first addressed in the single user case in the landmark paper of Berry and Gallager [4]. There have been several subsequent variations and improvements on this work and an extensive literature survey can be found in [14]. My aim here is to summarize a 'learning' approach to this problem that has been developed in [14], [15], which in turn depends on the theoretical groundwork laid in [3], [8]. The aim there is to address the realistic problem of transmission with unknown channel characteristics, on top of the aforementioned issue of the latter varying stochastically with time. When the channel characteristics are known, the standard approach has been to cast the problem as a constrained Markov decision problem [2], which seeks to minimize one cost (such as average power consumption) while imposing a bound on another cost (such as average delay). When the channel characteristics are unknown, one has to build on top of this a learning scheme. We use reinforcement learning based on the notion of 'post-state'. This is proposed, analyzed and

---
* Work supported in parts by a grant from CEFIPRA and a J. C. Bose Fellowship. This is an overview of work done over a period, some of which is joint with Mukul Agarwal, Abhijit Bhorkar, Abhay Karandikar and Nitin Salodkar.

E. Altman and A. Chaintreau (Eds.): NET-COOP 2008, LNCS 5425, pp. 62–69, 2009.

supported by simulations for the single user case in [14] and for the multi-user case in [15]. The latter in turn crucially uses the structural properties of the optimal policies for the constrained Markov decision problem that are established in [3]. Its convergent learning scheme is based on cooperative dynamics as in [8].

The next section describes the single agent problem and its formulation as a Markov decision process. It also summarizes the results of [3] concerning the optimal policy. Section 3 describes the learning scheme for the single user scenario from [14]. Section 4 sketches its extension to the multiuser case from [15]. Section 5 summarizes the conclusions.

2   Single User: Structural Properties

In the single user case, the queue dynamics is given by

$$Q_{n+1} = Q_n - U_n + W_{n+1}, \ n \geq 0, \tag{1}$$

where $\{Q_n\}$ is the queue length at the beginning of n-th slot. $U_n \leq Q_n \wedge R$ is the number of packets transmitted during this slot, R being the maximum number of packets that can be transmitted in a slot, and W_{n+1} is the i.i.d. arrival process with law ζ. We assume that there is a finite buffer with a very large capacity so that buffer overflow effects can be ignored. (This is purely for sake of simplicity.) We assume that the channel state $\{X_n\}$ is a finite state irreducible Markov chain with state space $S \subset (0, \infty)$ and transition probabilities $\kappa(\cdot|\cdot)$. We assume $\{Q_n\}$ to be non-negative integer valued. The aim is to minimize the long run average cost

$$\limsup_{n \uparrow \infty} \frac{1}{n} \sum_{m=0}^{n-1} E[X_m f(U_m)], \tag{2}$$

subject to the constraint

$$\limsup_{n \uparrow \infty} \frac{1}{n} \sum_{m=0}^{n-1} E[Q_m] \leq C, \tag{3}$$

Here $C > 0$ is a prescribed constant and f is a strictly convex strictly increasing function taking positive values such that the power as a function of the channel state x and the number u of packets transmitted is given by $xf(u)$. This expression matches the information theoretic formula for power if one sets $x =$ the inverse norm square of the complex channel gain and $f(u) = c(2^{c'u} - 1)$ for suitable $c, c' > 0$ [15]. We seek to minimize average power consumption subject to a constraint on average queue length, which by a standard argument akin to Little's theorem is equivalent to putting a constraint on average delay. From known results in the theory of constrained Markov decision processes [2], [6], we can consider the equivalent single objective Markov decision process that seeks to minimize

$$\limsup_{n \uparrow \infty} \frac{1}{n} \sum_{m=0}^{n-1} E[X_m f(U_m) + \lambda Q_m], \tag{4}$$

where $\lambda > 0$ is the Lagrange multiplier.

In [3], this problem is considered for more general state spaces for queue length (positive real line) and the channel state (it also considers Markov arrivals), and the dynamic programming equation for the long run average control problem with cost (4) is rigorously justified. See [10] for analogous results for the finite state case. For the discrete case, this equation is

$$V(q, x) = \min_u [c(q, x, \lambda, u) - \beta + \sum_{q', y} p(q', y|q, x, u)V(q', y)], \quad q \geq 0, x \in S, \quad (5)$$

where $p(\cdot)$ is the controlled transition kernel for the controlled Markov chain $\{(Q_n, X_n)\}$, and $c(q, x, \lambda, u) \overset{def}{=} xf(u) + \lambda q$. Under suitable irreducibility hypotheses, (5) specifies β uniquely as the optimal cost and V uniquely up to an additive scalar.

Using this and arguments based on convexity and supermodularity, [3] proves that the optimal transmission policy is stationary, i.e., depends only on the current state, and is 'stable', i.e., leads to a positive recurrent Markov chain. (Of course, this requires that we assume the existence of at least one stable stationary policy, which we do.) Furthermore, it has the property that the optimal number of packets to be transmitted in a slot is an increasing function of the queue length and a decreasing function of the channel state.

3 Single User: The Learning Scheme

In principle, the optimal policy can be obtained from (5), which in turn can be solved by the relative value iteration (assuming λ to be known) given by [13]

$$V_{n+1}(q, x) = \min_u [c(q, x, \lambda, u) - V_n(q_0, x_0) + \sum_{q', y} p(q', y|q, x, u)V_n(q', y)], \quad n \geq 0.$$
$$(6)$$

Here (q_0, x_0) is an arbitrarily prescribed state and V_0 is arbitrary.

The problem arises when the statistics of $\{X_n\}$ and / or $\{W_n\}$ is unknown. The reinforcement learning based algorithms for approximate dynamic programming are precisely meant for this situation [5], [12]. In the present case, it is convenient to use the so called post-state framework. We define the post-state as the 'state' immediately after the control action, but before the action of noise, i.e., as $\tilde{Q}_n \overset{def}{=} Q_n - U_n$. Then viewing $\{(\tilde{Q}_n, X_n)\}$ as the controlled Markov chain in place of $\{(Q_n, X_n)\}$, the dynamic programming equation becomes

$$\tilde{V}(q, x) = \sum_{w, x'} \zeta(w)\kappa(x'|x) \min_{u \leq q+w} [c(q + w, x', \lambda, u) - \beta + \tilde{V}(q + w - u, x')]. \quad (7)$$

Once again, under suitable irreducibility hypotheses, (7) specifies β uniquely as the optimal cost and $\tilde{V}$ uniquely up to an additive scalar. The advantage here is that the minimization is now inside the averaging operation. The corresponding relative value iteration would be

$$\tilde{V}_{n+1}(q, x) = \sum_{w, x'} \zeta(w)\kappa(x'|x) \min_{u \leq q+w} [c(q + w, x', \lambda, u) - \tilde{V}_n(q_0, x_0)$$
$$+ \tilde{V}_n(q + w - u, x')]. \quad (8)$$

Taking advantage of the preceding observation, one can write a stochastic approximation counterpart of this by first replacing the average on the right hand side by an actual evaluation at an observed transition, and then making an incremental move towards this 'correction', letting stochastic approximation to do the averaging. Specifically, the scheme is

$$V_{n+1}(q, x) = (1 - a(n))V_n(q, x) + a(n)I\{Q_n = q, X_n = x\} \times$$
$$\min_u[c(q + W_{n+1}, x, \lambda, u) + V_n(q + W_{n+1} - u, X_{n+1}) - V_n(q_0, x_0)]$$
$$= V_n(q, x) + a(n)I\{Q_n = q, X_n = x\} \min_u[c(q + W_{n+1}, x, \lambda, u)$$
$$+ V_n(q + W_{n+1} - u, X_{n+1}) - V_n(q_0, x_0) - V_n(q, x)].$$

Here $\{a(n)\}$ is a stepsize sequence satisfying the usual conditions in stochastic approximation: $\sum_n a(n) = \infty$, $\sum_n a(n)^2 < \infty$. We consider the scheme

$$V_{n+1}(q, x) = V_n(q, x) + a(n)I\{Q_n = q, X_n = x\} \min_u[c(q + W_{n+1}, x, \lambda_n, u)$$
$$+ V_n(q + W_{n+1} - u, X_{n+1}) - V_n(q_0, x_0) - V_n(q, x)], \qquad (9)$$

with λ no longer constant. In fact, it is replaced by λ_n, which is updated by a separate iteration

$$\lambda_{n+1} = \Gamma\Big(\lambda_n + b(n)(Q_n - C)\Big). \qquad (10)$$

Here Γ is a projection to the interval $[0, M]$ for a large M, which serves to keep the iterates bounded. Also, $\{b(n)\}$ satisfies: $\sum_n b(n) = \infty$, $\sum_n b(n)^2 < \infty$, and in addition, $b(n) = o(a(n))$. The latter ensures that (10) moves on a slower timescale than (9) and the 'two time-scale' analysis of [9], Chapter 6, applies.

As described in [9], we can analyze (9) by freezing $\lambda_n \approx$ a constant λ and looking at the limiting o.d.e.

$$\dot{y}(t) = \Lambda(t)(h(y(t)) - y(t)),$$

where $\Lambda(t)$ is a diagonal matrix with nonnegative elements summing to 1 on the diagonal, and $h(y) = [h_{q,x}(y)]$ is given by

$$h_{q,x}(y) = \sum_{w,x'} \zeta(w)\kappa(x'|x) \min_u[c(q + w, x, \lambda, u) + y_{q+w-u,x'} - y_{q_0,x_0}].$$

Under reasonable conditions, the diagonal elements of $\Lambda(t)$ remain uniformly bounded away from zero. One can then prove the convergence of $y(t)$ to the solution $\tilde{V}$ of (7) corresponding to $\tilde{V}(q_0, x_0) = \beta$ along the lines of [1]. In turn, the 'scaled limit' as in [9], Chapter 3, of the above o.d.e. is the same o.d.e. as the above, but with $c(\cdot) \equiv 0$. This has the origin as its globally asymptotically stable equilibrium. Arguing as in [9], Chapters 2 and 3, one concludes that $\sup_n V_n < \infty$ a.s., and furthermore, $V_n \to \tilde{V}$, defined as above, a.s.

However, this analysis treated $\lambda_n \approx$ a constant, so what one really has is that $\{V_n\}$ closely track $\{\tilde{V}_{\lambda_n}\}$, where $\tilde{V}_\lambda$ is $\tilde{V}$ with its λ-dependence made explicit. By an argument adapted from [7] which uses the 'envelope theorem', one can argue that the limiting o.d.e. for the λ_n's is in fact a steepest ascent for the Lagrangian minimized over the primal variables. This converges to the correct Lagrange multiplier, which is the corresponding maximizer. Then so do the λ_n's, a.s. This completes the convergence proof.

4   The Multi-user Scenario

Suppose that there are $K > 0$ users competing for access to a common channel, which is allocated to exactly one of them at a time by a central receiver. Let $\{Q_n(i)\}, \{X_n(i)\}, \{\xi_n(i)\}, \{W_n(i)\}$ denote the corresponding queue length, channel state, departure and arrival processes. Write $Q_n = [Q_n(1), \cdots, Q_n(K)]^T$, with analogous convention for ξ_n's, X_n's and W_n's. Suppose that each user (say, i-th) employs the above scheme to arrive at time n with a quantity $U_n(i) \in [0, Q_n(i) \wedge R]$, which is what she wishes to transmit. She can do so if the channel is allocated to her, but can transmit nothing otherwise. We assume that the channel is allocated to the user with the maximum demand, i.e., to the j-th user where $j = \text{argmax}_i U_n(i)$, at time n. (In case of more than one candidate, one of them may be picked at random.) We wish to analyze this scheme. It is convenient (as in machine learning literature) to work with 'softmax', i.e., the channel is allocated to user i with probability

$$F_i(U_n) \stackrel{def}{=} \frac{U_n(i)^m}{\sum_j U_n(j)^m}, \tag{11}$$

where $m \geq 1$ is a prescribed integer. Thus $\xi_n(i) = U_n(i)$ if the channel is allocated to i and $= 0$ otherwise. In the $m \uparrow \infty$ limit, one gets the original scheme.

We now adapt the arguments of [8] to analyze the behavior of the overall scheme. The analysis of the learning schemes proceeds exactly as before. The fact that the channel is not available at each instant only affects the manner in which the states are being sampled and therefore the process $\Lambda(\cdot)$. As long as $\Lambda(\cdot)$ satisfies the stipulated conditions, viz., that its diagonal elements remain uniformly bounded away from zero, the conclusions are not affected. The queue length dynamics for user i is then

$$Q_{n+1}(i) = Q_n(i) - \xi_n(i) + W_{n+1}(i), \ n \geq 0.$$

Let $\gamma(i) = E[W_n(i)]$. Then the above can be rewritten as

$$Q_{n+1}(i) = Q_n(i) + (\gamma(i) - F_i(U_n)U_n(i)) + \Big((W_{n+1}(i) - \gamma(i))$$
$$+ (F_i(U_n)U_n(i) - \xi_n(i))\Big).$$

Let $\tilde{F} = [\tilde{F}_1, \cdots, \tilde{F}_K]^T$ be defined by: $\tilde{F}_i(x) = F_i(x)x_i \ \forall i$. We assume that this is continuously differentiable. Then the above is of the form

$$Q_{n+1}(i) = Q_n(i) + (\gamma(i) - \tilde{F}_i(U_n)) + M_{n+1}, \ n \geq 0, \tag{12}$$

where $\{M_n\}$ is a martingale difference sequence. Recall that $U_n(i)$ depends on $(Q_n(i), X_n(i))$, i. e., $U_n(i) = \ell_i(Q_n(i), X_n(i))$ for some $\ell_i(\cdot)$. We assume $\ell_i(\cdot, x)$ to be continuously differentiable. Write $\ell(Q_n, X_n)$ for

$$[\ell_1(Q_n(1), X_n(1)), \cdots, \ell_K(Q_n(K), X_n(K))]^T.$$

Let π denote the (unique) stationary distribution of the Markov chain $\{X_n\}$. Define $\hat{F} = [\hat{F}_1, \cdots, \hat{F}_K(\cdot)]^T$ by: for $q = [q(1), \cdots, q(K)]^T$,

$$\hat{F}_i(q) = \sum_x F_i(\ell(q, x))\ell_i(q(i), x(i))\pi(\{x\}).$$

We analyze (12) by looking at its 'fluid' approximation, which is given by the o.d.e.

$$\dot{\tilde{q}}(t) = \gamma - \hat{F}(\tilde{q}(t)), \tag{13}$$

restricted to the positive orthant (i. e., it follows the projected dynamics on the boundary of this orthant). One way to arrive at this is to consider the scaled version of the discrete iteration above, given by

$$Q_{n+1}(i) = Q_n(i) + \eta[(\gamma(i) - \tilde{F}_i(U_n)) + M_{n+1}], \; n \geq 0, \tag{14}$$

for a small $\eta > 0$. The idea is that we consider smaller and smaller time slots of width η with $\gamma(i)$, resp. $\tilde{F}_i$ being 'rates per unit time' rather than 'per slot' quantities. We shall assume that

$$\sum_i \gamma(i) < R, \tag{15}$$

which ensures existence of stable stationary policies (see below). With η small, one may think of (14) as a constant stepsize stochastic approximation iteration analyzed in Chapter 9 of [9]. As argued there, one can conclude that with probability $1 - O(\eta)$, $\{Q_n\}$ will concentrate near the set of equilibria of (13) were the latter itself converging to this set. But our results on structural properties imply that (13) is a cooperative dynamics, i.e., $\frac{\partial \hat{F}_i}{\partial q_j} > 0$ for $i \neq j$. By the Hirsch theorem [11], if its trajectories approach a bounded set, then they converge for almost all initial conditions. Under mild additional assumptions, one can argue as in [9], Chapter 10, that (12) will then concentrate near the set of equilibria with a high ($\approx 1 - O(\eta)$) probability.

This leaves the task of establishing the fact that the trajectories do indeed approach a bounded set. Here's a suggestive, though not completely rigorous argument: Let A_n denote the set of maximizers of $i \to U_n(i)$. Then for $m >> 1$, $F_i(Q_n, X_n) \approx \frac{1}{|A_n|}I\{i \in A_n\}$. Let $\mathcal{V}(q) \stackrel{def}{=} \sum_i q_i$. Thus

$$\dot{\mathcal{V}}(\tilde{q}(t)) = \sum_i \gamma(i) - \sum_i \hat{F}_i(\tilde{q}(t))$$

$$\approx \sum_i \gamma(i) - \sum_x \pi(\{x\})\ell_{i^*(t,x)}(q_{i^*(t,x)}(t), x(i^*(t,x))),$$

where $i^*(t, x)$ is the maximizer of $i \rightarrow \ell_i(\tilde{q}_i(t), x(i))$. If any $\tilde{q}_i(t)$ becomes very high, then one expects the r.h.s. $\approx \sum_i \gamma(i) - R$, thus leading to

$$\dot{\mathcal{V}}(\tilde{q}(t)) \leq \sum_i \gamma(i) - R < 0.$$

Thus $\mathcal{V}$ serves as a Liapunov function for (12), leading to bounded trajectories.

To summarize, the scheme will allocate the channel with very high probability to one or more users whose rate requirement is the highest. In [8], the analogy between this and the so-called Wardrop equilibrium in transportation theory has been pointed out. Wardrop equilibrium means that only those routes that have the minimum disutility (i.e., delay / congestion) get traffic. Analogously, here only those users with the maximum rate requirement get the channel. Thus we can think of this as an approximate Wardrop-like equilibrium. Note that when a user with lower rate requirement is not allocated the channel for a while, her queue length and therefore the rate requirement will build up and she will eventually be allocated the channel. The equilibria q^* of the limiting o.d.e. correspond to situations where $\gamma(i) = \hat{F}_i(q^*) \; \forall i$, i.e., the mean arrivals and departures balance out as they should. The discussion above then shows that the stochastic behavior fluctuates around this. Two issues that need further study are an estimate of the actual channel utilization by the users and incentive compatibility of the scheme.

5   Conclusions

This is a brief survey of research done and in progress on the problem of opportunistic communication across a randomly varying channel when the channel characteristics themselves have to be learnt in real time. While the present account confines itself to the theoretical analysis, there are also accompanying simulation results in [14], [15], which give empirical justification for the scheme. They suggest that this line of research is a promising approach to this and related problems.

References

1. Abounadi, J., Bertsekas, D.P., Borkar, V.S.: Learning algorithms for Markov decision processes with average cost. SIAM Journal of Control and Optimization 40(3), 681–698 (2001)
2. Altman, E.: Constrained Markov Decision Processes. Chapman and Hall / CRC, Boca Raton (1999)
3. Agarwal, M., Borkar, V.S., Karandikar, A.: Structural properties of optimal transmission policies over a randomly varying channel. IEEE Transactions on Automatic Control 53(6), 1476–1491 (2008)
4. Berry, R.A., Gallager, R.G.: Communication over fading channels with delay constraints. IEEE Trans. on Information Theory 48(5), 1135–1149 (2002)

5. Bertsekas, D.P., Tsitsiklis, J.N.: Neuro-Dynamic Programming. Athena Scientific, Belmont (1996)
6. Borkar, V.S.: Convex analytic methods in Markov decision processes. In: Shwartz, A., Feinberg, E. (eds.) Handbook of Markov Decision Processes, pp. 347–375. Kluwer Academic, Dordrecht (2002)
7. Borkar, V.S.: An actor-critic algorithm for constrained Markov decision processes. Systems and Control Letters 54(3), 207–213 (2005)
8. Borkar, V.S.: Cooperative dymanics and Wardrop equilibria. Systems and Control Letters 58(2), 91–93 (to appear, 2009)
9. Borkar, V.S.: Stochastic Approximation – A Dynamical Systems Viewpoint. Hindustan Publ. Agency/Cambridge Uni. Press, New Delhi/Cambridge (2008)
10. Djonin, D.V., Krishnamurthy, V.: Structural results on the optimal transmission scheduling policies and costs for correlated sources and channels. In: IEEE Conference on Decision and Control, pp. 3231–3236 (2005)
11. Hirsch, M.W.: Systems of differential equations that are competitive or cooperative II: convergence almost everywhere. SIAM Journal of Mathematical Analysis 16(3), 423–439 (1985)
12. Powell, W.: Approximate Dynamic Programming. Wiley Interscience, Hoboken (2007)
13. Puterman, M.: Markov Decision Processes. John Wiley, New York (1994)
14. Salodkar, N., Bhorkar, A., Karandikar, N., Borkar, V.S.: An on-line learning algorithm for energy efficient delay constrained scheduling over a fading channel. IEEE Trans. on Selected Areas in Communications 26(4), 732–742 (2008)
15. Salodkar, N., Karandikar, A., Borkar, V.S.: A stable on-line algorithm for energy efficient multi-user scheduling (in preparation)

On the Variance of the Least Attained Service Policy and Its Use in Multiple Bottleneck Networks

Matthias Auchmann[1] and Guillaume Urvoy-Keller[2]

[1] Technische Universität Wien, Austria
m.auchmann@artech.at
[2] Eurecom, France
Guillaume.Urvoy@eurecom.fr

Abstract. Size-based scheduling has proved to be effective in a lot of scenarios involving Internet traffic. In this work, we focus on the Least Attained Service Policy, a popular size-based scheduling policy. We tackle two issues that have not received much attention so far. Firstly, the variance of the conditional response time. We prove that the classification proposed by Wierman et al. [11], which classifies LAS as an always unpredictable policy, is overly pessimistic. We illustrate the latter by focusing on the M/M/1/LAS queue. Secondly, we consider LAS queues in tandem. We provide preliminary results concerning the characterization of the output process of an M/M/1/LAS queue and the conditional average response time of LAS queues in tandem.

1 Motivation

Size-based scheduling has proved to be very effective in increasing performance in a lot of scenarios: Web servers [4], Internet traffic [8] or 3G networks [6]. The key idea behind size-based scheduling is to favor short jobs while ensuring that large jobs do not starve. The net result is better interactivity from the user point of view as short jobs correspond to interactive applications, while large job correspond to bulk transfers when considering Internet traffic. The extent to which large jobs suffer depends on the statistical characteristics of the job size distribution and especially onhow the mass is distributed among short and large jobs. Broadly speaking, the larger the mass carried by the large flows, the smaller the penalty since short flows, that have the highest priority, can not monopolize the server. Heavy-tailed distributions, which have often been observed in the Internet [3], feature such a property.

In this paper, we consider the Least Attained Service (LAS) policy, a.k.a the Foreground-Background policy [7]. LAS has been initially proposed and studied in the context of time-sharing computers in the late 60s [10]. Under LAS, priority is given to the job that has received the least amount of service. In case of ties, jobs share the server in a round-robin manner. A salient feature of LAS is that it has no internal parameter to tune.

E. Altman and A. Chaintreau (Eds.): NET-COOP 2008, LNCS 5425, pp. 70–77, 2009.
© Springer-Verlag Berlin Heidelberg 2009

Our focus in this work is twofold. First, we focus on the conditional variance of LAS. Few results exist concerning the variance of LAS [11,2]. In [2], the asymptotic conditional variance is considered. In [11], the authors propose a classification of scheduling policies based on their variance. In particular, they propose to classify scheduling policies as: (i) always predictable, (ii) sometimes predictable or (iii) always unpredictable - precise definitions will be given in Section 2. LAS falls in the latter category, which seems at first sight disappointing. Indeed, LAS does a good job at providing low response time to small jobs but despite this nice property, the results in [11] seem to restrict the interest of LAS.

We revisit the variance of LAS by considering the case of an M/M/1/LAS queue. This case is interesting for two reasons. First, it is mathematically tractable. Second, the performance of LAS and especially the fraction of flows that receive a better service under LAS than under PS is known to increase with the variability of job size distribution [8]; and empirical distributions observed for Internet traffic have a much higher variability than the one of an exponential distribution [5].

Considering the M/M/1/LAS queue, we analytically bound the fraction of flows that are treated in a predictable manner. We obtain that at least 75% of flows are treated predicably, irrespectively of the load. Numerical studies further demonstrate that the actual fraction of such flows should be closer to 95%.

Second, we focus on the problem of using LAS queues in tandem. The motivation behind this scenario is to determine the benefits that could be obtained with LAS in a multiple bottlenecks scenario. A typical example is wireless mesh networks based on the 802.11 protocol where the available bandwidth is known to be highly varying, as has been exemplified by the roofnet experiment (http://pdos.csail.mit.edu/roofnet/doku.php). In such a situation, LAS could be highly beneficial as it allows to maintain a minimum level of interactivity, even when congestion is high. However, using LAS at multiple queues in tandem can also be detrimental to large flows that could be penalized multiple times.

To the best of our knowledge, no work has tackled the problem of studying LAS in tandem queues. We rely on numerical evaluations to address this issue as the analytical approach seems too complex at the moment, even for the case of M/M/1/LAS queues. We make the following contributions: (i) We demonstrate that while the departure process of an M/M/1/LAS queue is apparently a Poisson process, the LAS scheduling policy introduces a negative correlation between departures times and job sizes; (ii) We evaluate the impact of the above correlation on the conditional average response times of LAS queues in tandem.

2   Conditional Variance of an M/M/1/LAS Queue

The variance of the conditional response time for an $M/G/1/LAS$ queue with arrival rate λ is given by [12]:

$$Var[T(x)]^{LAS} = \frac{\lambda x \tilde{m}_2(x)}{(1 - \tilde{\rho}(x))^3} + \frac{\lambda \tilde{m}_3(x)}{3(1 - \tilde{\rho}(x))^3} + \frac{3}{4}\left(\frac{\lambda \tilde{m}_2(x)}{(1 - \tilde{\rho}(x))^2}\right)^2 \qquad (2.1)$$

Where $\{\tilde{m}_i(x)\}_{i\geq 1}$ are the truncated moments of the service time distribution. Truncated moments converge to the moments $\{m_i\}_{i\geq 1}$ when the job size tends to infinity. In particular, $\tilde{m}_1(\infty) = m_1 = \frac{1}{\mu}$ is the mean job service time. $\tilde{\rho}(x) = \lambda \tilde{m}_1(x)$ is the (truncated) load of the jobs up to size x, where $\tilde{\rho}(\infty) = \rho = \frac{\lambda}{\mu}$ is the load of the $M/G/1/LAS$ queue. Truncated moments for an exponential distribution $Exp(\mu)$ are given by:

$$\tilde{m}_i(x) = \int_0^x y^i \mu e^{-\mu y} dy + x^i e^{-\mu x}$$

In [11], scheduling policies were classified based on the variance of conditional response times as always predictable, always unpredictable or sometimes predictable. For a policy P, jobs of size x are treated predictably if:

$$\frac{Var[T(x)]^P}{x} \leq \frac{\lambda m_2}{(1-\rho)^3} \tag{2.2}$$

Otherwise jobs of size x are treated unpredictably. See [11] for a justification of the right side term in Eq. (2.2). A policy is predictable for a given load ρ and a given service time distribution if all job sizes are treated predictably. More generally, a scheduling policy P is:

- **Always predictable.** If it is predictable under all loads and service distributions;
- **Sometimes predictable.** If it is predictable under some loads and service distributions, and unpredictable under others;
- **Always unpredictable.** If it is unpredictable regardless of service distribution and load.

In [11] a variance bound was derived to show that LAS is always unpredictable. In contrast, PS is shown to be always predictable. Comparison of LAS to PS is important as it is shown in [9] that the $M/G/1/LAS$ queue is an accurate model for a LAS router while the $M/G/1/PS$ queue is an accurate model for a FIFO router for connections with homogeneous RTT.

Our initial motivation in this paper is to show that LAS outperforms PS not only in terms of conditional response time offered to a majority of short jobs [8], but also in terms of conditional variance. Figure 1 illustrates the relative performance of LAS and PS for an $M/M/1$ queue with $\lambda = 1$ and $\mu = 1.25$, i.e. a load $\rho = 0.8$. We observe that while LAS offers both low average and variance of response time for most of the jobs, its performance becomes eventually worse than PS for the largest jobs.

The large variance observed for the large jobs in Figure 1 illustrates why LAS is classified as always unpredictable, but it is for the largest jobs only that Eq. (2.2) is violated. The question we address here is to determine the fraction of jobs that are treated predictably under LAS for the case of an $M/M/1/LAS$ queue.

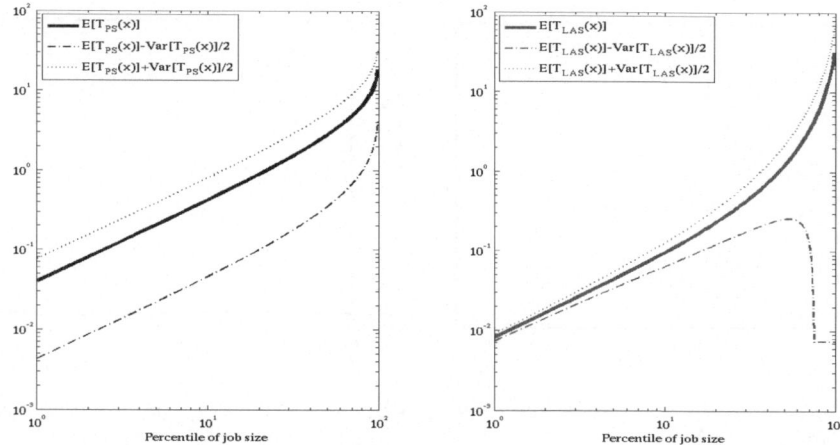

Fig. 1. M/M/1/LAS against M/M/1/PS: mean and variance of response time

2.1   M/M/1/LAS Variance Bounds

In this section, we first present two bounds on the variance of the conditional response time for an M/M/1/LAS queue. We next derive corresponding bounds on the fraction of jobs that are treated predictably under LAS. Due to space constraint, proofs are omitted, but can be found in our technical report [1].

Bound 1: For M/M/1/LAS,

$$Var[T(x)]^{LAS} \leq \frac{\lambda x m_2}{(1 - \tilde{\rho}(x))^4}\left(1 + \frac{2}{e^2} - (\frac{1}{4} + \frac{2}{e^2})\tilde{\rho}(x)\right) \qquad (2.3)$$

Bound 2: For M/M/1/LAS,

$$Var[T(x)]^{LAS} \leq \frac{8e\rho + 9\rho^2 - 8e\rho^2}{3e^2(1 - \rho)^4}x^2 \qquad (2.4)$$

Bounds 1 and 2 complement each other in the sense that bound 1 is more accurate for large job sizes while bound 2 is more accurate for small job sizes. Using these two bounds we further derive the percentage of jobs which are treated predictably in an M/M/1/LAS queue.

Bound 3: For M/M/1/LAS and a given ρ, at least a fraction of $\dfrac{1 - \left((1-\rho)^3(1 + \frac{2}{e^2})\right)^{1/4}}{\rho}$ of the jobs is treated predictably.

Bound 4: For M/M/1/LAS and a given ρ, at least a fraction of $1 - e^{-\frac{6e^2(1-\rho)}{8e+9\rho-8e\rho}}$ of the jobs is treated predictably.

Note that bounds 3 and 4 depend on ρ only, not on λ and μ. Bounds 3 and 4 show that the majority of jobs are in fact treated predictably in a $M/M/1/LAS$

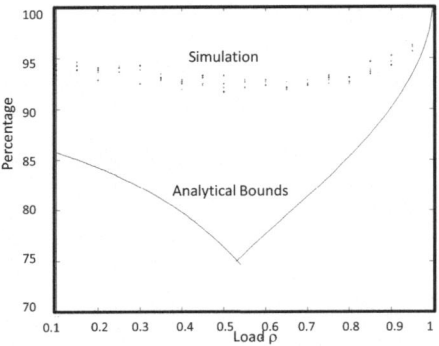 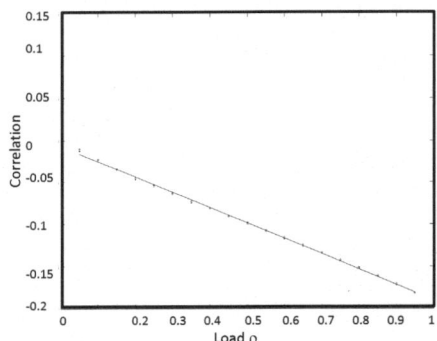

Fig. 2. Bounds 3 and 4 (solid line) and simulations (dots)

Fig. 3. Correlation of interdeparture times and jobsize for LAS

queue, as can be seen in Figure 2 where we plot the maximum of the two bounds (solid line). The minimum job percentage that is guaranteed to be treated predictably in this case, is about 75 percent.

As the above approach relies on lower bounding the number of jobs that are treated unpredictably under LAS, we further evaluated the percentage of jobs treated predictably using simulations. Figure 2 reports the results obtained by a simulator written in Matlab. Each simulation involved more than 500,000 jobs, and 4 different factorizations of ρ by using four different (λ, μ) pairs, which is why there are 4 points for each ρ value. We observe from Figure 2 that the fraction of flows that are treated predictably seems to depend on ρ only, not on the exact factorization of ρ. In addition, one can see that the actual percentage of jobs being treated predictably is very high: at least 90 percent of the jobs are treated predictably, regardless of the actual load value.

Note that for the case of Internet traffic, observed job size distributions are in general more skewed than the exponential one. As a consequence, we can expect that the fraction of jobs treated predictably is even higher than for the exponential case. As an illustration, for a Lognormal distribution with a coefficient of variation of 2, we observed that at all the load values we tested, between 10 and 90%, at least 99% of the jobs were treated predictably.

3   LAS in Tandem Queues

In this section, we focus on LAS in tandem queues where fresh arrivals occur only at the first queue and follow a Poisson process and service requirements follow an exponential distribution. We first study the output process of an isolated LAS queue and then, we will discuss the impact of the characteristics of the output process to the total response time of two LAS queues in tandem. Note that, to the best of our knowledge, no work has tackled this issue so far.

3.1 Characterization of the Output Process of an M/M/1/LAS Queue

LAS being a work-conserving and blind scheduling policy (job sizes are not known in advance), Burke's theorem is valid for an M/M/1/LAS queue. Hence, the output process for this queue is a Poisson process. We however show in the next section that job sizes and inter-departure times become correlated at the output of an M/M/1/LAS queue.

Correlation of Inter-departure Time and Job Size. To further characterize the output process of an M/M/1/LAS queue, we investigated whether job size is independent of interdeparture time. Figure 3 shows the correlation between job sizes and interdeparture times for LAS, plotted for different utilizations ρ. Again, different (λ, μ) pairs are used for the plots, but since curves overlap, correlation seems to depend on ρ only. Correlation is of negative type and increases with increasing load. We believe that this correlation stems from the fact that as load increases, large jobs are interrupted more frequently by shorter jobs. As a consequence, their remaining service requirement can reach very low values, lower than the service requirements of short jobs. When a large job leaves the queue, it is highly likely to be in a short period of time where load is low. During this period, many large jobs that were stuck in the queue, with small remaining service times, leave the system. We believe this explains the negative correlation we observe.

Note that we did not observe such a correlation for the PS queuing discipline (we do not present results here due to space constraint).

3.2 Impact on Tandem Queue Performance

The negative correlation observed above relates to the behavior of LAS that tends to sort jobs in the queue in ascending order, which means that short jobs tend to leave the LAS queue in groups and the same for large jobs. When considering the case of a tandem queues, this sorting introduced by the scheduler can have a detrimental impact on the performance of large flows. Indeed, when large flows reach the second queue, they again have to compete with the large flows they were in competition with in the first queue.

We quantitatively evaluated the previous intuition by comparing the conditional average response times[1] of two LAS queues in tandem with the sum of response time for the same system where we "re-draw" the job sizes of the job leaving the first queue using the initial distribution, thus wiping out the correlation observed in the previous section.

Figure 4 illustrates the above scenario for the case where load is 0.8. The left plot of Figure 4 represents the actual measured response time of the tandem system versus the added theoretical values (called independent queues in the graph). The right plot depicts the relative difference of the two systems.

---

[1] Results on the variance of the response time can be found in [1].

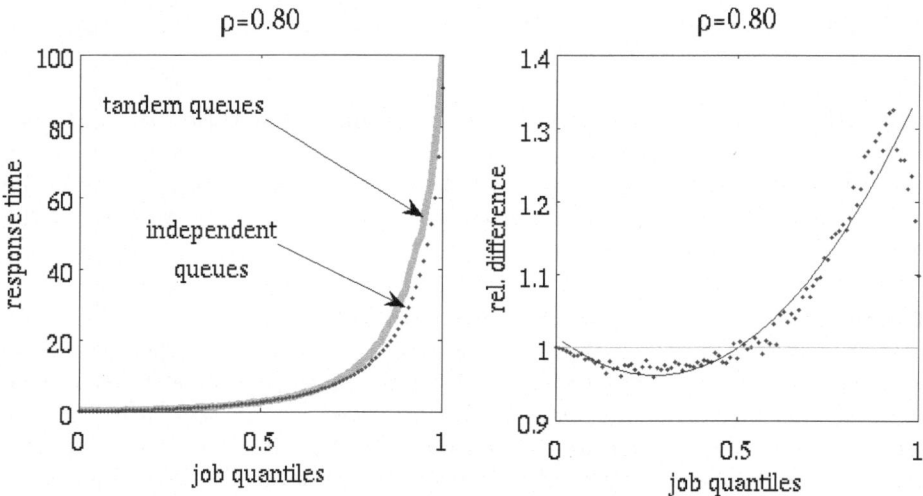

Fig. 4. Tandem Queue simulation results for LAS, $\rho = 0.80$

One can observe from Figure 4 that the observed negative correlation has a strong effect on the plots. While the response time is better than in the independent model for small jobs, LAS further penalizes large jobs in the tandem system.

4   Discussion

In this paper, we have focused both on the variance of the conditional response time of an M/M/1/LAS queue and the use of LAS in tandem queues.

For the variance, we proved that the fraction of jobs that are treated predictably is very high even in the unfavorable case of exponential service requirements. The practical implication of this result is that it is likely that when LAS is used for real Internet traffic, the variance in response time it offers to the majority of the flows be small as compared to the legacy FIFO scheduling policy.

Concerning the use of LAS in tandem queues, we demonstrated that while the output process of an M/M/1/LAS queue is Poisson, LAS tends to group jobs of similar sizes together, which results in a high penalty for the large jobs that cross the two queues. Practical implications of this result are less clear than for the variance case. Indeed routers work on a packet basis and do not output all the packets of a connection simultaneously as it happens in an M/M/1/LAS queue. This should dampen the effect we have observed.

As future work, we plan to continue working on the use of LAS in wireless mesh networks to precisely assess its performance. Note that a typical path in a wireless mesh network from an end user to an Internet gateway should be quite small, no more than 4 hops. As a consequence, we can expect that the nice properties of LAS, namely its ability to maintain interactivity even when the load is high, outweighs its side effect, namely the penalty experienced by large flows crossing multiple bottlenecks.

References

1. Auchmann, M., Urvoy-Keller, G.: On the variance of the least attained service policy and its use in multiple bottleneck networks. Technical Report RR-08-224, Institut Eurecom, France (June 2008),
   `http://www.eurecom.fr/util/popuppubli.fr.htm?page=copyright&id=2497`
2. Brown, P.: Comparing fb and ps scheduling policies. Technical report, Orange Labs (2008)
3. Crovella, M.E., et al.: A Practical Guide to Heavy Tails, ch. 3. Chapman and Hall, New-York (1998)
4. Harchol-Balter, M., Schroeder, B., Bansal, N., Agrawal, M.: Size-based scheduling to improve web performance. ACM Trans. Comput. Syst. 21(2), 207–233 (2003)
5. Hernandez-Campos, F., Karaliopoulos, M., Papadopouli, M., Shen, H.: Spatio-temporal modeling of traffic workload in a campus wlan. In: WICON 2006, p. 1 (2006)
6. Hu, M., Zhang, J., Sadowsky, J.: Size-aided opportunistic scheduling in wireless networks. In: GLOBECOM 2003. IEEE, Los Alamitos (2003)
7. Nuyens, M., Wierman, A.: The foreground-background queue: A survey. Perform. Eval. 65(3-4), 286–307 (2008)
8. Rai, I.A., Urvoy-Keller, G., Biersack, E.W.: Analysis of las scheduling for job size distributions with high variance. In: Proc. ACM SIGMETRICS, June 2003, pp. 218–228 (2003)
9. Rai, I.A., Urvoy-Keller, G., Vernon, M., Biersack, E.W.: Performance models for las-based scheduling disciplines in a packet switched network. In: ACM SIGMETRICS-Performance (June 2004)
10. Schrage, L.E.: The queue m/g/1 with feedback to lower priority queues. Management Science 13(7), 466–474 (1967)
11. Wierman, A., Harchol-Balter, M.: Classifying scheduling policies with respect to higher moments of conditional response time. ACM SIGMETRICS Performance Evaluation Review 33(1), 229–240 (2005)
12. Yashkov, S.: Processor-sharing queues: some progress in analysis. Queueing Systems: Theory and Applications 2(1), 1–17 (1987)

A Marginal Productivity Index Rule for Scheduling Multiclass Queues with Setups

José Niño-Mora*

Universidad Carlos III de Madrid
Department of Statistics
Avda. Universidad 30
28911 Leganés (Madrid), Spain
jnimora@alum.mit.edu
http://alum.mit.edu/www/jnimora

Abstract. This paper addresses the problem of designing a tractable scheduling rule for a multiclass $M/G/1$ queue incurring class-dependent linear holding costs and setup costs, as well as class-dependent generally distributed setup times, which performs well relative to the discounted or average cost objective. We introduce a new dynamic scheduling rule based on priority indices which emerges from deployment of a systematic methodology for obtaining marginal productivity index policies in the framework of restless bandit models, introduced by Whittle (1988) and developed by the author over the last decade. For each class, two indices are defined: an active and a passive index, depending on whether the class is or is not set up, which are functions of the class state (number in system). The index rule prescribes to engage at each time a class of highest index: it thus dynamically indicates both when to leave the class being currently served, and which class to serve next. The paper (i) formulates the problem as a semi-Markov multiarmed restless bandit problem; (ii) introduces the required extensions to previous indexation theory; and (iii) gives closed index formulae for the average criterion.

Keywords: Stochastic scheduling, optimal service control of queues, multiclass queues, setup times, setup costs, polling systems, index policies, marginal productivity index, queues with hysteresis.

1 Introduction

Consider a multiclass $M/G/1$ queue where the controller must dynamically allocate the server to one of M job classes, labeled by $m \in \mathbb{M} = \{1, \ldots, M\}$, which incurs linear holding costs at rate $h_m > 0$ per unit time per class m job in

---

* The author's research has been supported in part by the Spanish Ministry of Science and Innovation project MTM2007-63140 and an I3 faculty endowment grant, by the European Union's Network of Excellence Euro-FGI, and by the Autonomous Community of Madrid grant CCG07-UC3M/ESP-3389. The approach deployed herein was first announced by the author in a talk at the 13th INFORMS Applied Probability Conference (Ottawa, Canada, 2005).

E. Altman and A. Chaintreau (Eds.): NET-COOP 2008, LNCS 5425, pp. 78–86, 2009.

system. Switching the server from one class to another is costly: setting up the server so that it is ready to work on class m jobs entails an upfront setup cost $c_m \geq 0$, followed by a random setup time $D_m > 0$ having a general distribution with Laplace-Stieltjes transform (LST) $\gamma_m(\alpha) = \mathbb{E}\left[e^{-\alpha D_m}\right]$, with a finite second moment. At a given time, we say that the server is *on for class m* if it is either undergoing a setup or already set up for that class. Otherwise, we say that the server is *off for class m*. If the server is off for every class we say that it is *off* (for the system). The server can be turned on or off at *decision epochs* τ_k given by the instants of arrival when the server is off, along with the service and setup completion epochs. If the server is set up for a nonempty class, it is required to work in a job of that class. Yet, *idling* (cf. [1]) is allowed, meaning that the server can remain idle either while it is off for the system or while it is set up at an empty class, even though there may be jobs waiting at other classes. Class m jobs arrive as a Poisson process with rate λ_m, and their service times ξ_m have a general distribution with LST $\psi_m(\alpha) = \mathbb{E}\left[e^{-\alpha \xi_m}\right]$, having finite first and second moments $1/\mu_m$ and σ_m^2. Interarrival, service and setup times are mutually independent. The necessary stability condition $\rho < 1$ is assumed to hold, where $\rho \triangleq \sum_{m=1}^{M} \rho_m$ and $\rho_m \triangleq \lambda_m/\mu_m$.

Consider the problem of designing a scheduling policy $\boldsymbol{\pi}$, drawn from the space $\boldsymbol{\Pi}$ of nonanticipative randomized policies, which prescribes the action to take at each decision epoch, in order to minimize the expected total discounted cost relative to a given discount rate $\alpha > 0$, or the expected long-run average cost rate per unit time. A policy must resolve the following questions: (i) If the server is set up for a class, When should it leave (be turned off for) that class? (ii) When the server leaves a class, Should it be turned off for the system, or be turned on for another class? And, in the latter case, For which class? Denote by $a_m(\tau_k) \in \{0,1\}$ the indicator of whether the server is on for class m at epoch τ_k, and let $a_m^-(\tau_k) \triangleq a_m(\tau_{k-1})$ denote the corresponding indicator for the previous epoch (where $a_m^-(\tau_0)$ indicates whether class m is initially set up, as $\tau_0 = 0$). Denote by $L_m(\tau_k)$ the number of class m jobs in system at epoch τ_k. Such processes are extended to piecewise constant right-continuous continuous time processes $a_m(t)$ and $L_m(t)$. The scheduling problems of concern are *semi-Markov decision processes* (SMDPs) having state and action processes $\mathbf{X}(\tau_k) = \big(X_m(\tau_k)\big)$ and $\mathbf{a}(\tau_k) = \big(a_m(\tau_k)\big)$, respectively, where $X_m(\tau_k) = \big(a_m^-(\tau_k), L_m(\tau_k)\big)$ is class m's *augmented state*. The discounted-cost problem is thus formulated as

$$\min_{\boldsymbol{\pi} \in \boldsymbol{\Pi}} \mathbb{E}_{\mathbf{x}}^{\boldsymbol{\pi}} \left[\sum_{m \in \mathbb{M}} \left\{ h_m \int_0^\infty L_m(t) e^{-\alpha t}\, dt + c_m \sum_{k=0}^\infty \big(1 - a_m^-(\tau_k)\big) a_m(\tau_k) e^{-\alpha \tau_k} \right\} \right],$$
(1)

while the average-cost problem is

$$\min_{\boldsymbol{\pi} \in \boldsymbol{\Pi}} \varlimsup_{T \to \infty} \frac{1}{T} \mathbb{E}_{\mathbf{x}}^{\boldsymbol{\pi}} \left[\sum_{m \in \mathbb{M}} \left\{ h_m \int_0^T L_m(t)\, dt + c_m \sum_{\tau_k \leq T} \big(1 - a_m^-(\tau_k)\big) a_m(\tau_k) \right\} \right],$$
(2)

where $\mathbb{E}_{\mathbf{x}}^{\boldsymbol{\pi}}[\cdot]$ denotes expectation under policy $\boldsymbol{\pi}$ conditioned on $\mathbf{X}(0) = \mathbf{x}$.

Researchers have extensively investigated the *performance analysis* of multiclass queues with setups under given policies, as such models are relevant in a variety of application areas, most notably in communication networks (*polling systems*) and in manufacturing systems. See, e.g., [2] and [3].

The *performance optimization* of multiclass queues with setups through dynamic scheduling has received substantially less attention, though interest has been steadily increasing over the last two decades. In [4], the special cases of (1) and (2) where there are two symmetric classes is investigated. It is shown that service at each queue should be exhaustive, and a threshold policy is proposed where the server switches from one empty class when the number of jobs in the other class exceeds a certain threshold. The design of optimal routing tables for polling in multiclass queues with setup times under the average criterion, relative to fixed policies for deciding when to leave a class, is addressed in [5,6]. In [7], an intuitive heuristic dynamic scheduling rule is proposed and assessed for the special case of (2) with only setup times. Such a rule is based on greedy indices defined for each class which represent reward rates, and which depend on whether the class is or not set up. The same authors use similar ideas to propose in [8] a rule for the corresponding problem with only setup costs. In [9], heavy-traffic Brownian approximations are used to design heuristic policies for the special cases of (2) where there are two classes and either only setup costs or times. Other heuristic policies are proposed in [10] and in [11]. The latter paper further proposed performance bounds based on fluid approximationss. Bounds based on mathematical programming relaxations are given in [12].

In contrast to the diversity of ad hoc heuristic ideas used in previous work, this paper introduces a novel approach to the design of dynamic scheduling policies for the above problems based on deployment of a unifying, systematic methodology. The latter applies to a versatile model termed the *multiarmed restless bandit problem* (MARBP), which concerns the optimal dynamic allocation of effort to multiple (semi-) Markovian *projects*, where at each time a project can be active or passive, resulting in different dynamics and/or cost rates. Problems (1)–(2) fit into such a framework by identifying the "projects" with job classes.

The MARBP was introduced in [13], as an extension of the classic *multiarmed bandit problem* (MABP). In the MABP, one project must be engaged at a time, and projects are assumed to be nonrestless, in that they do not change state while passive. In such a case, it was first proven by Gittins and Jones in [14] that there exists a priority *index* $\nu_m^*(i_m)$ attached to each project m as a function of its state i_m, such that the corresponding *index policy* that engages at each time a project of currently highest index is optimal. While the MARBP extension is generally intractable, [13] introduced a heuristic index rule based on indices $\nu_m^*(i_m)$ attached to restless projects. Yet, such an index only exists for a limited class of projects termed *indexable*. Over the last decade, the author has developed a body of theoretical and algorithmic work on restless bandit indexation, motivated by and illustrated on a variety of applications. See, e.g., [15,16,17,18,19] and the review paper [20]. Such work gives sufficient conditions for a restless project to be indexable, along with an adaptive-greedy algorithm for index computation, and furnishes an economically intuitive foundation for the indexation approach based on the concept of *marginal productivity index* (MPI), which unifies and extends previous indices proposed in the literature. The incorporation of switching penalties in bandit models has been addressed by the author in classic bandits [19,21] and in restless bandits [22].

Yet application of such an approach to the model of concern is not straightforward, as it requires significant extensions of previous results —which applied either to finite-state projects or to countable-state projects with a linearly ordered state space— whereas the projects herein have a countable partially ordered state space. This paper outlines the required extensions, and shows how to deploy them to obtain new dynamic index policies for problems (1) and (2).

The remainder of the paper, which focuses for concreteness in the discounted problem (1), is organized as follows. Section 2 formulates the problem as a MARBP, and outlines the indexation approach to the design of a dynamic index policy. Section 3 introduces the required extensions of previous results. Section 4 deploys such results to obtain the new index rule, which is given in closed form for the average-cost problem. Finally, Section 5 ends the paper with some concluding remarks.

Due to space constraints no proofs are given. These will be included in the full paper version, along with the results of an extensive computational study.

2   Restless Bandit Indexation Approach

In the MARBP reformulation of the problem of concern, project m has state $X_m(t) = (a_m^-(t), L_m(t))$. Consider now the subsystem consisting of class m *in isolation*, as a controlled queue in which the server can be turned on or off at each decision epoch. Let us introduce a parameter ν which represents the *wage rate* to be paid to the server per unit time that it is on, and consider the optimal dynamic control subproblem for such a queue:

$$
\min_{\pi_m \in \Pi_m} \mathbb{E}^{\pi_m}_{(a_m^-, i_m)} \left[\left\{ \int_0^\infty \{ h_m L_m(t) + \nu a_m(t) \} e^{-\alpha t}\, dt \right. \right.
$$
$$
\left. \left. + c_m \sum_{k=0}^\infty \left(1 - a_m^-(\tau_k) \right) a_m(\tau_k) e^{-\alpha \tau_k} \right\} \right], \tag{3}
$$

where Π_m is the space of nonanticipative server-operating policies, and $\mathbb{E}^{\pi_m}_{(a_m^-, i_m)}[\cdot]$ denotes expectation under policy π_m conditioned on $X_m(0) = (a_m^-, i_m)$.

Note that several variations of problem (3), typically focusing on its time-average counterpart and assuming only setup costs, have been extensively investigated in the literature on optimal control of queues. See, e.g., [23,24,25,26,27,28].

We allow the server's wage ν to take any real value, and investigate the structure of optimal policies for (3) obtained by varying it as a parameter $\nu \in \mathbb{R}$. Let us say that problem (3) is *indexable* if the set of states (a_m^-, i_m) where it is optimal to take the active action $a_m = 1$ at a decision epoch decreases monotonically from the full state space $\mathbb{X}_m \triangleq \{0,1\} \times \mathbb{Z}_+$ to the empty set $\emptyset$ as the server's wage ν increases from $-\infty$ to ∞, where $\mathbb{Z}_+ \triangleq \{0,1,2,\ldots\}$. In such a case, optimal policies for (3) are characterized by an *index* $\nu_m^*(a_m^-, i_m)$ for $(a_m^-, i_m) \in \mathbb{X}_m$, which we will term the class' *marginal productivity index* (MPI): it is optimal to take action $a_m = 1$ in state (a_m^-, i_m) iff $\nu_m^*(a_m^-, i_m) \geq \nu$. Such an index measures the marginal productivity of the server's effort in each state, as elucidated in the economic interpretation in [17]. Note that the index decouples into an *active index* $\nu_m^*(1, i_m)$, which applies when the server is set up, and a *passive index* $\nu_m^*(0, i_m)$, which applies otherwise.

Assume now that each class m is indexable, having MPI $\nu_m^*(a_m^-, i_m)$. The economic interpretation of such indices suggests the following (priority-) index rule for the multiclass scheduling problem (1). Suppose that at a decision epoch τ_k class m occupies state $X_m(\tau_k) = (a_m^-, i_m)$, for $m \in \mathbb{M}$, and consider the index values $\nu_m^*(a_m^-, i_m)$ at such states. If none of them is positive, i.e., if $\nu_m^*(a_m^-, i_m) < 0$ for $m \in \mathbb{M}$, then turn or keep off the server. Otherwise, pick a class m^* which attains the largest index value among those that are positive at the current state, and turn or keep the server on for such a class.

Intuition suggests that such indices should satisfy the *hysteretic property*

$$\nu_m^*(1, i_m) \geq \nu_m^*(0, i_m), \quad i_m \geq 0, \tag{4}$$

so, other things being equal, one should keep the server in a class where it is set up rather than switching and setting it up for another class.

3   Outline of Required Extension of Indexation Theory

In order to deploy the indexation approach outlined above we need to (i) establish that the projects of concern are indexable, and (ii) give a tractable approach to compute the index. This turns out to require significant extensions of previous results on restless bandit indexation introduced by the author. We next outline such extensions as they apply to the model of concern.

Consider an individual project representing a single queue with setups subject to service control, where we drop henceforth the class label m from the notation. In such a setting, we evaluate the value of a policy π for operating such a single-server queue using the discounted *cost measure*

$$f_{(a^-,i)}^\pi \triangleq \mathbb{E}_{(a^-,i)}^\pi \left[\int_0^\infty hL(t)e^{-\alpha t}\, dt + c \sum_{k=0}^\infty \left(1 - a^-(\tau_k)\right)a(\tau_k)e^{-\alpha \tau_k} \right],$$

and further evaluate the server's work expended (where thet time spent in setups is counted as work) using the discounted *work measure* (cf. [16])

$$g_{(a^-,i)}^\pi \triangleq \mathbb{E}_{(a^-,i)}^\pi \left[\int_0^\infty a(t)e^{-\alpha t}\, dt \right].$$

We can thus formulate problem (3) as

$$\min_{\pi \in \Pi} f_{(a^-,i)}^\pi + \nu g_{(a^-,i)}^\pi. \tag{5}$$

We will refer to (5) as the ν-*wage problem*, as it concerns finding an optimal server-operating policy that minimizes the sum of holding, switching and server's labor costs. We can then use such a parametric problem to define the concept of *indexability* and MPI $\nu^*(a^-, i)$ as in the previous section.

Now, the key to achieving goals (i) and (ii) above is to exploit special structure, by being able to *guess* a family of stationary deterministic policies among which an optimal policy for (5) exists for any wage $\nu \in \mathbb{R}$. We will any such policy by its *active (state) set*, which is the set of states where the policy prescribes to take the active action at a decision epoch. Such an active set is conveniently represented by giving two sets $S_0, S_1 \subseteq \mathbb{Z}_+$, with the following interpretation: in state $(0, i)$, turn the server on iff $i \in S_0$; in state $(1, i)$, keep the server on iff $i \in S_1$. We will also denote by $S_0 \oplus S_1$ the corresponding policy.

Intuition suggests that it suffices to consider *hysteretic* policies given by a passive (k) and and active (l) threshold satisfying $k \geq l \geq 0$, so $S_0 = \{k, k+1, \ldots\}$ and $S_1 = \{l, l+1, \ldots\}$, as well as policies where $S_0 = \emptyset$ and $S_1 = \{l, l+1, \ldots\}$, where we take $k = \infty$. We will also denote by (k, l) the corresponding policy, writing, e.g., $g_{(a^-, k)}^{(k,l)}$. We will denote by $\mathcal{F}$ the family of all such active sets, and will refer to the family of $\mathcal{F}$-*policies*.

Let us say that problem (5) is $\mathcal{F}$-*indexable* if (i) it is indexable; and (ii) for every wage $\nu \in \mathbb{R}$ there is an optimal $\mathcal{F}$-policy for (5). Note that, in such a case, the MPI $\nu^*_{(a^-, i)}$ satisfies the hysteretic property (4).

In the finite-state case, previous indexation theory (cf. [20]) prescribes to use the *adaptive-greedy index algorithm* introduced in [15] to compute the MPI. In the present setting, however, the fact that the augmented state space $\mathbb{X} \triangleq \{0, 1\} \times \mathbb{Z}_+$ is countable yet not linearly ordered calls for a suitable extension, which we introduce next as follows. We must identify a *linear ordering* $\preceq$ of the state space $\mathbb{X}$ which satisfies certain conditions, where we write

$$\mathbf{S}_x \triangleq \{y \in \mathbb{X} : x \prec y\}, \quad x \in \mathbb{X}.$$

Such conditions are: (i) $\mathbf{S}_x \in \mathcal{F}$ for every $x \in \mathbb{X}$; (ii) the work measure is monotone consistently with such an ordering, in that $\left(g_y^{\mathbf{S}_{x'}}\right)_{y \in \mathbb{X}} \precsim \left(g_y^{\mathbf{S}_x}\right)_{y \in \mathbb{X}}$ if $x \prec x'$; and (iii) the *marginal productivity rates*

$$\nu^*(x) \triangleq \frac{f_x^{\mathbf{S}_x} - f_x^{\mathbf{S}_x \cup \{x\}}}{g_x^{\mathbf{S}_x \cup \{x\}} - g_x^{\mathbf{S}_x}}$$

are monotone consistently with the ordering $\preceq$, i.e., $\nu^*_x \leq \nu^*_{x'}$ if $x \preceq x'$. Instead of (iii), one can use the alternative condition (iii'): $\mathcal{F}$-policies are optimal for problem (5) under any wage $\nu \in \mathbb{R}$.

Theorem 1. *Under the stated conditions, the restless project is $\mathcal{F}$-indexable and $\nu^*(x)$ is its MPI.*

4   Application to the Scheduling Model

To deploy the above results in the model of concern it must be established that the required conditions (i)—(iii) in Theorem 1 hold relative to a certain linear ordering of $\mathbb{X}$. The following result ensures that such is indeed the case.

Lemma 1. *There exists a linear ordering $\preceq$ on $\mathbb{X}$ satisfying conditions (i)—(iii) in Theorem 1, under which $(0, i) \prec (1, i)$ and $(a^-, i) < (a^-, i+1)$ for $(a^-, i) \in \mathbb{X}$.*

The required ordering $\preceq$ can be readily constructed through a suitable modification of the adaptive-greedy algorithm referred to above, which is not included here due to space constraints.

Further, by taking appropriate Maclaurin expansions as the discount factor α vanishes, one obtains a corresponding index rule for the (long-run) average criterion. Under the latter, we can actually obtain closed-form formulae for the index. In such a case, the nested decreasing active-set ordering corresponding to the state ordering $\preceq$ has the form

$$(1, 0), \ldots, (k^* - 1, 0), (k^*, 0), (k^*, 1), (k^* + 1, 1), (k^* + 2, 1), \ldots, (\infty, 1), (\infty, 2), \ldots$$

where k^* is a critical threshold value given by

$$k^* = \max_{k \geq 1} \left\{ c\left(\frac{\lambda}{k} + \frac{1}{\mathbb{E}[D]}\right) - h\frac{(k + \lambda\mathbb{E}[D])\left((k-1)k - \lambda^2\mathbb{E}[D^2]\right)}{2k\lambda(1-\rho)\mathbb{E}[D]} > 0 \right\}.$$

We obtain that the discounted MPI of state $(1, i)$, for $i \geq 1$, has the Maclaurin expansion

$$\nu^*(1, i) = \frac{h\mu}{\alpha} + O(1), \text{ as } \alpha \searrow 0.$$

Further, the MPI of state $(1, 0)$ is given by

$$\nu^*(1, 0) = c\frac{\lambda}{k^*} + h\frac{(k^* - 1)(k^* + 2\lambda\mathbb{E}[D]) + \lambda\left(2\mathbb{E}[D] + \lambda\mathbb{E}[D^2]\right)}{2k^*(1-\rho)} + O(\alpha).$$

The MPI of state $(0, i)$, for $i \geq k^*$ is

$$\nu^*(0, i) = h\frac{i(1 + 2\lambda\mathbb{E}[D]) + i^2 + \lambda^2(\mathbb{E}[D]^2 - \text{Var}[D])}{2\lambda(1-\rho)\mathbb{E}[D]} - \frac{c}{\mathbb{E}[D]} + O(\alpha),$$

and, for $0 \leq i < k^*$,

$$\nu^*(0, i) = h\frac{i + \lambda\mathbb{E}[D]}{1 - \rho} + O(\alpha).$$

Note that in the multiclass model, for a discount rate α small enough, and two distinct classes m, n, with $i_n \geq 1$, it holds that $\nu_n^*(1, i_n) > \nu_m^*(0, j_m)$, the MPI scheduling rule is *exhaustive*. Other qualitative properties of such a rule are readily obtained from the above formulae, which are consistent with the properties of optimal policies established under symmetry assumptions in [29].

Such index formulae are valid for the case of positive setup times $D > 0$. In the case where there are no setup times yet there are positive setup costs, a similar analysis can be carried out which yields different index formulae.

5   Conclusions

This paper introduces a novel approach to the design of tractable dynamic scheduling policies of priority-index type for multiclass queues with both setup costs and times, based on formulating such models as multiarmed restless bandit problems and then deploying the general theoretical and algorithmic results available for the latter, suitably extended to the present setting. A full version of this paper will report on an experimental study to assess both the degree of suboptimality of the resultant index rules and their relative performance compared to other policies previously proposed in the literature.

References

1. Eisenberg, M.: The polling system with a stopping server. Queueing Syst. 18, 387–431 (1994)
2. Takagi, H.: Analysis of Polling Systems. MIT Press, Cambridge (1986)
3. Levy, H., Sidi, M.: Polling systems: Applications, modelling and optimization. IEEE Trans. Comm. 38, 1750–1760 (1990)
4. Hofri, M., Ross, K.W.: On the optimal control of two queues with server setup times and its analysis. SIAM J. Comput. 16, 399–420 (1987)
5. Boxma, O.J., Levy, H., Weststrate, J.A.: Efficient visit frequencies for polling tables: Minimization of waiting cost. Queueing Syst. 9, 133–162 (1991)
6. Boxma, O.J., Levy, H., Weststrate, J.A.: Efficient visit frequencies for polling systems. Performance Evaluation 18, 103–123 (1993)
7. Duenyas, I., Van Oyen, M.: Heuristic scheduling of parallel heterogeneous queues with setups. Management Sci. 42, 814–829 (1996)
8. Duenyas, I., Van Oyen, M.: Stochastic scheduling of parallel queues with setup costs. Queueing Syst. 19, 421–444 (1995)
9. Reiman, M.I., Wein, L.M.: Dynamic scheduling of a two-class queue with setups. Oper. Res. 46, 532–547 (1998)
10. Olsen, T.L.: A practical scheduling method for multiclass production systems with setups. Management Sci. 45, 116–130 (1999)
11. Lan, W.M., Olsen, T.L.: Multiproduct systems with both setup times and costs: fluid bounds and schedules. Oper. Res. 54, 505–522 (2006)
12. Bertsimas, D., Niño-Mora, J.: Optimization of multiclass queueing networks with changeover times via the achievable region approach: Part I, the single-station case. Math. Oper. Res. 24, 306–330 (1999)
13. Whittle, P.: Restless bandits: Activity allocation in a changing world. In: Gani, J. (ed.) A Celebration of Applied Probability; J. Appl. Probab. Applied Probability Trust 25A (spec. vol.), 287–298, Sheffield, UK (1988)
14. Gittins, J.C., Jones, D.M.: A dynamic allocation index for the sequential design of experiments. In: Gani, J., Sarkadi, K., Vincze, I. (eds.) Progress in Statistics (European Meeting of Statisticians, Budapest, 1972), pp. 241–266. North-Holland, Amsterdam (1974)
15. Niño-Mora, J.: Restless bandits, partial conservation laws and indexability. Adv. Appl. Probab. 33, 76–98 (2001)
16. Niño-Mora, J.: Dynamic allocation indices for restless projects and queueing admission control: a polyhedral approach. Math. Program. 93, 361–413 (2002)

17. Niño-Mora, J.: Restless bandit marginal productivity indices, diminishing returns and optimal control of make-to-order/make-to-stock $M/G/1$ queues. Math. Oper. Res. 31, 50–84 (2006)
18. Niño-Mora, J.: Marginal productivity index policies for scheduling a multiclass delay-/loss-sensitive queue. Queueing Syst. 54, 281–312 (2006)
19. Niño-Mora, J.: A faster index algorithm and a computational study for bandits with switching costs. INFORMS J. Comput. 20, 255–269 (2008)
20. Niño-Mora, J.: Dynamic priority allocation via restless bandit marginal productivity indices. TOP 15, 161–198 (2007)
21. Niño-Mora, J.: Computing an index policy for bandits with switching penalties. In: ValueTools 2007: Proceedings of the Second International Conference on Performance Evaluation Methodologies and Tools (Nantes, France). ACM International Conference Proceedinsg Series, ICST, Brussels, Belgium (2007)
22. Niño-Mora, J.: Marginal productivity index policies for scheduling restless bandits with switching penalties. In: Albers, S., Möhring, R.H., Pflug, G.C., Schultz, R. (eds.) Algorithms for Optimization with Incomplete Information. Number 05031 in Dagstuhl Seminar Proceedings (2005)
23. Yadin, M., Naor, P.: Queueing systems with a removable service station. Oper. Res. 14, 393–405 (1963)
24. Bell, C.E.: Characterization and computation of optimal policies for operating an $M/G/1$ queuing system with removable server. Oper. Res. 19, 208–218 (1971)
25. Bell, C.E.: Optimal operation of an $M/G/1$ priority queue with removable server. Oper. Res. 21, 1281–1290 (1973)
26. Heyman, D.: Optimal operating policies for $M/G/1$ queuing systems. Oper. Res. 16, 362–382 (1968)
27. Sobel, M.J.: Optimal average-cost policy for a queue with start-up and shut-down costs. Oper. Res. 17, 145–162 (1969)
28. Borthakur, A., Medhi, J., Gohain, R.: Poisson input queueing system with startup time and under control-operating policy. Comput. Oper. Res. 14, 33–40 (1987)
29. Liu, Z., Nain, P., Towsley, D.: On optimal polling policies. Queueing Syst. 11, 59–83 (1992)

A Heuristic Approach to the Passive Detection of Reno-Like TCP Flows[*]

Miguel Rodríguez-Pérez, Manuel Fernández-Veiga, Sergio Herrería-Alonso,
and Cándido López-García

E.T.S.E. Telecomunicación
Campus universitario s/n
36 310 Vigo, Spain

Abstract. Traditional TCP-Reno like congestion control protocols exhibit poor performance when deployed in fast or very large network paths. Delay based congestion avoidance mechanisms (DCA), like FAST-TCP, get much higher performance, in the same circumstances. However, when mixed with TCP-Reno or alike traffic they are unable to attain their fair share of bandwidth. In this paper we present a new mechanism that can indirectly detect the present of non DCA-friendly traffic that can be used by new DCA algorithms to auto-tune themselves with more aggressive parameters to achieve their fair share.

Keywords: Congestion control, Delay-based, FAST-TCP, TCP-Vegas.

1 Introduction

TCP congestion control protocols are having problems in keeping fully utilized current high-speed links. Very high-throughput implies very big congestion window sizes, which in turns needs negligible packet losses. For protocols that just employ packet losses as a signal of congestion, increasing the bandwidth means a substantial waste of resources if transmission errors were confused with packet losses really caused by congestion. Hence, new congestion control mechanisms are needed to fully use the installed network capacity under this scenario. The research community has come up with new protocols more aggressive than Reno to compensate for the lack of feedback that packet losses provide [1,2]. Another promising approach consist in adapting the techniques of Delay-based congestion avoidance (DCA) [3,4,5] protocols that gather more information feedback from the net, and thus should be able to better allocate its resources.

Delay-based congestion avoidance (DCA) control protocols, and FAST-TCP [5] in particular, are known for their effectiveness when used in isolation: low queueing delay, convergence to a constant transmission rate, low packet losses, full utilization of the links bandwidth, ... [6,4] However, when confronted against

---

[*] This work was supported by the "Ministerio de Educación y Ciencia" through the project TSI2006-12507-C03-02 of the "Plan Nacional de I+D+I" (partly financed with FEDER funds).

E. Altman and A. Chaintreau (Eds.): NET-COOP 2008, LNCS 5425, pp. 87–94, 2009.

Reno traffic they overreact to congestion, leading to an unnecessarily poor performance [6]. This has prevented wide-scale deployment of these kind of protocols despite being available, although not enabled by default, in the Linux kernel since at least 2004 for Vegas.

Thus, in the absence of fair-queueing mechanisms in the network, the ability to reliably and rapidly detect the presence of loss-reacting congestion control protocols in a network path is key for the successful deployment of DCA protocols in the Internet.

Because in a network with only DCA flows packet losses should be really scarce, the existence of quasi-periodic packet losses can be taken as an indication of the existence of Reno-like TCP flows. However, DCA sources cannot usually detect directly the losses, because dropped packets are more likely to belong to Reno flows. This happens for two reasons: firstly, Reno flows have a much higher chance of suffering losses because they get a higher share of the bandwidth, and send more packets per second. The second is that, as the queue gets full, DCA flows decrease their sending rate due to the increased queueing delay, so it is just when a link is closest to congestion that DCA flows throttle their traffic, decreasing even more the chance that the dropped packet will be theirs. In the evaluation section of this paper we show some scenarios in with FAST flows get no direct losses, while Reno flows share a common bottleneck.

In this paper we propose a simple but effective mechanism to detect the presence of loss-based congestion control algorithms (like Reno and its variants) in a given network path. This proposal permits the creation of new dual algorithms that are able to rapidly adapt to the presence of Reno flows. Our proposal tries to look at the effects of AIMD traffic in the network and, as such, predicts episodes of packet losses in the network caused by the tendency of Reno variants to fill the router queues. Compared with [7], we can detect and thus react to Reno flows in the timescale of the RTT and, in contrast to [8], we do not mistake the presence of many DCA flows with Reno flows, unless the network is under-provisioned. But in that case DCA algorithms behave almost exactly like Reno.

The rest of this paper is organized as follows. Section 2 provides information about DCA algorithms and their compatibility with Reno. Section 3 presents the basis of our passive loss detection algorithm. Then, in Section 4 representative results from experimental evaluation are shown. The conclusions are in Section 5.

2   Background

DCA algorithms work on the assumption that it is possible to infer the network status by observing the variations in the RTT. The difference between the RTT and the propagation delay is directly related to the amount of data in transit, this amount being a measure of the level of congestion. So, adjusting the window size based on these variations, DCA flows keep an appropriate transmission rate without causing congestion. In contrast, TCP-Reno and its variants need to drive the network close to congestion in order to receive the feedback needed to adjust the window. The window size is slowly increased until it reaches a point that buffers overflow and a packet loss occurs. This leads sources to abruptly reduce the sending rate and the slow increment begins again. This prevents Reno flows to fully use all the available bandwidth. Thus, DCA algorithms are more suitable in long fat pipes where packet losses are too scarce to properly adjust the rate or for those applications negatively affected by sudden changes in the transmission rate.

Both TCP-Vegas and FAST-TCP employ a similar *modus operandi*, in fact, FAST-TCP can be treated as an improved (faster) version of the former [5].

To adjust its window size w in the absence of packet losses FAST-TCP sources keep an estimation of both the current RTT, r, and the propagation delay r_0, approximated in practice as the minimum RTT measured throughout the connection lifetime. Then, w is periodically updated according to

$$w \longleftarrow \gamma \left(\frac{r_0 w}{r} + \alpha \right) + (1 - \gamma)w. \tag{1}$$

Here, α and γ are configuration parameters: α plays the same role that α and β play in Vegas, representing the amount of data enqueued in the network when stability is reached, while γ controls the speed of convergence and is usually set to 0.5. Several papers deal with the conditions that both α and γ must met to reach equilibrium. More details can be found in [9,10,11,12].

In comparison, TCP Reno and its variants induce packet losses to estimate the available bandwidth in the network. To do so, they slowly increase their transmission rates up to the point of filling network buffers. When this happens, the transmission rate is halved and the cycle repeats again.

Although Reno behavior leads to fair bandwidth share between Reno flow and network stability, it causes an unfair bandwidth share against DCA protocols. In fact, according to [13] if $k < \alpha$ is the number packets DCA flows have enqueued at a given bottleneck of capacity B packets, then the relative throughput of DCA flows is given by

$$\rho = \frac{2k}{B - k}. \tag{2}$$

If the buffer is overprovisioned, which is usually the case, $B \gg k$ and DCA flows are unable to attain their fair share.

In the last couple of years there have started to appear new hybrid congestion control proposals that try to combine the behavior of DCA flows with the aggressiveness of Reno variants depending on the network state [7,8]. In [7] the authors propose a way to adapt FAST-TCP α parameter that takes into account both loss rate and queueing delay. However, the configuration is updated only once every two minutes, leading to slow reaction and long convergence times. Alternatively, the authors of [8] use queueing delay to decide whether to switch between DCA or AIMD algorithms, employing DCA when the measured queueing-delay is sufficiently small. The drawback is that they also unnecessarily employ AIMD algorithms when there are many DCA flows in the network path, degrading overall performance.

3   Procedure

In a properly dimensioned network shared only by delay-based flows the equilibrium point is maintained with a complete lack of packet losses caused by congestion. On the contrary, loss-reacting congestion control protocols —like TCP-Reno or its variants— cannot reach a complete equilibrium and cause periodic packet losses. With this in mind, a FAST-TCP flow could look for packet losses to infer the presence of non DCA-friendly TCP flows.

However, the unfair sharing of a bottleneck between flows employing different congestion control algorithms makes FAST-TCP less likely to suffer from direct packet losses that the Reno-like flows, so a method to detect packet losses, even if not own, is needed. We provide simulation scenarios later in this paper that show this phenomenon.

In a bottleneck shared by TCP-Reno flows, the queue occupation follows cyclic patterns, first getting filled up while flows struggle to reach the highest sustainable throughput, to be drained later while traversing flows halve their windows to adapt to congestion. Thus, an observer could detect packet losses monitoring the dynamics of the queue length.

Queue length is precisely what FAST-TCP flows indirectly monitor to react to congestion. In fact, they estimate their own queueing delay to maintain α packets enqueued along its network path by measuring both the round-trip-time (r) and the round-trip propagation delay (r_0). These data can be reused to estimate not only its own queueing delay, but the total delay caused by all flows sharing the network path. In fact, the difference $r - r_0$ is directly proportional to the amount of data enqueued at the bottleneck link.

Let $r(n)$ be the round trip time measured by a FAST-TCP flow after the arrival of acknowledgment n. Then, the queueing delay can be calculated as $d(n) = r(n) - r_0$. To avoid having all values dependant on the network characteristics and packet length, define $\bar{q}(n) \triangleq \frac{d(n)}{r_0}$ as the normalized queueing delay (which is clearly proportional to the normalized queue length). Lastly, let $\Delta\bar{q}(n) = \bar{q}(n) - \bar{q}(n-1)$ be the per-packet variation of the queue length.

The ideal loss signal

$$l(n) = \begin{cases} 1 & \text{if losses occurred between packets } n-1 \text{ and } n \\ 0 & \text{in any other case,} \end{cases} \tag{3}$$

can be tried to be recovered using an heuristic based on the variations of the queueing delay as

$$\tilde{l}(n) = \begin{cases} 1 & \text{if } \frac{-\Delta\bar{q}(n)}{\bar{q}(n-1)} > \tau \\ 0 & \text{in any other case.} \end{cases} \tag{4}$$

Equation (4) merits several comments. We deduce that there must have been packet losses when the decrement of queueing delay represents a significant portion of the total queueing delay. It is important to note that the value of the threshold τ should be chosen carefully. There is certainly a tradeoff between a too low value that could yield many false positives, for instance when a flow leaves the network, and a too high value that would miss many losses.

4   Experimental Results

Throughout this section we will present some of the results we have obtained
testing the accuracy of our estimated loss signal. Recall that it is the ability to
detect the presence of AIMD flows what we are interested in testing, and not the
detection of every packet loss event. To this end, we have modified the FAST-
TCP implementation for the ns-2 [14] simulator so that it is able to report the
recovered $\hat{l}(n)$ vector.

For our first set of experiments we used a topology like that shown in Fig. 1.
There is a set of n_F FAST-TCP flows competing for bandwidth with n_R Reno
flows. Unless otherwise stated, all FAST-TCP flows have been set up with $\alpha = 3$
and network buffers with capacity for $B = (\alpha+1)n_F + 10n_R$ packets. The decision
threshold has been set experimentally to a 20 percent reduction ($\tau = 0.2$). All
the flows carry a endless stream of application data from S_i towards D_i.

Our first experiment measures the time needed to detect a given packet loss.
We show the results for $n_F = 1$ and $n_R = [1, 50]$ in Fig. 2. The propagation delay
in the links $S_i \rightarrow R_1$ has been modified so as to make round-trip propagation
delay of the FAST-TCP flow one tenth, equal and ten times as large as the one
of the competing Reno flows. As the figure shows, it takes about two RTT for
loss detection, which is quite fast indeed, given that what is used for detection
is the reaction of Reno flows to packet losses.

Our second experiment shows both $l_i(n)$ and $\hat{l}_F(n)$. Fig. 3 represents with a
little mark packet losses suffered by Reno flows, and by dashed lines the losses
detected by a modified FAST-TCP flow. Each TCP flow is assigned an unique
sequential identifier to help to identify them in the y-axis. Again, we modify link
propagation delays so as to compare the results for different ratios of the RTT
of the Reno flows against that of FAST-TCP. The results are for fifty Reno flows

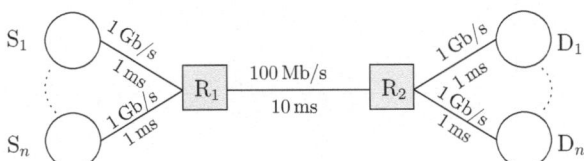

Fig. 1. Network test bed

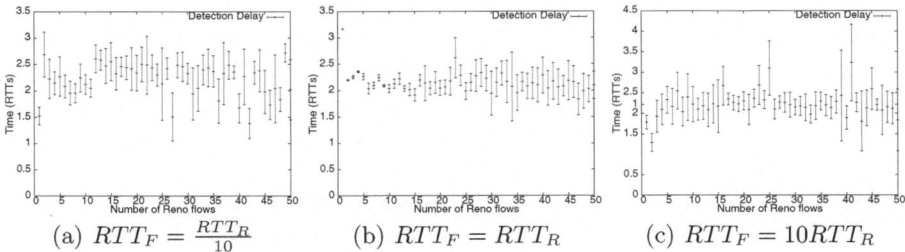

(a) $RTT_F = \frac{RTT_R}{10}$ (b) $RTT_F = RTT_R$ (c) $RTT_F = 10RTT_R$

Fig. 2. Average delay in detection of a packet loss for different propagation delays

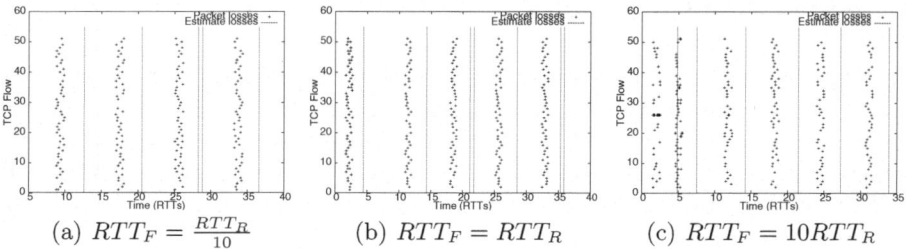

(a) $RTT_F = \frac{RTT_R}{10}$ (b) $RTT_F = RTT_R$ (c) $RTT_F = 10RTT_R$

Fig. 3. Loss pattern for a dumb-bell topology with 50 Reno flows for different propagation delays

and a single FAST-TCP flow. Observe how losses are heavily correlated between TCP flows, and how, despite the appearance of some false positives (RTT 28 in Fig. 3(a) and RTTs 22 and 36 in Fig. 3(b), for instance), those are always a double positive and not a false indication of packet losses.

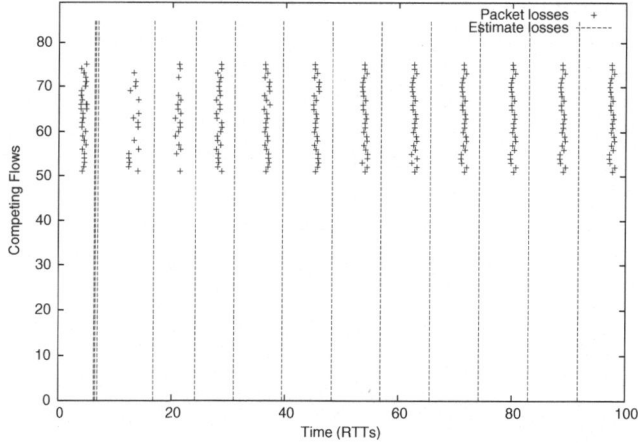

Fig. 4. Loss pattern for a dumb-bell topology with 50 FAST-TCP flows for 25 number of Reno flows

We have repeated the above experiments, but this time employing fifty FAST-TCP flows competing against one, 25 and 50 Reno flows. The results for the 25 Reno flows case appear in Fig. 4. FAST-TCP flows have ids between one and fifty while Reno flows have ids from 51 onwards. We have only run the loss detection algorithm in a single FAST-TCP flow.

Again, the recovered signal $\hat{l}(n)$ follows closely the measured $l(n)$ for any of the Reno flows. It is also important to note that the FAST-TCP flows get almost no losses, so, in absence of a loss detection algorithm they would be unable to discern whether they are competing with more aggressive AIMD flows and react

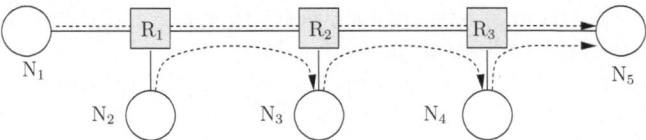

Fig. 5. Network with multiple bottlenecks to test the algorithm in the presence of background web traffic

accordingly. This confirms the need for an indirect way to detect packet losses anticipated in the introduction.

Finally, to validate our model in a more realistic scenario we used the network topology depicted in Fig. 5. In this setting, a single FAST-TCP flow carries data from N_1 to N_5 while thirty Reno flows carry web traffic from N_2 to N_3, N_3 to N_4 and N_4 to N_5. The loss pattern is shown in Fig. 6, where flows ids between 1 and 10 correspond to flows running from N_2 to N_3, ids in the range 11 to 20 belong to flows between N_3 and N_4, and the rest ids are to flows between N_4 and N_5. Note that, now, packet losses occur in three different bottlenecks and

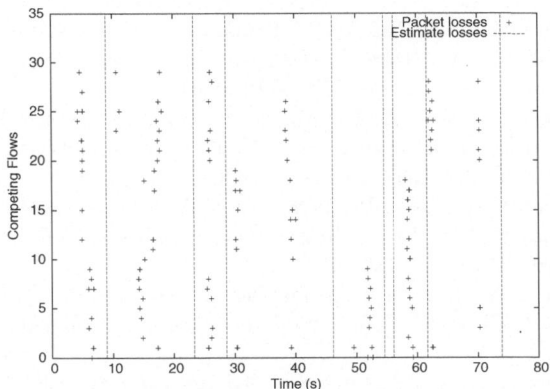

Fig. 6. Loss pattern in the presence of background web traffic in a network with multiple bottlenecks

not always simultaneously. Even so, the FAST-TCP flow from N_1 to N_5 is able to detect them, albeit with a lower accuracy, because simultaneous departures of HTTP sessions can be confused with the response to packet losses. Finally, some losses go undetected as the throughput of the FAST flow drops to 0 during heavy congestion episodes.

5   Conclusions

In the previous sections we have presented and described a new mechanism for the rapid passive detection of AIMD flows in a network path. Our proposal does not need of cooperation of any involved network agent and is able to accurately detect the occurrence of loses in just a few RTT.

The availability of this mechanism should help the creation of new hybrid congestion control protocols that exploit DCA advantages when in isolation, but can adapt to Reno-like protocols when needed, thus paving the way for the deployment of the first.

References

1. Floyd, S.: Highspeed TCP for large congestion windows. RFC 3649 (December 2003)
2. Rhee, I., Xu, L.: CUBIC: A new TCP-friendly high-speed TCP variant. In: PFLD-Net 2005 (February 2005)
3. Jain, R.: A delay-based approach for congestion avoidance in interconnected heterogeneous computer networks. SIGCOMM Comput. Commun. Rev. 19(5), 56–71 (1989)
4. Brakmo, L.S., O'Malley, S.W., Peterson, L.L.: TCP Vegas: New techniques for congestion detection and avoidance. SIGCOMM Comput. Commun. Rev. 24(4), 24–35 (1994)
5. Wei, D.X., Jin, C., Low, S.H., Hegde, S.: FAST TCP: Motivation, architecture, algorithms, performance. IEEE/ACM Trans. Netw. 14(6), 1246–1259 (2006)
6. Martin, J., Nilsson, A., Rhee, I.: Delay-based congestion avoidance for TCP. IEEE/ACM Trans. Netw. 11(3), 356–369 (2003)
7. Tang, A., Wei, D., Low, S.H.: Heterogeneous congestion control: Efficiency, fairness and design. In: IEEE International Conference on Network Protocols, Santa Barbara, CA, USA, 127–136 (November 2006)
8. King, R., Baraniuk, R., Riedi, R.: TCP-Africa: An adaptive and fair rapid increase rule for scalable TCP. In: Proceedings of the IEEE INFOCOM, Miami, FL, USA, vol. 3, pp. 1838–1848 (March 2005)
9. Wang, J., Wei, D.X., Low, H.S.: Modelling and stability of FAST TCP. In: Proceedings of the IEEE INFOCOM, April 2005, vol. 2, pp. 938–948, Pasadena, CA, USA (2005)
10. Choi, J.Y., Koo, K., Lee, J.S., Low, S.H.: Global stability of FAST TCP in single-link single-source network. In: 44th IEEE Conference on Decision and Control, Seville, Spain, pp. 1837–1841 (2005)
11. Choi, J.Y., Koo, K., Wei, D.X., Lee, J.S., Low, S.H.: Global exponential stability of FAST TCP. In: 45th IEEE Conference on Decision and Control, San Diego, CA, USA, December 2006, pp. 639–643 (2006)
12. Tan, L., Zhang, W., Yuan, C.: On parameter tuning for FAST TCP. IEEE Commun. Lett. 11(5), 458–460 (2007)
13. Mo, J., La, R.J., Anantharam, V., Walrand, J.: Analysis and comparison of TCP Reno and Vegas. In: Proceedings of the IEEE INFOCOM, New York, NY, USA, March 1999, vol. 3, pp. 1556–1563 (1999)
14. NS: ns Network Simulator (October 2005), http://www.isi.edu/nsman/ns/

Oscillations of the Sending Window in Compound TCP

Alberto Blanc[1], Denis Collange[1], and Konstantin Avrachenkov[2]

[1] Orange Labs, 905 rue Albert Einstein, 06921 Sophia Antipolis, France
[2] I.N.R.I.A. 2004 route des lucioles, 06902 Sophia Antipolis, France

Abstract. One of the key ideas of Compound TCP is to quickly increase the sending window, until full link utilization is detected, and then to keep it constant for a certain period of time. The actual Compound TCP algorithm does not hold the window constant but, instead, it makes it oscillate around the desired value. Using an analytical model and ns-2 simulations we study these oscillations on a Linux implementation of Compound TCP, in the case of a single connection with no cross traffic. Even in this simple case we show how these oscillations can behave in different ways depending on the bandwidth delay product. We also show how it is important to take into account, in the analytical model, that some implementation subtleties may introduce non-negligible differences in the behavior of the protocol.

1 Introduction

Tan et al. have introduced Compound TCP [5] to improve the performance of TCP on networks with large bandwidth delay products. One of the main ideas of this new high speed TCP variant is to quickly increase the sending window as long as the network is underutilized and then stabilizing it when a certain number of packets is buffered in the network. To achieve this goal the sender monitors the round trip time: as long as the network is underutilized (i.e. no packets are queued) the round trip time will not change. This corresponds to the case where the window is smaller than the bandwidth delay product. As the window is increased the sending rate will eventually surpass the capacity of the bottleneck link and the round trip time will start to increase. In particular the sender estimates the number of packets currently backlogged in the network. When this estimate is greater than or equal to a threshold γ the sender stops increasing its window. Figure 4 in [5], and some of the comments in that paper, give the impression that the window is then kept constant for a certain time.

While this might be a useful approximation in explaining and thinking about this new TCP version, it is easy to see, from equation (5) in [5], that the window will indeed oscillate during this phase. Figure 1 shows the evolution of the sending window from an ns-2 simulation. Clearly, at least in this case, the oscillations have a non-negligible amplitude. In the remainder of this paper we are going to analyze these oscillations in the case of a single Compound TCP connection with no competing traffic and no random losses (packets are dropped only when

E. Altman and A. Chaintreau (Eds.): NET-COOP 2008, LNCS 5425, pp. 95–102, 2009.
© Springer-Verlag Berlin Heidelberg 2009

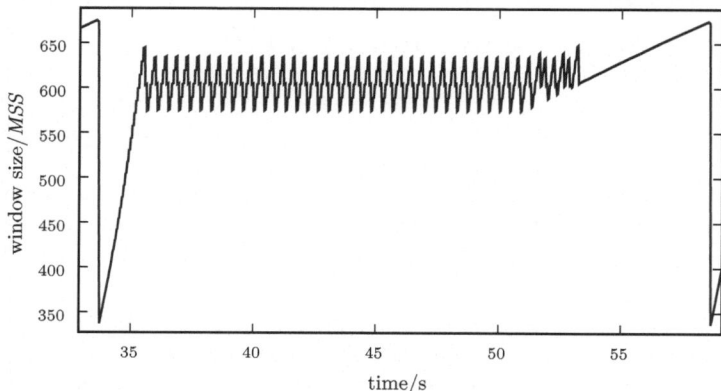

Fig. 1. The evolution of the sending window between two packet drops (ns-2 simulation, $\mu = 100\,\text{Mb/s}$, $\tilde{\tau} = 69\,\text{ms}$)

the buffer is full). While this is clearly the simplest possible scenario, even in this case, the oscillations have several possible patterns and, based on simulation results, their amplitude increases with the bandwidth delay product.

These oscillations may have many consequences on Compound TCP flows. Firstly, the packet loss probability in presence of other flows, using Compound TCP or not, will be increased during this phase. This may reduce the proportion of time during which the congestion window is larger than the bandwidth delay product, and then the efficiency of the protocol. Secondly, as these oscillations increase with the bandwidth delay product, the probability to saturate the bottleneck's buffer and will be higher and the efficiency will be lower in case of large round-trip times, as observed in [2]. Thirdly, these oscillations of the window, and, therefore of the buffer occupancy, may also degrade the performance of the network, increasing the delay, the jitter and the loss rate experienced by the other flows.

2 Evolution of the Compound TCP Window during the "Constant Window" Phase

During the "constant window" phase, every round trip time, the sender estimates the current backlog in the buffer of the bottleneck through the variable Δ (*diff* in [5]). An objective of Compound TCP is to keep Δ positive, to use the bottleneck at full speed, but small (close to γ), to minimize the buffer occupancy.

Let $w(t)$ be the window size at time t and let t_i be the end of the i-th round trip, when the window is increased from w_i to w_{i+1}. In order to make the $w(t)$ a left continuous function we set $w(t) = w_i$ if $t_{i-1} < t \leq t_i$. This way $w(t_i) = w_i$. Throughout this paper we will assume that w is expressed in terms of packets, or Maximum Segment Size (MSS). Note that $t_{i-1} - t_i$ is one round trip time so that the expression "every round trip time" refers to the time between two increments of the window. In the absence of loss, Compound TCP increments the window in the following way (see [5] for a complete description):

$$w_{i+1} = \begin{cases} w_i + \alpha w_i^k & \text{, if } \Delta_i < \gamma \\ w_i - \zeta \Delta_i + 1 & \text{, if } \Delta_i \geq \gamma \end{cases} \tag{1}$$

with

$$\Delta_i = w_i \left(1 - \frac{\tilde{\tau}}{\tau_i}\right). \tag{2}$$

Where $\tilde{\tau}$ is the smallest round trip time observed so far, and τ_i is the latest estimate of the round trip time. For the remainder of the paper we assume that $\zeta = 1$, and for all numerical example we use $\alpha = 1/8$, $\gamma = 30$, and $k = 3/4$, as suggested by the authors of CTCP [5]. While selecting these values is an interesting problem in itself it is outside the scope of this work (see [5] for more details).

Clearly as w increases so does Δ_i and, as the round-trip time is an increasing function of window, eventually $\Delta > \gamma$; and the window will be decreased, provided no packets are dropped in the meantime. Similarly, as smaller values of w imply smaller values of Δ, the window will be increased again. In other words one or more increasing phases are followed by one or more decreasing phases. We call a "cycle" the collection of increasing and decreasing phases starting with the first increasing phase and ending with the last decreasing phase. Figure 2 shows two possible cycles, the one on the left has 3 increasing phases and 1 decreasing phase, while the one on the right has 4 and 2, respectively. We will use two integers to classify cycles, with the first one representing the number of increments and the second one the number of decreasing phases. A 5:2 cycle, for example, has 5 increments and 2 reductions. In the figure dots and circles represents the value of the window *before* and *after* each increment, respectively.

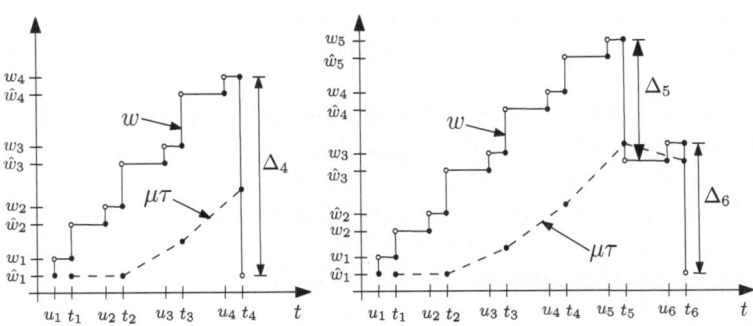

Fig. 2. The 3:1 and 4:2 cycles

The sending window of Compound TCP is the sum of two components that are incremented independently during each round trip time. The congestion component is incremented by one each round trip time, just like the window in TCP

Reno. While the delay component (w_{d}) is incremented, once per round trip time as well, as $w_{\mathrm{d}} = w_{\mathrm{d}} + \alpha w^k - 1$. The minus one compensates for the increase of the congestion component so that the total window grows as $w = w + \alpha w^k$. Similarly the plus one in (1) comes from the increment of the congestion window component, which happens also during the round trip time when the delay component is decreased. So that in a $m{:}n$ cycle there are m increments of the delay component and $m + n$ increments of the congestion component. In Figure 2 the smaller increments, between $\hat{w}_i$ and w_i, represent the increments of the congestion component and they take place at time u_i while the bigger increments are due to the delay component and take place at time t_i. Note that w_1 is the value *after* the initial increment of the congestion window, such increment represents the increment of the congestion window corresponding to the last reduction of the delay component at the end of the previous cycle.

2.1 Linux Implementation

In order to study the behavior of Compound TCP we ran simulations using ns-2 version 2.33 [4] with a Compound TCP implementation for Linux [1]. This implementation uses a slightly different formula to compute Δ_i: instead of w_i it uses w_{i-1} so that (2) is replaced by:

$$\Delta_i = w_{i-1}(1 - \tilde{\tau}/\tau_i). \tag{3}$$

Recall that w_i is the value of the window *before* the increment at time t_i so that w_{i-1} is the value of the window during (t_{i-2}, t_{i-1}). While [5] is somewhat vague about the details of these computations, it is appropriate to use w_{i-1} instead of w_i. One way of thinking about Δ_i is that it tries to estimate the number of backlogged packets by comparing the current round trip time with the smallest round trip time observed so far. Given that the sender uses acknowledgments to measure the round trip time, any such sample corresponds to the round trip time experienced by the packet last acknowledged and such a packet was sent when $w = w_{i-1}$. In other words all the round trip samples are "one round trip time old."

Another aspect to take into account is that, while it is possible to find several equivalent expression for Δ_i, the Linux kernel does not use floating point operations. So that all the operations have to be approximated with integer ones. This introduces an error that can be minimized but that can lead to non-negligible differences between the implemented protocol and a theoretical model. In order to minimize the approximation error Δ_i is computed as:

$$2\Delta_i = 2w_{i-1} - \left\lfloor \frac{2w_{i-1}\tilde{\tau}}{\tau} \right\rfloor \tag{4}$$

and γ is multiplied by 2 whenever it is compared with Δ_i. (We use $\lfloor x \rfloor$ to represent the integer part of x.) Computing the window increment αw_n^k presents a similar problem. As $\alpha = 1/8$ and $k = 3/4$ (as suggested in [5]) the following formula is used:

$$\alpha w_n^k = \left\lfloor \frac{1}{2^3} \left\lfloor \frac{2^8 w_n}{\sqrt{2^{16} \sqrt{w_n}}} \right\rfloor \right\rfloor \tag{5}$$

where all the multiplications (and divisions) by a power of 2 are implemented as shift operations and the square root is implemented using the int_sqrt() function of the Linux kernel.

2.2   Modeling the Linux Implementation

For the case of a single connection with no other traffic $\mathring{\tau}$ is equal to the propagation delay, which we assume to be known. In this case it is also possible to express τ_i (the latest estimate of the round trip time) as a function of the window and the bottleneck capacity μ. In the Linux kernel the round trip times are measured in microseconds so that, even if integers are used, the precision is extremely high.

Assuming that the backlog is non-zero, we can compute the round trip time dividing the window by the bottleneck capacity so that:

$$\tau_i = \min \left[\left\lfloor \frac{w_{i-2} + 1}{\mu} \right\rfloor, \tilde{\tau} \right]. \tag{6}$$

This is is because the implementation in question uses the smallest round trip time sample among all the samples collected during the last round trip time, between t_{i-1} and t_i. (One comment in the source code explains that the choice of using the smallest round trip sample is to minimize the effect of delayed acknowledgments.) As the window, and therefore the round trip time, is an increasing function of time, the smallest value corresponds to the smallest time value; that is the beginning of the round trip. For example in Figure 2, at time t_4 the sender considers all the samples relative to the packets sent between times t_2 (excluded) and t_3 (included), whose acknowledgments were received between t_3 (excluded) and t_4 (included). At time t_2 the window was increased from w_2 to w_3, but, while this increment is instantaneous, the round trip time grows by smaller increments (more precisely by $1/\mu$) so that the smallest round trip sample *observed* between t_3 and t_4 corresponds to the packet that was sent when the window was $w_2 + 1$. Clearly τ_i cannot be smaller than the propagation delay, hence the minimum with $\tilde{\tau}$. This can indeed happen as w_i can be smaller than $\mu\tilde{\tau}$, either during the initial growing phase during the oscillation phase in the case of multiple reductions.

In [5] the authors say that the window should be updated "once per round trip time." The implementation we used accomplishes this as follows: whenever the window is updated the sequence number of the next segment to be transmitted (say n_i) is recorded. Once the corresponding acknowledgment arrives the window is updated another time. As a consequence, whenever the window is reduced because $\Delta \geq \gamma$ the next segment cannot be sent immediately (the window is smaller than the number of unacknowledged packets). The sender resumes transmission only after receiving acknowledgments for Δ packets. Due to this pause in the transmission the backlog experienced by packet n_i is smaller. When the corresponding acknowledgment arrives the round trip time (for this packet) is:

$$\tau_i = \min\left[\left\lfloor \frac{w_{i-1} - \Delta_{i-1}}{\mu} \right\rfloor, \tilde{\tau}\right]. \qquad (7)$$

Where $w_{i-1} - \Delta_{i-1}$ is the window size after the reduction. Therefore, if at time t_{i-1} the window was reduced, t_i (i.e. the beginning of the new round trip time) corresponds with the arrival of the acknowledgment for packet n_i. As we have already mentioned, the implementation we have used takes the smallest of all the round trip samples collected between the last window update, at time t_{i-1} (excluded), and the current time t_i (included). This implies that, each time the window was reduced at t_{i-1}, the smallest round trip time sample is due to the last acknowledgment received. And the corresponding packet is the first one sent after the transmission pause.

Note that, provided the queue at the bottleneck link does not empty during the pause, when the sender resumes sending packets the backlog size will not change until the window is updated at time t_i. This implies that the value given by (7) is actually the "true" value of the round trip time between $t_{i-1} + \Delta_{i-1}/\mu$ and t_i , where Δ_{i-1}/μ is the duration of the transmission pause (it is the time needed to receive enough acknowledgments to compensate for the reduction of the window).

Given that we have defined a cycle as a series of increasing phases followed by one or more decreasing phase, the first phase of a cycle will always follow a window reduction so that, at t_1 (7) is used. In this case we also have that $w_m - \Delta_m = w_1 - 1$, where m is the last phase of the previous cycle. (Recall that we have defined w_1 as the value after the first increment of the congestion component.) And we can write $\tau_1 = (w_1 - 1)/\mu$. At time t_2 the smallest round trip samples received between t_1 and t_2 is again τ_1 because the packets whose acknowledgments arrive during $(t_1, t_2]$ were sent between during $(t_m + \Delta_m/\mu, t_1]$. As previously observed, all the packets sent during this time experience the same round trip time: $(w_m - \Delta_m)/\mu$.

In general, τ_i is given by (6) unless the window was reduced at time t_{i-1}, in which case (7) should be used, or if the window was reduced at time t_{i-2} and incremented at time t_{i-1}, in which case $\tau_i = \tau_{i-1}$. Using these formulas, together with those for Δ_i (3) and for the window increment (5) it is possible to model the evolution of the window. At the same time it is important to use the same integer approximations used in the Linux kernel: for example if we compute $w_4(w_1)$ (that is the value of the window after three increments with a starting value of w_1) using the same formulas used in the Linux Kernel or using floating point operations the difference between the two quantities is between 0 and 2. Where we use the formula αw_n^k to compute the window increment and compute Δ_i as $\Delta_i = w_i(1 - \tilde{\tau}/\tau)$ when we use floating point operations. Finally, Figure 3 compares Δ_5 using integer and floating point operations.

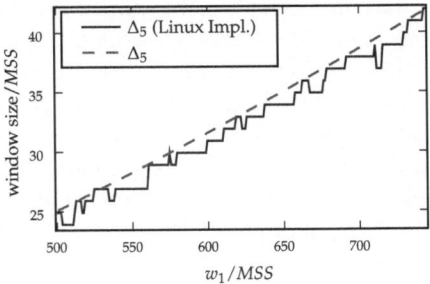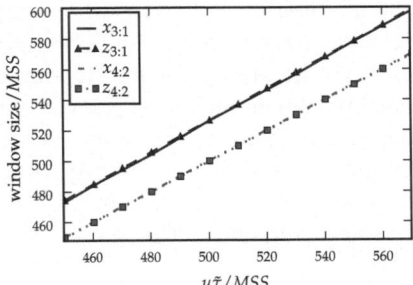

Fig. 3. Δ_5 using floating point and integer operations

Fig. 4. Solutions of the fixed point equation for the 3:1 and 4:2 cycles using floating point (z) and integer (x) operations

3   Fixed Points

Given that, as previously discussed, a series of increasing phases is always followed by one or more decreasing phases it is natural to ask if such oscillations follow a specific pattern and, above all, if they reach a steady state. It is sufficient to look at a few simulations to guess that oscillations do reach a steady state very quickly (after one or two cycles). Depending on the system parameters, we have observed 5 types of cycles: 3:1, 2:1, 5:2, 4:2 and 3:2. For each cycle type it is possible to find the steady state solution by numerically solving a fixed point equation. For the 3:1 cycle, for example, if w_1 is the value of the window at the beginning of each phase the value at the end of the cycle is $f_{3:1}(w_1) \triangleq w_4(w_1) - \Delta_4(w_1) + 1$ where $w_{n+1} = w_n + \alpha w_n^k$ and Δ_4 is given by (3). Note that the only independent variable is w_1 so that solving the fixed point equation $f_{3:1}(w_1) = w_1$ it is possible to find the steady state solution. The plus one takes into account the fact that, during each cycle, there are three increments of both window components and one increment (by one) of the congestion component combined with one reduction of the delay component. To be precise, here w_1 corresponds to the initial value of the total window after an increment by one of the congestion component (see Figure 2).

For each cycle $m{:}n$ it is possible to define the corresponding function $f_{m:1}(w_1) = w_{m+1}(w_1) - \Delta_{m+1}(w_1) + 1$ if $n = 1$ and $f_{m:n} = w_{m+1}(w_1) - \Delta_{m+2}(w_1) + 2$ if $n = 2$. For the latter case the plus two compensates for the two increments of the congestion component corresponding to the two reductions of the delay component. Figure 4 shows the solution of $f_{3:1}$ and $f_{4:2}$ as a function of the bandwidth-delay product $(\mu\tilde{\tau})$. In this case the difference between using floating point and integer operations is not very significant, especially for the 4:2 case where the error is negligible. While Figure 4 shows only two cases, they are the most representative ones. The solutions for the 2:1 case are close to those of the 3:1 case. And the solutions for all the $m{:}2$ cases are almost identical. It is interesting to note how the solutions for the $m{:}2$ cases are very close (and in some cases equal) to $\mu\tilde{\tau}$. As $w_1 - 1$ is the minimum value of the window is

$w_1 = \mu\tilde{\tau}$ then $w_1 - 1 < \mu\tilde{\tau}$ which implies that the buffer will be empty for the first part of each oscillation. The simulations do confirm this, showing that the buffer will be empty for half a round trip time during each oscillation. This is caused by the increment of the congestion component, which usually takes place after half a round trip time after the last reduction. While half round trip time over a cycle of a few round trip times is not a big portion it does nonetheless lead to an under utilization of the bottleneck link during this "constant window" phase negating one of the main design ideas of Compound TCP.

4 Conclusions and Future Work

Contrary to what suggested by one of the figures in [5], we have shown how the Compound TCP window does oscillate during the "constant window" phase. These oscillations converge quickly to a cyclic behavior whose mode (number of increases:number of decreases) depends on the bandwidth delay product. Some implementation details on Linux have also an influence on the mode, and on the amplitude of these cycles, especially the discretization of the state variables, increments of the window and backlog estimates.

These oscillations may explain some of the inefficiencies observed for Compound TCP on some tests, especially when the round-trip times are large or the buffers small [3,2]. This phenomenon may also degrade the performance of the other simultaneous flows. We plan on further analyzing the influence of these oscillations on the performance of long lived Compound TCP connections and on other simultaneous flows. We would also like to understand the relationship between the parameters of the system and the type of cycles followed by the oscillations. While the simulations seem to indicate that this depends on the bandwidth delay product we do not yet know the exact relationship.

References

1. Andrew, L.: Compound TCP Linux module (April 2008),
   http://netlab.caltech.edu/lachlan/ctcp/
2. Baiocchi, A., Castellani, A., Vacirca, F.: YeAH-TCP: Yet Another Highspeed TCP. In: Proc. 5th Int. Workshop on Protocols for FAST Long-Distance Networks (March 2007)
3. Li, Y.-T.: Evaluation of TCP congestion control algorithms on the Windows Vista platform. Technical Report SLAC-TN-06-005, Stanford Linear Accelerator Center (June 2005)
4. McCanne, S., Floyd, S., et al.: ns network simulator,
   http://www.isi.edu/nsnam/ns/
5. Tan, K., Song, J., Zhang, Q., Sridharan, M.: A compound tcp approach for high-speed and long distance networks. In: INFOCOM 2006. Proc. 25th IEEE Int. Conf. on Computer Communications (2006)

Optimum Channel Allocation in OFDMA
Multi-cell Systems

Andrea Abrardo[1], Paolo Detti[1], Gaia Nicosia[2],
Andrea Pacifici[3], and Mara Servilio[4]

[1] Università degli Studi di Siena,
Dipartimento di Ingegneria dell'Informazione, Siena, Italia
{abrardo,detti}@dii.unisi.it
[2] Università degli Studi Roma Tre,
Dipartimento di Informatica e Automazione, Roma, Italia
nicosia@dia.uniroma3.it
[3] Università degli Studi Tor Vergata,
Dipartimento di Ingegneria dell'Impresa, Roma, Italia
pacifici@disp.uniroma2.it
[4] Università degli Studi di L'Aquila,
Dipartimento di Informatica, via Vetoio, I-67010 Coppito, L'Aquila, Italia
servilio@di.univaq.it

Abstract. This paper addresses the problem of allocating users to radio resources (i.e., sub-carriers) in the downlink of an OFDMA cellular system. We consider a classical multi-cellular environment with a realistic interference model and a *margin adaptive* approach, i.e., we aim at minimizing total transmission power while maintaining a certain given rate for each user. We discuss computational complexity issues of the resulting model and present a heuristic approach that finds optima under suitable conditions, or "reasonably good" solutions in the general case. Computational experiences show that, in a comparison with a commercial state-of-the-art optimization solver, our algorithm is quite effective in terms of both infeasibilities and transmitted powers and extremely efficient in terms of CPU times.

Keywords: Radio resource allocation, network flow models, heuristic algorithms.

1 Introduction

IEEE 802.16 Air Interface Standard [6], which is the basis of the WiMAX technology, is the most recent solution for the provision of fixed broadband wireless services in a wide geographical scale and proved to be a real effective solution for the establishment of wireless metropolitan area networks (WirelessMAN). The most flexible physical layer implementation provided by the IEEE 802.16e standard is the OFDMA. It provides a sub-channelization structure with variable FFT (Fast Fourier Transform) sizes accommodating different channel bandwidths. The active sub-carriers are divided into subsets called sub-channels,

E. Altman and A. Chaintreau (Eds.): NET-COOP 2008, LNCS 5425, pp. 103–111, 2009.

being one of the basic units of resource allocation. In OFDMA systems, the concept of multi-user and single-user diversities are strictly connected. Indeed, for fixed or portable applications where the radio channels are slowly varying, an intrinsic advantage of OFDMA over other multiple access methods is its capability to exploit the multi-user diversity embedded in diverse frequency-selective channels [2,9]. Assigning the available sub carriers to the active users in an adaptive manner is a viable method to achieve multi-user diversity: the propagation channels are independent for each user and thus the sub carriers that are in a deep fade for one user may be good ones for another. Several papers have recently focused on the problem of optimum channel allocation of OFDMA cellular systems, and some of them have also considered the joint scheduling-allocation problem [10,12]. In general, resource allocation and scheduling tasks consist of either minimizing a cost measure (e.g. transmit power [5,10]) or maximizing a benefit (e.g. throughput [7,8,11]) while considering system hardware constraints, service specific quality of service (QoS) requirements and the overall system state. Assuming that the transmitter knows the instantaneous channel state of all users, significant performance improvements can be achieved in OFDMA if the sub-carrier, modulation, coding and power management is performed in an adaptive channel aware manner.

Most of the above studies have so far concentrated on the single cell scenario, where interference among users can be easily avoided by orthogonal assignments. In this context, it is shown that a high multi-user diversity gain can be obtained by means of cross layer approach, even in presence of a high degree of single user diversity. An interesting approach for considering more realistic interference model is considered in [1], where a classical cellular environment is studied. In [1], a realistic interference model is considered, where the ability of two nodes to communicate reliably depends not only on their distance but also on actual interference level which is produced by other users which are assigned the same resource, i.e., the same sub-carrier.

The paper is organized as follows. In Section 2, the problem is formally defined and its complexity is addressed. In Section 3, we proposed a heuristic algorithm for solving the radio resource allocation problem, based on a network flow model, which provides an optimal solution for a simplified version of the problem. Finally, computational results are presented and discussed in Section 4.

2   Problem Statement

In this section we describe the interference model used throughout the paper and give a formal statement of the optimization problem that we address.

We are given (i) a set of sub-carriers or radio resources $\{1, \ldots, m\}$; (ii) a set of cells $\{C_1, \ldots, C_k\}$, and (iii) for each cell C_h a set of n_h users $U_h = \{1, \ldots, n_h\}$. For each user i, we denote by $b(i)$ the cell i belongs to. Hence, $b(i) = C_h$ for all $i \in U_h$. If we set a certain target spectral efficiency η_i for user i, the transmission requirements correspond to a certain number of sub-carriers $r_i = R_i/\eta_i$, where R_i is the transmission rate required by user i, and η_i is set in a such a way that r_i is integer.

In general, users belonging to different cells can share the same sub-carrier, while interference phenomena do not allow two users in the same cell to transmit on the same sub-carrier. However, the power required for the transmission on a given sub-carrier increases with the number of users transmitting on that sub-carrier. More precisely, let S_j be the set of users which are assigned to (i.e., that are transmitting on) the same sub-carrier j. The transmission powers $p_i(j)$ requested by users in S_j on sub-carrier j satisfy the following system.

$$
\begin{aligned}
p_i(j) &= A_i(j) + \sum_{\substack{\ell \in S_j \\ \ell \neq i}} B_i^{b(\ell)}(j) p_\ell(j) & i \in S_j \\
p_i(j) &\geq 0 & i \in S_j
\end{aligned}
\tag{1}
$$

where $A_i(j)$ and $B_i^{b(\ell)}(j)$ are given data taking into account the target signal-interference-ratio (SIR_i), the channel gain of user i on sub-carrier j $(G_i(j))$, and the channel gain between user i and the base station of cell $h \neq b(i)$ on sub-carrier j $(G_i^{b(h)}(j))$. More precisely, $A_i(j)$ is proportional to $SIR_i/G_i(j)$ and $B_i^{b(\ell)}(j) = SIR_i G_i^{b(\ell)}(j)/G_i(j)$. In the following, we refer to the quantities $A_i(j)$ and $\sum_{h \in S_j, h \neq i} B_i^{b(h)}(j) p_h(j)$ of System (1) as *fixed costs* and *variable costs*, respectively. Note that, System (1) may not have a feasible solution.

A *feasible radio resource allocation* consists in assigning sub-carriers to users in such a way that (i) for each user i, r_i radio resources are assigned to it, (ii) users in the same cell are not assigned to the same radio resource, (iii) given the set S_j of users assigned to radio resource j, System (1) has a feasible solution, for any sub-carrier $j = 1, \ldots, m$. Clearly, a necessary condition for a feasible allocation to exist is $m \geq \max_{h=1,\ldots,k} \sum_{i \in U_h} r_i$. The problem, that we call *Cellular Radio Resource Allocation* (RAP), consists of finding a feasible radio resource allocation that minimizes the total transmission power, i.e., the sum of the transmission powers required by all the users. Iteratively solving instances of RAP, on a radio-frame basis, may be used for dynamically assigning radio resources. In fact, practically a carrier is allocated to different users over time.

In Table 1, we summarize some results about the computational complexity for some special cases of the problem. All the details of the polynomial time algorithms and the NP-completeness proofs are reported in [4].

Table 1. Computational complexity results

Cells	Special Features	Complexity
2	cost as in (1)	open
2	identical resources	polynomial (Perfect Matching)
fixed k	indistinguishable users	polynomial (min cost flow)
3	identical resources	strongly NP-hard (from 3-dim axial assignment, [4])
-	identical $A_i(j)$ $\forall i, j$	strongly NP-hard (from 3-dim matching)
-	convex variable costs (Sect. 3)	polynomial (Min cost flow)
-	limited cell power	strongly NP-hard (from 3-Partition, [1])

In the first column of the table, the number of cells of the system is indicated, while the second column reports the special characteristics of the problems. In the problem with "identical resources", the fixed and variable costs do not depend on the particular resource the users are assigned to. The term "indistinguishable users" refers to the case in which the transmission power on a resource depends only on the number of users transmitting on it, and by the cell the users belong to. The case with convex variable costs is thoroughly addressed in Section 3. In the last row of the table, "Limited cell power" means that an upper bound on the transmission power of the users in the same cell is given. In this latter case, NP-hardness holds even if $n_h = 1$ for any cell $h = 1, \ldots, k$ and identical values of the $B_i^h(j)$'s.

3   A Network Flow Based Algorithm

In this section we propose a heuristic algorithm for solving RAP which is based on a minimum cost flow problem. To this purpose, we exploit a procedure that *exactly* solves a simplified version of RAP in which the transmission power of any sub-carrier j assumes a special structure.

3.1   A Simplified Model

Given a sub-carrier j and a set of users S assigned to it, suppose that the transmission power $T(j) = \sum_{i \in S} p_i(j)$ has the following special form:

$$T(j) = g(|S|) + \sum_{i \in S} A_i(j). \tag{2}$$

where $g(\cdot)$ is a convex function. Then $T(j)$ is comprised by the (usual) fixed cost part, which depends on the set S of users assigned to j, plus a *convex* variable cost which *only depends on the number* $|S|$ of users assigned to resource j. When the transmission power on resource j is expressed as in Equation (2) for all $j = 1, 2, \ldots, m$, we may find an optimal solution of RAP with the network flow model described hereafter.

Consider the marginal variable cost $\Delta_\ell(j) = g(\ell) - g(\ell - 1)$ corresponding to assigning an additional user to resource j when $\ell - 1 \geq 1$ users have been already assigned to it (let $\Delta_1(j) = 0$). Since g is convex, $\Delta_{\ell+1}(j) \geq \Delta_\ell(j) \geq 0$, for all $\ell \geq 1$.

On these grounds, we may define the following flow network $G = (V, A, c)$ illustrated in Figure 1. We distinguish four layers of nodes plus a demand node t. The first layer of nodes contains a supply node per each user. We denote the node associated to user i of cell C_h, as u_h^i. In the second and third layer, for any pair (j, h) associated to resource j and cell C_h, there is a node $v'_{j,h}$ for the second layer and $v''_{j,h}$ for the third layer . The fourth layer contains one node for any possible number of users ℓ assigned to resource j, for all $j \in R$. Since the maximum possible value for ℓ equals the number of cells k, we have mk nodes in this layer. We refer to the ℓ-th node corresponding to resource j as $w_{j,\ell}$. The arcs of the network are defined as follows.

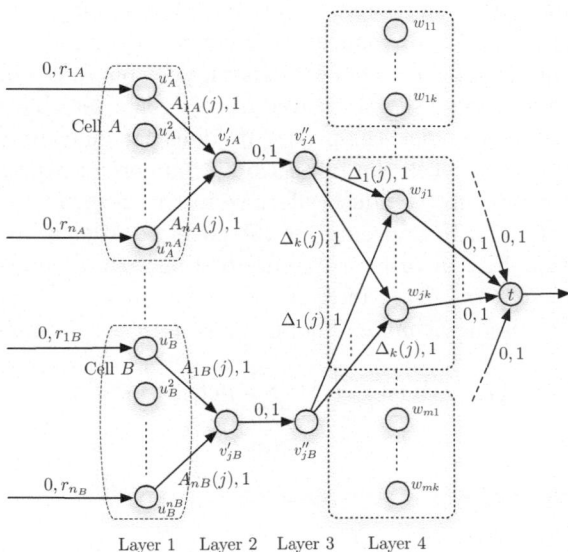

Layer 1   Layer 2   Layer 3   Layer 4

Fig. 1. The network flow model for the simplified RAP

1. For all $j \in R$, $h \in C$ and $i \in C_h$, arc $(u_h^i, v_{j,h}')$, with unit capacity and cost equal to $A_i(j)$, connects first and second layer nodes.
2. There is a unit capacity, null cost arc for each pair of nodes $v_{j,h}'$ to $v_{j,h}''$ between second and third layer.
3. For all $j \in R$, $C_h \in C$ and $1 \leq \ell \leq k$, unit capacity arc $(v_{j,h}'', w_{j,\ell})$ connect third and fourth layer nodes. The cost of such an arc is $\Delta_j(\ell)$.
4. All the arcs $(w_{j,h}, t)$ exist, with unit capacity and null cost, for all the nodes $w_{j,h}$ in the fourth layer.

The amount of commodity supplied by each node u_h^i in the first layer is r_i, the demand at node t is $\sum_i r_i$, while all other nodes are neither supply nor demand nodes. It is not hard to prove that there is a one-to-one correspondence between any integer feasible flow on G and a feasible solution of the instance of RAP. Therefore, the minimum cost flow in this supply-demand network provides an optimal solution to the simplified version of RAP.

3.2 A Heuristic for RAP

In this section, we propose a heuristic algorithm for RAP based on the network $G = (V, A, c)$ introduced in the previous section. Clearly, the cost structure of RAP does not allow to use the network model introduced above to determine an optimal solution. However, a feasible integer flow on G corresponds to an assignment of users to resources. The idea of the heuristic algorithm is that of approximating the actual costs of RAP with a cost structure satisfying Equation (2) and then applying the network flow model in order to obtain an *initial* assignment of users to the resources. Note that, such an initial assignment may not be feasible in the original problem, since System (1) may not be feasible for some set of users assigned to a resource. In most cases (and as long as a feasible solution of the original instance of RAP exists), possible infeasible assignments can be adjusted, via a local search procedure, to get a feasible solution. Even when feasible assignments exist, the procedure does not guarantee to find one of these solutions. However, as shown in Section 4, numerical experiments give an evidence that the procedure is indeed effective in this regard.

We proceed as follows, to approximate the costs in order to apply the model described in Section 3.1. In order to compute the variable costs part, we set $A_i(j) = \bar{A}(j)$ and $B_i(j) = \bar{B}(j)$ in System (1) for all $i \in U$ and $j \in R$, thus making the users indistinguishable. The linear system (1) becomes

$$p_i(j) = \bar{A}(j) + \bar{B}(j) \sum_{\substack{h \in S_j \\ h \neq i}} p_h(j) \quad i \in S_j. \tag{3}$$

After some algebra, the total transmission power required on resource j becomes

$$T'_t(j) = \sum_{i \in S_j} p_i(j) = \frac{t\bar{A}(j)}{1 - (t-1)\bar{B}(j)} = t\bar{A}(j) + \frac{t\bar{A}(j)(t-1)\bar{B}(j)}{1 - (t-1)\bar{B}(j)} \tag{4}$$

where $t = |S_j|$. Note that $T'_t(j)$ only depends on the number t of users assigned to j. According to the last expression of (4), $T'_t(j)$ can be decomposed into a fixed part, $t\bar{A}(j)$, and variable cost part, $g_j(t) = \frac{t\bar{A}(j)(t-1)\bar{B}(j)}{1-(t-1)\bar{B}(j)}$, as in (2). It is easy to show that $g(\cdot)$ is a convex function in t.

In our heuristic, we use the network described in Section 3.1, in which the costs of arcs connecting first and second layer nodes are the actual fixed costs coefficients $A_i(j)$, while the costs $\Delta_\ell(j)$ of arcs connecting the nodes of third and fourth layers are equal to $g_j(\ell) - g_j(\ell - 1)$. Observe that $g_j(t)$ could be negative for some value of t. In such cases, we say that it is *infeasible* to allocate t or more users to resource j, and we set $\Delta_\ell(j) = +\infty$, for all $\ell \geq t$. Observe that the flow between the second and third layer nodes defines a user-resource assignment and, as already mentioned, a feasible solution of the network flow problem may not correspond to a feasible solution for the original problem. Hence, the correspondence between the feasibility of the solutions of the two problems strictly depends on the choice of $\bar{A}(j)$ and $\bar{B}(j)$ parameters used to compute $g_j(\cdot)$.

We are now in the position to give a sketch of a heuristic, called NETWORK, for RAP. The procedure inputs a numerical instance of RAP and iteratively solves the network flow problem described above, as follows:

1. the parameters $\bar{A}(j)$ and $\bar{B}(j)$ are initially set to suitable values;
2. network $G = (V, A, c)$ is built and an optimal solution on G, i.e., an assignment $\mathcal{A}$ of users to resources, is found;
3. if an infeasibility is detected in $\mathcal{A}$, say on resource j, NETWORK carries out a local search in which, basically, the assignment of two users are exchanged: one user i is chosen in S_j and it is substituted by another user ℓ of the

same cell $b(i)$ (thus $\ell \notin S_j$). This search is performed for a given number of iterations or until all the infeasibilities are removed;

4. if $\mathcal{A}$ is feasible, some of the parameters $\bar{A}(j)$ and $\bar{B}(j)$ are updated, in order to improve the quality of the solution (i.e., the total transmission power). To this purpose, the fixed costs of those users requiring the highest transmission powers in the current assignment are increased.

Steps 1–4 are repeated for a limited number of iterations. Eventually, NET-WORK returns an assignment of all the users to the sub-carriers, if a feasible assignment has been found. If this is not the case, i.e., infeasibilities cannot be removed, the procedure returns an assignment of a subset of users (partial assignment). It is worthwhile to mention again that, given that the time required for collecting data and computation times are short enough, NETWORK may be used for dynamically assigning radio resources on a radio-frame basis.

4   Computational Experiments and Conclusions

In this section, computational results of the heuristic NETWORK on randomly generated instances are presented. The algorithm has been coded in standard C; CPLEX 9.1 has been used for solving the network flow problems. The performances of the heuristic have been compared with a truncated branch and bound algorithm that uses an Integer Linear Programming formulation solved with CPLEX 9.1 (most of the solutions are, in fact, optima or near-optimal solutions). In the instances, the number of cells is $K = 7$, the cell radius is 500 m, and the overall signal bandwidth is $B_{tot} = 5$ MHz. We assume a fixed throughput per cell equal to R_{tot} bit/s and that such a per-cell throughput is evenly shared among $|U_k| = n_k$ users, which are uniformly distributed in hexagonal cells of radius R. In all the instances, $m = 16$ sub-bands, each with a bandwidth of $B = 312.5$ kHz, and $n_k = 4$ users per cell have been considered. Hence, each user has a target throughput of $R_{tot}/4$ bit/s. As in [1], we assume that all users adopt the same transmission format, i.e., $\eta_i = \eta$ for all users on all sub-carriers. Since the rate per sub-carrier is $B\eta$, the condition to achieve the requested R_{tot} is that $\eta = \frac{R_{tot}}{16 \times B}$. Note that, in this case, each user is assigned a fixed number of sub-carriers $r_i = 4$. In all the instances $R_{tot} = B_{tot} \times \eta$. Hence, the bigger is η the bigger is the cell (fixed) target throughput. Three scenarios have been considered ($\eta = 2$, 2.5, 3.0) each corresponding to one hundred instances.

Table 2 illustrates a comparison of the results obtained by applying our NET-WORK heuristic (columns 2–4) and the CPLEX truncated branch and bound (columns 5–6). Average values of the following data are given: (i) solution, i.e., total transmission power, (ii) computation times in seconds, and (iii) a measure of rate loss. More precisely, column 3 reports the percentage of *resources with infeasible assignments* obtained by the NETWORK heuristic. Column 6 reports the *number of instances*, out of 100, in which the branch and bound cannot find any feasible solution within the time limit (these results have been presented in [1]). In fact, for the infeasible instances, the branch and bound algorithm cannot return an allocation for any user request. Note also that column 4 reports power

Table 2. Computational results

η	Network			Branch and Bound		
	Sol.value	Time	% Rate loss	Sol.value	Time	# Infeas.
2.0	67.59	0.31	0.0	48.56	201.68	0
2.5	251.18	0.64	0.07	101.92	268.78	2
3.0	710.92	1.51	0.46	215.58	339.56	18

values that are indeed computed over the set of instances for which a feasible solution exists. In most cases, NETWORK can find a feasible solution of reasonable quality in less than one second (which is less than one hundredth than the time required by the branch and bound.) This proves that an implementation of our algorithm on a dedicated processor is suitable for usage in an iterative scheme that solves the problem dynamically.

The power values (at least for the first scenario with $\eta = 2.0$) obtained by applying NETWORK, exceed those of the branch and bound by about 28% over all the 100 instances. However, if we compare the results, restricting our observations to the best (i.e., less congested) 85 and 70 instances, the gap decreases to 17% and 11%, respectively.

Possible future directions of research include (*i*) computational complexity characterization of "open" special cases of RAP; (*ii*) improvement of the proposed heuristic via the more effective local search scheme; (*iii*) design of *distributed* algorithms for RAP.

References

1. Abrardo, A., Alessio, A., Detti, P., Moretti, M.: Radio resource allocation problems for OFDMA cellular systems. Computers & Operations Research 36(5), 1572–1581 (2009)
2. Bender, P., Black, P., Grob, M., Padovani, R., Sindhushayana, N., Viterbi, A.: CDMA/HDR: a bandwidth-efficient high-speed wireless data service for nomadic users. IEEE Communications Magazine 38(7), 70–77 (2000)
3. Burkard, R.E., Rudolf, R., Woeginger, G.J.: Three-dimensional axial assignments problems with decomposable cost coefficients. Discrete Applied Mathematics 65, 123–139 (1996)
4. Detti, P., Nicosia, G., Pacifici, A., Servilio, M.: Optimal power control in OFDMA cellular networks. Tech. Report n. 2008-4, Dipartimento di Ingegneria dell'Informazione, University of Siena (2008)
5. Ergen, M., Coleri, S., Varaiya, P.: QoS aware adaptive resource allocation techniques. for fair scheduling in OFDMA based broadband wireless systems. IEEE Transactions on Broadcasting 49(4) (2003)
6. IEEE Standard for Local and Metropolitan Area Networks. Part 16: Air Interface for Fixed Broadband Wireless Access Systems, IEEE 802.16-2004 revision
7. Pietrzyk, S., Jannsen, G.: Multiuser subcarrier allocation for QoS provision in OFDMA systems. In: IEEE Vehicular Technology Conference, VTC (2002)

8. Rhee, W., Cioffi, J.M.: Increase in capacity of multiuser OFDM system using dynamic subchannel allocation. In: Proc. IEEE Vehicular Technology Conference, VTC (2000)
9. Shakkottai, S., Rappaport, T.S., Karlsson, P.C.: Cross-Layer Design for Wireless Networks. IEEE Communications Magazine, 41(10) (2003)
10. Wong, C., Cheng, R., Lataief, K., Murch, R.: Multiuser OFDM with adaptive subcarrier, bit and power allocation. IEEE Journal on Selected Areas in Communications 17(10), 1747–1758 (1999)
11. Yin, H., Liu, H.: An efficient multiuser loading algorithm for OFDM based broadband wireless systems IEEE Globecom (2000)
12. Zhang, Y., Letaief, K.: Energy-efficient MAC-PHY resource management with guaranted QoS in wireless OFDM networks. In: Proc. IEEE ICC, Seoul, Korea (2005)

Transmission Power Control Game with SINR as Objective Function[*]

Eitan Altman[1], Konstantin Avrachenkov[1], and Andrey Garnaev[2]

[1] INRIA Sophia Antipolis, France
{altman,k.avrachenkov}@sophia.inria.fr
[2] St. Petersburg State University, Russia
agarnaev@rambler.ru

Abstract. We consider the transmission power control problem with SINR as objective function in the two scenarii: selfish and cooperative. We show that in the selfish (non-cooperative) scenario several Nash equilibria can arise. In particular, the game can take the form of the Hawk-Dove game, where the users can choose either conciliation or conflict fighting for shared sub-carriers. We fully characterize different types of Nash equilibria. In the cooperative scenario, we show that the parameter area where users employ pure strategies is essentially narrower than the area where users employ mixed strategies. Moreover, we identify an area where Nash equilibrium and Pareto equilibrium coincide. If one of the users has a large power resource (called a stronger user) for both scenarii and his rival has small power resource (weaker user) then the behaviour of the stronger user drastically changes in cooperative scenario compared to the selfish one. Namely, in the selfish scenario the stronger user squeezes the weaker one from the best channel meanwhile in the co-operative scenario he allows the weaker user to employ the best channel and himself applies a mixed strategy.

Keywords: Wireless networks, Power Control, Nash Equilibrium, Cooperation.

1 Introduction

We consider the transmission power control problem with SINR as objective function in the two scenarii: selfish and cooperative. In particular, in the selfish scenario we consider two users who try to send information through n resources. The strategy of user j ($j = 1, 2$) is $T^j = (T_1^j, \ldots, T_n^j)$ with $T_i^j \geq 0$ such that $\sum_{i=1}^n \pi_i T_i^j = \bar{T}^j$, where $\bar{T}^j > 0$. Here we assume that resource i has a "weight" of $\pi_i > 0$. The resources may correspond to capacity available at different time slots; we assume that there is a varying environment whose state changes among a finite set of states $i \in [1, n]$, according to some ergodic stochastic process with stationary distribution $\{\pi_i\}$. Either the resources may correspond to frequency

[*] The work was supported by EGIDE ECO-NET grant no.18933SL "Game Theory for Wireless Networks" and RFBR and NNSF Grant no.06-01-39005.

E. Altman and A. Chaintreau (Eds.): NET-COOP 2008, LNCS 5425, pp. 112–120, 2009.
© Springer-Verlag Berlin Heidelberg 2009

bands (e.g. as in OFDM) where one should assign different power levels for different sub-carriers [9]. In that case we may take $\pi_i = 1/n$ for all i.

In the selfish (non-cooperative) scenario each user tries to maximize its average SINR:

$$v^j(T^1, T^2) = \sum_{i=1}^{n} \pi_i \frac{\alpha_i^j T_i^j}{N_i^0 + \alpha_i^{\hat{j}} T_i^{\hat{j}}},$$

where N_i^0 is the noise level and $\alpha_i^j > 0$ are fading channel gains of user j when the environment is in state i, and $\hat{j} = 3 - j$. We assume that all the fading channel gains α_i^j, the noise levels N_i^0, the total powers $\bar{T}^j$ are known to both users or they can be quickly inferred [4]. The authors of [1] have studied the case of incomplete information.

The SINR as an objective function in the power control game was also considered in [6]: all users have a single common channel and choose between several base stations. We note that in the regime of low SINR the present objective can serve as an approximation to the Shannon capacity. A central motivation to consider SINR as an objective function and not Shannon capacity, is that current technology for voice over wireless does not try to achieve Shannon capacity but rather uses given codecs that can adapt the transmission rate to the SINR; these turn out to adapt the rate in a way that is linear in the SINR over a wide range of throughput. The SINR has therefore been used very often to represent directly the throughput see [7,8]. The validity of this can be seen e.g. in [5, p. 151, 222, 239]. As we see from [5, Fig. 10.4, p. 222], the ratio between the throughput and the SINR is close to a constant throughout long range of bit rates. For example, between 16Kbps and 256Kbps, the maximum variation around the median value is less than 20%.

We finally note that with an SINR objective we are able to characterize fully cooperative and non-cooperative scenarii. In [2] with the Shannon capacity as an objective we have dealt only with the symmetric case. An interested reader can find more relevant literature on Gaussian Interference Game in [2,4]. In the present work we restrict ourselves to the case of two users. We believe that the two user case is good for illustration and many techniques of this paper apply to the case of more than two users which we leave as a topic for future research.

In the non-cooperative scenario we look for a NE (Nash Equilibrium), that is, we want to find such couple of strategies (T^{1*}, T^{2*}) that for any (T^1, T^2) the inequalities hold: $v^1(T^1, T^{2*}) \leq v^1(T^{1*}, T^{2*})$, $v^2(T^{1*}, T^2) \leq v^2(T^{1*}, T^{2*})$.

In the cooperative scenario, both users want to maximize $v^1 + v^2$. We shall show that in some parameter settings cooperative and non-cooperative strategies coincide.

It is worth to note that in [3] one of the results concerns a game which can be considered as a game with the SINR as object function in the jamming scenario the first user wants to maximize the objective function v_1 and the second user wants to minimize this objective function. For this game the jammer in his optimal behaviour tends to equalize the quality of the best sub-carriers to as low level as his power constraint allows.

We will assume that all channels differ by their quality for both users. Namely, we assume that for each user j ($j = 1, 2$) $\alpha_{i_1}^j/N_{i_1}^0 \neq \alpha_{i_2}^j/N_{i_2}^0$ for any $i_1 \neq i_2$. Without lost of generality we can assume that $\{a(j,1), a(j,2), \ldots, a(j,n)\}$ is a permutation of $\{1, 2, \ldots, n\}$ such that the sub-carriers are arranged in the following decreasing order by their quality: $\alpha_{a(j,1)}^j/N_{a(j,1)}^0 > \ldots > \alpha_{a(j,n)}^j/N_{a(j,n)}^0$.

2   Non-cooperative Scenario

2.1   The Best Sub-carriers Differs for the Users

Since v^i is linear in T^i the optimal strategy of user i can be nonnegative only for sub-carriers where the compound SINR is maximal. So, we have the following result describing the structure of the optimal strategies.

Theorem 1. (T^1, T^2) *is a Nash equilibrium if and only if there are non-negative* ω^1 *and* ω^2 *(which present the maximal compound SINR for the corresponding user) such that for* $j = 1, 2$ *and* $i \in [1, n]$:

$$T_i^j \geq 0 \text{ for } \frac{\alpha_i^j}{N_i^0 + \alpha_i^{\hat{j}} T_i^{\hat{j}}} = \omega^j \text{ and } T_i^j = 0 \text{ for } \frac{\alpha_i^j}{N_i^0 + \alpha_i^{\hat{j}} T_i^{\hat{j}}} < \omega^j.$$

The payoffs corresponding to these strategies are $(\omega^1 \bar{T}^1, \omega^2 \bar{T}^2)$.

The strategy when user j ($j = 1, 2$) transmits all the signal through just one sub-carrier (say, i) will be called a pure one and we will denote it by $\mathcal{T}_i^j$. So, the pure strategy is $\mathcal{T}_i^j = (T_1^j, \ldots, T_n^j)$ such that $T_k^j = \bar{T}^j$ for $k = i$ and $T_k^j = 0$ otherwise. The strategies when users employ more than one sub-carrier to transmit signal will be called mixed strategies.

If the best sub-carriers are different for users, namely $a(1,1) \neq a(2,1)$, then by Theorem 1 the NE has time sharing form, namely the following result holds.

Theorem 2. *If* $a(1,1) \neq a(2,1)$, *then the game has the unique NE and it is the pure one* $(\mathcal{T}_{a(1,1)}^1, \mathcal{T}_{a(2,1)}^2)$.

It is worth to note that if there are more than one best quality sub-carrier the NE is not unique at all since there is enough room for the users to share these best quality channels.

So, our assumption that all sub-carriers are different by its quality is quite reasonable. But as it will be shown in the next section even then if the best sub-carriers coincides a variety of NE is possible.

2.2   The Best First Sub-carriers Coincides for Users

Let the first best sub-carriers coincides for users, i.e. $a(1,1) = a(2,1) = a(1)$. Then some variety of cases arise depending on the quality of the second best sub-carriers and the power of signal the users can apply.

The SINRs for the best sub-carrier with the induced noise are big enough for both users

If the SINRs for the best sub-carrier with the induced noise are greater than the SINRs with the natural noise for the second best sub-carriers for both users, then each of them could manage to transmit all the signal just through the best sub-carrier. The next theorem follows straighforward from Theorem 1 and supplies the formulas describing the corresponding conditions on SINRs.

Theorem 3. *Let the following inequalities hold*

$$\frac{\alpha^j_{a(1)}}{N^0_{a(1)} + \alpha^{\hat{j}}_{a(1)}\bar{T}^{\hat{j}}} \geq \frac{\alpha^j_{a(j,2)}}{N^0_{a(j,2)}} \; for \; j = 1, 2. \tag{1}$$

Then there is the unique NE and it is the pure one $(T^1_{a(1)}, T^2_{a(1)})$.

Note that inequalities (1) can be rewritten in the following equivalent form

$$A^j \geq \bar{X}^j \; for \; j = 1, 2, \tag{2}$$

where $A^{\hat{j}} = \alpha^j_{a(1)}N^0_{a(j,2)}/\alpha^j_{a(j,2)} - N^0_{a(1)}$ and $\bar{X}^j = \alpha^j_{a(1)}\bar{T}^j$.

The SINR for the best sub-carrier with the induced noise is big enough only for one user

If the SINR for the best sub-carrier with the induced noise is greater than the SINR with the natural noise for the second best sub-carriers only for one user (say, user $\hat{j}$), then the other user (user j) could threaten to jam the best sub-carrier and user $\hat{j}$ has nothing to threaten back. This makes him to withdraw and to use the second best sub-carrier. The next theorem follows straightforward from Theorem 1 and supplies the formulas describing the corresponding relations between SINRs.

Theorem 4. *Let* $A^j > \bar{X}^j$, $A^{\hat{j}} < \bar{X}^{\hat{j}}$ *hold either for* $j = 1$ *or* $j = 2$*: Then the game has the unique NE and it is the pure one* (T^1, T^2) *where* $T^j = T^j_{a(j,2)}$ *and* $T^{\hat{j}} = T^{\hat{j}}_{a(1)}$.

Thus, the weaker user is squeezed out from the common best sub-carrier by the threat from the stronger user.

The SINRs for the best sub-carrier with the induced noise are small for both users

If the SINRs for the best sub-carrier with the induced noise are less than the SINRs with the natural noise for the second best sub-carriers for the both users, then each user could threaten to jam the best sub-carrier for his opponent. The situation becomes very competitive and Hawk-Dove type strategies are possible.

The next theorem follows straightforward from Theorem 1 and supplies the formulas describing the corresponding relations between SINRs and Hawk-Dove type strategies.

Theorem 5. *Let $A^j < \bar{X}^j$ hold for $j = 1, 2$. Then there are two pure NE equilibria $(\mathcal{T}^1_{a(1)}, \mathcal{T}^2_{a(2,2)})$ and $(\mathcal{T}^1_{a(1,2)}, \mathcal{T}^2_{a(1)})$.*

In the first pure NE user 1 presents an aggressive (Hawk) player always fighting for the best quality sub-carrier meanwhile user 2 is a withdrawing (Dove) player escaping any fighting. In the second pure NE the users exchange the roles. In Figure 1 possible pure NE are pointed out depending on power signals they have to transmit.

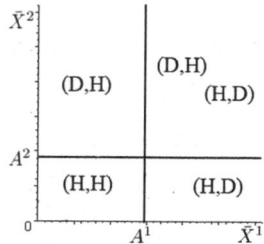

Fig. 1. Pure NE strategies

Besides the two pure NE a mixed NE can take place. Let us consider the case when the second best sub-carriers are different for users. Then by Theorem 1 we can see that in the mixed equilibrium both users at first take care about the opponent by equalizing quality of the opponent's two best by quality sub-carriers. It allows users to transmit all the rest of the signal through the second best sub-carriers. Of course, this strategy assumes some cooperation between the users.

Theorem 6. *Let $A^j < \bar{X}^j$ hold for $j = 1, 2$ hold and $a(1, 2) \neq a(2, 2)$, so the second best sub-carriers are different for users. Then there is the unique mixed NE, using only two first by quality sub-carriers, given by the following strategies which equalize the first and second by quality sub-carriers and transmit the rest power through the second sub-carriers:*

$$
T^j_i = \begin{cases}
\dfrac{\alpha^{\hat{j}}_{a(1)}}{\alpha^j_{a(1)}} \left(1/\omega^{\hat{j}} - N^0_{(1)}/\alpha^{\hat{j}}_{a(1)} \right), & \text{for } i = a(1), \\[2ex]
\bar{T}^j - T^j_{a(1)}, & \text{for } i = a(j, 2), \\[1ex]
0, & \text{otherwise},
\end{cases}
\tag{3}
$$

where $\omega^j = \alpha^j_{a(j,2)}/N^0_{a(j,2)}$, $j = 1, 2$.

2.3 The K Best Sub-carriers Coincide

In this subsection we consider situation when the K $(K \le n)$ best sub-carriers coincide for users, i.e. $a(1,i) = a(2,i) = a(i)$, $i \in [1,K]$ and $a(1,K+1) \neq a(2,K+1)$ if $K < n$. Theorem 6 can be generalized as follows:

Theorem 7. *Let $k^1 = k^2 < K$ where $k^j (j = 1,2)$ are integers such that*

$$H^{\hat{\jmath}}(\alpha^j_{a(j,k^j)}/N^0_{k^j}) < \bar{T}^{\hat{\jmath}} \le H^{\hat{\jmath}}(\alpha^j_{a(j,k^j+1)}/N^0_{k^j+1}),$$

where $\alpha^j_{a(j,n+1)}/N^0_{n+1} = 0$ and

$$H^{\hat{\jmath}}(\omega) = \sum_{i=1}^{n} \frac{\alpha^j_{a(j,i)}}{\alpha^{\hat{\jmath}}_{a(j,i)}} \left[1/\omega^j - N^0_{a(j,i)}/\alpha^j_{a(j,i)} \right]_+.$$

Then the NE is given by the strategies (T^1, T^2) where

$$T^{\hat{\jmath}}_i = \frac{\alpha^j_{a(i)}}{\alpha^{\hat{\jmath}}_{a(i)}} \left[1/\omega^j - N^0_{a(i)}/\alpha^j_{a(i)} \right]_+, \quad i \in [1,n]$$

for $j = 1,2$, and ω^j is the unique root of the equation $H^{\hat{\jmath}}(\omega^j) = \bar{T}^{\hat{\jmath}}$.

Thus, if the powers of signal to transmit are approximately equal then the equilibrium mixed strategies have water-filling structure.

Theorem 8. *Let $K = k^1 = k^2$ and $a(1,K+1) \neq a(2,K+1)$. Then if the power of signals allows to equalize the first $K+1$ channels, so*

$$H^{\hat{\jmath}}\left(\alpha^j_{a(j,K+1)}/N^0_{a(j,K+1)} \right) < \bar{T}^{\hat{\jmath}}$$

then the NE is given by the strategies (T^1, T^2) where

$$T^j_i = \begin{cases} \dfrac{\alpha^{\hat{\jmath}}_{a(i)}}{\alpha^j_{a(i)}} \left[1/\omega^{\hat{\jmath}} - N^0_{a(i)}/\alpha^{\hat{\jmath}}_{a(i)} \right]_+ & \text{for } i = a(1), \dots, a(k), \\ \bar{T}^j - H^j(\omega^{\hat{\jmath}}) & \text{for } i = a(j,K+1), \\ 0 & \text{otherwise,} \end{cases}$$

and where $\omega^j = \alpha^j_{a(j,K+1)}/N^0_{a(j,K+1)}$, $j = 1,2$.

3 A Cooperative Scenario

In this section we assume that the users cooperate and they want to maximize their joint payoff $v = v^1 + v^2$. Of course, if the best sub-carriers are different for users, then, time sharing strategies $T^1_{a(1,1)}$, $T^2_{a(2,1)}$ are the optimal ones. Next, let us consider the case when the best sub-carriers coincide for the users, namely $a(1,1) = a(2,1) = a(1)$. The next theorem supplies the complete solution of this problem where the second best sub-carriers are different, namely $a(1,2) \neq a(2,2)$.

Theorem 9. *Let* $a(1,1) = a(2,1) = a(1)$ *and* $a(1,2) \neq a(2,2)$. *(i) If*

$$F^j(\bar{X}^1, \bar{X}^2) \geq \bar{\alpha}^j \text{ for } j = 1,2, \tag{4}$$

where

$$F^j(\xi^1, \xi^2) = \alpha^j_{a(1)} \left(\frac{1}{N^0_{a(1)} + \xi^{\hat{j}}} - \frac{\xi^{\hat{j}}}{(N^0_{a(1)} + \xi^j)^2} \right), \quad \bar{\alpha}^j = \frac{\alpha^j_{a(j,2)}}{N^0_{a(j,2)}} \tag{5}$$

then $(T^1_{a(1)}, T^2_{a(1)})$ *is optimal.*
(ii) If

$$F^1(\bar{X}^1, \bar{X}^2) < \bar{\alpha}^1 \text{ and } F^2(\bar{X}^1, \bar{X}^2) > \bar{\alpha}^2 \tag{6}$$

then (T^1, T^2) *is optimal, where* $T^2 = T^2_{a(1)}$, $T^1 = (t, \bar{T}^1 - t, 0, \ldots, 0)$, $t = \max\{0, T\}$ *and* T *is the maximal root of the equation:*

$$\alpha^1_{a(1)} \left(\frac{1}{N^0_{a(1)} + \alpha^1_{a(1)} \bar{T}^2} - \frac{\alpha^1_{a(1)} \bar{T}^2}{(N^0_{a(1)} + \alpha^2_{a(1)} T)^2} \right) = \bar{\alpha}^1. \tag{7}$$

(iii) The case $F^1(\bar{X}^1, \bar{X}^2) > \bar{\alpha}^1$ *and* $F^2(\bar{X}^1, \bar{X}^2) < \bar{\alpha}^2$ *is symmetric to (ii).*
(iv) If

$$F^j(\bar{X}^1, \bar{X}^2) < \bar{\alpha}^j \text{ for } j = 1,2 \tag{8}$$

then (T^1, T^2) *is optimal, where* $T^j = (x^j/\alpha^j_{a(1)}, \bar{T}^j - x^j/\alpha^j_{a(1)}, 0, \ldots, 0)$ *and* (x^1, x^2) *is the positive solution of the system* $F^j(x^1, x^2) = \bar{\alpha}^j, j = 1,2$.

This theorem allows us to depict (see Figure 2) in coordinate system $(\bar{X}^1, \bar{X}^2)$ how NE and cooperative equilibria differ depending on the power signal users can apply. The area $\{(\bar{X}^1, \bar{X}^2) : X^j \leq A^j, j = 1,2)$, where the pure equilibrium $(T^1_{a(1)}, T^2_{a(1)})$ is NE, is essentially larger than the area $\{(\bar{X}^1, \bar{X}^2) : F^j(\bar{X}^1, \bar{X}^2) \geq \bar{\alpha}^j\}$ where it is also the cooperative equilibrium. Meanwhile the area $\{(\bar{X}^1, \bar{X}^2) : F^j(\bar{X}^1, \bar{X}^2) > \bar{\alpha}^j\}$ where in cooperative behavior the users prefer to employ mixed strategies include the corresponding area for NE as well as a part of the area where in NE a user is squeezed from the best sub-carrier. Thus, in the cooperative scenario in comparison with the non-cooperative scenario the area where users prefer to employ pure strategies is essentially narrower.

The conditions that $F^j(\bar{X}^1, \bar{X}^2) > \bar{\alpha}^j\}$ and $\bar{X}^j < \bar{A}^j$ can be interpreted as if user j has a small power resource for cooperative and selfish scenarii, respectively, meanwhile the conditions that $F^j(\bar{X}^1, \bar{X}^2) < \bar{\alpha}^j\}$ and $\bar{X}^j > \bar{A}^j$ can be interpreted as if user j has a large power resource. If one of the users has a large power resource (called a stronger user) for both scenarii meanwhile his rival has small power resource (weaker user) then behaviour of the stronger user drastically changes in the cooperative scenario compared to the selfish one. Namely, in selfish one the stronger user squeezes the weaker one from the best channel meanwhile in the cooperative scenario he allows the weaker user to employ the best channel and himself applies a mixed strategy. Finally note that the lines on Figure 2 can be also interpreted as switching lines for the cost of anarchy.

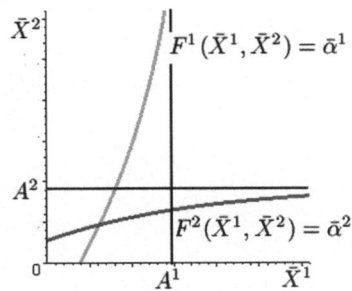

Fig. 2. Cooperative and Nash equilibria

4   Appendix

Proof of Theorem 6. Since $a(1,2) \neq a(1,2)$ the users do not have colluded interests in the second by quality sub-carriers which are different for them. Also, $T^1_{a(1)} > 0$ and $T^2_{a(1)} > 0$ since the users apply mixed strategies. Thus, by Theorem 1, $\omega^1 = \alpha^1_{a(1,2)}/N^0_{a(1,2)}$, $\omega^2 = \alpha^2_{a(2,2)}/N^0_{a(2,2)}$, and

$$\frac{\alpha^1_{a(1)}}{N^0_{a(1)} + \alpha^2_{a(1)} T^2_{a(1)}} = \omega^1, \qquad \frac{\alpha^2_{a(1)}}{N^0_{a(1)} + \alpha^1_{a(1)} T^1_{a(1)}} = \omega^2.$$

Solving these equations for T^1 and T^2 implies (3).

Proof of Theorem 9. Since $a(1,2) \neq a(2,2)$ and $a(1,1) = a(2,1)$ the optimal strategy T^j, $j = 1,2$ has to be of the form

$$T^j_i = \begin{cases} t^j & \text{for } i = a(1), \\ \bar{T}^j - t^j & \text{for } i = a(j,2), \\ 0 & \text{otherwise,} \end{cases}$$

where $t^j \in [0, \bar{T}^j]$ and the optimal t^1 and t^2 are the ones which maximize the following function

$$v(t^1, t^2) = \frac{\alpha^1_{a(1)} t^1}{N^0_{a(1)} + \alpha^2_{a(1)} t^2} + \frac{\alpha^2_{a(1)} t^2}{N^0_{a(1)} + \alpha^1_{a(1)} t^1} + \sum_{i=1}^{2} \frac{\alpha^i_{a(i,2)}}{N^0_{a(i,2)}} (\bar{T}^i - t^i).$$

To find the optimal t^1 and t^2, we need to calculate the derivatives of v with respect to t^1 and t^2:

$$v_j(t^1, t^2) := \frac{\partial v}{\partial t^j} = \frac{\alpha^j_{a(1)}}{N^0_{a(1)} + \alpha^{t^j}_{a(1)} t^j} - \frac{\alpha^1_{a(1)} \alpha^2_{a(1)} t^{\hat{j}}}{(N^0_{a(1)} + \alpha^{t^j}_{a(1)} t^{\hat{j}})^2} - \frac{\alpha^j_{a(j,2)}}{N^0_{a(j,2)}}, \quad j = 1,2.$$

It is clear that

$$v_j(t^1, t^2) = \tilde{v}_j(\xi^1, \xi^2) := F^j(\xi^1, \xi^2) - \bar{\alpha}^j,$$

where $\xi^j = \alpha^j_{a(1)} t^j$ and $\xi^j \in [0, \tilde{T}^j]$ with $\tilde{T}^j = \alpha^j_{a(1)} \bar{T}^j$, $j = 1,2$.

$\tilde{v}_j$ has the following properties:

$$\tilde{v}_j \text{ is increasing in } \xi^j \text{ and decreasing in } \xi^{\hat{j}}, \tag{9}$$

$$\tilde{v}_1(t,0) = \frac{\alpha^1_{a(1)}}{N^0_{a(1)}} - \frac{\alpha^1_{a(1,2)}}{N^0_{a(1,2)}} > 0, \; \tilde{v}_2(0,t) = \frac{\alpha^2_{a(1)}}{N^0_{a(1)}} - \frac{\alpha^2_{a(2,2)}}{N^0_{a(2,2)}} > 0 \text{ for } t \geq 0. \tag{10}$$

By (10) the points $(0,0)$, $(0,\xi)$, $(\xi,0)$ cannot be the maximal ones.

In Figure 3 we depict signs of $\tilde{v}_1$ and $\tilde{v}_2$ in the coordinate system (ξ^1, ξ^2). Namely, the region $(+,+)$ presents the set $\{(\xi^1, \xi^2) : \tilde{v}_1(\xi^1, \xi^2) > 0, \tilde{v}_2(\xi^1, \xi^2) > 0\}$, the region $(-,-)$ is $\{(\xi^1, \xi^2) : \tilde{v}_1(\xi^1, \xi^2) < 0, \tilde{v}_2(\xi^1, \xi^2) < 0\}$ and so on. If $(\tilde{T}^1, \tilde{T}^2) \in (-,-)$ which corresponds to (5) then the maximum is at $(\tilde{T}^1, \tilde{T}^2)$ and (i) is proved. If $(\tilde{T}^1, \tilde{T}^2) \in (+,+)$ which corresponds to (8) then the maximum is at (ξ^1, ξ^2) which is the unique positive solution of the system $\tilde{v}_i(\xi^1, \xi^2) = 0, i = 1, 2$ and (iv) is proved. Similarly, the cases $(\tilde{T}^1, \tilde{T}^2) \in (+,-)$ and $(\tilde{T}^1, \tilde{T}^2) \in (-,+)$ correspond to (8) respectively and are investigated similarly.

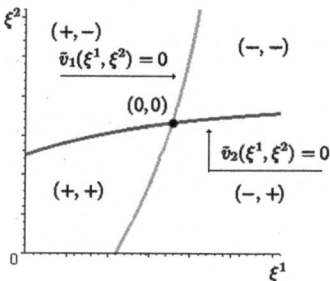

Fig. 3. Signs of $\tilde{v}_1$ and $\tilde{v}_2$

References

1. Adlakha, S., Johari, R., Goldsmith, A.: Competition in Wireless Systems via Bayesian Interference Games. Arxiv.org, no.0709.0516
2. Altman, E., Avrachenkov, K., Garnaev, A.: Closed form solutions for symmetric water filling games. In: Proc. of IEEE INFOCOM (2008)
3. Altman, E., Avrachenkov, K., Garnaev, A.: Fair resource allocation in wireless networks in the presence of a jammer. In: Proc. of ValueTools 2008 (2008)
4. Etkin, R., Parekh, A., Tse, D.: Spectrum Sharing in Unlicensed Bands. IEEE J. on Selec. Areas Comm. 25(3), 517–528 (2007)
5. Holma, H., Toskala, A.: WCDMA for UMTS
6. Ji, H., Huang, C.-Y.: Non-cooperative uplink power control in cellular radio systems. Wireless Networks 4, 233–240 (1998)
7. Kim, S.L., Rosberg, Z., Zander, J.: Combined power control and transmission selection in cellular networks. In: Proceedings of IEEE Vehicular Technology Conference (Fall 1999)
8. Koo, I., Ahn, J., Lee, H.A., Kim, K.: Analysis of Erlang capacity for the multimedia DS-CDMA systems. IEICE Trans. Fundamentals E82-A(5), 849–855 (1999)
9. Tse, D., Viswanath, P.: Fundamentals of Wireless Communication. Cambridge University Press, Cambridge (2005)

Battery State-Dependent Access Control in Solar-Powered Broadband Wireless Networks[*]

Hamidou Tembine[1], Eitan Altman[2], Rachid El-Azouzi[1], and Yezekael Hayel[1]

[1] LIA/CERI, University of Avignon. 339, chemin des Meinajaries Agroparc BP 1228
84911 Avignon Cedex 9 France
[2] INRIA B.P 93, 2004 Route des Lucioles 06902 Sophia Antipolis Cedex France

Abstract. This paper studies both power control and multiple access control in solar-powered broadband wireless networks. We assume that the mobiles use power storage element, such as rechargeable Solar-powered batteries, in order to have energy available for later use. By modeling the energy-level of Solar-powered batteries as a stochastic process, we study noncooperative interactions within large population of mobiles that interfere with each other through many local interactions. Each local interaction involves a random number of mobiles. The actions taken by a mobile determine not only the immediate payoff but also the state transition probabilities of its battery. We define and characterize the evolutionary Stable Strategies (ESS) of the stochastic evolutionary game.

Keywords: Power Control, Access Control, Evolutionary games, Markov Decision Processes.

1 Introduction

Power control and multiple access control in wireless networks have become an important research area. Since today's technology cannot provide batteries with small weight and large energy capacity, design of tools and protocols for efficient power control are needed in order to improve the energy capacity for small batteries. For a comprehensive survey of recent results on power control in wireless networks, an interested reader can consult e.g., [4] and the references therein.

Environmental energy is becoming a feasible alternative for many low-power systems, such as wireless sensor and mesh networks. However, this provides an ubpredictable and limited amount of energy over time. The power storage elements, such as rechargeable batteries or super-capacitors, become very useful to increase the system lifetime and the system availability. In particular, solar power is made possible with the use of Photovoltaic cells. Comprised of several layers of material, these cells are able to produce electrical power from exposure to sunlight. Since in many geographic areas, nice weather is not guaranteed and is

[*] This work was partially supported by the INRIA ARC Program POPEYE and the European Project BIONETS.

unpredictable, the nodes should be able to recover from blackout periods caused by the unavailability of energy. In [3], a stochastic model for a solar powered wireless sensor/mesh networks is used to analyze the following QoS measures for several stochastic policies proposed: the average battery capacity, the sleeping probability and the average delay.

In this paper, we consider an evolutionary game approach with dynamic rechargeable battery depending on the weather (solar energy). Evolutionary games have been used to model the evolution of population sizes as a result of competition between them that occurs through many local interactions. Central in evolutionary games is the concept of Evolutionary Stable Strategy (ESS), which is a distribution of (deterministic or mixed) actions such that if used, the population is immune against penetration of mutations. This notion is stronger than that of Nash equilibrium as ESS is robust against a deviation of a whole fraction of the population where as the Nash equilibrium is defined with respect to possible deviations of a single player.

We make use of a recent dynamic version of stochastic evolutionary games, which we call "Markov Decision Evolutionary Games" (MDEG)[1], in solar-powered broadband wireless networks. There are many local interactions among individuals belonging to large populations of mobiles. The result of the interaction between mobiles depends on their current individual state. ¿From time to time the individual state of a mobile varies. The actioni choice of mobiles involved in a local interactions as well as their individual states determine the not only the result of the interactions but also the transition probabilities to the other possible individual states. Each individual is thus faced with an Markov Decision Process (MDP) in which it maximizes the expected average cost criterion. Each individual knows only the state of its own MDP, and does not know the state of the other mobiles it interacts with.

The destination of some transmission occasionally may receive simultaneously a transmission from another terminal which results in a collision. It is assumed however that even when packets collide, one of the packets can be received correctly if transmitted at a higher power. As state of the MDP of a user we take its energy level. The immediate fitness (rewards) is the number of successful transmissions. By allowing the mobiles to be equipped with rechargeable solar powered batteries, the mobiles may have infinite life time and the criteria that is maximizing is the limit average Cesaco-type payoff.

The remainder of this paper is organized as follows. In Sections 2 and 3, we present the description and notation used in our modeling approach and study the special case of three pure strategies in battery-state dependent power and access control. Section 5 concludes the paper.

2   The Model

Consider the following setting of evolutionary games: there is a large populations of mobiles; each mobile has a finite number of transmission power level available. There are many local interactions at the same time. At each slot, some of the terminals have to take a decision on their transmission power based on their own battery state. At the lowest state of the battery no power is available and the mobile has to wait the time to have good weather for regain some energy. Each player has its individual states set $S = \{0, 1, 2, \ldots, n\}$. Each mobile of the population has a finite action set in each state $s : A(s)$. We assume that there are a random number of interacting mobiles in each local interaction. At time t, each mobile knows its own state s_t and selects an action $a_t \in A(s_t)$. The mobile receives some payoff $r(s_t, a_t, \alpha_t)$ where α_t is the composition of the population at time t (the j-th element of $\alpha_t^{s_t}$ represents the fraction of mobiles choosing the action j) and the state of mobile goes to the state s_{t+1} with the probability $q(s_{t+1}|s_t, a_t)$. Each individual is thus faced with an MDP in which it maximizes the expected average cost criterion. Each individual knows only the state of its own MDP, and does not know the state of the other players it interacts with. The transition probabilities of a player's MDP are only controlled by that player. Let $\Delta(S)$ be the $(|S| - 1)$-dimensional simplex of the Euclidean space $\mathbb{R}^{|S|}$. The set of all action profiles at all states is given by $All = \{(s, a), \ s \in S, \ a \in A(s)\}$, then $q : \ All \times \Theta \ \to \ \Delta(S)$ is a transition rule between the states where $\Theta = \prod_{s \in S} \Delta(A(s))$, $\Delta(A(s))$ is the set of probability distribution on $A(s)$. The vector $[q(s_{t+1} = 0|s_t, a_t), \ldots, q(s_{t+1} = n|s_t, a_t)]$ satisfies $\forall \ j \in S$, $q(s_{t+1} = j|s_t, a_t) \geq 0$, $\sum_{j \in S} q(s_{t+1} = j|s_t, a_t) = 1$. A state s is absorbing state if $q(s|s, a) = 1$, $\forall \ a \in A(s), \forall \alpha \in \Theta$. We examine the limit average Cesaro-type payoff given a population profile σ and an individual trajectory u,

$$F_n(u, \sigma) = \liminf_{T \longrightarrow +\infty} \mathbb{E}_{u,\sigma} \left(\frac{1}{T} \sum_{t=1}^{T} r(s_t, a_t, \alpha_t) \right)$$

where $\mathbb{E}_{u,\sigma,n}$ denotes the expectation over the probability measure $\mathbb{P}_{u,\sigma,n}$ induced by u, σ on the set of histories endowed with the product σ-algebra (initial state of the battery is n). Define further

- The subset $\mathcal{U}_S$ of stationary policies; a stationary policy u is a policy in which the probability to choose an action a depends only on the current state s; it is denoted by $u(a|s)$.
- The subset $\mathcal{U}_D \subset \mathcal{U}_S$ of pure or deterministic stationary policies $\mathcal{U}_D$. A policy of this type can be viewed as a function from the states to the actions.
- The set $\mathcal{U}_M$ of mixed strategies: A mixed strategy is identified with a probability γ over the set of pure stationary strategies. It can be considered as first choosing a pure stationary policy u with probability $\gamma(u)$ and then keeping choosing forever the actions according to u. A general mixed strategy is a mixture of behaviorial strategy.

Occupation Measure. Often we encounter the notion of individual states in evolutionary games; but usually the population size at a particular state is fixed. In our case the choices of actions of an individual determine the fraction of time it would spend at each state. Hence the fraction of the whole population that will be at a given state may depend on the distribution of strategies in the population. In order to model this dependence we first need to introduce the expected average frequency $f_{n,u}(s)$ that an individual spends at a given state s when it follows a strategy u and its initial state at time 1 is n. Moreover, we define $f_{n,u}(s,a)$ the expected average frequency during which it is at state s and it chooses action a, $f_{u,n} = \lim_{T_o\infty} \frac{1}{T} \sum_{t=1}^{T} Q^t(u)$ where $Q(u) := [q(s'|s,a,u)]_{s',s,a}$.

We now define the equilibrium concept in the context of evolutionary games. A behaviorial stationary strategy $u = (u_1,\ldots,u_n)$ with $u_i = (x_i, y_i)$ is an evolutionary stable strategy (ESS) if for all strategy mut such that $f_{mut} \neq f_u$ there exists $\epsilon_{mut} > 0$ such that

$$\sum_{s,a} (f_u(s,a) - f_{mut}(s,a)) r(s,a,\alpha^\epsilon) > 0 \text{ where } \alpha^\epsilon = (1-\epsilon)\alpha(u) + \epsilon\alpha(mut).$$

Interpretation: Suppose that, initially, the population profile is $\alpha(u)$. Now suppose that a small group of mutants enters the population playing according to a different profile $\alpha(mut)$. If we call $\epsilon \in (0,1)$ the size of the subpopulation of mutants after normalization, then the population profile after mutation will be $\epsilon\alpha(mut) + (1-\epsilon)\alpha(u)$. After mutation, the average payoff of non-mutants will be given by $\sum_{s,a} f_u(s,a) r(s,a,\alpha^\epsilon)$. Analogously, the average payoff a mutant is $\sum_{s,a} f_{mut}(s,a) r(s,a,\alpha^\epsilon)$. That is, u is ESS if, after mutation, non-mutants are more successful than mutants. In other words, mutants cannot invade the population and will eventually get extinct. In case where the payoff function r is linear in last variable α (it is not the case in this model) then this definition is equivalent to $\alpha(u)$ is a strict symmetric Nash equilibrium or $\alpha(u)$ is a strictly better response than $\alpha(mut)$ given that the others mobiles mut. Note that if α is not linear, we can have $\alpha(\epsilon mut + (1-\epsilon)u) \neq \epsilon\alpha(mut) + (1-\epsilon)\alpha(u)$.

3   Stochastic Modeling of the Energy Levels of Solar-Powered Battery

In this subsection, we suppose that a battery has $n+1$ energy states $S = \{0,1,\ldots,n\}$. The state 0 corresponds to the state *Empty* and the state n is the *Full* state of the battery. The other states $1,\ldots,n-1$ are intermediary states of the battery. We associate with each mobile a Markov Decision Process (MDP) which represents the transition probabilities between energy levels. Let X_t^i be the energy level of battery at time t. Given a stationary policy σ and a strategy of all the population $\alpha = (\alpha_t)_{t\geq 1}$, the transition probability of the energy level of battery is is described by the (first order, time-homogeneous) Markov process (X_t) where the transition probability law q which is given by

$$q_{sas'} = \begin{cases} 1 - R_{\gamma,s}(a) - Q_{\gamma,s}(a) & \text{if } s' = s-1 \\ R_{\gamma,s}(a) & \text{if } s' = s+1 \\ Q_{\gamma,s}(a) & \text{if } s' = s \\ 0 & \text{otherwise} \end{cases}, \forall 1 \leq s \leq n-1, \forall a_s \in A(s),$$

$$q_{nas'} = \begin{cases} 1 - Q_{\gamma,n}(a) & \text{if } s' = n-1 \\ Q_{\gamma,n}(a) & \text{if } s' = n \\ 0 & \text{otherwise} \end{cases}, \quad q_{0as'} = \begin{cases} \gamma & \text{if } s' = 1 \\ (1-\gamma) & \text{if } s' = 0 \\ 0 & \text{otherwise} \end{cases},$$

where $\gamma \longmapsto R_{\gamma,s}(a) \in [0,1]$ is an increasing function $\forall s, a$ with $R_{0,s}(a) = 0$, $0 \le R_{\gamma,s}(a) + Q_{\gamma,s}(a) \le 1$. The factor γ represents the probability to have a "good weather". If γ is zero, the state 0 is unique absorbing sate and expected lifetime of the battery is finite. For $\gamma \ne 0$, the Markov chain is irreducible i.e., there is only one class, that is, all states communicate with each other for stationary policy.

3.1 Battery-State Dependent Access Control in Solar-Powered System

This subsection studies is a generalization of the *random access game* with unknown number of mobiles, finite state, and three strategies.The channel is ideal for transmission and all errors are due to collision. A mobile can transmit a packet using a power level among three available levels: transmit with high power P_h, transmit with low power P_l or does not transmit 0. We consider a general capture model where a packet transmitted by a mobile is received successfully when if and only if that mobile uses a transmission power which is greater than the power used by the others transmitters at that time slot. Given a population profile $\alpha = (x, y, 1-x-y)$ with $0 \le x, 0 \le y, \ x+y \le 1$, the expected probability to have a successful transmission:

(i) When the mobile chooses P_l, the reward is the probability that the others mobiles choose zero i.e no others mobiles transmit, i.e.,

$$r(s, P_l, \alpha) = \sum_{k \ge 0} \mathbb{P}(K = k) (1 - x - y)^k = \mathbb{E}((1 - x - y)^K) = G_K(1 - x - y)$$

where G_K is the generating function of K.

(ii) When the mobile chooses P_h, the reward is the probability that no other mobiles transmit with the high power i.e.,

$$r(s, P_h, \alpha) = \mathbb{E}_K \sum_{l=0}^{K} \binom{K}{l}(1 - x - y)^l y^{K-l} = \mathbb{E}_K(1 - x)^K = G_K(1 - x). \quad (1)$$

where $\binom{K}{l}$ is the binomial coefficient of K and l.

(iii) When the terminal chooses 0, the reward is zero, i.e., $r(s, 0, \alpha) = 0$

Since there are three strategies P_h, P_l and 0, the population aggressiveness can be described by a process $(x_t, y_t)_{t \ge 1}$ where x_t (resp. y_t) is the fraction of the population using the high power level (low power) at time t. However, for each state $s \ne 0$, the action space becomes $M := \{(x, y), \ x \ge 0, \ y \ge 0, \ x + y \le 1\}$. A stationary policy of an user is a map $\beta : S \longrightarrow M$. The expected reward of a user when its battery is at the state $s \ne 0$ is then given by

$$\tilde{r}(s, \beta, \alpha) = x'_s r(s, P_l, \alpha) + y'_s r(s, P_l, \alpha),$$

where $\beta(s) = (x'_s, y'_s) \ \forall s \in S$.

4 Computing Equilibria and ESS

4.1 Nash Equilibria and Pareto Optimality

In this subsection, we study the existence and uniqueness of Nash equilibrium in different scenarios:

Two mobiles $K = \delta_2$. The interaction in each slot and each non-empty individual state is described in the following tabular. Mobile 1 chooses a row, mobile 2 chooses a column. The payoff of mobile 1 (resp. mobile 2) is the first (resp. the second) component of the vector payoff.

$1\backslash 2$	”0”	P_l	P_h
”0”	$(0,0)$	$(0,1)^\diamond$	$(0,1)^{\diamond\star}$
P_l	$(1,0)^\diamond$	$(0,0)$	$(0,1)^{\diamond\star}$
P_h	$(1,0)^{\diamond\star}$	$(1,0)^{\diamond\star}$	$(0,0)^\star$

The Nash equilibria are represented by $\star$ and Pareto optimal allocation[1] are represented by $\diamond$.

Three mobiles $K = \delta_3$. The instantaneous reward is presented in the matrix game. Mobile 1 chooses a row, mobile 2 chooses a column and mobile 3 chooses an array M_i.

$$M_1 := \begin{array}{|c|c|c|} \hline (0,0,0) & (0,1,0)^\diamond & (0,1,0)^\star \\ \hline (1,0,0)^\diamond & (0,0,0) & (0,1,0)^\star \\ \hline (1,0,0)^{\diamond\star} & (1,0,0)^{\diamond\star} & (0,0,0)^\star \\ \hline \end{array} \quad M_2 := \begin{array}{|c|c|c|} \hline (0,0,1)^\diamond & (0,0,0) & (0,1,0)^{\diamond\star} \\ \hline (0,0,0) & (0,0,0) & (0,1,0)^{\diamond\star} \\ \hline (1,0,0)^{\diamond\star} & (1,0,0)^{\diamond\star} & (0,0,0)^\star \\ \hline \end{array}$$

$$M_3 := \begin{array}{|c|c|c|} \hline (0,0,1)^{\diamond\star} & (0,0,1)^{\diamond\star} & (0,0,0)^\star \\ \hline (0,0,1)^{\diamond\star} & (0,0,1)^{\diamond\star} & (0,0,0)^\star \\ \hline (0,0,0)^\star & (0,0,0)^\star & (0,0,0)^\star \\ \hline \end{array}$$

Proposition 4.2. *In any state $s \neq 0$, the one-shot local interaction between $p \geq 2$ mobiles has an infinite (Nash) equilibria, $\binom{p}{1}2^{p-1} = p2^{p-1}$ of them are Pareto optimal, and a unique symmetric (Nash) which is the strategy h (independently of the state).*

Note that this one-shot game has a unique evolutionary stable strategy (see [2]).

Proof. The Nash equilibria and Pareto optimality of the local interaction in state $s \neq 0$ can be described as follows:

(i) **Symmetric Equilibrium:** It is clear that $r(s, P_h, \alpha) \geq r(s, P_l, \alpha) \geq r(s, 0, \alpha)$, $\forall \alpha$ i.e P_h weakly dominates P_l which weakly dominates 0. Hence, the strategy P_h is an equilibrium. Moreover the best reply to the population profile $\alpha = (x, y, 1 - x - y)$ is to play P_h if $x \neq 1$, and to play any strategy

---

[1] An allocation of payoffs is Pareto optimal or Pareto efficient if there is no other allocation that makes every node at least as well off and at least one node strictly better off.

$z \in [0,1]$ if $x = 1$. Thus, $(P_h, P_h, \ldots, P_h)$ is the unique symmetric equilibrium. At the equilibrium $(P_h, P_h, \ldots, P_h)$, the reward of each mobile is zero. Thus, $(P_h, P_h, \ldots, P_h)$ is not Pareto optimal because the allocation obtained at $(P_h, P_l, \ldots, P_l)$ or $(P_h, 0, 0, \ldots, 0)$ Pareto dominates zero.

(ii) **Pure Equilibria:** Fix a mobile m which uses the action P_h. Then any action profile of the others mobiles $b^{-m} \in \in \{0, P_l, P_h\}^{p-1}$ leads to a Nash equilibrium (no mobile can improve its probability of success by deviating unilaterally). In particular, if k $(0 \leq k \leq p-1)$ of the $p-1$ mobiles choose P_l and the $p-k-1$ others use 0 then no mobile can improve its probability of success by deviating unilaterally. The mobile m has exactly $\sum_{k=0}^{p-1}\binom{p-1}{k} = 2^{p-1}$ pure equilibria in which he/she has successful transmission. By changing the role of m, we get $\binom{p}{1}2^{p-1} = p2^{p-1}$ pure equilibria with successful transmission. All these pure equilibria are Pareto optimal: if only one terminal uses the high power P_h and the others mobiles use 0 or P_l,, then the mobile with the high power P_h gets the payoff 1 and the others gets the payoff 0.

(iii) **Mixed Equilibria:** Any situation where at least one of the mobiles use the strategy P_h , and other mobiles use an arbitrary mixed strategies, gives a mixed Nash equilibria. The allocation of payoff obtained in these mixed strategy are not Pareto optimal if at least one mobile chooses the strategy P_h with positive probability.

In the figure 1, we plot the best response (power level) of a mobile for a given trajectory of a profile population, with $P_h = 10$ and $P_l = 2$. We observe that the best response is is to use a low power when the population is very aggressive $(x = 1)$, and to use the high power in any state $s \neq 0$ when the population is less aggressive $x < 1$. In the figure 2, we plot the sojourn time of a mobile to stay in a state as function of its stationary strategy $\beta = (x, y)$ with $s \neq 0, Q_s(0) = 0.95, Q_s(P_l) = 0.65$ and $Q_s(P_h) = 0.25$. We observe that the sojourn time is decreasing function in aggressiveness of that mobile.

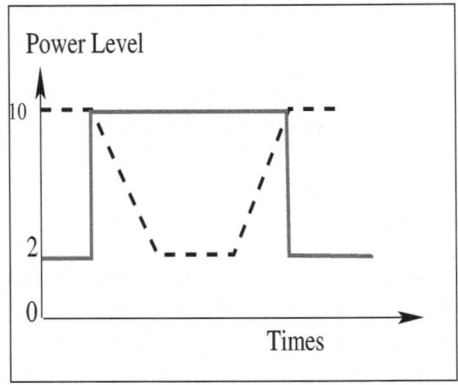
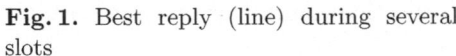
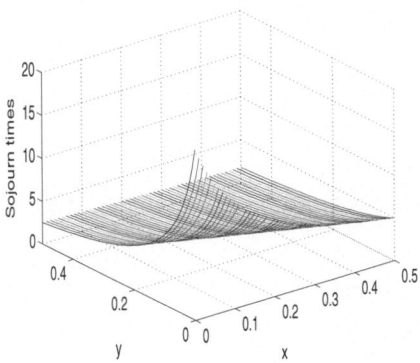

Fig. 1. Best reply (line) during several slots

Fig. 2. Sojourn time

4.3   Evolutionary Stable Strategy

Under the condition $\gamma > 0$, we have the following result [1]:

Proposition 4.4. *The payoff function has a representation in term of occupation measure, i.e., $F_{n,u}(\sigma) = \sum_{s,a} f_u(s,a) r(s,a,\alpha)$ where $\alpha = (x,y)$ is the profile of population under stationary strategy σ.*

Proposition 4.5. *The fully aggressive strategy $\bar{P}_h$ which consists to transmit with the maximum power (P_h) in each state $s \neq 0$ is an Evolutionarily Stable Strategies.*

Proof. Let mut such that $\alpha'(mut) \neq 1$. For $u = \bar{P}_h$ the time average payoff is $F_u(\alpha^\epsilon)$ $= G_K \left(\epsilon(1 - \alpha'_{P_h}(mut)) \right) \sum_{s=1}^{n} f_{\bar{P}_h}(P_h)$, and $F_{mut}(\alpha^\epsilon) = \sum_{s=1}^{n} f_{mut}(s, mut_s) \times$ $\left[mut_{P_h} G_K(\epsilon(1 - \alpha'_{P_h}(mut))) + mut_{P_l} G_K(\epsilon(1 - \alpha'_{P_h}(mut) - \alpha'_{P_l}(mut))) \right]$. Since the generating is increasing, $G_K(\epsilon(1 - \alpha'_{P_h}(mut) - \alpha'_{P_l}(mut))) \leq G_K(\epsilon(1 - \alpha'_{P_h}(mut))$ with equality if and only $\alpha'_{P_l}(mut) = 0$. We deduce that $F_{mut}(\alpha^\epsilon)$ is strictly greater $F_{mut}(\alpha^\epsilon)$ for all mut such that $\alpha'_{P_h}(mut) < 1$.

4.6   Power Control in Clouded Weather

We assume now that the solar-powered system is in a clouded weather ($\gamma = 0$, "no sunlight") during a long period (clouded sky, raining time or due to the season). Power storage elements, such as supercapacitors (but finite in practice), in order to have energy available for later use has been proposed. Because of limited capacity (hence energy of the battery), the aggressive terminals (which use the high power) will be rapidly in the state 0 which becomes an absorbing state. The terminals with empty battery need an alternative solution such as external recharge or to buy a new battery. So there is an additional cost to survive in this situation. If the maximum lifetime of the battery (for example using the power "0") is finite then the power control in clouded weather can be modeled by the stochastic evolutionary game with total successful transmission before to reach to the absorbing state 0.

Lemma 4.6.1 *The total expected successful transmission during the lifetime of the battery under the strategy u is given by*

$$\frac{1}{1-\gamma} \times 0 + \sum_{s=1}^{n} \frac{u_s(P_l) G_K(1 - \alpha_{P_l} - \alpha_{P_h}) + u_s(P_h) G_K(1 - \alpha_{P_h})}{1 - Q_{0,s}(u_s)}$$

where $Q_{0,s}(u_s) := u_s(P_h) Q_{0,s}(P_h) + u_s(P_l) Q_{0,s}(P_l)$.

Proof. This says that the total reward total is the sum over the states of the expected successful transmission times the expected sojourn times spent in this state. The sojourn time in state s under the policy u_s is $\frac{1}{1 - Q_{0,s}(u_s)}$. This completes the proof.

The following Proposition holds in the stochastic evolutionary game with total reward.

Proposition 4.7. *(i) The strategy "stay quiet" (plays "0" in each state) cannot be an ESS. (ii) A necessary condition for the full aggressive strategy to be an ESS is* $G_K(0) = P(K = 0) = 0$. *Moreover if* $G_K(1 - \alpha_{P_h}) \sum_{s=1}^{n} \frac{1}{1 - Q_{0,s}(P_h)} >$ $\max_{mut \in \{P_h, P_l\}^n} \left\{ \sum_{s=1}^{n} \frac{r(s, mut_s, \alpha)}{1 - Q_{0,s}(mut_s)} \right\}$ *then* $\bar{P}_h$ *is an ESS. (iii)Similarly, if* G_K $(1 - \alpha_{P_h}) \sum_{s=1}^{n} \frac{1}{1 - Q_{0,s}(P_l)} > \max_{mut \in \{P_h, P_l\}^n} \left\{ \sum_{s=1}^{n} \frac{r(s, mut_s, \alpha)}{1 - Q_{0,s}(mut_s)} \right\}$ *then* $\bar{P}_l$ *is an ESS.*

Proof. The strategy "stay quiet" (play "0" in each state) cannot be an ESS because it is best reply to itself. Hence, the strategy *not transmit* can be invaded by mutations. If $\bar{P}_h$ is an ESS then $G_K(0) \sum_{s=1}^{n} \frac{1}{1 - Q_{0,s}(P_h)}$ must be greater than $G_K(0) \sum_{s=1}^{n} \frac{1}{1 - Q_{0,s}(P_l)}$. Since the power consumption is greater with P_h than P_l ($P_h > P_l$), one has, $\sum_{s=1}^{n} \frac{1}{1 - Q_{0,s}(P_h)} < \sum_{s=1}^{n} \frac{1}{1 - Q_{0,s}(P_l)}$. This implies that $G_K(0) = P(K = 0) = 0$. The other results are immediate by best response conditions.

5   Concluding Remarks

Thanks to the renewable energy techniques, designing autonomous mobile terminal and consumer embedded electronics that exploit the energy coming from the environment is becoming a feasible option. However, the design of such devices requires the careful selection of the components, such as power consumption and the energy storage elements, according to the working environment and the features of the application. In this paper we have investigated power control interaction based on stochastic modeling of the remaining energy of the battery for each user in each local interaction. We have showed existence of equilibria and conditions for evolutionary stable strategies.

References

1. Altman, E., Hayel, Y.: A Stochastic Evolutionary Game of Energy Management in a Distributed Aloha Network. In: Proc. of INFOCOM 2008 (2008)
2. Altman, E., Elazouzi, R., Hayel, Y., Tembine, H.: Evolutionary Power Control Games in Wireless Networks. In: Proc. 7th IFIP Networking 2008 (2008)
3. Niyato, D., Hossain, E., Fallahi, A.: Sleep and wakeup strategies in solar-powered wireless sensor/mesh networks: Performance analysis and optimization. IEEE Transactions on Mobile Computing 6(2), 221–236 (2007)
4. Meshkati, F., Poor, H., Schwartz, S.: Energy-Efficient Resource Allocation in Wireless Networks. IEEE Signal Processing Magazine 58 (2007)
5. Susu, A.E., Acquaviva, A., Atienza, D., De Micheli, G.: Stochastic Modeling and Analysis for Environmentally Powered Wireless Sensor Nodes. In: Wiopt 2008 (2008)
6. Tembine, H., Altman, E., El-Azouzi, R., Hayel, Y.: Evolutionary games with random number of interacting players applied to access control. In: WiOpt 2008 (2008)

Author Index